Regionalism in East Asia

Regional co-operation and integration have emerged as key issues for East Asia following the financial crisis. This book explores these issues, and examines the degree to which a new paradigm is emerging. It reviews the evolution of the concepts and practices of regionalism in East Asia, and considers the factors which are shaping new patterns of regional co-operation and integration. It includes discussions of historical developments, economic co-operation, socio-political factors, and defence and security. It considers the role of those states, including China and Japan, which have distinctive approaches to international relations, and assesses the role of regional international bodies such as ASEAN, ASEM, ARF and 'ASEAN plus three'.

Fu-Kuo Liu is Associate Research Fellow at the Institute of International Relations, the National Chengchi University and Adjunct Associate Professor at the Graduate Institute of Political Science, the Chinese Culture University, Tapei. He has researched on regional integration, Asia Pacific security and Taiwan security.

Philippe Régnier is Senior Lecturer at the Graduate Institute Development Studies (GIDS), the University of Geneva, Switzerland. Since 1992 he has also been the director of the Modern Asia Research Centre in Switzerland. He specializes in East Asian political economy and small enterprise development in the Asian emerging economies.

Regionalism in East Asia

Paradigm shifting?

Edited by
Fu-Kuo Liu and Philippe Régnier

RoutledgeCurzon
Taylor & Francis Group

First published 2003
by RoutledgeCurzon
11 New Fetter Lane, London EC4P 4EE

Simultaneously published in the USA and Canada
by RoutledgeCurzon
29 West 35th Street, New York, NY 10001

RoutledgeCurzon is an imprint of the Taylor & Francis Group

Editorial matter © 2003 Fu-Kuo Liu and Philippe Régnier; individual chapters
© the individual contributors

Typeset in Times by LaserScript Ltd, Mitcham, Surrey
Printed and bound in Great Britain by
Antony Rowe Ltd, Chippenham, Wiltshire

British Library Cataloguing in Publication Data
A catalogue record for this book is available from the British Library

Library of Congress Cataloging in Publication Data
Regionalism in east Asia : paradigm shifting? / edited by Fu-Kuo Liu and Philippe Régnier.
    p. cm.
    Includes bibliographical references and index.
    1. East Asia–Economic integration. 2. East Asia–Economic conditions. 3.
Regionalism–East Asia. I. Liu, Fu-Kuo, 1958- II. Régnier, Philippe.
HC460.5 .R443 2002
337.5–dc21   2002075138

ISBN 0–7007–1612–2

Contents

Contributors

Pablo Bustelo is Associate Professor of Applied Economics at Complutense University of Madrid, Spain, and Head, Group of East Asian Economic Studies (GEAES) in the Department of Applied Economics 1 of Complutense University. He has published several books and more than 50 articles in Spanish on the East Asian economies. He has contributed to journals such as *The European Journal of Development Research* (London), *Emerging Markets Review* (Amsterdam), *The Indian Journal of Quantitative Economics* (Amritsar), *Comercio Exterior* (Mexico DF), and *Ciclos* (Buenos Aires).

Christopher M. Dent is Lecturer in the East Asian Economy and Director of the Institute for Pacific Asia Studies at the University of Hull, UK. His main research interests focus on the international political economy of East Asia; the foreign economic policy of Singapore, South Korea and Taiwan; and East Asia's economic relations with the European Union. Recent published books include *The European Economy: The Global Context* (Routledge, 1997) and *The European Union and East Asia: An Economic Relationship* (Routledge, 1999). He has also written over 30 articles and chapters.

Jörn Dosch is Lecturer in Asia–Pacific Studies at the University of Leeds, Great Britain. He was a Fulbright scholar at the Asia/Pacific Research Center, Stanford University and an Assistant Professor at the University of Mainz, Germany. Former affiliations also include the Center for Strategic and International Studies, Jakarta. He has widely published on cooperation and integration in Southeast Asia and the Asia–Pacific, US foreign policy and Europe–Asia relations. Recent publications include Jörn Dosch, Manfred Mols, eds. *International Relations in the Asia–Pacific* (St. Martin's Press, New York, 2000).

Heiner Hänggi is Assistant Director at the Geneva Centre for the Democratic Control of Armed Forces (DCAF) and Lecturer in Political Science at the University of St. Gallen (Switzerland). Previously, he was a Senior Research Fellow at the Geneva-based Modern Asia Research Centre (MARC), of which he was Acting Director from July 1999 till February 2000. He has published *inter alia* on regional security in Southeast Asia and Asia–Europe relations.

Tsutomu Kikuchi is Professor of International Politics and the Director of the Institute of Research and Development of International Studies, Aoyama Gakuin University, Tokyo, and Adjunct Research Fellow, Japan Institute of International Affairs (JIIA). For years, he has been an active member of PECC, APEC and CSCAP process. His publications on the nature of APEC and regional political economy have received broad respect from all over the region.

Nadhavathna Krishnamra is the Second Secretary of the Asian Department, at the Ministry of Foreign Affairs, Thailand. He was educated at Oxford University for his postgraduate studies and received his Ph.D. degree from the Graduate Institute of International Studies (IUHEI), the University of Geneva. His current assignment includes involvement in ASEAN internal coordination.

Tse-Kang Leng is Associate Research Fellow at the Institute of International Relations, National Chengchi University, Taipei. He received his Ph.D. degree from the Department of Government and Foreign Affairs, the University of Virginia, USA. Dr. Leng's main research focus includes international political economy, cross-Taiwan Straits relations, and sustainable development.

Fu-Kuo Liu is Associate Research Fellow at the Institute of International Relations, National Chengchi University and Adjunct Associate Professor at the Graduate Institute of Political Science, Chinese Culture University, Taipei. He was a visiting research fellow at the Asian Studies Program, Edmund Walsh School of Foreign Service, Georgetown University from August 2000 to August 2001. His former academic affiliations include the Department of International Politics, Aoyama Gakuin University, Tokyo. He has researched on regional integration, Asia Pacific security and Taiwan's security.

Philippe Régnier is Senior Lecturer in East Asian Political Economy at the Graduate Institute of Development Studies (GIDS), University of Geneva, Switzerland. Since 1992, he has also been the Director of the Modern Asia Research Centre, an academic unit unique in Switzerland and sponsored by the Graduate Institute of International Studies and GIDS.

Wei-Wei Zhang is Senior Research Fellow at the Modern Asia Research Centre, Geneva University, and Professor at the College of the Humanities, Fudan University, China. His publications include *Ideology and Economic Reform under Deng Xiaoping (1978–1993)* (Kegan Paul, London, 1996) and *Transforming China: Economic Reform and its Political Implications* (Macmillan, London, 2000).

Abbreviations

ADB	Asian Development Bank
AFTA	ASEAN Free Trade Area
AICO	ASEAN Industrial Cooperation Scheme
AMF	Asian Monetary Fund
ANIEs	Asian Newly Industrializing Economies
APEC	Asia–Pacific Economic Cooperation
APMC	ASEAN Post Ministerial Conferences
ARATS	Association for Relations across the Taiwan Straits
ARF	ASEAN Regional Forum
ASEM	Asia-Europe Meeting
CAEC	Council of Asia-Europe Cooperation
CEA	Chinese Economic Area
CSCAP	Council for Security Cooperation in the Asia Pacific
EAEC	East Asian Economic Caucus
EAGA	East ASEAN Growth Area
EALAF	East Asia Latin America Forum
EAS	East Asian Summit
ECAFE	Economic Commission for Asia and the Far East
EFTA	European Free Trade Association
EMU	Economic and Monetary Union
ERM	Exchange Rate Mechanism
ESCAP	Economic and Social Commission for Asia and the Pacific
EVSL	Early Voluntary Sectorial Liberalization
FDI	Foreign Direct Investment
FEZs	Free Economic Zones
FTAA	Free Trade Area of the Americas
IEOs	International Economic Organizations
IMF	International Monetary Fund
JERC	Japan Economic Research Center
KEDO	Korean Peninsula Energy Development Organization
MNCs	Multinational Corporations
NAFTA	Northern America through the North American Free Trade Area
NATO	North Atlantic Treaty Organization

NEAEF	Northeast Asian Economic Forum
NEAREA	Northeast Asian Regional Economic Association
NGOs	Non-Governmental Organizations
OECD	Organization for Economic Cooperation and Development
OSCE	Organization for Security and Cooperation in Europe
PAFTA	Pacific Free Trade Area
PBEC	Pacific Basin Economic Council
PTA	Preferential Tariff Arrangements
REC	Regional Economic Co-operation
REI	Regional Economic Integration
SEATO	South East Asia Treaty Organization
SEF	Straits Exchange Foundation
UNCTAD	UN Conference on Trade and Development
WEF	World Economic Forum
WPO	Warsaw Pact Organization

Preface

Although many of us have been interested in looking at and studying regionalism as a rather fashionable topic, we have never attempted to understand what exactly the strength of regionalism is based upon, comes from, and may lead to. We generally see it as a complicated or ambiguous concept, simply summing it up from a number of factual developments in certain regions, particularly drawn from European integration. As the concept remains to be clearly defined, most critiques have concluded that much of the study approaches to regionalism have been based upon a European understanding of regional cooperation.

This book constitutes the output of the first Sino–European Joint Research Project, and as such has been a cooperative effort between two research centres: the Institute of International Relations at National Chengchi University (Taipei) and the Modern Asia Research Centre at the University of Geneva. Beginning as early as 1998, contributors to this book – including European and East Asian experts and practitioners – have met several times to discuss and debate among themselves the issues at hand. The major intention has been to try to raise a series of questions and initiate debates on the concept and current development of regionalism.

The mission of this work has been to review contemporary trends relating to the concept of regionalism and to explore developing and changing trends of regionalism in East Asia, especially the impact of the changing regional context of regionalism *per se*. The argument of the book brings together the varying approaches of this field and covers critical issues that generate regional development in Southeast and Northeast Asia. Our efforts in this book have been channelled into trying to pinpoint the emergence of new paradigms of regionalism in the region. It has been strongly suggested that the post-Cold War scenario has changed in terms of the fundamental ingredients of regional cooperation. Given the natural economic course of East Asian regionalism, the demands for an economic momentum have come to rejuvenate and newly shape the utility of regionalism, with greater emphasis on the approaches of inter-regionalism, exclusiveness, and networking. Above all, the most updated move by regional countries has evolved in a new form of regional cooperation: 'ASEAN plus three.' This also has potential implications for future development.

The book concludes by suggesting a few emerging paradigms of regionalism in East Asia, which would in all likelihood, we believe, come to determine the future direction of regional cooperation in the region. It is our intention to draw attention to the most recent developments of inter-regionalism, exclusive regionalism, and regional networking in East Asia.

During this extended research period, we would both especially like to thank the two institutions for their continuous support of this work and all contributors of this book for their patient and knowledgeable comments. We are indebted to Professor Stephen Kirby and Dr Mya Than for their thoughtful advice on the topic overall. Thanks also go to a number of colleagues in Taipei and Geneva for their immense help. We would finally like to make a special note to thank Chanel Grubner for her great assistance in wrapping up the project.

Fu-Kuo Liu and Philippe Régnier

Prologue

Whither regionalism in East Asia?

Fu-Kuo Liu and Philippe Régnier

Regionalism has become a truly fashionable construct in East Asia of late. However, what the notion of regionalism really refers to is much more complicated in the case of East Asian development than of elsewhere. Since the concept of regional cooperation had been considered foreign in most of the East Asian region, the original driving forces of regionalism did not come from political ends but rather were derived from a vast variety of the social spectrum throughout the region. During the Cold War era, although regionalism arrived in Southeast Asia intact and with a certain institutional form, its rationale was closely associated with the balance and counterbalance of power strategies, and not so much with any sense of regional awareness. The promotion of regional cooperation was an expediency and/or strategy of foreign policy of individual nations in the subregion. However, in Northeast Asia the concept of regionalism was literally non-existent in those early days.

The sources of regionalism have accumulated over the years in East Asia and have mainly grown out of an increasing degree of interdependence, intensive cross-border economic interactions, subregional economic groupings, as well as the experience of regional organisations. Most studies on regionalism however, especially of East Asia, concentrate on the process of regional institutions and emphasise that regionalism is the outcome of trade mechanisms and regime buildup.[1] The simplicity of this designated perspective may not catch the whole spirit of a community-building process. However, other approaches have gone on to depict regionalism as a way of building network power among the business community and as a natural economic area across national borders.[2] In this book, we take multi-dimensional perspectives on regionalism, which is more than an 'expression of regional consciousness' and relates not only to the interstate level but also to the regional and subregional levels.[3] Based on the identification of an exact geographic region of East Asia,[4] where economic, political, societal and cultural links are substantially tied in with each other, in this book the concept of regionalism may be understood in a twofold manner: first, as *a natural progress of regional convergence*, through which the economic, political and societal interactions among states with specific features of geographical proximity is bound to bring about the effect of regional identity and of regional community; second, as *a driving force of regional coherence*, through which certain regional mechanisms are seen to further stimulate regional cooperation among regional countries, promote a common interest in the region, as well as guide the regional order.

The post-Cold War regional setting has seen a variety of regional mechanisms flourish, and as a result there has been a new order in the making. In the late 1990s, the Asian financial crisis was a severe challenge for the region but at the same time it triggered a new dynamism for closer regional cooperation. In rebounding from financial turbulence, regional countries learned the dangers of being ineffective in their collective cooperation. This lesson has prompted East Asia to activate a new wave of regionalism in favour of managing a regional order. We intend to look back at the process of East Asian regionalism and divide it into three phases: the 'old regionalism' (inward-looking, politico-military orientation, Euro-centric), the 'new regionalism' (openness, outward-looking, economic orientation, linkage with nationalism, transnationalism),[5] and the 'second wave of new regionalism' (Asianness,[6] financial integration). We will attempt to answer the following questions: Why is regionalism once again attracting so much of our attention today? What are the salient differences between the 'old regionalism' and the 'new regionalism'?[7] With this new dynamism recurring in East Asia, what will we make of the new changes to regionalism and the implications of any possible emerging new paradigms for future regional development? During the past two decades, East Asia has experienced vital transformations of regional economic and political development with which regionalism is closely associated. Due to a lack of cooperative experience at the regional level, the development of regionalism in East Asia has not been directed by political will but is largely driven by the natural course of economic forces. It is therefore obvious that this form of regionalism is characterised by market dynamism. Since the 1980s, the pace of economic development has been pushing ahead the changes to regional economic structures. Regional countries have shifted their industrial focus further up the developmental ladders from primitive industries to manufacturing or from labour-intensive industries to capital- and technology-intensive industries. Nowadays, the progress of economic development has gone so far as to bring forth information- and knowledge-intensive industries.

In addition, the post-Cold War regional setting has stimulated numerous advantageous factors in the development of regionalism. In the economic field, the transformation of the economic structure coupled with an ever-increasing interdependence among regional countries has activated the changing phases of regionalism in East Asia. Throughout East Asia, a number of subregional economic groupings are flourishing, which are driven simply by economic dynamism. In the political field, the tight bipolarity of the Cold War structure has been eased somewhat. The fault line of national confrontation has been replaced by a range of factors that encompasses regional mechanisms, regional dialogues, regional regimes, economic interactions and cross-border networks. The Association of Southeast Asian Nations (ASEAN) has actively driven the pace of regionalism in order to broaden regional cooperation and thus to gain international parity in relation to other regional powers. For countries of ASEAN, through advocating regionalism it comes to stand at the centre of their foreign policy and regional strategy. The most important single factor influencing East Asia regional development today is China's internal development and attitude towards the region. Through successful economic developmental progress so far, China has been congregated into regional systems and markets. Economically, there seems to be no way back. Politically, it has become much harder for China to pull back, even if its policy changes at some future point. These thriving regional effects have led some to suggest that Kenichi Ohmae's 'region-state' is in fact in existence in East Asia.[8]

While the 1997 Asian financial crisis severely battered the region, regional countries including China and Japan, two of the most influential regional powers, joined forces to push for closer cooperation and to try to deepen the process of regional integration. An unprecedented step forward has been taken on issues directly related to financial and economic policy, which has traditionally fallen into the domain of national sovereignty. These dynamics have since aroused much attention among academics and practitioners in terms of the development of regional cooperation, the review of present regional mechanisms, the possible direction of regional integration, and the effect of the second wave of new regionalism as it emerges.

The recent development of regional processes in East Asia has indeed transformed the nature of the 'new regionalism.' In going beyond the previous understanding of that new regionalism, the region has already begun to centre its efforts under the complex of open regionalism and Asianisation, which would allow regional countries to keep up with global economic development and to advocate regional consciousness. One of the most serious and immediate effects of the Asian financial crisis was to cause disintegration in the region. This has provoked both a concerted effort to construct a means to manage a future crisis of this sort as well as revived the momentum for updating the 'new regionalism.' Unlike the cooperative nature of the new regionalism, the present endeavour has put forward concrete mechanisms of regional integration. Galvanised by the globalisation process, this new drive towards an unprecedented direction of regional integration is likely to lead to some form of regional paradigm shifting in East Asia, the notion of which is tentatively explored within this book.

After all these years, there is an abundance of literature seeking to examine the development of Asian regionalism, yet many fundamental questions remain unsolved. What is the main difference between the Western and Eastern understanding of regional concepts and, for that matter, regionalism itself? What kinds of cooperative regional experience is East Asian regionalism based upon? Do we truly have to measure regional development under the terms and definitions drawn from European experience? If not, where and what kind of regional economic cooperation experience is East Asian regionalism based upon? Regionalism has been an evolving process in East Asia; what exactly is the impact on regionalism in the aftermath of the Asian financial crisis? How significant are these new dynamics and what are the implications for the future direction of regional cooperation? What new features have emerged in the present dynamics of regionalism? What now? In asking all these questions, many would especially like to know in which direction regionalism may be heading from now on. Although regionalism may turn out to be another trend of political expediency for many, academics and practitioners in the region have tried to figure out the profound implications of these updated dynamics for regionalism. What has made East Asian regionalism so unique is its multiple forces of regional dynamism for further cooperation, which have appeared not only at official, non-official and individual levels, but also at the edge of illegal transnational activities across many national borders.

The principal objective of this book is twofold: first, it aims to produce a critical review of the evolution of the concept and practice of regionalism in East Asia since the 1960s; second, it explores the factors directing the future development of regional cooperation such as the emergence of a new paradigm. The major thrust of the book is based on the innovative approaches of examining the implications of this new regional dynamism for regionalism and it attempts to suggest various emerging new paradigms.

The book takes a historical, socio-politico approach while encompassing the discipline of international relations, and its subdiscipline of international political economy. It moves beyond traditional theoretical approaches such as realist, structuralist analysis and neoliberal institutionalism, arguing that while structure and power are obviously important, so too are process-oriented approaches. To this end, the book is highly definitive, and seeks to draw out the constraints and opportunities for economic and security cooperation by analysing the processes of East Asian regionalism. As such it explores the evolution of the concept of regionalism, the means by which progress is being made as well as the mechanisms through which this progress is carried out.

The regional concepts

The idea of regional cooperation as a means to bring forth peace, stability, reconstruction and development both for traditional states and newly independent states in the region had not been high on the agenda in East Asia. With the semi-exception of ASEAN, regional cooperation has either been largely absent or has tended to embrace politico-military arrangements manipulated by superpowers for most East Asian nations during the Cold War period. The whole concept of regionalism has been perceived as foreign to East Asia, and East Asian nations were tied up with various domestic and external priorities which, on the contrary, have had very little to do with any regional commitment. Due to the emergence of a range of new regional, inter-regional and global factors during the late 1980s and 1990s, however, regional cooperation has gradually come to be a declared objective of the majority of East Asian nations.

It is true that regionalism is prevailing in East Asia and that it encompasses notions like 'regional cooperation', 'regional integration', and 'regionalisation'. It is somewhat problematic that, without clarifying the definition of these notions, they are almost interchangeable depending on what approach is taken. Obviously, it is necessary to note their differences before we proceed with any further discussion on regionalism. Regional cooperation has been widely used to describe the nature of East Asian regionalism, since it has evolved as a certain process and condition of the cooperation between states and between other regional actors without becoming entangled in any legal form of commitment. It is imagined that throughout the regional process, some common awareness of interdependence will gradually come about. This does not however imply that regional countries may merge into a new body, although it has become apparent that, as a consequence of intensive interactions among regional countries in East Asia, there has indeed been a developing sense of a loosely knit community. The main function of regional cooperation in this context has been to promote mutual understanding and mutual trust, so that regional consensus may be reached and regional tension largely reduced.

Regional integration is measured by theoretical disciplines in more delicate terms than regional cooperation. Notwithstanding that it could mean a process and/or a condition (product), most arguments, especially those directed towards East Asia, are concerned with a process. In no way would it refer to an end-product in the region as acquired through the regional process. The main thrust behind defining integration as a process is that 'two or more states form a new entity' and may become a political community.[9] In terms of a general understanding, regional integration 'can refer to the legal and institutional relationship within a region in which economic transactions take place, or it can refer to the market relationship among goods and factors within the region.'[10] It is clear then that in terms of agenda-setting, regional integration can proceed in the sense of a legal and institutional relationship but not under that of the market relationship. Displaying quite a different turnout of events, East Asia has experienced a certain institutional process; however, the existing regional institutions do not imply any sense of legalised regional integration. On the whole, what ASEAN, Asia–Pacific Economic Cooperation (APEC), ASEAN Regional Forum (ARF) and Asia Europe Meeting (ASEM) have exercised is the institutional instrumental approach to regional integration.[11] In this regard, East Asian countries envisage regional cooperation as a way of extending foreign policy and would therefore wish to maintain it as an interstate affair.

The main debate, which has followed the major distinctions of regional integration in European analysis, may also have set the scene in East Asia for the convergence between the 'state-model' and the 'community-model.'[12] Regional integration in East Asia has always implied for attainment of distant hopes as held up by integrationists. In fact, the process of regional integration has not had a clear interim goal – such as a customs union, free-trade area, common market, economic union – since there has been no true legal and institutional process in the region. Significantly, however, the present practice in monetary integration under the 'ASEAN plus three' process might serve as the first-ever bold attempt to revive these past hopes.

'Regionalisation' was originally used in accounting for the regional economic process, through which economic interactions and industrial cooperation among regional economies would be integrated into a mainstream of development and promote certain coherent conditions for economic policy. This conceptualisation later came to be broadened as both a *de jure*, 'driven by political forces that are motivated by security, economic or other concerns' and as a *de facto* development, 'driven by the same microeconomic forces that drive globalisation.'[13] On the other hand, regionalisation paired with globalisation emphasises the process of transforming various policy domains from 'relative heterogeneity' to 'increased homogeneity.'[14]

There is no fixed formulation on when and where one notion is best selected to define regionalism. Rather, since regionalism in practice is a developing process, it is likely to transform in conceptualisation as different circumstances arise.

Characteristics of regionalism in East Asia

Ever since the end of the Second World War, the world has witnessed a constant yet gradual development of regionalism in recent international relations. The emergence of regionalism has become the ethos of bipolar confrontational international systems. Following in the vein of Cold War thinking, various regional alliance systems appear to have been pushing forward regional cohesion within each camp. Under this view, it has been a natural outcome to defend the group's common external threats, since regional countries have sensed that the only alternative has been to strengthen cooperation as a mechanism with which to protect their national interest and thus extend the welfare of individual societies. Regionalism in this period was characterised by this sort of inward-looking nature and politico-military orientation.[15] Most economic, political and social interactions in certain parts of the region have been largely motivated by the same political, security and, to some extent, the same economic issues.

When economic interactions across national borders began later to take shape more fully, and as economic processes came under the effects and dynamism of economic interdependence, we started to see an acceleration of world development. In this process, economic incentives came to be the main determining factors pushing forward a worldwide development of regionalism. In other words, the desire for foreign trade and direct foreign investment has shaped the way that regionalism has come about. For the first time in history, more and more countries have been able to become involved in increasing regional processes of economic interaction. Surprisingly for some, the momentum has not been totally dictated by political reasons but to a larger extent by economic demands calling for mutual benefit. As a result, economic interactions are further intensified by the all-out activities of the private sectors.

It is true to say that both private sector contributions and market forces have emerged as critical factors of regional cooperation. This economic trend has persistently stimulated much academic effort to explore regionalism from the perspective of regional trade establishments. Hence, arguments about whether regional trade blocs would lead to the emergence of a regional fortress, or rather, further momentum for economic cooperation, have continuously aroused major debate among academics and practitioners.[16]

Over time, the nature of regionalism has gradually come to be characterised by the broader aspects of regional and national development rather than by simple economic incentives for the region. Previous understandings of regionalism seen largely through the lens of trade concentration could not define and explain exactly what has been accelerated in the past decade or so. In particular, when we take the need to generate economic welfare as the basis for and the economic explanation of regionalism, this has not been able to reflect the political nature and its profound implications for regional and national development. Although regionalism in Europe and elsewhere is largely formed and noted by way of economic cooperation, the process of regional integration may have developed further than anticipated. Regionalism has thus been referred to and analysed in terms of a wide variety of regional interactions: regionalisation, regional identity, regional interstate cooperation, regional integration and regional cohesion.[17]

The process of regionalism in East Asia contains a set of unique characteristics. Due to the complicated recent past history of nations in the region, an accordant concept of regional unity is largely non-existent. Nor does East Asian regionalism *per se*, retain sufficient experience in cooperation at the regional level. It is also worth noting that the 1980s East Asia did not have any region-wide cooperative mechanisms in existence. ASEAN as a subregional grouping is an exception. Although the establishment of ASEAN was motivated by politico-military concerns, it has been anchored in terms of its economic formation. In Northeast Asia, enduring politico-security tensions along the Korea Peninsula continue to dominate much of the regional scene and thus have continued to dictate a major area of national priority. For decades, apart from certain bilateral (alliance) relationships (the US–South Korea, the US–Japan, and China–North Korea), and excluding the private sectors' endeavours to explore regional economic benefits, the subregion has been found lacking in experience with respect to region-wide official cooperation, let alone in terms of developing full-fledged regional cooperation mechanisms. Nevertheless, with economic dynamism acting as a catalyst, regionalism is gradually emerging and becoming fashionable in the rest of East Asia. Moreover, the momentum of economic integration has further accelerated the pace of political reconciliation in the Peninsula.

More recently, due to emergence of a novel set of regional, inter-regional and global factors during the late 1980s and 1990s, regional cooperation has gradually become one of the declared objectives of most East Asian nations. A range of new factors relating to environment, economic development, transnational crimes, human security, narcotics, disease, weapons, refugees and migrants have come to be common concerns among all regional countries and, concurrently, have become pressing issues in terms of national and regional policy. In the post-Cold War era, these concerns have even stepped up the progress and force of regional interdependence as well as directly generating a new momentum for regionalism. However, it remains to be seen whether recent initiatives at different levels (such as at the subregional level of ASEAN, ASEAN Free Trade Area (AFTA), the Growth Triangle and the Greater China; at the inter-regional level of APEC, ARF, ASEM; or even the East Asian Economic Caucus (EAEC), and the latest development of the 'ASEAN plus 3' process at the intra-regional level) may be considered as substantial commitments to the construction of regionalism in East Asia.

Into the new century, the region has also come to envision a renewed momentum toward reviving what has been termed 'the new regionalism.' The dynamism behind this wave of regionalism has been driven largely by the collective efforts of regional countries in responding to the Asian financial crises and the effects of globalisation.[18] Although the Asian financial crisis and its profound effects in the near term did result in a disintegration progress in the region, the region bounced back under the ever-ambitious initiative of regional integration. This has to some extent changed the pace of Asian regionalism. Frustrated by the inactivity of existing regional establishments to resist effects of the crisis, many in the region have felt the pressing necessity to come up with an agenda to enable the enhancement of cooperation. As a result, this renewed attempt to bring closer cooperation among regional countries has also brought forth a new agenda aimed at setting up a regional monetary integration scheme for the region. What is even more significant through the process is the intensification of the sense of 'Asianness.' Against this background, in parallel to existing or newly established intergovernmental arrangements, other substantial forms of regional cooperation seem to be emerging and being reinforced in East Asia (e.g. inter-regionalism and business networks). This appears to suggest that under the shadow of the previous scope of regional cooperation, 'the second wave of new regionalism' is emerging and may become the potential key behind the development of East Asia well into the twenty-first century. Yet it remains to be seen whether or not such a new contribution to regionalism buildup will firmly lead to greater concrete commitment towards the construction of an East Asian community.

Regionalism with regional network power

From the late 1960s, the increasing demand for a newer form of regionalism began to emerge in both Europe and the Asia Pacific as a result of growing global economic interdependence between trading countries. In the Asia Pacific region, many initiatives aimed towards regional economic cooperation (e.g. the Pacific Free Trade Area (PAFTA) and Organisation for Pacific Trade and development (OPTAD)) were put forward but later failed in their attempts.[19]

Despite this fact, throughout the post-war era, the dynamism of regional cooperation has never been completely erased. Its persistent effort was not carefully planned by states but encouraged by the momentum of catching up in economic development, increasing intra-regional economic transactions, and the effort of promoting economic liberalization. In 1975, regional businessmen established a private regional organisation, the Pacific Basin Economic Cooperation (PBEC), as a mechanism to support multinational economic cooperation and to encourage transnational business cooperation in the region. Later, in 1980, the momentum of regionalism led to the establishment of the Pacific Economic Cooperation Conference (PECC), which involved a combination of academics, businessmen and government officials in its informal set-up. It was out of this successful experience of PECC that growing demands for closer economic cooperation brought forward an early initiative of building a Pacific community to establish APEC in 1989.

Throughout this growing trend of regionalism, one might wonder what exactly is the driving force behind this constant regional economic integration process. As has been characterised by the spontaneous efforts of the private sector, the economic rationale to catch up on the developmental ladder and the vision to further promote economic transactions within the region have inspired the process. Apparently, this increasing integration process in East Asia initially, had more to do with general hopes for promoting joint efforts in economic interaction rather than with political consideration. Although Asian culture may play a substantial part in forming loose regional mechanisms for cooperation, many East Asian countries do not have sufficient confidence to become involved in and to some extent are even reluctant to commit seriously to multilateral cooperation. They wonder whether the effects of regional cooperation may in the long term lead to their loss of sovereignty, which for them would be a significant loss, since obtaining sovereignty has become a symbol of successful nation-building. In addition, most regional countries could not face the fear of being dominated by regional powers in the process of regional integration. It is not surprising to learn that, unlike the case in Europe, regional countries in East Asia would not want to push forward an institutional approach of regional integration. Instead, they have over the years shown minimal satisfaction with the progress of regional cooperation.

Early on, due to the fact that regional countries showed minimal enthusiasm towards the idea of regional integration, it is natural to suggest that market forces have taken over and directed progress. The momentum for regionalism in East Asia mainly derives from the endeavours of the private sector and the progressive economic development process. Moreover, it is fair to say that over the years the degree of regional economic interdependence has dramatically increased among regional countries, which has led to growing interactions of the private sector across national boundaries. In particular, Japanese enterprises and overseas Chinese business groups have expanded in the region and have stimulated the further regional progress of economic development. As a result of the globalisation and regionalisation process, civil societies are gradually emerging in the region. Apart from nominal regional establishments and the private sector, regional networks have become well extended among government officials, politicians, academics and individual citizens.

New regionalism and the second new regionalism in East Asia

Into the post-Cold War era, regionalism has seen prospering growth throughout the world. In East Asia, the momentum of regionalism has even been seen to drive much harder across the board of economic, political, security and social domains. With the advent of a post-Cold War environment, the globalisation process and subsequent changes, many have witnessed that East Asia is quickly transforming itself, and has thus gradually changed the usual norms of interaction across countries and economies. In a broader sense, East Asian regionalism in fact refers to inter-regionalism, intra-regionalism, subregionalism and the effects of globalism. Not only has cooperation in the economic field been at the centre of the regional process, but a growing aspiration for security cooperation has also become one of the key pillars of regionalism. In the past decade, the ASEAN Post-ministerial Meeting (ASEAN-PMC) has become the first regional forum tackling regional security issues. This practice generated further the momentum for the establishment of the Council for Security Cooperation in the Asia Pacific (CSCAP) and ARF, which have served as regional open forums for dialogue over regional security issues with inter-regional representation.

As the 1997 financial crisis swept through East Asia it seriously eroded not only regional economies *per se* but also people's confidence in continuing the pursuit of prosperous regional development. One of the after-effects of the Asian financial crisis in East Asia has been to bring about a serious commitment of regional governments to pushing forward regional economic cooperation. A new environment, new demands and a new framework have enhanced the desire among regional countries for the establishment of 'ASEAN plus three'. In terms of regional cooperation programmes, 'multilateralism has suffered because of the perceived impotency of the major regional institutions during the crisis'.[20] What really matters in the intermediate term is how regional countries may recover from the past experience of regional institutional inertia. Certainly, the lesson taught by the crisis has further inspired many down-to-earth proposals for closer regional cooperation; for example, the Japanese initiative on the Asian Monetary Fund and the 'New Miyazawa Initiatives' on economic aid programmes,[21] the 'Chiang Mai Initiative' by the 'ASEAN plus three' process,[22] as well as the proposals for regional free-trade zones.

The way in which regional countries came to recognise the most urgent task of rebuilding the cooperative process has implied a new regionalism in the making. By and large, there are seven important features of regionalism that deserve our attention as the process of regionalism continues.

First, as new security issues have come to head the policy agenda in many regional countries, and since regional security mechanisms have been taken ever more seriously, the regional integration progress has seen a new impetus in the joint forces of economic and security aspects for regional cooperation. With APEC, PECC, ASEM, the Korean Peninsula Energy Development Organization (KEDO), ARF and CSCAP in place, different forms of regional and inter-regional efforts are indeed bringing regional countries ever closer to each other. It is not far-fetched to suggest that the present effort has broadened the practical scope of regional integration in East Asia.

Second, East Asian regionalism is gradually progressing in the vein of 'ASEANization.' In the post-Cold War setting, ASEAN countries have stood together in an attempt to deal with external powers collectively and so to enhance relative parity in international politics. To non-ASEAN members, this united front is regarded as ASEAN unity, which becomes a major drive for establishment of a regional community. The experience of APEC, ASEAN PMC process, ARF, ASEM, and most recently the 'ASEAN plus three', indicates that ASEAN has played a leading role in driving regional agendas forward.[23] In terms of the structure and decision-making process, all existing regional architectures have more or less accorded, if not linked, with ASEAN's vision of community-building. Even though immediately after the Asian financial crisis the unity of ASEAN was seriously crippled internally and externally, and although China, Japan and South Korea have taken up leadership in the 'ASEAN plus three' process, it does not fundamentally change the trend of the ever-developing ASEANisation.

Third, although the 'ASEAN plus three' process has been established for four years (since 1997), it has quickly become one of the most decisive and promising forums of regional cooperation. It also has great prospects and has gained substantial attention from regional countries. Based on the thinking of fashioning fresh attempts to counter the Asian financial crisis, the main focus of the process is to manage regional challenges incurred by the globalisation effect and to ensure the future direction of regional integration collectively. One of the incentives behind establishing this process was that regional countries were fed up with the incompetence of existing regional establishments during the Asian financial crisis. It shows in part that regional countries hope for something more effective and perhaps with a more accountable capacity for their purposes. Taking into account recent developments, 'ASEAN plus three' (thirteen governments) will in the near term be the major driving force of the regional agenda (regionalism).

Fourth, the geographic domain of Asian regionalism has become more comprehensive. In the past, Southeast Asia has shown deviation from development in Northeast Asia. Although East Asian regional integration has gained ground in many ways, it can actually be divided into two geographic subregions. Most issue areas that the existing regional establishments cover are inter-regionalist or subregionalist in nature rather than intra-regionalist. This current new development for a more comprehensive Asian regionalism however is in line with a conventional approach, where the formation of regionalism is confined to neighbouring countries within immediate geographic proximity.

The financial crisis has taught an important lesson to the region: an individual economy alone does not have the sufficient strength to counter global economic challenges and, for that matter, inter-regionalism or subregionalism cannot be relied on to prevent the region from being attacked again. The economic and political reality gives rise to a rationale that is in favour of enhancing regional integration progress in a wider region. As a result, the dynamism of the 'ASEAN plus three' that encourages the tying together of Southeast Asia with Northeast Asia has changed the overall nature of Asian regionalism. In regional security, the first participation of North Korea in the seventh meeting of ARF in July 2000 marked the milestone of a joint effort in developing East Asian regionalism.

Fifth, governments' engagement in regional integration has always played a decisive role in the whole process. In the past, East Asian regionalism was unable to fulfil the critical element of theoretical requirements since the process lacked government support. This has changed now that the 'ASEAN plus three' process has seen the firm commitment of regional governments towards development.[24] As the process enhances discussions on regional consciousness, the region seems increasingly to embrace the regional community-building effort. With governments' involvement, awareness of regional identity is increasingly more salient than ever before.

Sixth, sovereign states may not have been the sole determining factor in the globalisation process. Current regionalism in East Asia nevertheless highlights the exact opposite feature. As a point of fact, ARF and the 'ASEAN plus three' process have been based on participation of sovereign states. Despite repeated assertions of the principle of inclusiveness, some other important countries in the region (i.e. Taiwan and North Korea) have, for obvious political reasons, been left out of the current endeavour for regionalism. While the major purpose of regionalism is to bring about an ever peaceful and prosperous region, the absence of both countries involved in major security concerns to date and the omission of Taiwan's economic influence in the region may prove to be incompatible with present regionalism.

Seventh, with the advent of the 'ASEAN plus three', a certain hierarchical structure of East Asian regionalism has emerged. While the 'ASEAN plus three' as intra-regionalism is designated at the head of the agenda, ARF (security cooperation), APEC (economic cooperation) and ASEM (specific regional focus) as inter-regionalism occupy second place, and are operating according to their functional division of labour. ASEAN, as a form of subregionalism, remains the backbone of East Asian regionalism and is in third place. Finally, down the base of the agenda, there is a vast variety of economic interactions and regional networks that are counted on.

Structural prospect for the new order

It is our goal in this book to critically identify the ways in which East Asians (scholars and practitioners) have answered explicitly or implicitly the central question raised in its title. Therefore, in considering this notion of paradigm shifting, the various chapters have concentrated not only on a review of past scholarly publications, but have also gone on to analyse regionalism in practice as well as to make predictions about the future directions of regionalism. Accordingly, the structure of this book may be divided into three parts: theoretical revisits, regional cooperation in practice, and new directions.

Although East Asia has not had much experience or understanding of regionalism in the past, what has been given credence is an Asian track record of regionalism, the nature of which has not necessarily been based on the Western experience of regional integration. By challenging the notion of a general trend of regionalism, Fu-Kuo Liu, (Chapter 1) begins with the assumption that there is East Asian regionalism, and examines the concepts of regionalism in East Asia. He suggests that although it may still be too early to seek a single definition, the concept of East Asian regionalism may be theorised in rather different ways from conventional thinking. Following on from this, in order to provide an effective framework for a new approach, he goes on to conceptualise several important concepts: informality, incrementalism, bottom-upism, consensus-building, minimalism, and ASEANisation.

In Chapter 2, Jörn Dosch reviews the arguments of integration theorists and contrasts their more traditional approaches to regionalism with that of literature within the context of the 'new regionalism'. He explores the meaning of the latter concept in the light of East Asian experience, and highlights important features which indicate that a general shift of paradigms has occurred in the study of regionalism since the end of the Cold War. More importantly however, Dosch finds that there has been a convergence of issues and actors in the study of regionalism in three main areas: first, he states that 'it is difficult, if not impossible in some cases, to draw an exact line between the views of academics and practitioners'; second, he finds that over time, views among West and East Asian scholars has shown a significant degree of overlap; and finally, he concludes that 'a striking element of the new regionalism is the convergence of analysis and advocacy'.

Chapter 3 undertakes both a theoretical and empirical review of East Asian economic cooperation. Similar to Dosch in his review, Philippe Régnier seeks to examine the degree of convergence between theoretical and empirical issues; however, he narrows the scope of his enquiry by treating ASEAN as a case study. He emphasises that the extreme heterogeneity of East Asia has constantly challenged two key aspects of regional theories; members of this regional entity reject the notion of institutionalised economic integration and, in turn, are reluctant to agree to any supranational transfers of competencies. Particularly since the 1990s, this issue of unity versus diversity has become central to ASEAN, although debate within the grouping has been limited to unity in the context of inter-regional cooperation under the guise of an open regionalism rather than being defined as closer integration among member states. He suggests that in opting for enlargement as opposed to a deepening of economic cooperation, ASEAN 'has widened the gap and disparities among the economic and social regimes of all member-states.' These findings also have important implications in light of recent developments in the wake of the financial crisis.

Along with Bustelo in Chapter 8, Régnier refers to the incapacity of ASEAN to face the crisis in a unified manner as a reason to question the relevant strengths as opposed to the weaknesses in this regional grouping of economic cooperation. He goes on to point out that an absence of mechanisms in place to rescue these member-states facing difficulty has in fact been an inherent feature of ASEAN throughout its evolution. This being the case, he nevertheless concludes with the comment that defining ASEAN as a Southeast Asian regional grouping may be too narrow, since 'Whether merged or not to wider regional or inter-regional concepts such as East Asia/EAEC or APEC/Pacific Rim, the ASEAN economies are more and more linked to *de facto* or *de jure* groupings, which associate both developing and developed nations.'

In undertaking a review of the economic, political and security perspectives towards regionalism, Chapter 4 by Fu-Kuo Liu has attempted to bring a closer insight into the development of those dimensions within the regional setting. Liu seeks to explore the implications of a progressive regionalism for national security in East Asia, and aims to develop an understanding of the political sector of security and the assumption that increased regional political fragmentation would jeopardise regional stability and thus result in greater security concerns. Since such fragmentation in this region would likely eliminate any opportunity of promoting cooperation at the international level, and may even render related states vulnerable to threats, its effects would give rise to security threats to individual states. Some regional practices have shown a corresponding impact upon the political fragmentation of regional security. As regionalism based on economic cooperation develops, he reminds us that we should place the whole process of regional progress on a more realistic basis of political disintegration. He suggests that the political sector of security could serve as the complementary dimension of studying East Asian security as well as the development of regionalism.

Chapter 5, by Nadhavathna Krishnamra, a practitioner within government, presents an inside view with a substantial focus on policy issues. He sets out to examine both the past and present mechanisms at work under the auspices of ASEAN. In addition to highlighting how the region has developed, his approach intends to give an insight into the possible future prospects for the Asia Pacific region as a whole, since Krishnamra argues that ASEAN and its processes will continue to be a central component of future regional cooperation among East Asian economies. In terms of region-building, voluntarianism and pragmatism have constituted the key foundations of ASEAN cooperation. In the wake of the financial crisis however, there has been speculation as to whether or not there may be an emerging divergence in direction for the members of ASEAN. Rejecting this notion completely, Krishnamra sees a continuance of state-to-state solutions and predicts that, while only at a tentative stage, ASEAN is showing signs of a more predictable and rule-based pattern of relations particularly in terms of economic spheres.

The notion of regional governance and the varying views towards regionalism itself have been clearly set out in Chapter 6 by Tsutomu Kikuchi, who begins by examining the characteristics of international relations in the region. He goes on to analyse the underpinnings of (global) regulatory regimes covering Northeast Asia, regionalism and bilateralism as well as the domestic political changes taking place in the respective countries. Perhaps most notable is his effort to point out the importance of developing multi-layered nested regimes. He argues that if such a construct were successfully implemented it would serve to effectively regulate the interactions among the countries of the region, and in turn would place mutual constraints on them. Reflecting back on the concerns over the various deficiencies of past efforts in the region, this chapter has, in a broader sense, been devoted to the bettering of prospects for regionalism. In conclusion, Kikuchi assures us that an effective and accountable regional mechanism in East Asia would require the following features: (1) reliance on multilateral consultations among the major powers to manage critical situations; (2) a commitment to protect all essential members, and (3) a mutual recognition that all the major powers must retain equal status and that none should be humiliated.

In Chapter 7, Christopher Dent has concentrated on the development of Northeast Asian regional economic integration. He makes efforts to put forward some creative proposals to future regional cooperation. Taking up the theoretical line, he begins by examining some propositions for economic integration in this region: first, that the fundamental principle for any substantive regional economic integration arrangement or project to be viable in Northeast Asia is inclusiveness; second, that the political economies of Japan, China, South Korea and Taiwan possess strong developmental characteristics, inferring that their respective national economic development has in various guises been strategised by the state. His third proposition points out that recent changes in the developmental political economies of Northeast Asian states have predisposed them to new regionalist possibilities. For Japan, South Korea and Taiwan this is in particular reference to the evolving nature of developmental statism and the shift from national to regional economic management. For China and, to a lesser extent Taiwan, the compliance to meet WTO membership will make an important impact on domestic economic and political processes, integrating them into wider regional and international frameworks. Dent concludes with a proposal for the creation of a Northeast Asian Regional Economic Association (NEAREA) as a flexible yet purpose-driven regional economic integration arrangement for the region. The initiative relates not only to helping Northeast Asian states come to common terms with the new developmental challenges identified, but also seeks to bring Northeast Asia's positive contributions towards a broader regional, transregional and multilateral economic order.

The devastating effects of the financial crisis upon East Asian economies has stimulated strenuous debate. While seeking to highlight the salient features underlying the crisis, in Chapter 8, Pablo Bustelo extends his analysis to examine the dynamic effects upon the region in the wake of the crisis and, in turn, questions the relevance of expecting a continuation of the pre-existing features of East Asian regionalism. Two main implications drawn from his analysis are that the East Asian developmental and state-led model of capitalism is likely to see reinforcement; and that the dynamics of the crisis have opened a window of opportunity for an enhancement of the prospects for an 'East Asian' understanding of the region. In addition, he argues that some kind of strictly East Asian formal integration may prove to be desirable.

Chapter 9 is both a review and critique of what Wei-Wei Zhang terms a 'diversified understanding' over the evolution of a Greater China, and takes a look at both Western and Eastern analyses of the concept. Beginning with an investigation of the economic implications, Zhang goes on to consider both its cultural and political meaning. In examining its economic implications, Zhang outlines a range of subconcepts that have been used to further define the term 'Greater China' with reference to economic goals. Each of these subconcepts, in terms of origin, reference and implication for greater integration, is explored in detail, with the conclusion that the most politically neutral term of the *Chinese Economic Area* is in fact the most commonly used term. Finally, Zhang also delves into the implications of a Greater China for East Asian regionalism, and highlights the effects of the financial crisis on such developments.

In his analysis of Taiwan and Mainland China as a subregion, in Chapter 10 Tse-Kang Leng emphasises that political factors have played a dominant role in any perceived regional cooperation and regime formation. In particular, the political distrust and misperception between these two actors has been identified as both a major obstacle and an impediment to the institutionalisation of economic integration and regional cooperation. Further to this, both the scope and direction of informal integration between Taiwan and Mainland China is seen to be determined by three main forces: economic globalisation, political distrust and national sovereignty issues. Similar to the development of East Asian regionalism, sovereignty issues loom large over economic integration processes, though on a much magnified scale. Drawing on a host of empirical evidence, Leng delves into the intricacies of business networking with reference to both Taiwanese and MNC alliances with Mainland Chinese counterparts. While political factors have been a counterforce to that of globalisation, Leng concludes with the observation that individual political elites could play a more important role in the process of regional integration and cooperation.

Chapter 11 explores the underpinnings of new developments in regionalism in the wake of the Cold War. Heiner Hänggi seeks to further enhance an understanding of the particular unique form of regionalism that has evolved in the Asia Pacific region. He takes a comparative approach, focusing upon the processes at work through which the three main regional entities – North America, Western Europe and East Asia – carry out group-to-group relations. To this end, the linkages between two relatively fresh concepts 'new regionalism and inter-regionalism' are clearly drawn out and defined. Inter-regionalism is seen to have a spillover effect on the development of regionalism for member-states of a particular regional entity. Since Hänggi seeks to undertake a deeper analysis of the causes and consequences stemming from such spill-over effects, he thereby utilises a case study of the Asia Europe Meeting ASEM in its biannual regional caucus.

This joint effort of exploring new ground for East Asian regionalism has followed the most recent developments currently occurring in the region, especially with respect to the effect of the post-Cold War development and the impact of the Asian financial crisis on regionalism. We have aimed to put forward a new set of characteristics that are able to describe the emerging dynamism of regionalism and, as such, hope to pave the way for the further exploration and perhaps deeper engagement in current debates. We believe that this new development as it is now occurring in East Asia will have profound implications for the region, and thus is worthy of further research.

Notes

1 The institutional perspective taken by most studies, for example: Louise Fawcett and Andrew Hurrell, eds, *Regionalism in World Politics: Regional Organization and International Order* (New York: Oxford University Press, 1995) and Robert Lawrence, *Regionalism, Multilateralism and Deeper Integration* (Washington, DC: The Brookings Institution, 1996); the perspective referring to trading blocs and mechanisms taken by Ross Garnaut and Peter Drysdale, eds, *Asia Pacific Regionalism: Readings in International Economic Relations* (Pymble: Harper Educational Publishers, 1994).

2 Peter J. Katzenstein and Takashi Shiraishi, eds, *Network Powers: Japan and Asia* (Ithaca, NY: Cornell University Press, 1997); Peter Kazenstein *et. al., Asian Regionalism* (Ithaca, NY: Cornell University Press, 2000); Edward K.Y. Chen and C.H. Kwan, eds, *Asia's Borderless Economy: The Emergence of Subregional Economic Zone* (St Leonards, Australia: Allen & Unwin, 1997).

3 There has not been much definition of regionalism prevailing in the region. One of the rare definitions of regionalism in East Asia offered by Hasnan Habib is widely noted. Habib, 'Defining the "Asia Pacific Region",' *Indonesian Quarterly*, Vol. 23, No. 4, pp. 302–312.

4 The East Asian region in this book covers mainly Japan, the Korean Peninsula, China, Taiwan, and the whole of Southeast Asia (ten countries).

5 The development of the regional integration process in the 1980s was seen as the revival of regionalism. According to its new features of regional systems, 'new regionalism' was broadly defined. For example, Norman D. Palmer, *The New Regionalism in Asia and the Pacific* (Lexington, MA: Lexington Books, 1991), pp. 1–8; Wilfred J. Ethier, 'The new regionalism', *The Economic Journal*, Vol. 108, No. 409 (July 1998), pp. 1149–1161; Bjorn Hettne, 'The new regionalism: a prologue', in Bjorn Hettne, Andras Inotai and Osvaldo Sunkel, eds, *Globalism and the New Regionalism* (Basingstoke: Macmillan, 1999), pp. xvi–xvii.

6 The notion of 'Asianness' emerges as an important symbol in identifying Asian groupings. Richard Higgot, 'The international political economy of regionalism: the Asia–Pacific and European compared', in William D. Coleman and Geoffrey R.D. Underhill, eds, *Regionalism and Global Economic Integration* (London: Routledge, 1998), pp. 59–61.

7 See the first section of Jörn Dosch's contribution (Chapter 2, this volume).

8 Kenichi Ohmae, *The End of the Nation State: The Rise of Regional Economies* (New York: The Free Press, 1995).

9 Charels Pentland, 'Functionalism and theories of international political integration', in A.J.R. Groom and Paul Taylor, eds, *Functionalism: Theory and Practice in International Relations* (New York: Crane, Russak & Company Inc, 1975), pp. 10–11.

10 Richard Cooper, 'Worldwide regional integration: is there an optimal size of the integrated area?', in Garnaut and Drysdale, eds, *Asia Pacific Regionalism: Readings in International Economic Relations,* p. 12.

11 Higgot, 'The international political economy of regionalism: the Asia–Pacific and European compared', p. 58.

12 Pentland, 'Functionalism and theories of international political integration', p. 11.

13 Charles Oman, 'The policy challenges of globalisation and regionalisation', Policy Brief No. 11 (Paris: OECD, 1996), p. 2.

14 Bjorn Hettne, 'Globalization and the new regionalism: the second great transformation', in Hettne, A, Inotai and O. Sunkel, eds, *Globalism and the New Regionalism,* pp. 11–12.

15 Palmer, *The New Regionalism in Asia and the Pacific;* Hettne, 'The new regionalism: a prologue'.

16 Edward D. Mansfield and Helen V. Milner, 'The new wave of regionalism', *International Organization,* Vol. 53, No. 3 (Summer 1999), pp. 605–606.

17 Some concrete categories of regionalism have been offered by Louise Fawcett, 'Regionalism in historical perspective,' in Fawcett and Hurrell, eds, *Regionalism in World Politics: Regional Organization and International Order*; International political and economic approaches to regionalism have been highlighted by Edward Mansfield and Helen Milner, 'The political economy of regionalism: an overview,' in their co-edited *The Political Economy of Regionalism* (New York: Columbia University Press, 1997).

18 Simon S.C. Tay, 'ASEAN and East Asia: a new regionalism?', in Simon Tay, Jesus Estanislo and Hadi Soesastro, eds, *A New ASEAN in a New Millennium* (Jakarta: Center for Strategic and International Studies, 2000), pp. 229–230.

19 The early development of the Asia Pacific regional proposal effort is elaborated by Peter Drysdale, *International Economic Pluralism: Economic Policy in East Asia and the Pacific* (New York: Columbia University Press, 1988), pp. 204–228; Hadi Soesastro, 'Pacific economic cooperation: the history of an idea', in Garnaut and Drysdale, eds, *Asia Pacific Regionalism: Readings in International Economic Relations,* pp. 77–88; also for later regional development see Kozo Kato, 'Open regionalism and Japan's systemic vulnerability,' in P. Kazenstein, *et. al., Asian Regionalism,* pp. 40–42.

20 Desmond Ball, *The Council for Security Cooperation in the Asia Pacific: Its Record and Its Prospects,* Canberra Papers on Strategy and Defence No. 139 (Canberra: the Australian National University, 2000), p. 45.

21 On 3 October 1998, in the hope of assisting Asian neighbouring countries in coping with their economic difficulties, Japan launched a new initiative of a US$30 billion supporting package, 'A new initiative to overcome the Asian currency crisis: new Miyazawa initiative', (http://www.mof.go.jp/english/if/ele042.htm).

22 'The joint statement of the ASEAN + 3 Finance Ministers' meeting', 6 May 2000, Chiang Mai, Thailand (http://www.mof.go.jp/english/if/if014.htm).

23 Abdullah Ahmad Badawi, 'Keynote address', in Stephen Leong, ed., *ASEAN Towards 2020: Strategic Goals and Future Directions* (KL: ISIS Malaysia, 1998), pp. 15–16; see also the comments on active regional effort of ASEAN in 'ASEAN: building the peace in Southeast Asia', by H.E. Rodolfo Severino, Secretary-General of the ASEAN, at the Fourth High-Level Meeting between the United Nations and regional organisations on cooperation for peace-building, United Nations, New York, 6–7 February 2001.

24 For instance, the leaders of ASEAN countries at their latest Informal Summit (the fourth) held between 22 and 25 November 2000 agreed to launch an Initiative for ASEAN Integration (IAI). 'Press statement by Chairman, the 4th ASEAN Informal Summit', Singapore, 25 November 2000 (http://www.asean.or.id/summit/infs4_cps.htm).

Part I

The critical review of regional concepts and theories of regionalism

1 East Asian regionalism

Theoretical perspectives

Fu-Kuo Liu

Over the years, East Asia as a region has become increasingly integrated through intense economic links, growing intra-regional trade, and, more recently, the general demand for regional security cooperation, all of which have been occurring at an unprecedented pace. The processes of economic development serve as an impetus for heightening regional cooperation, which continues to hold the politically divided region together. At first, it was the momentum of economic growth, coupled with market forces that propelled the whole progress of regional economic cooperation and the emergence of regional arrangements. Later, East Asian outward-looking economies had to come to terms with tighter international trade competition and the pressures of trading constraints, since trade blocs elsewhere in Europe and North America had emerged and were attempting to regulate trade relations with outsiders according to their preferences. During the period when the global trade regimes were under the prolonged negotiation process of the Uruguay Round, East Asian countries began to respond to these external challenging new factors and came to realise that they did not have much choice but to stand together and work collectively. Economic regionalism has thus taken shape in East Asia. Its characteristics may be explored from three dimensions: economic dynamic division of labour, institutional characteristics through industrial cooperation, and regional organisations.[1] While economists may have focused more on the first two dimensions, political scientists tend to look at the effect of the last dimension on regional process in a broader perspective. Apart from the above-mentioned dimensions, several other dimensions within the regional process may also have been emerging; for example, integration of labour markets, underground transnational movements and illegal business networking across borders have also been accelerated by the process of regional economic growth. These potentially resilient regional dynamics will obviously also have substantial effects on the development of regionalism as much as the above-mentioned dimensions, and may have paved the way for future regional integration. They have however not yet been sufficiently explored, and deserve our closer attention and further analysis.

Economic regionalism in East Asia is characterised by a prevailing outward-looking tendency and thus has come to be depicted as the 'new regionalism.'[2]

The open regionalism that has prevailed in the Asia–Pacific Economic Conference (APEC) process has been at the centre of this new regionalism.[3] In addition to an economic-based regionalism, the post-Cold War environment has found itself observing the multi-dimensional development of regionalism. These new circumstances have supplied the region with an exceptional opportunity within which to include the broader security aspect, which is based upon a comprehensive concept of security still within the thrust of the existing regionalism.[4] The development of regional cooperation with both economic and security aspects has substantively enriched the development of regionalism. To some extent, the desire for regional security cooperation and the buildup of security establishments has implied that regional countries are attempting to step up efforts to deepen the process of regional cooperation. Although right from the very beginning the security aspect has not been an outcome of any deliberate regional integration, the process of security cooperation has so far at least been conducive to the continuous process of fostering mutual understanding and enhancing the degree of confidence-building within the region. It may not yet have produced something credible to long-term regional integration, but it is certainly beneficial to the process.

In the same vein, the general structure of regional cooperation in East Asia was severely shaken in the wake of the Asian financial crisis in 1997, which left numerous economic, political and social scars throughout the region. It has even challenged the long-standing dominant thinking of regional cooperation, which has for the past few decades favoured external powers' involvement in the regional process. The conventional East Asian view of international politics conceives that the theories of the balance of power and of hegemony would work better for the region because of the protracted political divisions in existence. Yet external powers, which presumably acts as a stabiliser to the regional order, were to blame for the impotency of existing regional establishments during the financial crisis. As a result, regional countries have responded to the crisis by putting up both a united and an ambitious regional attempt to establish a new regional mechanism, or perhaps a regional decision-making establishment, while strictly limiting participation to regional countries. Regional identity emerges and is rigidly reinforced during the process. To begin with there have been efforts to manage the regional financial rather than the trade order, and some have even termed the present move under the 'ASEAN plus three' process 'Asia's monetary regionalism.'[5] Although the future of this new dynamism remains to be seen, it is now working to combine both Southeast and Northeast Asian regionalism, and is likely to dominate the regional scene as well as possibly lead the way to constructive and extensive regional arrangements and even regional integration. The progress of regional cooperation has thus evolved with new features and regenerated what had already been termed the 'new regionalism.'

This chapter concentrates on theoretical arguments encompassing regional integration and regional cooperation in East Asia by proposing that there are distinctive features of 'East Asian regionalism.'[6] It is important to identify the more inclusive features of regionalism with economic and security perspectives in the changing East Asian setting and, more significantly, to explore the perspective of regionalism prevailing in the region to date. As such, by studying the implications of developing regionalism for further regional cooperation in East Asia, it will certainly help us survey the analytical underpinnings of the necessity to reappraise the current understandings on regionalism and regional cooperation. Thus, regionalism with an East Asian perspective could be further defined and perhaps may even be conceptualised, which bears out the major intention of this chapter.

In search of defining regionalism with an East Asian outlook

In the past few decades, the outgrowth of regional cooperation and the subsequent formation of regionalism has become one of the landmarks by which we depict the changing world system. The development of regional efforts has been largely characterised by the transforming nature of the regionalisation and globalisation processes. Since the 1980s, the world has witnessed several new waves of emerging regionalism. Essentially, this trend has been a result of the rising degree of economic interdependence and trade competition among regional trade blocs as well as among countries. What is even more salient is the fact that the increasing impetus for economic, social, political, security, and other interactions across national borders has pushed forward strongly to link together regional countries. As the scale of the market has gradually come to attract more attention than that of the national boundaries, to many, the relationships between international trading partners has become more significant than those between states. Many analysts have been inclined to explore this arising phenomenon as a way of leading towards the 'borderless economy' or the 'borderless world.'[7]

With the abrupt end of the Cold War, though to the surprise of many, a new international context began to emerge and has since allowed the transformation of the worldview from an insistence on ideological confrontation to the realisation of economic interdependence. Thereafter, it has been more than fair to argue that the international norms have quickly shifted towards a multidimensional and cooperative nature. Promoting cooperation has become the central theme of new international norms rather than confrontation, and the nature of this new trend in international relations emphasises competition rather than conflict. Along with these new norms for international relations, we have seen that regional cooperation coupled closely with the economic regionalisation process is thriving everywhere.

In East Asia, dynamic regional cooperation within the economic and security fields is greatly encouraged by these new international norms. With more and more regional mechanisms emerging in the post-Cold war regional scene, it is reasonable to push forward the ideas of trade liberalisation, the principle of non-discrimination and security cooperation through dialogue mechanisms and so on in order to strengthen the course of economic growth and to seek persistent prosperity. Even after the Asian financial crisis, East Asia began to take up an ambitious regional proposal and, as a result the building of effective regional arrangements has been given due attention. Through various regional cooperation schemes commonly in practice, the region has bounced back from the crisis with new hopes for generating further regional integration. It will be interesting to see whether there will be a continuation of the existing regional cooperation or whether the region is marching towards regional integration. What kinds of regionalism are we referring to? How, in fact, might one define Asian regionalism while there is as yet no universal one in existence? Will this new dynamism to date bring forth any new implications for the definition of regionalism?

Definition of regionalism: a brief review

To begin with, regionalism seems to be regarded more generally as *a notion* that describes the outcome or the tendency of regional efforts by varying regional actors, including state and non-state actors. Most economists and perhaps some political scientists however tend to see regionalism in a rigid way as *a synonym* of regional trade mechanisms.[8] These different standpoints that have been projected on to the term 'regionalism' may of course promote quite a diverse trail of thinking.

Moreover, the concept of regionalism has gradually come to be defined by various analysts in a rather ambiguous and much broader scope than exists in practice. Some regard regionalism as the making of regional associations in which a government's involvement will be drawn into the process through a formal gathering among regional countries.[9] Thus, this explication envelops an analytic focus of regional activities within an existing formal set-up of regional establishments and their related functional development. Based on the idea of cooperation as a means to enhance national interest, one attempt defines that regionalism is 'cooperation among governments or non-government organizations in three or more geographically proximate and interdependent countries for the pursuit of mutual gain in one or more issue-areas.'[10]

Following the same vein, economists have tended to define regionalism in more concrete terms as 'preferential trade agreements among a subset of nations.'[11] Another analogue takes a similar view that regionalism is regarded as 'an economic policy choice of governments' 'in the form of regional economic integration schemes.'[12] It seems that the dynamics of national trade, economic transactions and foreign direct investment among neighbouring countries has come to determine the main features of regionalism. Accordingly, regionalism may be depicted as 'the expression of regional consciousness that develops from a sense of identity among states situated in geographical proximity.'[13] To sum up with one last contribution, regionalism has also been described as 'the disproportionate concentration of economic flows or the coordination of foreign economic policies among a group of countries in close geographic proximity to one another.'[14] According to the definition line-up, there are a few elements of regionalism that should be spelled out. First, to make sense, regionalism should occur around a group of geographically proximate countries. Second, the density of regional economic interactions among the regional countries should be considerably higher than that of external interactions. Third, through certain regional arrangements, the economic policy of an individual country will be coordinated at the regional level. Fourth, regional cooperation should commit to one or more issue areas (e.g. economic, security and social issues).

A useful and thorough definition of regionalism offered by Andrew Hurrell generally refers to five different categories: the regionalisation process, the emergence of regional identity, regional interstate cooperation, state-promoted regional integration, and regional cohesion.[15] This comprehensive definition touches upon the interrelation of *de facto* and *de jure* regional integration, the involvement of state and non-state actors, the dynamism of market and politics, emerging regional consciousness, and a process leading to a political goal of a regional union. It has supplied certain useful indicators for analysis to inspect specific regional experience. If we use these categories to examine particular features of East Asian regionalism, it would be interesting to know how much of a difference exists. I believe that each form of regionalism that exists in certain particular regions stems from its cultural, economic, political and social circumstances. It may not be that comfortable or wise to pursue a universal theory of regionalism, but it is certainly fair to push forward for a theory of an identified regionalism.

Defining East Asian regionalism

What is East Asian regionalism? It is very common to say that the concept of regionalism in East Asia is really referring to 'regional cooperation' but not necessarily to 'regional integration'. In some particular circumstances, regionalism may be loosely defined. All referred terms are thus interchangeable. In fact, a number of interpretations on East Asian regionalism are already emerging in discussion (e.g. '*de facto* regional integration', 'conditional regional integration', 'subregional groupings', 'economic zones or sphere' and 'trade bloc'). When we discuss regionalism in East Asia, do we always need to be confused by this conglomeration of terms? Or for that matter do we need to be using all of them? It seems that due to its ambiguous nature, regionalism *per se* is rather metamorphic. In varying circumstances and different countries, it might refer to quite different dimensional arguments. Therefore, there may not be an urgent need to take on a broad and overarching concept at one time.

Based on economic development in the region, this form of regionalism is characterised by 'dynamic developments in markets rather than by formal political institutions.'[16] It is inclined to be a network style arrangement, and creates overlapping identities of economic and political actors. With its emphasis on informal networks, this approach defines regionalism in market terms and also suggests that regionalism will be built on business organisational characteristics.[17] In most parts of East Asia, the experience of regionalism is relatively new and limited; hence the subsequent cognition of regionalism has resulted from the outcome of regional cooperation. Although general perceptions of regionalism have been largely based on economic development, in this study, regionalism can be more specifically categorised into two conceptual groups: ASEAN regionalism and general East Asian regionalism.

In terms of extrapolating the meaning of regionalism, the existing ASEAN version implies and is more inclined towards an institutionalised regional integration than the rest of regional development found in the region; on the other hand, it is not as sophisticated as that of regional integration among European countries. In the East Asian experience, regional integration is generally considered to be a regional process rather than an ultimate objective of regional evolvement. By its nature, it is 'just a non-coercive process leading to the formation and maintenance of collective entities the members of which are willing to relinquish some aspects of their sovereignty for the sake of other national gains, such as security.'[18] It thus refers to the joint decisions taken by a group of countries to be involved in a regional grouping voluntarily, and may or may not lead the related countries to sharing or pooling part of their sovereignty. This seems to have been the original idea of building ASEAN regional integration back in the early days when it was first established.

Although ASEAN affords the most advanced example of regionalism (or of regional integration) in East Asia, in terms of regional integration as a product and condition, it has not quite reached and does not want to trace down the required level of regional integration (building transnational institutions) set by theorists. Whenever the process of regional integration directly touches upon sovereign issues, ASEAN has been reluctant to give support. One obvious example would be that of APEC's 1994 declaration of a trade liberalisation agenda of which some regional countries commented in what was in effect a joint statement as 'merely indicative and non-binding.'[19] In regard to the progress of regional integration, most importantly ASEAN has picked up the favourite ingredients of integration but has left those it considers to be unfavourable. This may be why we always get a vague picture about whether ASEAN is taking up a regional integration process that may be directed at a more European experience. It does not however imply that ASEAN has gone or will be going through the progress of regional integration, although some misconceptions as to committing to regional integration has occurred in the past. Instead, it may be more accurate to say that ASEAN regionalism will potentially be led towards a conditional regional integration under its own version of regionalism, one which, for now, ASEAN countries prefer to see as a process, not a designated goal.[20] This is the area where policy advisers have advocated that ASEAN members would have to exercise their political will in order to materialise the goals of regional integration set in the new proposal – 'ASEAN 2020 Vision.'[21]

In East Asia, the terms of regional integration and of regional cooperation have been somewhat confused and even misused. Regional integration is generally understood within the context of the development of European institutionalised processes. By taking this as an understanding of economic regionalisation, market integration in the region may have been more conspicuous. During the past decade, the region has witnessed a mushrooming of regional organizations; however, in no way does this refer directly to the institutionalised regional integration process that is taking place in East Asia. Many countries in the region see market integration as 'a way of retaining government involvement in markets rather than a process of weakening state institutions.'[22] What differs greatly is from regional cooperation is that the major feature of regional integration is directed through the process of insitutionalised regional formation, while regional cooperation refers to an interstate voluntary cooperative set-up without being restricted in policy. In most cases, the European Community's experiences have been held up as an example of what regional integration should reflect; however, this is not how East Asian regional arrangements have progressed. In general, there are two persistent lines of argument in the process of regional integration: intergovernmentalism and transnationalism. In a state-centred international system, regional involvement of a state is regarded as an undertaking of the state's foreign policy. Cooperation with other states in the regional context would be based on a state-to-state intergovernmental approach, while neighbouring states join together to form regional mechanisms through which a transnational structure is the anchor to regulate and coordinate common policy.

In terms of East Asian regionalism, the regional process is built on a coherence of national policy, market integration, informal business networks and spontaneous economic interaction. Open regionalism has centred the concept of regionalism through the APEC process.[23] As yet there has been no proposal to build political institutions for regional integration that has survived in the regional process. Significant business networks by Japanese and Chinese enterprises represent their unique versions of regionalism that are actually in existence and are not simply at a proposal stage.[24] Thus one major aspect of East Asian regionalism may be closely defined as building on informal regional networks among business groups through industrial cooperation formulae and encouraging natural coherence among regional economies by the consideration of economic complementarity. Although a government's commitment can fuel the hope for further regional integration, regionalism does not rely on political and formal institutions to manage its development. Therefore, it may be more appropriate to describe regional cooperation as central to general East Asian regionalism, while regional integration lies more at the heart of ASEAN's regionalism. However, on the whole, East Asian regionalism shows a general tendency to develop along the lines of regional cooperation.

As is obviously apparent to many, there is no single prevalent definition of East Asian regionalism. Rather, the existing regional establishments actually feature under a diverse set of dimensions. The Pacific Economic Cooperation Conference (PECC), APEC, ASEAN-PMC, Council for Security Cooperation in the Asia–Pacific (CSCAP), ASEAN Regional Forum (ARF), Asia Europe Meeting (ASEM) and the 'ASEAN plus three' may each represent certain visible features of regional formations in the process of regional integration. On the other hand, the emergence of subregional groupings illustrates yet another set of distinctive features of East Asian regionalism, which contains certain definitions commonly accepted by regional countries. This is the notion that it is more promising for the development of regionalism to build upon business networks and across-the-board industrial linkages already existing in the region. Hopefully these analyses further highlight and consolidate the framework within which an approach to the study of East Asian regionalism may be developed.

The sources of East Asian regionalism

The concept of regionalism itself has traditionally been distinctly unfamiliar in Asia's long history apart from those memories relating to imperial expansionism. Why then has it come to prevail today? Where in fact did it begin? How has it evolved? Passing through the recovery of war-torn hardship immediately after the Second World War, most parts of East Asia, like many other regions in the world, began to forge ahead in the process of economic development and nation-building in the 1950s. Economic development became a fundamental task not only for the enhancement of an individual state's well-being, but also for accelerating the coherence of the region as a whole. Nevertheless, since there was no regional congruity in place, the process of economic development and the goal of national economic policy were mainly based on a state-oriented approach and featured relatively few regional features. It was obvious that regional, especially newly independent countries were very cautious and even sensitive to issues of sovereignty and economic gains in any kind of international cooperation. After all, during its nation-building process, independent sovereignty had stood as an uncompromising position and is still regarded as a symbol of gaining international identification.

Not surprisingly then, most early regional cooperation was only able to be initiated one way or another by various countries or international organisations through the auspices of the United Nations agencies and the USA. In parallel with the progress of economic development, intergovernmental organisations were at that stage primarily promoting functional cooperation in the region through such mechanisms as the Economic Commission for Asia and the Far East (ECAFE), Economic and Social Commission for Asia and the Pacific (ESCAP), Asian Development Bank, Asian Coconut Committee, Asian, Clearing Union, and so on.[25] It is understandable that particularly during this time the sensibility of a sovereign state was emphasised and even reinforced as the process continued. Therefore, regional cooperation was regarded as a way of forming 'a voluntary association among sovereign states for mutual benefit.'[26] This intergovernmental thinking clearly dominates the thrust of regional cooperation and delineates how East Asian countries observe the development of regional cooperation in general. Nevertheless, an increasing recognition of seeking a regional solution for some of the pending regional issues, especially economic ones, was highlighted, and came to be one of the dominant trends towards regionalism.[27]

Economic development and production cycle

There has long been recognition of the wide diversity existing in the region and among East Asian countries. Although those early attempts to build functional organisations did help the region to be aware of cooperation across national boundaries, there seemed little hope of the region bringing about any kind of applicable regional integration. Nevertheless, when the momentum of economic development started to gather pace in the region in the early 1950s and subsequently changed the regional structure, frequent interactions and increasing common economic interests intensified the needs for further regional efforts. As regional countries gradually began to catch up with the upper rungs of the developmental ladder, the centripetal of market integration began to take effect and the process of regionalisation to take place. Since then, shares of regional market in their total foreign trade (goods) and foreign direct investment (capital) in the region have risen dramatically.[28] It is therefore fair to state that once economic forces bring about profound effects to the region from the bottom, a combination of other regional production factors, such as service, information (services), and work forces (persons) may then further accelerate the economic integration process.

How do we come to estimate regional progress? The example derived from European integration illustrates that to start with integration of the single market hinges upon fully implementing free movements of goods, services, capital and persons on which a closer regional integration has been based. It is understandable that the momentum of regionalism therefore relies upon a comprehensive web of interaction between regional countries. Quite clearly then, East Asia has seen quite different approaches of developing regionalism from Europe's, since most of these interactions among regional countries are not necessarily initiated by the state authorities. Rather, market forces and the momentum of economic interdependence have to a large extent driven the process of regionalism. What many analysts have seen of the development at the level of regional organisations or economic interactions may not be sufficient to justify the origins of East Asian regionalism. Drawing on Doner's three dimensions of regionalism – economic dynamic division of labour, institutional characteristics through industrial cooperation, and regional organizations – one more dimension of transnational movement needs to be added in order to effectively examine how regionalism has gathered pace in the region.

Despite the fact that East Asia has not had much experience in regionalism, there is no reason to believe that activities related to developing those dimensions should respectively begin within a different time scale. Rather, they should have evolved almost at the same time, within a favourable regional context, since the international system under the context of East Asia has not only changed dramatically but has also given rise to regional networking (by both the public and private sectors). Ever since progress towards outward-looking economic development has taken shape in the region,[29] regional countries have virtually become tied in with each other in terms of economic structure. In other words, based on export-oriented economic strategy, on the whole the region has developed a product-concentrated economic area. Not only has increasing capital from the region itself been invested in the region through economic production processes, but also a certain regional division of labour has been widely developed through industrial cooperation. Significantly, up to the 1980s Japanese investment in the region accelerated the economic structural changes of regional trade partners, especially among the newly industrialised countries (NICs: South Korea, Taiwan, Singapore, Hong Kong) and the ASEAN countries. Since then, the NICs have shifted their industrial structure upward towards technology- and capital-intensive industries, and ASEAN has taken over from the NICs and moved towards unskilled labour-intensive industries. Economic complementarity among East Asian countries has become even more salient. As a result, we have seen how a continuous flow of Japanese investment and structural changes in the region have brought about horizontal and intra-firm division of labour.[30]

Structural changes and investment dynamism

Taking a retrospective view on the development of regionalism in East Asia, one should be aware that it has almost been carried alongside the progress of economic development. Japanese investors and industries have obviously played critical roles in promoting regional cooperation, though in fact they meant to create business institutions that aimed only to further their own economic goals and may not be that insightful in the direction of regionalism-building. What is even more significant for regional cooperation is the influence of Japan's organised capitalism, since Japan's model of economic development and industry has systematically spread into the rest of the region through extending a coordinating structure of Japan's industry, inter-firm cooperation, trading companies, and subcontracting relationships.[31] The effect of Japanese trans-national industrial cooperation has unwittingly served to heighten the feeling of a regional economic grouping among regional countries.

Since the late 1980s, the Asian NICs have become regional leading capital suppliers along with Japan. This new wave of unprecedented investment in the region has brought about a lively regionalisation process and has resulted in the emergence of subregional groupings throughout East Asia. No matter what the development of subregional groupings is derived from, the investment of Japan and the Asian NICs is definitely fuelling large part of this dynamism. The basis of the booming South China Economic Zone is propelled by investment mainly from Hong Kong and Taiwan. Correspondingly, the momentum of the Northeast Asia Economic Zone has seen significant generation of Japanese and South Korean capital. Although ASEAN countries have devoted much energy to the emergence of the Indochina Economic Zone, those countries involved have also been seeking Taiwan, Hong Kong and Japan's investment, while the growth triangle began with Singapore's serious commitment to constructing infrastructure, management know-how and other supporting services.[32] Within the hierarchical structure of economic development, Japan, Asian NICs, ASEAN countries and China have all been able to fit in under the wider aspects of the division of labour. The region as a whole once again meets the changes in economic structure, and the regionalisation process has further materialised through the deepening of economic integration inside these subregional groupings.

Apart from an industrial division of labour, the new wave of regional labour migration supplies a favourable note for developing regionalism. Theoretically, increasing labour migration throughout the region, whether legal and illegal, will strengthen regional labour market integration and enhance the sense of rising regionalism. In the progress of economic development, labour shortages in Japan and the NICs in particular have appeared to be of concern. Economic demand for various skilled labour has stimulated a massive scale of long- and short-term as well as legal and illegal labour migration to the region.[33] With the existing wide wage differentials, workers from many ASEAN countries and China have been destined for Japan and the NICs. Under this process, while they came to advanced countries for capital and at the same time returned home with better skills for economic development, the advanced countries gained access to a labour supply that could serve to generate their economic development.[34] In the process of economic development, workers with new skills returned home to help their own countries move up the product-cycle ladder. Although many continue to be concerned with social tensions caused by immigrating foreign workers throughout the region, in order to solve their respective transnational problems, governments and business groups of regional countries will now have to work ever more closely. In this regard, labour migration has joined with other favourable factors stimulating the progress of regional economic integration.

The weight of regional mechanisms

The appearance of regional organisations has been regarded as one of the most obvious indicators of regionalism, since this is where a government's influence on regionalism comes in. In fact, the development of regional organisations and all that have been associated with them is a major starting point of most of the analyses on regionalism. Particularly, in the case of East Asia, however, regionalism is not characterised by political motives but by non-political forces of economic interdependence. Despite this obvious fact, it is still true to say that, following the thinking of regional integration theorists on the progress of regional formations, one can quite simply determine the degree to which the progress of regional integration has been developed.

Throughout much of the postwar period in East Asia, we have been able to observe three main trends of regionalism which can be defined in the following way: the 'old regionalism' or the 'first regionalism' in the 1950s and 1960s, the 'new regionalism' or the 'second regionalism' starting from the 1980s, and the 'second wave of new regionalism' which has literally begun since the Asian financial crisis.[35] One of the most important characteristics embedded in the thinking of the old regionalism is illustrated by the political mission-driven orientation and 'an interlinkage approach', which appeared to build regionalism between the two accounts of unilateralism and multilateralism.[36] Although the old regionalism did occur under the establishment of regional organisations of functional cooperation and hopeful regional free-trade areas such as the EFTA and the Pacific Free Trade Area, they later failed as a result of a stiff international framework and multiple political disagreements among major countries. During the period when economic interdependence became an indispensable element in world systems, the new regionalism, which is characterised by the outward-looking nature of economies, openness of regional economic systems and varying regional actors, began to formulate in the region and has been supported by abundant economic advantageous factors. The origin of regional organisations in East Asia has much to do with responding to external pressures, especially pending negotiations on the global trade regime in the 1980s and the rising trend of protectionism in the EC and the North American Free Trade Area (NAFTA).

As the progress of economic development among regional economies further deepens the intensity of regionalisation and the process of regional cooperation, up to the mid-1990s various regional arrangements have flourished as a result, some of which include the Pacific Basin Economic Cooperation (PBEC), PECC, APEC, CSCAP, the Korean Peninsula Energy Development Organisation (KEDO), ASEAN-PMC and ARF.[37] Up until now, these regional organisations have continued to serve as excellent arenas, allowing member-states to build mutual understanding and confidence along the dialogue process and to coordinate their policy on set issues at the levels of policy adviser and decision-maker. In terms of regional decision-making and policy-forming processes, first-track diplomacy has in practice joined with efforts in the second track. At least for now, through varying regional mechanisms, regional cooperation has been much reinforced at governmental policy level. In addition, regionalism in East Asia has undertaken its deepening course of regional integration by linking economic issues with those of security cooperation, as may be seen in the issues tackled by regional arrangements.

Transnational movement: real world of interactions

After the Cold War ended, state-centred sentiments that people used to hold to began to give way to the endeavour of regional community-building. Economic, social, political and security interactions in East Asia have become prosperous. There is no doubt that this new context has brought about a fresh dynamism in regional cooperation. One important factor, which continues to be largely ignored by mainstream academics, is the scope of transnational interactions developed in the interdependent world as well as the subsequent effects on regionalism. Accelerated by the process of regionalisation, transnational business conducted by various underground transnational groups is also prospering. This is to suggest that illegal business networking across national borders, such as drugs/arms trafficking, human smuggling, money laundering, pirating, cybercrime[38] and so on, is rapidly spreading to every corner of East Asia. Similar to business networks as stated above, they have set up their own division of labour in the region and perhaps have also contributed greatly to the regionalisation process.

Another type of transnational movement may refer to non-governmental organisations and various international groups (e.g. environmental, human rights, charity, religious, etc.) in the region. In fact it is clear that these two general types of transnational movement may contribute much to the process of making a regional community, which is also a deserving subject for students of regionalism to take a closer look.

New dynamism and the second wave of new regionalism

Since the Asian financial crisis of summer 1997, the entire region has suffered seriously from economic downturns and a setback of confidence. At best, the financial crisis granted the region a chance to review the efficiency of regional mechanisms in existence. Out of this we can see that East Asia has rebounded by generating a new regional process – 'ASEAN plus three', which has in turn paved the way for new paradigms to occur in regional cooperation. Since this new regional process is still under the developing momentum of the new regionalism, it makes complete sense to characterise it as 'the second wave of new regionalism'. From its decisive exercises shown so far, the 'ASEAN plus three' process has led regional countries to an unprecedented high commitment in terms of policy cooperation, especially, in the field of financial management.

A theory of East Asian regionalism in evolution

Regionalism prevailed throughout most of the postwar era in the twentieth century, since by nature the ideas at its very core promote cooperation among geographically proximate countries. It builds on a belief that a regional community will be of more interest to an individual state, serve as a mechanism for settling differences, and increase the chance of regional countries gaining advantages from regional cooperation. These favourable factors explain why regionalism is increasingly significant in international relations and regional development. How will regionalism function? Apart from the positive factors that are obviously apparent in the nature of regionalism, regional cooperation has became desirable, because, based on security considerations, states have perceived that regional cooperation could stimulate economic development, provide a framework for the peaceful settlement of intra-regional disputes, and serve as a device for the promotion and stabilisation of a regional political balance of power.[39] The making of the old regionalism was largely inspired by the general anxiety over uncertainty and dissatisfaction with international *realpolitik* of bipolarity, under which European countries discovered that they did not have much leverage in positioning themselves between superpowers. The old regionalism surfaced within the Cold War setting following on from the belief that security cooperation would be much easier to coordinate at the regional than the universal level. In this sense, regional cooperation was regarded as an 'adjunct' not a 'substitute' to global cooperation.[40] For small countries, being part of the regional effort would guarantee their security, dilute the dominant influence of big powers, and at the same time would serve to gain substantial benefits from the enhanced interactions with neighbouring countries. Therefore, regional cooperation was seen to be able to retain the balance of power and stabilise the region.

To some extent, we must not deny that regional arrangements were used to serve as a complement to the grand strategy of superpowers in coping with the East–West confrontation and to an economic strategy of liberalising and opening up individual national markets during the Cold War era.[41] Prominent examples include those regional political, security and economic establishments in Europe and Asia (e.g. North Atlantic Treaty Organization (NATO), Warsaw Pact Organization (WPO), South East Asia Treaty Organization (SEATO), the Association of South East Asian Nations (ASEAN), the European Community (EC), and the European Free Trade Association (EFTA)). No matter whether they later transformed to something else or even faded away, it is always important to recognise that these organisations did serve to realise the idea of regional cooperation and also strengthened the understanding of regional cooperation in certain regions. Furthermore, they may have paved the way for further joint efforts.

Based on dissatisfaction with the existing world trade system and apprehension over an uncertain future, the emergence of the new regionalism has once again repeated the experience as seen earlier. When the EC triumphed in its proceedings with an internal market programme in the late 1980s, the potential trend of protectionism accompanied the perception of a European fortress, the notion of which worried many trading countries around the world. As a result, many regions responded to regional integration in Europe by accelerating the pace in their undertaking to establish regional trade groupings, such as NAFTA and APEC. Regional economic cooperation was seen not only as a means by which to strengthen the joint stand of regional countries in dealing with trade issues in those global and regional arenas in which an individual country standing alone may find immovable, but it also enabled smaller economies to gain access to other regional markets. This wave of regional interaction and buildup is what is recognised as the new regionalism. It is based more on a realisation of economic interdependence and of the reality of existing business networking, which mainly refers back to common economic interests and security needs in the region, more than to any considerations of political strategy against one another.

Identification of essential elements

The emergence of both the old and the new regionalism owes some credit to the critical role of pressing external factors. In particular, when we consider a region that does not have much understanding of regional cooperation and lacks a consensus on regional development, external factors become very important accelerators of regional cooperation. Security concerns within a confrontational international system and sharp market competition among trade blocs aggravated by the worst scenario of pending world trade negotiation have in different circumstances heightened the need for regional countries to cooperate with one another. Just as security concern over communist aggression was to give birth to NATO and SEATO (under the old regionalism), so misapprehension of rising protectionism in the EC and NAFTA was to give rise to the advent of APEC (under the new regionalism).

On that account, there appear to be at least six sets of general criteria which fall into the conceptual domain of regionalism, namely assurance of national and regional security, benefit of economic development, credibility of conflict resolution, management of regional order through an existing mechanism, external incentives, and psychological acceptance of regional coherence. Hence, this implies that, in whatever circumstances, any region involved in interaction would have to satisfy these criteria of regionalism in order to endure and prosper. It is these necessary and sufficient elements that I will take into account in examining the theory of regionalism.

1 Security assurance

Common security concerns render countries into a regional unified front. In a solely state-centred international system, this is the area where the traditional thinking of national boundaries can see some yielding ground. For instance, the Southeast Asia countries joined together under the security structure of SEATO and later transformed into ASEAN, while the six original members of the European Community perceived their security in accordance with a strengthening regionalism. While most of the ensuing regionalism then came to address security concerns, their basic assumption well reflected the thinking of enhancing regional security through developing regionalism. The establishment of regional security organisations implied that national security concerns of an individual state were not only closely tied with regional countries, but also with outside powers. Once it was accepted that this imperative purpose of assuring security could be delivered, the formation of regionalism would be able to endure.

2 Benefit of regional economic development

In terms of the conceptual analysis of regionalism, there have often been arguments based upon economic approaches. They focus on the fact that an increasing amount of intra-regional trade with geographic neighbours can result in the appearance of regionalisation, which is also a prerequisite for bringing about regionalism.[42] As the world economy has gone through a process of concurrent development of regionalisation and globalisation, the EC, APEC and

NAFTA have emerged almost equally in their share of economic resources of the world. Most literature relating to regional cooperation in the past few years has been inclined to suggest that the worldwide emergence of regionalism in the 1980s and 1990s has been characterised by the demand for the opening of more national markets and the liberalising of individual economies.[43]

While economic interactions among states were relatively limited during the Cold War era, the formation of economic organisations generated some hopes of gaining access to various markets and subsequent economic benefits. An individual economy had to go through the political will of its government to make this choice. The respective economic gains will of course be given due significance. However, in an interdependent world, an individual economy is bound to be part of any regional efforts one way or another, since the regionalisation process and regional organisations are in practice driving along the line of regionalism. The centripetal force of economic regionalisation has come to reinforce the continuous buildup of regionalism. Although varying particular regional buildups may stress rather different focuses, they are working on ways to strengthen regional unifying stands in meeting with the rest of the world. Therefore, global trade liberalisation and market access are claimed to be based on the principal agenda of regionalism.

3 Conflict resolution

One of the most important functions of regionalism is to serve as a peaceful settlement mechanism, especially since many interstate conflicts or disputes would normally have much regional derivation and implication. The arguments as to whether regionalism or universalism could better deal with regional conflicts are of traditional concern.[44] While there is no absolute answer to these arguments, the interests of regional countries always head the agenda of regionalism. ASEAN's successful settlement of intraregional disputes and the Cambodian problem in the 1980s and early 1990s demonstrates that regionalism can be an excellent conflict resolution mechanism.[45] It is important that regionalism at the organisational level should be provided with a certain identifiable mechanism for sorting out differences among regional countries. Under the regionalisation process, regionalism could serve to encourage more communication and increase mutual understanding, so that the potentiality of conflict might be reduced.

4 Management of the regional order

No matter what form of regionalism is concerned, the process of regional cooperation among states is likely to take on common issues in the region and establish certain acceptable norms. In addition to conflict resolution, regionalism *per se* is moving towards establishing competence over the managing of regional issues. In the economic field, the arrangement of a custom union, a free-trade area and economic policy integration tends to regulate regional development and thus places regional order within the terms of management. Presumably, regional arrangements could effectively ease away potential trade tensions among regional economies. On the security front, most regional organisations or regional regimes attempt to develop new structures and to introduce international norms from which new developments in certain regions would be shaped accordingly.

5 Regional identity

Economic, security and political motivations may be the most critical factors in the buildup of regionalism. They do not however guarantee regional integration to go any deeper, unless grass-roots perceptions of regional identity can be recognised. This is to suggest that beyond practical motivation, regionalism concerns must build on some common shared values and create a certain cohesive awareness in a region. Therefore, regional identity may be seen as a kind of common feeling and as the values that are generally shared by the people in the same region and which may help them find out what they really believe in and what they wish to be like.

Although awareness of regional identity will undoubtedly be gradually rising along the process of regionalisation, it is all the more important to go beyond visible cooperation and to create a regional sense of psychological similarity among regional countries and people. The emergence of regional identity will be from voluntary acceptance and should in no way be imposed on anyone. Regional consciousness will help further stimulate regional coherence and send an image of a unifying region to the rest of the world. It seems fair to state that the development of regionalism is similar to the shifting of national and individual consciousness of state to a new centre – a region.

East Asian theory of regionalism in evolution

Over the past two decades, the world has experienced dramatic changes in the nature of international relations. Increasingly, the scope of regional and inter-regional cooperation has broadened to the fields of trade, economics, culture, security and even politics, all of which are the elements upon which new regionalism has been based. In the East Asian region, a general observation of regionalisation concentrates on economic development with the increasing impetus of regional business networking. In particular, the networking of Japanese enterprises and overseas Chinese business has brought about wider effects of regionalism.[46] Paralleled with growing economic development, the evolution of regionalism has generated the momentum for closer regional cooperation from all levels of regional effort. This momentum has been characterised by across-the-board industrial cooperation, the building of a regional network by the business community, and the establishment of regional organisations.

Increasing economic transactions have built multi-channel networks as well as multi-cultural webs in the region. Despite the lack of much political will to lead regional efforts in the past, East Asian regionalism is quickly emerging and approaching maturity. It remains to be seen, however, whether regional arrangements with the characteristic of security cooperation will also be involved in this process of regionalisation. A growing sense of regional consciousness has raised hopes of bringing about the process of regional integration among East Asian states.

Nevertheless, whenever any regional arrangement emerges in the real world, people need to be more realistic about how it could reasonably originate common interests and hence hold the region together. On the theoretical front, no matter what regional form has been or will be taken, it will have to be firmly based upon a prospect for gaining practical and potential economic advantages in various time ranges. Without economic incentives in place, any regional arrangement would be difficult to implement for states, especially while a regional consensus in East Asia has yet to be established.

Against the background of conventional theoretical approaches to regionalism, such as neo-liberalism and neo-realism, it may be worthwhile to work on some concrete concepts which have been closely associated with the developing regionalism in East Asia. Although it may still be premature to say that there is a theory, even for this particular region, I intend to break through these stereotyped approaches and probe the basis of East Asian regionalism by exploring specifically selected regional characteristics and conceptualising all related factors. As regards to theory-making, six central and common concepts of East Asian regionalism could be selected for further exploration: informality, incrementalism, bottom-upism, consensus-building, minimalism, and ASEANisation.

1 Informality

Due to the recent past memory and experience of distrust among regional countries, it has been less than comfortable for them to form any formal and regular regional institutions, at least before mutual confidence can be fully built. Most East Asian countries instead prefer informal dialogues to formal talks and a consultative nature to legitimate institutions in dealing with regional issues collectively. Under the context of East Asian regionalism, regional cooperation has taken informal approaches to begin the process, which would leave some flexibility for policy coordination among them. Although Southeast Asian structural regionalism is different from Northeast Asian loose regionalism, the informality normally occurs in two features: official but informal regional engagements and unofficial networks. As part of Asian culture, interstate cooperation relies more on friendship between leaders than on regional institutions.[47] ASEAN does not want to go along with the idea of transnationalism; nor do Northeast Asian countries like the idea of heading for a regional centralised mechanism. Unlike regional organisations elsewhere, we often see statements or joint declarations from regional meetings in East Asia (or the Asia Pacific setting), but not agreements or the like being produced.

In addition to this political exercise, East Asian regionalism has been closely linked with market forces. This has also developed a unique informality of business networks, which continues to push forward regional cooperation without involving much political consideration. From Japanese enterprises and ethnic Chinese business groups to varying newly established active business groups and multinational corporations in the region, unofficial networks, which become a trigger for regional integration, are emphasised and further strengthened along the way to economic development.

2 Incrementalism

At the official level of regional cooperation, much of the progress made is really a step forward in a long process of evolvement. One ASEAN senior official has wisely suggested that in East Asia 'events evolve gradually and subtly, rather than in a series of dramatic breakthroughs.'[48] Because the region is so diverse in so many ways, any proposal by any particular country to promote sudden changes to new structures will be considered unsuitable, unacceptable, and in danger of threatening another's national interest. Through regional cooperation mechanisms regional countries always progress with caution. What really matters is the surrounding atmosphere of cooperation among regional countries. Sometimes, it is more sensible to meet regularly with regional leaders and to move gradually rather than to dig in on substantive issues. At best, this incrementalism does tend to develop a remarkable process of regional cooperation along with official channels, and has even survived in the region for several decades.

3 Bottom-upism

Since regional cooperation with strong economic incentives has taken place in much of the region, the private sectors in carrying on their grass-roots efforts have started to network with one another in different countries and this has further stimulated the momentum to extend and consolidate regional efforts in the region. This is one of the areas that students of regional integration find exceptionally encouraging, as intensive economic cooperation has gradually triggered rising expectations among political players that has led to furthering the progress of regional integration. Regarded as functional cooperation, once it reaches the threshold at certain points, such development will start to have spill-over effects from the realm of economic cooperation into the political domain. Without involving much in the way of political determinants, the experiences of subregional groupings around the region and of developing all sorts of networking or mechanisms have partly reflected that the drive for regionalism is mainly derived from ever-dynamic business groups. Subsequently, regional governments are obliged to make moves and join together in establishing regional mechanisms. It is without doubt that should there be no prevailing grass-roots efforts paving the way, regionalism may not yet have occurred.

4 Consensus-building

At the core of ASEAN's decision-making process we have seen the principles of consultation and consensus, which have, together with informality and non-interference, constituted the major features of the 'ASEAN way'.[49] The essence of consensus-building is about 'agreeing to disagree rather than allowing disagreements to cloud and undermine the spirit of regionalism'.[50] Being the most advanced example of regional cooperation throughout the region, ASEAN's experience is embedded within the centre of East Asian regionalism.

Moving into a larger East Asian setting, consensus is in fact no stranger to most Asian societies. After all, decisions taken by way of democratic voting are not deeply rooted in regional systems. All existing regional arrangements in the region seem to be in accord with the ASEAN experiment of regional cooperation with special regard to their decision-making process, to consultative nature of their decisions and the corporate partnership. It has been argued that an 'Asia Pacific way' in the making has been transplanted from the 'ASEAN way'.[51]

5 Minimalism

In the regional process, the concept of minimalism is little known but perches at the core of the approach to regionalism. In general, there may be two sets of thinking on how minimalism operates. First, in terms of regional cooperation, East Asian countries tend to be reluctant to support any grand strategy that the whole region may need to rush ahead for big changes, and as such this notion is the cause of controversy. Rather, on many occasions, regional leaders favour muddling through. Even if they tend to realise how confusing and ineffective this approach might turn out to be, the process of being continuous is considered to be more important than doing something practical. Second, the concept finds a definite echo in a Chinese proverb '*yi-zhong-qiu-tong, tong-zhong-tzuen-yi*' (*getting to agreement on a minimal niche while acknowledging major difference among related parties*). In a diverse regional setting, the direction of regional cooperation often begins with the identification of working issues where they can easily be seen as in the common interest. It serves to remind us that the development of regionalism in East Asia is not articulated by political goals but by the interest-seeking motive.

6 ASEANisation

In terms of geographic scale, East Asian regionalism over the years has taken various forms at institutional level: subregionalism (i.e. ASEAN, the growth triangle, etc.), intra-regionalism (i.e. 'ASEAN plus three') and inter-regionalism (i.e. APEC, ARF, ASEM). The whole process of regionalism in East Asia has been somewhat ASEANised in its norms. The concrete features of ASEAN regionalism have become implanted in the general framework of East Asian regionalism. No formal kinds of decision-making institutions have been established, and no majority voting has been added to the decision-making process of regional mechanisms. Much of the existing regional cooperation relies on the pattern of dialogue structure, especially in the security field. Therefore, this kind of regionalism would prefer to admit differences among participants and allow individual countries to opt out in any circumstance, whence they do not feel comfortable with being pushed further.

An East Asian theory of regionalism is indeed evolving at an unprecedented pace. Stimulated by a set of countermeasures proposed in response to the Asian financial crisis, this new dynamism of regionalism has emerged and is forging ahead of any exclusive East Asian type of regional integration. The identity of the existing regionalism has been put to the test and subsequently calls for redefinition. Although many existing regional mechanisms remain in place as overarching frameworks to link up with external powers, the exercise of the second wave of new regionalism has shifted a decade-long conventional paradigm. Apart from Taiwan and North Korea, almost all the major countries in the region have been linked since 1997 under the 'ASEAN plus three' process at the height of the crisis. To date, under this process there is continuing effort to organise regular foreign, economic and finance ministerial meetings and we have seen the pushing ahead of pioneer proposals of regional integration, such as an East Asian summit meeting, monetary integration (the currency swap plan) and an East Asian trade bloc.[52] These new drives correspond with a shifting regional paradigm that would certainly help to redefine the theory.

To sum up, I will attempt to summarize the features of regionalism to date in East Asia, which I strongly believe will be of great benefit to a general understanding of regionalism.

Conclusion: The future tendency in East Asia

By pointing to the necessity of reappraising the current understanding of regionalism in East Asia, this chapter sees through the basic regional nature of East Asia and defines the 'second wave of new regionalism' as 'East Asian regionalism.' The development of regionalism to date has had profound implications for the rest of the world and the entire region, and even the study of theory, as found under some new initiatives of regional cooperation, such as Asian financial integration and the free-trade area, has effectively brought forward regional integration and has met with no disagreement among regional countries. If there were to be an ever-developing regional integration in East Asia, it would almost certainly start from financial integration rather than from trade integration, which is a more conventional approach.[53] The stereotype of regional cooperation in East Asia would be transformed into a dynamic regional integration while integrating the current course of regionalism in the process.

In general, the concept of regionalism in East Asia refers not only to one but to several forms, namely interstate regional cooperation, regional institution buildup, networking force, and subregional groupings. The concept itself does not yet imply any political intention of institutionalising the process of regional cooperation. Between the existing regional approaches of transnationalism and intergovernmentalism, East Asian regionalism is to a large extent characterised by the latter. At this stage, it would be more accurate to refer to East Asian regionalism as a form of regional cooperation rather than as regional integration as such. Nevertheless, the new dynamism of regionalism has tested fresh ground in pushing forward finance integration and has put forth the idea of forming a regional trade bloc.[54] The outcome will, as predicted or requested, touch upon some kind of transformation of national sovereignty to regional mechanism over certain policy-making areas.

The emergence of regionalism certainly relies upon the acknowledgement of a relatively cohesive policy among related countries, apart from frequent interactions and a higher degree of interdependence. Therefore, before all related factors can be identified, one should not jump to any conclusions too soon; nor should any concept be too narrowly defined. Keeping this in mind, the following four dimensions of regionalism should form the thrust of the arguments on regionalism: (1) economic dynamic division of labour; (2) institutional characteristics through industrial cooperation; (3) regional organizations; (4) transnational movements. Especially in the case of East Asia, throughout the pre-financial crisis era political commitment from regional governments was rather vague and uncertain. Accordingly, business and unofficial efforts have generally led the drive for further regional cooperation.

What I have reviewed with respect to the development of regionalism in East Asia has focused mainly on the characteristics of the new regionalism from which I conceive the second new wave of regionalism stems. Therefore, it would be more appropriate to divide the regionalism in East Asia into three characteristics: the old regionalism, the new regionalism, and the second wave of new regionalism.

In retrospect, during the high politics-centred Cold War era, the efforts of forming regional groupings were directed by the assumption of alliance, and its reasoning was therefore rooted in the forms of intergovernmental cooperation. According to the realist perspective, states have not only been the dominant players in international politics, but have also continued to be the determinants of an international agenda. It is thus reasonable to say that the momentum of regional arrangements worldwide was mainly politics-driven in the light of the top–down operational pattern. Although many regional establishments turned out to be economic in form, nevertheless, political motivation obviously served as the only realistic rationale of regional establishments.

In the context of the new regionalism, with special reference to East Asia, more and more international actors (e.g. regional organisations, informal regional dialogue mechanisms (track I and II diplomacy), indigenous and external multinational corporations) have emerged and have even taken the lead in forming regional coherence. Over the years, business, private and public groups and governmental institutions have all managed to establish well-connected regional networks right across the region, and their efforts have been relied upon. Along with all these dynamic developments, a theory of regionalism based upon East Asian experience has been put to the test through a conceptualising process. The main specific features of regionalism; namely informality, incrementalism, bottom-upism, consensus-building, minimalism, and ASEANisation, are thus identified.

The exploration of a regionalism theory incorporating the updated developments has suggested that as progress continues, there are at least three profound implications deserving of greater attention. First and foremost, as a result of the new developments within the 'ASEAN plus three' process, regionalism is actually seeing further progress in terms of geographic integration. It would however be more meaningful to see the region converging around a delineated regional structure, if such regional integration is truly to take place. In terms of regional attributes and development experience, Southeast Asia and Northeast Asia were quite different from each other in many ways. Apart from economic ties activated by Northeast Asian countries, there has been little opportunity for Southeast Asian countries to become involved in the subregional development of their northern neighbours, especially in the security field. In geographic terms, most regional cooperation and issues tackled in regional establishments in East Asia that we have seen today are subject more to the individual context of these two subregions than to the region as a whole. However, their variance has diminished and inter-involvement has been assured as a result of interdependent incentives and of new overarching regional structures.

For the first time ever, East Asia can really put together these fragmented pieces. Now, with APEC in economic cooperation, ARF in security cooperation and 'ASEAN plus three' in the overall prospective picture, East Asian regionalism has begun to march into a new era. This does not mean that all remaining regional controversial issues can be automatically sorted out under this new dynamism. Rather, the regionalism that is emerging supplies us with a better-communicated and more effective mechanism for the future. What it would imply for the region is the need to opt for deepening progress of regional integration in the near future.

Second, while East Asians are trying to make up for the financial crisis by moving towards financial integration, 'a three-block configuration' is quietly emerging in the world.[55] The imaginary scenario of competition among the trio – the EU, NAFTA and East Asian regionalism – may have come into further effect. This development implies new relationships among them, not only economic but also political. In this respect, East Asian regionalism could potentially push ahead a change for the whole world system. What their future relationships will turn out to be remains an interesting topic to follow through. Over the next few years, East Asian countries will have to make adjustments to new partnerships within and outside the region, as do American and European countries. For so long, Asians have been suppressed by the world system that continues to be dominated by the Western powers. Now, it is time for the West to respect the achievement of East Asian regionalism and yield a fair ground to share.

Last but not least, given the fact that the new dynamism is driving towards a new paradigm, East Asian regionalism is now on the verge of turning a new page of regional development. Regional paradigm shifting, an evolving regionalism theory and the refocusing of regional integration have characterised the second wave of new regionalism. Even ASEAN regionalism itself is increasingly facing pressure to make adjustments to its traditional perceptions of regional cooperation. The debate on whether it should seriously take into account the redefining of the 'ASEAN way' on regional cooperation is now underway among policy-thinkers.[56] The Asian financial crisis has taught the region the fundamental lesson that the establishment of regionalism has to be based on the principles of feasibility, effectiveness, accountability, reliability and capability. Therefore, the implementation of all listed principles should transform the nature of this new regionalism. Once the current East Asian regionalism prevails, it is more likely that this new dynamism will lead to serious regional integration.

With all these specific features in mind, whither will the second new wave of regionalism go? What are the broader implications of this regionalism for the region? In the near term, the prospects that the East Asian region will become inclined to move towards an institutionalised process of regional integration seem rather convincing.

Notes

1 Richard Doner, 'Japanese foreign investment and the creation of a Pacific Asian region', in Jeffrey Frankel and Miles Kahler, eds, *Regionalism and Rivalry: Japan and the United States in Pacific Asia* (Chicago, IL: the University of Chicago Press, 1993), p. 159.

2 The term is generally used by Norman Palmer, *The New Regionalism in Asia and the Pacific* (Lexington, MA: D.C. Heath, 1991), pp. 1–6; Bjorn Hettne, 'The new regionalism: a prologue', in Bjorn Hettne, Andras Inotai and Osvaldo Sunkel, eds, *Globalism and the New Regionalism* (Basingstoke: Macmillan, 1999), pp. xvi–xvii. But, In other cases, the revival of regionalism is called the 'second regionalism'. Jagdish Bhagwati, 'Regionalism and multilateralism: an overview', in Ross Garnaut and Peter Drysdale, eds, *Asia–Pacific Regionalism: Readings in International Economic Relations* (Sydney: HarperEducational Publishers, 1994), p. 146.

3 Cameron Van Brunt, 'Introduction', in Francisco Rojas Aravena and Paz Buttedahl, eds, *Open Regionalism: Strengthening the Net – Perspectives from APEC Countries* (Santiago, Chile: FLACSO-Chile, 1999), p. 11.

4 The central theme of this concept (comprehensive security) is that 'security must be conceived in an holistic way – to include both military and non military threats to a state's overall well being.' David Capie, Paul Evans and Akiko Fukushima, *Speaking Asia Pacific Security: A Lexicon of English Terms with Chinese and Japanese Translations and a Note on the Japanese Translation* (Toronto: University of Toronto-York University, 1999), p. 25.

5 Heribert Dieter, 'Asia's monetary regionalism', *Far Eastern Economic Review*, 6 July 2000, p. 30.

6 In many previous analyses, Asia–Pacific regionalism and Asian regionalism have been interchangeably used. East Asian regionalism is mainly to reflect new regionalism in the region to date and geographically refers more specifically to East Asia – Northeast and Southeast Asia. It is a combination of both subregions and has also developed new features in its own course.

7 Edward K.Y. Chen and C.H. Kwan, eds, *Asia's Borderless Economy: The Emergence of Subregional Economic Zones* (St Leonards, Australia: Allen & Unwin, 1997); Knichi Ohmae, *The End of the Nation State: The Rise of Regional Economies* (New York: The Free Press, 1995).

8 This view is taken by most contributors in Garnaut and Drysdale, eds, *Asia–Pacific Regionalism: Readings in International Economic Relations*.

9 Mordechai Kreinin, Shigeyuki Abe and Michael Plummer, 'Regional integration in Asia', in Kohsrow Fatemi, ed., *The New World Order: Internationalism, Regionalism and the Multinational Corporations* (Oxford: Elsevier Science, 2000), p. 97.

10 Muthiah Alagappa, 'Regionalism and conflict management: a framework for analysis', *Review of International Studies*, No. 21 (1995), p. 362.

11 Jagdish Bhagwati, 'Regionalism and multilateralism: an overview', p. 145.

12 Paul Bowles, 'Regionalism and development after the global financial crises', *New Political Economy*, Vol. 5, No. 3 (November 2000), p. 433.

13 Wilfred J. Ethier, 'The new regionalism', *The Economic Journal*, Vol. 108, No. 449 (July 1998), p. 1152.

14 Edward D. Mansfield and Helen V. Milner, 'The political economy of regionalism: an overview', in their co-edited *The Political Economy of Regionalism* (New York: Columbia University Press, 1997), p. 3.

15 Andrew Hurrell, 'Regionalism in historical perspective', in Louise Fawcett and Andrew Hurrell, eds, *Regionalism in World Politics* (Oxford: Oxford University Press, 1995), pp. 38–45.

16 Peter Kazenstein, 'Introduction: Asian regionalism in comparative perspective', in Peter Kazenstein and Takashi Shiraishi, eds, *Network Power: Japan and Asia* (Ithaca, NY: Cornell University Press, 1997), pp. 5–7; also Kishore Mahbubani argued in a different way of network, and he took on small- and medium-sized powers for pushing through regional institutions. Mahbubani, 'The Pacific way', *Foreign Affairs*, Vol. 74, No. 1 (January 1995), pp. 100–111.

17 Peter Kazenstein *et. al.*, *Asian Regionalism* (Ithaca, NY: East Asian Program, Cornell University, 2000), pp. 16–17.

18 Hans H. Indorf, *Impediments to Regionalism in Southeast Asia: Bilateral Constraints among ASEAN Member States* (Singapore: Institute of Southeast Asian Studies, 1984), p. 6.

19 Peter Kazenstein, 'Regionalism and Asia', *New Political Economy*, Vol. 5, No. 3 (November 2000), p. 358.

20 Jörn Dosch and Manfred Mols, 'Short papers, notes and comments – Why ASEAN co-operation cannot work as a model for regionalism elsewhere – a reply', *ASEAN Economic Bulletin*, Vol. 11, No. 2 (November 1994), pp. 213–214.

21 Jusuf Wanandi, 'The ASEAN-10 and its international and regional implications', in Mohamed Jawhar Hassan, ed., *A Pacific Peace: Issues & Responses* (Kuala Lumpur: ISIS, 1998), p. 202; Carolina G. Hernandez, 'The future role of ASEAN: a view from an ASEAN ISIS member', in *East Asia at A Crossroads Challenges for ASEAN* (Hanoi: Institute for International Relations, 1998), p. 99.

22 Peter Kazenstein, 'Regionalism and Asia', p. 358.

23 Open regionalism has generally five definitions: open membership, unconditional MFN, conditional MFN, global liberalisation, and trade facilitation. C. Fred Bergsten, 'Open regionalism', Working Paper (Washington, DC: Institute for International Economics), No. 97–3 1997.

24 Peter Katzenstein, 'Introduction: Asian regionalism in comparative perspective', pp. 35–44.

25 For details, see Michael Haas, 'Asian intergovernmental organisations and the United Nations', in Berhanykun Andemicael, ed., *Regionalism and the United Nations* (Dobbs Ferry, NY: Oceana Publications, 1979), pp. 403–405.

26 Ibid., p. 402.

27 Arthur Paul, 'Regionalism in Asia: a new thrust for development', Occasional Paper No. 1 (San Francisco: Asia Foundation, 1967), p. 7.

28 Evidence of regional integration was explored by Mordechai Kreinin, Shigeyuki Abe and Michael Plummer, 'Regional integration in Asia', pp. 101–105.

29 The process is headed by Japan and known as the 'flying geese' pattern.

30 Richard Doner, 'Japanese foreign investment and the creation of a Pacific Asian region', p. 174.

31 Ibid., pp. 191–197.

32 Above subregional groupings refer to Edward K.Y. Chen & C.H. Kwan, 'The emergence of subregional economic zones in Asia', in their co-edited *Asia's Borderless Economy: The Emergence of Subregional Economic Zones* (St Leonards, Australia: Allen & Unwin, 1997), pp. 15–21.

33 For migration and economic development refer to Yasuo Kuwahara, 'Economic development in Asia and its consequences for labour migration', in OECD Proceedings – *Migration and Regional Economic Integration in Asia* (Paris: OECD, 1998), pp. 20, 24.

34 Richard Doner, 'Japanese foreign investment and the creation of a Pacific Asian region', p. 177.

35 For comparison of the old and new regionalism, refer to Bjorn Hettne, 'The new regionalism: a prologue', pp. 7–8; see also Chapter 2 (this volume): Jörn Dosch gives an excellent analysis on the comparison.

36 A. Hasnan Habib, 'Defining the "Asia Pacific Region",' *The Indonesian Quarterly*, Vol. 23, No. 4 (1995), p. 305.

37 There are already a number of literatures contributing to regional groupings and regionalism in the Asia Pacific. To name just a few: for early development of regional establishments refer to Peter Drysdale, *International Economic Pluralism: Economic Policy in East Asia and the Pacific* (New York: Columbia University Press, 1988); for APEC refer to M. Dutta, *Economic Regionalization in the Asia–Pacific: Challenges to Economic Cooperation* (Cheltenham, Glos: Edward Elgar, 1999); for ARF see Michael Leifer, *The ASEAN Regional Forum*, Adelphi Paper No. 302 (London: IISS, 1996); for CSCAP refer to Desmond Ball, *The Council for Security Cooperation in the Asia Pacific: Its Record and Its Prospects*, Canberra Papers on Strategy and Defence No. 139 (Canberra: The Australian National University, 2000).

38 Transnational criminal groups have been using the Internet to broaden their sales networks in the region (e.g. car smugglers in China, women smugglers in Japan). Hamish McCardle *et. al.*, Sub Group report – 'Cybercime and its effects on the Asia Pacific Region', Transnational Crime Working Group, Council for Security Cooperation in the Asia Pacific, 2000.

39 The comments are taken from Norman Padelford and Ronald Yalem, *Regionalism and World Order* (Washington, DC: Public Affairs Press, 1965), p. 7.

40 Ibid., p. 8.

41 Robert Z. Lawrence, *Regionalism, Multilateralism, and Deeper Integration* (Washington, DC: The Brookings Institution, 1996), p. 6.

42 Wilfred J. Ethier, 'The new regionalism,' p. 1152.

43 For example, Edward D. Mansfield and Helen V. Milner, eds, *The Political Economy of Regionalism: New Direction in World Politics* (New York: Columbia University Press, 1997); Robert Lawrence, *Regionalism, Multilateralism, and Deeper Integration* (Washington, DC: The Brookings Institution, 1996); Andrew Gamble and Anthony Payne, eds, *Regionalism and World Order* (New York: St Martin's Press, 1996).

44 Ronald Yalem, *Regionalism and World Order,* p. 9.

45 Jusuf Wanandi, 'ASEAN's past and the challenges ahead: aspects of politics and security', in Simon S.C. Tay, Jesus Estanislo and Hadi Soesastro, eds, *A New ASEAN in a New Millennium* (Jakarta: CSIS, 2000), p. 28.

46 Peter Katzenstein, 'Introduction: Asian regionalism in comparative perspective', pp. 35–44.

47 Amitav Acharya, 'Culture, security, multilateralism: the "ASEAN Way" and regional order', *Contemporary Security Policy*, Vol. 19, No. 1 (1998), p. 58.

48 Rodolfo Severino, 'The ASEAN way in Manila', *Far Eastern Economic Review* (23 December 1999), p. 27.

49 The sources and origins of the 'ASEAN way' have been elaborated by Amitav Acharya, 'ideas, identity and institution-building: from the "ASEAN Way" to "Asia Pacific Way"?', *The Pacific Review*, Vol. 10, No. 3 (1997).

50 Amitav Acharya, 'Culture, security, multilateralism: the "ASEAN Way" and regional order', p. 61.

51 Ibid., p. 65.

52 Joint Ministerial Statement of the ASEAN+3 Finance Ministers meeting, 6 May 2000, Chiang Mai, Thailand, http://www.mof.go.jp/english/if/if014.htm; 'Japan, China, Korea forge closer economic links', Reuters, 24 November 2000, http://taiwansecurity.org/reu/reuters-112400.htm.

53 As argued by Fred Bergsten, 'East Asian regionalism: towards a tripartite world', *The Economist*, 15 July 2000, p. 23.

54 Ibid.

55 Ibid.

56 Carolina Hernandez, 'Challenges for society and politics', in Simon S.C. Tay, Jesus Estanislo and Hadi Soesastro, eds, *A New ASEAN in A New Millennium,* p. 119.

2 The post-Cold War development of regionalism in East Asia

Jörn Dosch

Introduction: 'old' versus 'new' regionalism

Contrary to the *regionalization* of international relations, which refers to the real existence of co-operation between adjoining states and their actors, the term *regionalism* is more complex. 'In the descriptive sense [it means] ... the formation of interstate associations or groupings on the basis of regions; and in the doctrinal sense, the advocacy of such formations.'[1] Or as Indonesia's Hasnan Habib puts it, 'Regionalism is the expression of regional consciousness that develops from a sense of identity among states situated in geographical proximity which motivates them to mutually cooperate in one or another mode to attain common goals, satisfy common needs, or to solve political, military, economic, and other practical problems.'[2] Hence, both the *emergence/existence* and the *advocacy* of regional co-operation are elements of regionalism. In addition, it is also useful to subsume the *analysis* of regional relations to the concept. There is a simple reason to do so: real life politics and social science theory are closely interrelated. They cannot exist independently from each other. 'Practice without theory' is an illusion, and 'theory without practice' will result in bad science.[3]

Obviously, early studies of regionalism were strongly influenced by the process of European community-building. The vast majority of integration theory's proponents, Ernst Haas, Philippe Schmitter, Karl W. Deutsch, Leon Lindberg, Amitai Etzioni or Joseph Nye based their work on hypotheses meant to primarily explain the origins, conditions and potentials of European integration as well as to prognosticate further developments.[4] Their approaches to the study of interstate co-operation and transnational community-building present the classic or old school of regionalism. This 'old regionalism' consists of the three broad strands, Functionalism/Neo-Functionalism, Federalism/ Neo-Federalism and Transactionism/Communications Theory. Although they differ significantly in detail, classic writings on integration have some features in common.

- They are concerned with the process by which loyalty is shifted from one centre to another;

- They share an interest in communications within units to be integrated (people learn to consider themselves members of a community because of human communications patterns);
- They hold that elite groups both in the governmental and societal sectors adopt integrative behaviour because of expectations of joint rewards or penalties;
- They assume that integration is a multidimensional phenomenon.[5]

The integration theories of the 1950s, 1960s and 1970s are typical children of their times when political scientists in the United States started to orient themselves towards the more rational and empirical natural sciences. Systems theory and Behaviourism present two prominent examples. Accordingly, scholars hypothesised that integration would present a dynamic, steady process under standardised conditions.[6] Neofunctionalists, such as Ernst Haas, believed that integration would 'spill over' from one policy area to another, thus leading to a transfer of national sovereignty to a supra-national level in a growing number of sectors. Eventually this process would result in general integration characterised by a whole new entity of integrated institutions. When it became obvious that the European Community did not develop in the way theory had predicted and when 'spill backs' began to hinder the process, the school of 'old regionalism' entered a stage of crisis and gradually almost vanished.

To an even greater extent, the end of bipolarity and East–West confrontation with its enormous global structural changes has posed a major challenge to international relations theory in general. For the most part of the 20th century international relations have been significantly global in focus and scale. 'Great-power rivalries, and the resulting hot and cold wars, were conducted world-wide by states with global interests and global reach.'[7] This has certainly changed in the post-Cold War era. Regional powers and regional organisations have gained more influence on the international stage. Consequently, middle-range and single case theories have more and more taken the place of universal approaches.[8] As far as the European integration process is concerned, most scholars and practitioners today agree that Europe's regionalism is unique and does not present a global model of integration. Consequently, students of regional co-operation have broadened their theoretical framework and empirical research focus. Questions on how phenomena such as nation-building and integration or globalisation and regionalization interrelate are typical for a new school of regionalism which no longer clings to the 'European model'. Instead, developments and experiences in other parts of the world are given prominent attention.[9] This new approach can be called 'new regionalism'[10] which is less inward-looking and Euro-centric and thus more proactive than reactive compared to its predecessor. The major differences between the old and new school of thought are summarised below.

Assuming that there has been a general shift of paradigms in the study and advocacy of regionalism, we have to ask if this trend holds true for East Asia, too. Can we observe new theoretical and practical approaches to regionalism in

Table 2.1 Features of 'old' and 'new' regionalism

	Old regionalism	New regionalism
Theoretical approach	'Classic' theories of integration: Federalism, Functionalism, Communications Theory	Wide range of different frameworks of analysis
Concept of 'region'	In general narrow and static: geographic proximity and features of cultural homogeneity and shared values are inevitable definition criteria	In general wide and dynamic: ranges from the traditional definition as a 'geopolitical unit' to the notion that regions are 'socially constructed'
Fundamental research questions	• Why and under what conditions do new political communities emerge among nations? • Why and under what conditions do élites of different states seek to make joint decisions and to shift their loyalty to a new centre of decision-making?	• What are the advantages of regional co-operation and integration over other forms and strategies of international interactions? • When and why do actors decide to participate in regional co-operation schemes?
Central assumption	• The growing complexity of governmental systems, the increasing importance of technical issues in the twentieth century and flourishing transactions between states and their people will inevitably generate new arrangements of political organization beyond the nation-state • Integration is sooner or later the quasi-automatic result of regionalism	• Regional co-operation can be a choice by policymakers to increase absolute or relative gains and/or the result of different international forces. • Integration is a possible but not inevitable result of regionalism; regional co-operation can be terminated without having reached the stage of political and/or economic integration
Empirical basis	European integration process as a model	Various phenomena of co-operation in different areas

East Asia since the end of the Cold War to the same extent as in the 'Western World'? In order to answer this question, this chapter follows three steps:

- Firstly, I will give a brief summary of what has been said and written by East Asian scholars and practitioners on regional co-operation efforts prior to the international watershed of 1989.[11]
- Secondly, some prominent examples of the East Asian regionalism debate in the Post-Cold War era will be presented, focussing a) on the continuous analysis and advocacy of co-operation within ASEAN, b) the quest for exclusive East Asian economic community-building as materialised in the EAEG proposal, c) sub-regional economic zones, and d) emerging regionalism in the Asia–Pacific.

- Thirdly, I will conclude with a few personal views on the difficulties of distinguishing between analysis and advocacy as well as between 'Western' and 'Eastern' Views in the era of 'new regionalism.'

The views and opinions of academics and practitioners presented in the following can only be a small selection of what has been written and said on East Asian regionalism. On ASEAN alone presumably more than a thousand books and articles have been published. I will try to highlight some concrete and illustrative contributions the debate.

Views on regionalism in the Cold War era: a brief retrospective

Some years ago the historian Muhammad Kamlin of Brunei Darussalam criticized non-Asian commentators and observers of regionalism in Asia in that they

> seem to believe, using [the] European Community as their model, that no genuine intra-regional cooperation, especially in economic activity, is possible unless there exists [a centralised decision making] structure ... In so arguing, they seem unable to read between the lines of the various declarations of hope and intention regularly renewed by ASEAN leaders, or even to appreciate the considerable constraints that keep ASEAN from developing into a cohesive force in regional cooperation.[12]

It is true on the one hand that contrary to their European and North American colleagues, East Asian intellectuals seldom, if ever, measured ASEAN or other Asian approaches to regionalism against the results and early successes of the European integration process. On the other hand 'Western' integration theories as well as the notion of the EC as a model for Asian regionalism were not alien to East Asian contributors to the debate. To get a clearer picture, it is useful to differentiate the views of scholars and practitioners.

The views of scholars: Is the 'Western concept' suitable?

Although East Asian scholars wrote fewer studies on regional integration than European and North American academics, they nevertheless contributed to the 'old regionalism' debate.[13] One of the pioneers is the Political Scientist Estrella D. Solidum of the Philippines. In her monograph on 'Towards a Southeast Asian Community' (1974) she gathers 'Western' ideas of integration, especially neo-functionalism, and applies them to the regionalism in Southeast Asia. She observes that co-operation among ASEAN nations as well as developing countries in general is more realistic and successful the more it deals with 'safe' or non-sensitive issues. Matters of high politics, such as the creation of defence alliances or common markets, would not be susceptible to the early stages of co-operation among heterogeneous polities. Therefore, according to Solidum, the case of the then five ASEAN states support Amitai Etzion's hypothesis that initially a cautious approach, amplifying close targets and underplaying the remote ones, is most effective in the early stages of regionalism.[14] Malaysian Political Scientist Pushpa Thambipillai primarily employs Karl W. Deutsch's hypotheses on community building in her dissertation on 'Regional Cooperation and Development: The Case of ASEAN and External Relations' (1980). She concludes that ASEAN differs from the process of community-building described by Deutsch.

Contrary to his assumption that adjoining states and societies strive for political amalgamation, within Southeast Asia the desire not to unite politically but to preserve autonomy would prevail. Accordingly, although interdependence (as conceptualised by Joseph Nye and Robert Keohane) among ASEAN members has been growing, the states of Southeast Asia are still be concerned with keeping their national identity by subscribing to the principle of non-interference in neighbouring countries' affairs.[15] In a similar vein, University of the Philippines graduate Bella R Lucas perceives that 'regional integration theory as developed by Westerners cannot be taken in its entirety to explain regionalism in the Southeast Asian milieu.'[16] She doubts, for instance, the universal validity of the functionalistic spill over concept, which predicts that integration starts in the economic area and then extends itself automatically to the political sector. Instead, Lucas believes that despite the Western view that economic unification would build up the foundation for political agreement, co-operative efforts within ASEAN are more political than economic.[17]

Thai scholar Somsakdi Xuto is even more sceptical about the validity of integration theory for the analysis of East Asian regionalism. An early article written in 1971 nevertheless demonstrates that students of regional co-operation in Southeast Asia followed the 'Western' concept of defining regionalism as integration:

> Newly independent countries of Southeast Asia are naturally sensitive about their newly-acquired independence and sovereignty, which tend to be jealously guarded against any real or imaginary infringement. Effective regionalism is likely to lead to weakening individual sovereignty and independence and Southeast Asian countries may be reluctant to commit themselves fully to it.[18]

As many other scholars' Hong Kong-based Professor Reuben Mondejar feels uncomfortable with the approach of applying integration theories to East Asian regionalism. He suggests employing organization theory instead. In a 1988 paper he explains that ASEAN-members,

> have agreed to create various inter-governmental organizations under the assumption that organizational maturity can be achieved through informal but coordinated handling of inter-state problems. There is no denying that the diverse outlooks and points of view of each state could present

themselves as forces of disunity, but the common desire for progress may also serve as a neutralizing element to the threats against unity.[19]

An important strand of the academic debate[20] focused on the historical burdens of East Asian regionalism and the relating obstacles to integration. Chung-Si Ahn, for instance, observes that the growth of regionalism in Asia is slow due to the bitter memories of colonialism and World War II. In his view, both contributed to tensions, disputes and distrust among the regions' nations. Therefore, Chung-Si Ahn regards regionalism as coexistent with strong tendencies of nationalism in Asia. The nation's political leaders would not accept any proposal for regional co-operation that may infringe upon the national sovereignty and independence.[21] It is interesting, however, that high-ranking politicians nevertheless continuously proposed far reaching co-operation schemes – at least in rhetoric.

The views of practitioners: European integration as a model?

Even if it is often denied nowadays, there is clear proof that many prominent politicians in Southeast Asia were influenced by the early successes of the European integration process and initially used the EC as a model for their own region. In 1962 Malaysia's ambassador to the Philippines, Inche Zaiton Ibrahim declared, 'look at the European Common Market. From its beginnings and its development we can learn a lot.'[22] The Finance Minister of Malaysia, Tan Siew Sin, joined him in 1966 when he confessed in an interview, 'I look to the ultimate creation of a Southeast Asian Common Market comparable to the European Common Market.'[23] And the former Foreign Minister of Thailand and one of ASEAN's founding fathers, Thanat Khoman, recollects, 'it should be put on the record that, for many of us and for me in particular, our model has been and is still the European Community'.[24] Indonesia especially, in its early days of 'New Order' was active in promoting integration as a model for regional development vis-à-vis extra-regional influences. To quote a statement by General Suharto before the Indonesian House of Representatives on 16 August 1966. 'If one day an integrated South-East Asia can be established, this part of the world may stand strongly in facing outside influences and intervention from whatever quarter it may come, be it of an economic nature, or a physical-military intervention.'[25]

It goes without saying that this political philosophy reflects exactly the spirit of the Bandung conference of 1955, which also stressed the necessity of becoming independent from outside influences by internal coherence. The term integration was used in speeches by Suharto and other senior officials of his administration, up until mid-1967. It was obviously understood as the 'natural' concept for the operational realisation of the above mentioned philosophy. There exist at least a dozen official statements by leading politicians like Ferdinand Marcos, Narciso Ramos, José Ingles, Sinnathamby Rajaratnam and many others made in the 1960s and early 1970s advocating the establishment of regional economic integration schemes modelled after the EC (see Dosch 1997 for details). These ideas were in line with concepts of the United Nations and their sub-organisations such as the UN Conference on Trade and Development (UNCTAD) enthusiastically praising regional economic integration as an appropriate action in fighting the problems of underdevelopment in the so-called 'Third World'. However, when the European integration process took more shape in the first half of the 1970s or so, it was realised in East Asia that the concept of integration means a partial transfer of sovereignty, a strong institutional framework, and a common and binding decision-making process. Hence, the term integration was constantly avoided and remained a taboo within ASEAN – at least on the higher political levels – up to the Manila Summit Meeting in 1987. Instead it was stressed that ASEAN never intended to emulate European integration.[26] It is evident that the actual policies carried out by several ASEAN governments, especially in the field of economic co-operation, did indeed show no evidence of any ambition to follow the European way.

Analysis and advocacy of regionalism in the post-Cold War era

The regionalism debate in the aftermath of the Cold War is clearly more complex and diversified than the one before 1989. Although ASEAN is still a relevant issue, the new school of regionalism also prominently focuses on other forms of co-operation and community-building. Among them are sub-regional schemes such as various so-called growth triangles or quadrangles. This discussion on the development and effects of economic integration below the nation state level is embedded in the general argument on globalisation in the post Cold War international order. Others concentrate on the advocacy and feasibility of new and exclusively East Asian trading blocks or groupings to counterbalance 'Western' regionalism such as NAFTA or the EU Common Market. The idea of an East Asian Economic Caucus (EAEC) first articulated by Malaysia's Prime Minister Mahathir Mohammad in 1990 is the most prominent example in this respect. Finally, the quest for wider Asia–Pacific co-operation has become a major pillar of the new regionalism. Although concepts of community building in the Pacific Rim date back to the 1960s, the issue became really relevant only with the founding of APEC (1989), ARF (1993) and CSCAP (1993). It is true on the one hand that co-operation efforts in the Asia–Pacific extend East Asian regionalism and are not the central concern of this volume. On the other hand, East Asian intellectuals and politicians are among the leading proponents of the Pacific community idea. Therefore, brief reference will be given to Asia–Pacific co-operation too.

As far as theory is concerned, any observer will immediately notice that the theoretical approaches of the old regionalism have lost their significance as frameworks of analysis. However, the question if and to what extent the European Union presents a model for possible steps towards integration in East Asia remains important especially among practitioners. A striking element of the new regionalism is the convergence of analysis and advocacy. And it is equally difficult, if not impossible in some cases, to draw an exact line between the views of academics and practitioners. Kenichi Ohmae's well received book 'The End of the Nation State' (1995) is only one of many examples. As a former Senior Partner of McKinsey, Ohmae obviously belongs to the group of practitioners but has stimulated the academic debate on the reshaping of markets more than almost anyone else in East Asia. The same holds true for the debate on regional co-operation in the Asia–Pacific, which is shaped by track two networks or epistemic communities[27] consisting of both scholars and government officials. Hence, contrary to the brief evaluation of the old school of regionalism, the following part will not be structured according to the two groups of actors but to the different discussion areas. I will start with views on ASEAN's development in the 1990s, followed by the discussion on sub-regional growth areas, the EAEC-concept, and eventually the Asia–Pacific argument.

The different concepts of ASEAN

The integration debate revisited

The first strand of the ASEAN debate continues to focus on the aspect of integration and the relevance of European community-building as a model for Southeast Asian regionalism without being linked however to the classic 'Western' theories.[28] Recent academic studies have instead drawn on more modern theoretical approaches, as excellently demonstrated by Suthiphand Chirathivat (1997) for instance.[29] The discussion on the pro and cons of integration reached its peak around 1991–1993 and was clearly stimulated by external influences. When the new post-Cold War order loomed large on the horizon, politicians in Southeast Asia searched for strategies to strengthen ASEAN's cohesion and the groups' international position. Firstly, the global tendency towards the regionalization of markets in general and the formation of NAFTA, the EU Common Market and the South American free trade area MERCOSUR in particular made Southeast Asians to think about the necessity and desirability of more integration within ASEAN. Secondly, the clear structure of bipolarity and East–West confrontation had served ASEAN well. It had kept the United States engaged in the region as a guarantor for a secure geopolitical environment. At the same time the Cold War had contained the power projection interests of all three major actors, i.e. the US, the Soviet Union, and China. Not surprisingly, uncertainties concerning the new regional political-security architecture arose in the wake of the Cold War[30] and even provided reason to evaluate the possibility of defense integration within ASEAN.

Senior officials and scholars especially from Singapore and Malaysia started talking in a seemingly deliberate way about regional economic integration in the early 1990s. A prominent senior official from Singapore put it as follows: 'Integration is our final objective. The EC as a model is our hope.'[31] In 1991, Singapore's Prime Minister Goh Chok Tong advised the association's fellow members in a speech, 'ASEAN economies are in different stages of economic development, but if we take steps now towards freer market linkages within the

ASEAN co-operative framework, we too will one day arrive at the level of co-operation and prosperity which the EC enjoys today.'[32] Around the same time, Philippine Foreign Minister Raul Manglapus suggested the negotiation of an 'ASEAN Treaty for Economic Cooperation' modelled after the EC (ibid.). However, Thailand's initiative to build an ASEAN Free Trade Area (AFTA) gained more support and was formally approved in 1992. Scholars like Chandran Jeshurun of ISEAS predicted a gradual process of *Brusselsization* of ASEAN leading at least to a more professional cluster of interactions at the inter-governmental level.[33]

Parallel to concepts of intensified economic co-operation, prominent politicians brought ideas of defence integration into the discussion. (It goes without saying that the EC/EU did not serve as a model in this respect since Europe has not managed to create its own institutional framework for effective common defence.) Among the most remarkable proposals was the one by former Indonesian Foreign Minister Mochtar Kusumaatmadja to establish a 'Malacca Straits Defence Pact'.[34] And Gen. Rafael Ileto, security advisor to President Aquino, launched the idea of creating a regional security alliance with the participation of the Indochina States in the case of a US withdrawal from the Philippines.[35]

Nonetheless, we should not blind ourselves to the fact that large parts of Southeast Asia's Foreign Policy elite have constantly refused the concept of integration both in the economic sector and even more strongly in the defence area. In the 1990s the governments of Southeast Asia have still been sensitive with regard to their independence. Any kind of supranational decision-making has so far been out of question for ASEAN. As far as the EU as a reference is concerned, for many practitioners European integration represents more an anti-model than something ASEAN should imitate. Decision-makers within ASEAN are well aware of the shortcomings and obstacles of European integration. At least until the outbreak of the Asian crisis in 1997, it was quite obvious that for many in Southeast Asia learning from Europe meant in the first place avoiding the mistakes of the Europeans in their efforts to grow together. On the basis of a most remarkable economic success and a related strong self-confidence, Southeast Asians became convinced that ASEAN was already strong enough to present a model on its own and that Europe could learn a lot from East Asia.[36]

Assessments in the light of the 'new regionalism'

From an analytical as well as practical-political point of view and contrary to the old school, the new debate does not consider regionalism as quasi identical with integration. Integration is regarded as one possible feature of regionalism but no longer the only one. In other words': while the old school had the tendency to deny the presence of regionalism in Southeast Asia because of the absence of integration, for the new school regionalism is a multidimensional phenomenon. Unlike Western scholars[37] most East Asian analysts have not compared ASEAN with regionalisms elsewhere but treated Southeast Asia as a single case. There has been the widespread opinion that ASEAN would *per se* not be comparable with other efforts of regional co-operation because of Southeast Asia's unique geopolitical, cultural and historical structure. The analysis of ASEAN's general achievements until the outbreak of the Asian Crisis generally focused on five broad arguments:

ASEAN as a successful collective actor on the international stage: The strong links that ASEAN-members have forged amongst themselves enable them to negotiate and bargain with third countries with greater confidence and success. Like no other group of non-western countries, ASEAN as a collective actor has managed to gain the industrial nation's attention through its well-established dialogue mechanisms belong to the most recognised international forums in the world.[38] Noordin Sopiee describes ASEAN as a 'politico-diplomatic coalition vis-à-vis the outside world.[39]

- *ASEAN as a regional conflict mediator*: The ASEAN has demonstrated its will to find regional solutions for regional problems: a) ASEAN contributed to the political solution of the Cambodian conflict as one – if not as the most important major player in peace negotiation process. b) At the Twenty-Fifth Meeting of the ASEAN Foreign Ministers in Manila 1992, ASEAN adopted the 'Declaration on the South China Sea', which is regarded as a first step towards a peaceful settlement of this dispute. c) At the ASEAN Summit in Bangkok (1995) a treaty was signed which bans the development, acquisition, use, testing, and stationing of nuclear arms in Southeast Asia. As Chin Kin Wah puts it, 'ASEAN's forte in the handling of intramural conflicts has been principally by way of conflict management or conflict avoidance rather than conflict resolution.'[40]

- *ASEAN as a security community*: ASEAN is a security community in the sense that probably no ASEAN member would seriously consider the use of military force as a means of problem solving in inter-member relations. ASEAN has successfully managed to keep the residual conflicts between the members – especially territorial disputes – on a low-key level. Armed confrontation in the ASEAN region had been avoided since the end of *Konfrontasi*.[41]

- *ASEAN as an inter-personal network*: High-ranking bureaucrats, government officials, scholars and the representatives of the private initiative within the ASEAN framework have forged a close network of personal links. In this way border-crossing communications and activities have increased and interactions have become much more easier. If one takes into consideration that only about 40 years ago the different national élites in Southeast Asia were practically not talking to each other, this network building within ASEAN is one major achievement of Southeast regionalism. It has resulted in transparency and confidence building.[42]

- *ASEAN as a framework for economic development*: Taking these four aspects together, ASEAN has created for itself a peaceful and stable regional situation. This situation in turn has contributed to a conductive climate for ASEAN countries to pursue their national economic development. In the words of the late ISEAS Director K.S. Sandhu: 'The [. . .] stability and security has allowed market forces to operate and these, together with generally outward-looking and development-oriented policies, have seen the region grow by leaps and bounds.'[43]

As far as specific issues of Southeast Asian regionalism are concerned, a substantial number of studies deal with the different member countries' policies towards ASEAN.[44] However, in recent years by far the largest quantity has been written on the concept, first results and prospects of the AFTA project.[45] In general, the picture painted of before the outbreak of the Asian crisis was positive. The assessment of Naya/Plummer is typical in this respect. 'AFTA is well on the way to full implementation by 2001. In fact, by the year 2000, ASEAN will already be a significantly-integrated market.'[46] Although euphoria has cooled down since then, many academics and practitioners agree that AFTA has not been harmed by the region's economic set back and might be even more relevant than before. 'AFTA needs to move forward so that ASEAN countries can better face challenges of globalization and competitive regionalism.'[47]

Recently however, for many economists, the ASEAN Foreign Ministers' Meeting in July 2000 in Bangkok came as a disappointment. Instead of coming up with new proposal to speed up the process, the Ministers only recalled an earlier decision to eliminate all import duties on intra-ASEAN trade by 2010 for the six original signatories and by 2015 for Vietnam, Laos, Myanmar and Cambodia 'with some flexibility'.[48] Since 1993, when ASEAN-6 enthusiastically signed the AFTA agreement and fixed the year 2003 as the deadline for the scheme's full implementation, the process has suffered many setbacks and delays. Some members seem to have spent more time drawing up long exclusion lists than trying to meet their obligations to gradually reduce tariffs as some observers have hinted.[49]

Considering the wide range of publications on different aspects of ASEAN, which are mentioned here only in fragment, it is interesting that the important question of widening versus deepening of regional co-operation has not stimulated any lively debate in East Asia. Apart from some isolated remarks on the value of an expanded ASEAN balanced against the advantage of intensified community building among the old members (assuming that both goals can hardly be reached at the same time),[50] most Southeast Asians never really questioned the organization's strategy of reaching the ASEAN-10 goal as quickly as possible and at almost all cost. Western scholars have been more critical in this respect.[51] Only now, after the completion of ASEAN-10, do senior officials in some ASEAN Foreign Ministries wish the organization had given second thoughts at least to the question of Mynamar's membership instead of rapidly enlarging the group.[52] In general, however, 'Western' and 'Eastern' analyses of ASEAN as well as recommendations for the organisation's further development are broadly similar in direction. This holds true for the more critical assessment of Southeast Asian regionalism in the wake of the Asian crisis, too. Not only ASEAN's handling of the regional financial crisis has been seen as ineffective in and outside the region. Also the ASEAN members' failure to effectively adopt a common, co-operative strategy in fighting the 'haze problem' has caused intra- and extra-regional criticism.[53] Maybe the region's intellectuals are even more outspoken than their non-Southeast Asian colleagues. Bantarto Bandoro writes,

> ASEAN will definitely become less cohesive and more distracted, and long-standing rivalries within the grouping may resurface. This will make the association a whole more susceptible to penetration by external powers or actors. ... ASEAN is not only at the crossroad, but it is also on the brink of depression and disintegration.[54]

High ranking politicians like Thailand's Foreign Minister Surin Pitsuwan are no longer satisfied with the traditional 'Asian way' of dealing with problems and challenges and thereby sound the bell for a new phase of regionalism. At the ASEAN Ministerial Meeting (AMM) in July 1998 in Manila, Thailand supported by the Philippines, proposed that ASEAN's non-interference policy should be replaced by 'flexible engagement'. Even though the concept was not well received by the majority of ASEAN's Foreign Ministers and finally re-named 'enhanced interaction', it is shaking up the status quo of foreign relations in Southeast Asia. Surin believes the time is right for reforms within ASEAN.

> In 31 years, diversity has become a problem for ASEAN [...]. Diversity, which used to be a source of strength has become a source of weakness [...]. We have no freedom and flexibility of expressing our views concerning some members. We have to be silent because we are members of the family. This is not fair, not just.[55]

Back then Surin's challenging of the sacrosanct 'ASEAN way' seemed to be premature. But the Foreign Minister has won a growing number of colleagues over to his idea. At their Bangkok meeting 2000, the foreign ministers formally approved Thailand's concept of an 'ASEAN Troika.' The new mechanism enables the sitting chair to activate a three-member task force to tackle specific problems that have regional implications. While the arrangement has to be considered as one of ASEAN's most important attempts at the institutionalized management of regional order, its effectiveness remains questionable among observers. Partly – and explicitly! – modelled after the 'EU troika', it seems hard to believe that, analogous to the European Union, ASEAN's present chairman, his immediate predecessor and designated successor would have a formal mandate to act on behalf of the other members.

If Thailand, Singapore, and Vietnam (the hypothetical present troika) had authority to deal with border-disputes between ASEAN-members, or even ethnic-religious violence and political instability in Indonesia, ASEAN would have reached the stage of a supra-national organization. However, according to Philippine Foreign Secretary Domingo Siazon, the troika-concept does not mean that ASEAN is becoming interventionist, but 'proactive'.[56] Many believe that in order to regain some momentum, ASEAN has to demonstrate that it does not simply add more buzzwords to its agenda but that there is institutional substance behind the new rhetoric. As Jesus P. Estanislao puts it, 'the biggest challenge for ... ASEAN ... is to match their rhetoric about community building with substance'[57].

New ideas on regionalism: trading blocks, sub-regional growth areas and mega-regional dialogue diplomacy

Different to the debate on Southeast Asian regionalism which already started decades ago, other concepts of East Asia regionalism were born only after the Cold War. Among them is the idea of a wider but exclusively East Asian economic bloc-building.

In December 1990, on the eve of the GATT negotiations' (temporary) failure, Malaysian Prime Minister Mahathir Mohamad proposed the establishment of an economic bloc including Southeast and Northeast Asia (with China, Japan and ASEAN as centres) and excluding external powers such as the United States and Australia. The idea was not only a reaction to the frustrating events within GATT but also stimulated by Japan's massive foreign investment within the region. Mahathir, who had since the early 1980s been openly pro-Japanese, was looking for a way to channel an even larger share of Japanese outbound capital and technology know-how to aid ASEAN's industrial development.[58]

This proposal of an East Asian Economic Group (EAEG) was problematic from the very beginning. Not only did the US, Australia and Japan strongly object but it also attracted negative reactions from several ASEAN nations.[59] Comments from Jakarta were especially harsh, partly because the Indonesian government had not been consulted by Mahathir beforehand. In a newspaper comment Hadi Soesastro, executive director of the Center for Strategic and International Studies, wrote, '... the proposal is too reactive, anti-American, not realistic and even dangerous.'[60] To ease the tension Malaysian government officials and also academics tried their best to downgrade the concept. Noordin Sopiee, head of Malaysia's leading foreign policy think tank (Institute for Strategic and International Studies), who was said to be closely connected to the idea's evolution, explained,

> ... it is not a bloc, a trading bloc. It is intended to start off as a low-level economic alliance, a pressure group, something like the Cairns group, that can act as a megaphone to magnify our voices in the current Uruguay round, and in future arenas of multilateral economic diplomacy.[61]

The EAEG has since been diluted and continuously deliberated within ASEAN as the East Asian Economic Caucus (EAEC). One of the problems with the proposal was the absence of a clear blueprint. The whole issue remained vague and highly politicised, culminating in 1993 when Mahathir refused to attend the APEC summit in Seattle. Although the idea has never fully materialised, it still bears importance as the most ambitious quest for a new East Asian regionalism in the era of globalisation and simultaneous economic bloc building. Interestingly, when the Asia-Europe Meeting (ASEM) constituted itself in 1996, the Asian side was entirely composed of those States that were supposed to form EAEG.

Given the current difficulties in implementing AFTA and ASEAN's long history of failed strategies to liberalize intraregional trade, it has been a logical move to focus more on the wider East Asian context. To this end, in November 1999 the Association launched an 'ASEAN plus three'-meeting (ATP) to confer with their counterparts from China, South Korea and Japan. The meeting presents the most serious evolution of the EAEC proposal, perhaps even a step closer towards a loose East Asian alliance. Jususf Wanandi explains the incentives for APT as follows.

> The Crisis made the need for East Asia to come together much more pertinent than ever. There were already economic factors pushing East Asia together when the financial crisis made the urgency obvious. How the Crisis was handled by the international financial institutions was so dismaying. These institutions are based on the balance of power in 1945. They have to adjust. The voice of Europe is too overwhelming in the International Monetary Fund, while East Asia including Japan has nothing. So that needs rebalancing. That is the idea behind the need for integrating Northeast Asia and Southeast Asia. The embryo has been put down with APT.[62]

The only tangible result of the first formal gathering in Bangkok (2000), however, was Japan's announcement of a US$ 15 billion five-year assistance plan to help regional countries to develop their IT infrastructure. From now on ATP will be an essential part of the association's annual conference package centered around the Foreign Ministers meeting and including also the Post Ministerial Conferences with the group's dialogue partners, such as the US and the EU, and the ASEAN Regional Forum (ARF).

Sub-regional co-operation: Emerging growth areas

The massive structural changes in the aftermath of the Cold War not only provoked a debate on regional bloc building but gave also reason to think about strategies of sub-regionalism. In this respect Hidetoshi Taga distinguishes two different types of post-Cold War regionalism. The first or 'defensive type' would be represented by the EU and NAFTA, whereas the second or 'positive type' could be found in East Asia. He names the 'Yellow Sea Rim region',[63] the 'Greater Hong Kong Area',[64] the 'Singapore-Batam-Johor Triangle' and the 'Bath or Indochina Economic Zone'[65] as examples.[66] Generally sub-regional economic zones are defined as 'a few neighboring provinces of different countries interlinked closely through trade, investment, and personal movement across national borders.'[67] Others also subsume so-called special economic zones within state borders, city-states and free ports to the concept.[68] For Keniichi Ohmae these economic zones or what he calls regional states 'may or may not fall within the borders of a particular nation. Whether they do is purely an accident of history.'[69]

Apart from a series of studies which primarily intend to supply information on certain growth areas,[70] the most ambitious strand of the debate (from an academic point of view) focuses on the effects of globalization, the role of government and private business interests on the emergence of sub-regionalism. There are broadly three lines of argumentation represented here by characteristic quotations.

- The first assumption refers to sub-regionalism as a result of the 'end of the nation state' after the Cold War: '... there is not much evidence to support the notion that economic activity in today's borderless world follows either the political boundary lines of traditional nation states or the cultural boundary lines of what Huntington calls "civilizations." But there is plenty of evidence that is does follow information-driven efforts.'[71]
- The second group of argumentation regards the role of the state as crucial to the evolution of sub-regionalism: 'Governments play a crucial role in the planning, establishment and implementation of policies within growth areas. Growth areas are designated to exploit the existing natural cross-border economic and socio-political links, with the intention of extending the range and scope of activities.'[72]
- The third or middle-position awards both nation-state and private sector an important role depending on the type of sub-regionalism: 'The evolution of FEZs [Free Economic Zones] highlights the relative roles of the nation-state and private capital in global, national and local development. The evolution of intra-national FEZs reveals the interaction between government policy and the private sector in shaping local and regional development within the boundary of nation-states. The recent emergence of cross-national growth zones in the Asia–Pacific region offers a fresh and timely opportunity to examine issues regarding the changing relationship between the nation-state and global capital.'[73]

Most authors agree on the emergence or presence of two sub-regional entities. One is regarded as the product of market-driven interactions. Here, official designation represents no more than an ex post recognition of an evolving economic fact. In the case of the other deliberate policy efforts are taken to generate closer integration within sub-regions.[74] The second type has also gained importance as an element of advocacy since growth areas bring 'together parts of countries without having to go through the laborious process of forming trade and investment blocs such as the European Union ... which unite whole countries.'[75]

Asia–Pacific community building

The third trend of regionalism in the Post Cold War era refers to wider Asia–Pacific co-operation. The Pacific Community idea dates back to the 1960s when especially Japanese politicians and economists formulated ideas of wider Asia–Pacific economic co-operation.[76] Among the first were the vision of a 'Pacific Association' by Foreign Minister Takeo Miki and the proposal for an 'Pacific Free Trade Area' (PAFTAD) by economists Saburo Okita and Kiyoshi Kojima.[77] After intensive academic lobbying the concept finally resulted 1980 in the creation of Pacific Economic Co-operation Council (PECC) and more importantly the founding of APEC 1989. Security-related co-operation schemes, especially ARF and CSCAP complemented for the time being the post-Cold War concept of Pacific Rim regionalism in 1993.

According to the traditional concept of the 'old regionalism', Asia–Pacific would not make up a region. Considering the fact that a non-stop flight from Los Angeles to Tokyo, for example, takes about 12 hours, one can hardly talk about geographical proximity. Cultural homogeneity is even less visible. The concept of Asia–Pacific as a region is hence a typical child of the 'new regionalism'. In this respect Pacific Rim regionalism is driven by the motivation and the common interests of the actors involved to 'create a prosperous, stable, secure and peaceful community of nations in the Asia Pacific . . .'.[78] Hence, the Asia–Pacific region is not defined in terms of material structures but based on a set of compatible identities interests among élites. However, it seems difficult to award Asia–Pacific and Southeast Asia, for instance, the same quality as a region. Analogous to the term sub-region, which describes parts of established regions, it might be helpful to use the term mega-region for a larger entity consisting of adjoining regions.

The process of multilateral – economic and security – cooperation in the Asia Pacific, referred to as 'the Asia–Pacific Way', is widely regarded as a unique form of interaction characterized by a combination of four principles.[79]

- *open regionalism:* a set of features including, in the first place, promotion of transparency, avoidance of discrimination among intraregional and between intra- and extraregional actors, mutual reassurance, and non-exclusive order-maintenance and conflict regulation.[80]
- *cooperative security:* inclusiveness as far as possible or a commitment that the dialogue must be open to all relevant actors and a concept of 'building security with others rather than against them';[81] in short the opposite of a military bloc which implies exclusive membership and a clear-cut perception of friends and enemies. The concept ideally also includes norms like non-interference, respect for national identity and territorial integrity.[82]
- *soft institution-building:* a non-legalistic approach to cooperation on the basis of voluntary membership (which means that every actor keeps an exit-option), non-binding decision-making, conventions and informal networks

(rather than formal contracts or treaties), a loose organizational structure and the absence of any supra-national agents.

- *consensus building:* a commitment to finding a 'way of moving forward by establishing what seems to have broad support.'[83] Thus, consensus should not be confused with unanimity and consequently does not require total agreement by all parties.

In total the Asia–Pacific Way, which reflects in most parts the well-established ASEAN model of inter-member relations, is

> not so much about the substance or structure of multilateral interactions, but a claim about the *process* through which such interactions are carried out. This approach involves a high degree of discreteness, informality, pragmatism, expediency, consensus-building, and non-confrontational bargaining styles which are often contrasted with the adversarial posturing and legalistic decision-making procedures in Western multilateral negotiations.[84]

Many East Asian authors writing on the 'new regionalism' in the Asia–Pacific seem to follow the path of neo-liberalism or institutionalism. The extensive work done in recent years is – at least implicitly – based on the liberal hypothesis that states and their actors have a strong interest in institution-building as a means of increasing transparency in international relations and thereby improving regional welfare and reducing security-related risks for all participants. According to this view, the presently existing dialogue mechanism centered around APEC, PECC, PMC, ARF and CSCAP are improving and widening channels of information gathering and sharing, policy consultation and coordination. The process, described as a positive sum game, is suited to facilitate multilateral (and as a side effect bilateral) agreements as well as to identify and preventing problems arising from unilateral actions and decisions. The inclusion of the PRC is widely regarded as the most valuable concrete result of Asia–Pacific regionalism.[85]

This is more a general observation and does not mean that East Asian intellectuals follow a specific theoretical way in dealing with Asian-Pacific regionalism. To the contrary: the bulk of literature is not theory-oriented at all. There are a few exceptions, however. A group connected with US institutes such as the Berkeley APEC Study Center (headed by Vinod Aggarwal) or the Institute of International Economies (Fred Bergsten) in Washington employ International Regimes theory as a framework for the analysis of economic co-operation in the Asia–Pacific.[86] Others use gravity-models or the flying-geese pattern as frameworks of analysis.[87] As a whole the literature on economic co-operation in the Asia–Pacific mega-region is richer in ambitious theoretical approaches than studies on the security-related dialogue mechanisms. Only occasionally contributions on the security environment go beyond descriptive stock-taking. Matake Kamiya, for instance, applies Karl Deutsch's ideas when he writes, 'there is justifiable reason to believe that the [Asia–Pacific] region as a whole is moving closer to becoming a "pluralistic security community"....'.[88]

A concluding observation: the phenomenon of multiple convergence

The early work on regionalism in East Asia, with a strong focus on ASEAN, draws heavily on classical integration theories. Although only a few scholars fully adopted 'Western concepts', a substantial number of academics discussed the relevance of these theoretical approaches for the analysis of regional-co-operation in Asia. At the same time many prominent politicians advocated the European integration process as a model for East Asia. Contrary to the ambitious theory-oriented approaches of the 'old school' the 'new regionalism' is much richer in topics but for the most part poorer in methodological concepts. Exceptions such as studies on sub-regionalism or partly on Asia–Pacific mega-regionalism do exist, as has been shown.

This remark should by no means be read as a 'Western' critique. The absence of theory or scientific methodology is intentional in most cases: a wide range of publications on Asia–Pacific regionalism deliberately do not strive for greater academic glory but instead aim at the information of a multidisciplinary public and the advocacy of community building. The Asia–Pacific debate, for instance, clearly shows the convergence of regionalism's analysis and advocacy. Yoichi Funabashi's highly regarded book on 'Asia–Pacific Fusion' (1995) gives an excellent example in this respect as does the APEC process in general. Among others, we owe to scholars like Suhadi Mangkusuwondo (Indonesia), Noordin Sopiee (Malaysia), Rong-I Wu (Taiwan), Ippei Yamazawa (Japan) or Jang Hee Yoo (South Korea) severe and stimulating writing on the topic. At the same time these personalities were members of APEC's Eminent Persons Group. In this function they advocated intensified economic co-operation by outlining the major steps of economic regionalization as materialised in the Bogor Declation of 1994 and other policy documents. One might even argue that unlike the 'old regionalism', analysis of the 'new regionalism' has to some extent lost its former academic independence since leading scholars in the field who are personally involved in the actual policy process have a naturally strong self-interest in promoting the existing dialogue schemes. On the other hand elder statesmen and senior government officials have joined academicians in analysing the efforts, shortcomings and obstacles of Asia–Pacific community building. Japan's former prime minister, Yasuhiro Nakasone, and Singapore's ambassador-at-large Tommy Koh are two active personalities in this respect.[89] These arguments are not about estimating the actual influence of individual East Asian intellectuals but meant to demonstrate the difficulty of drawing an exact line between, firstly, academic analysis and political advocacy and, secondly, between scholarly and practical-political contributions.[90]

The third and final element of convergence refers to overlapping views among Western and East Asian scholars and practitioners. More than in the days of the 'old regionalism', a substantial part of today's work on regional co-operation is carried out under the umbrella of epistemic communities and international second track networks, international conferences and research projects bringing together Asian *and* Western intellectuals on a regular basis. A wide range of volumes[91] provides demonstration of the fact that typical, characteristic European/American standpoints versus East Asian opinions on East Asian regionalism are hard to find in the post-Cold War era.

It can be concluded that more than a general shift of paradigms (which has taken place but does not seem to be of far-reaching importance) we can today observe a multiple convergence of issues and actors in the study and advocacy of regionalism.

Notes

1 Joseph Nye, 1968, p. vii.
2 Habib, 1995, p. 305.
3 Risse-Kappen, 1996, p. 8.
4 However, Western Europe does not present the first prominent example of regionalism, which started in the early nineteenth century on the eve of Latin America's independence movement, experienced a gradual evolution through the US-dominated inter-American system following the Pan-American conference in Washington of 1889–1890 and reached a new dimension in 1945 with the founding of the League of Arab States (Mols 1996b: 11).
5 Dougherty/Pfaltzgraff, 1990, p. 434.
6 See Mols, 1996a, p. 17 for details.
7 Lake/Morgan, 1997, p. 3.
8 This does not mean, however, that grand theories have to be considered as completely irrelevant. Structural Neo-Realism as presented by the work of Kenneth Waltz for instance, is still of significance in international relations theory (if wrongly or rightly has to be left open here).
9 The volumes 'The challenge of Integration' (1993) and 'Cooperation or Rivalry' (1996), edited by Peter H. Smith and Smith/Soji Nishijima respectively presenting the views of acknowledged scholars from Europe, the Americas and Asia are good examples for this new line of academic thinking.
10 The distinction between old and new regionalism is borrowed from Norman Palmer (1991). The term 'new regionalism' is also used by Soesastro 1998b: 88.
11 The year 1989 which marks the tearing down of the Berlin Wall is used here more in a symbolic way. It goes without saying that the end of the Cold War refers more to a process than a single date or event.
12 Kamlin, 1991, p. 10.
13 Only very few evaluations of East Asian contributions to integration theory exist. One of the most interesting is the unpublished thesis by Bella R. Lucas: 'Towards a Methodology for Assessing ASEAN regionalism: A study of intra-ASEAN interactions in 1976–1982. Manila: University of the Philippines, March 1983, especially pp. 14–22.
14 Solidum, 1974, p. 95.
15 Thambipillai, 1980, p. 274.
16 Lucas, 1983, p. 22.
17 Ibid, p. 26.
18 Xuto, 1982 [reprint], p. 49.
19 Mondejar, 1988, p. 12.
20 There are other strands which cannot be mentioned here in detail. One is the work on decision-making processes within ASEAN represented by monographs and books published in the 1980s by R.P. Anand and Purificacion V. Quisumbing (1981); Pushpa Thambipillai and J. Saravanamuttu (1985) or Renato de Castro (1989), to name only a

few. They are characterised by an approach of finding 'Asian explanations' to 'Asian phenomenon' employing concepts of bargaining and decision-making models (the concept of 'musyawarah' for instance). A selection of the most relevant articles on ASEAN up to circa 1990 can be found in 'The Asian Reader', complied by K.S. Sandhu *et. al.* (1992b).

21 Chung-Si Ahn, 1980, pp. 106–109.
22 *Straits Times*, 22 November 1962.
23 *Straits Times,* 05 June 1966.
24 Khoman, 1992, p. xix.
25 Quoted from Leifer, 1983, p. 119.
26 Rieger, 1986, p. 92.
27 Track two cooperation is basically a non-governmental academic activity, where government officials also participate in private capacity. This brings both official input and academic feedback but also flexible and free discussions in the cooperation process (Wanandi 1995b: 56). Epistemic communities are networks of 'professionals with recognized expertise and competence in a particular domain and an authoritative claim to policy-relevant knowledge within that domain or issue-area' (Haas 1992: 3; Kahler 1994: 31).
28 To avoid possible misunderstanding: the concept of integration and the case of the EC/EU are not necessarily linked from an analytical point of view. However, both aspects have so far often been discussed in conjunction.
29 One of the most comprehensive studies in recent years applying the theories of regional economic integration on ASEAN was carried out by Michael Plummer (1997). Although he is not an East Asian Plummer's article might be relevant here since his research was sponsored by the Japan Foundation and the results were published in an Asian journal, the ASEAN Economic Bulletin.
30 See for example Singh, 1997, pp. 128–131.
31 Personal communication, July 1993.
32 Quoted from Rieger, 1991, p. 162.
33 Personal communication, March 1993.
34 Kusumaatmadja, 1990.
35 *Straits Times*, 28 March 1991.
36 The 1996 Asia-Europe Meeting (ASEM) in Bangkok for example provided evidence for the new way of thinking. ASEM 'produced a number of milestones. Not least was an ironic reversal of historical roles. Where before European powers had single-mindedly stamped their own agenda during earlier encounters, Asia's former colonizers now came courting, attracted by the region's big economic potential. Eager to secure a bigger share of the business action, European leaders made notable efforts to accommodate their Asian counterparts. The visitors even acknowledged that any lapse in regional ties was largely Europe's fault.' (*Asiaweek*, 22 March 1996: 19).
37 See for example Dosch/Wagner 1999; Proff/Proff 1996, De La Torre/Kelly 1992.
38 Parreñas 1989.
39 Sopiee, 1991, p. 320.
40 Chin, Kin Wah 1997, p. 154.
41 Samad/Mokhtar 1995; Khoo How San 1994; Acharya 1991; Alagappa 1991.
42 Wanandi 1995a; Mak 1998.
43 Sandhu 1992a: 4.
44 Sing 1997; Rocamora 1994; Anwar 1994; Karim *et. al.* 1990 and many others.
45 Chia 1998; Ariff 1997; Tan 1996; Pangestu 1995 and many others. For a good summary of AFTA and other regional Free Trade projects in the Asia–Pacific see Soesastro 2000.
46 Naya/Plummer 1997; 121.
47 Chia 1998: 231.

48 See paragraph 39 of the Joint Communiqué of the 33rd ASEAN Ministerial Meeting, Bangkok, Thailand 24–25 July 2000 (http://www.asean.or.id, as of 3 January 2001).
49 *Asiaweek*, 01 September 2000: 'Tariff Troubles' (http://www.*Asiaweek*.com/*Asiaweek*/magazine/2000/0901/asean.tariff.html, as of 3 January 2001).
50 Chrirathivat/Pachusanond/Wongboonsin 1999: 30; Snitwongse 1998: 190–194; Mutalib 1997: 82–83; Abad 1996: 242.
51 Glad 1997; Dosch/Mols 1998: 176.
52 Personal communications in ASEAN capitals 1998–99.
53 See Funston 1998 for a summary.
54 Bandoro 1998: 298–299.
55 Speech at the Foreign Correspondence Club, Bangkok, 11 August 1998; transcript by J.D.
56 *Asiaweek*, 25 July 2000: 'Intelligence. New Realities' (http://www.*Asiaweek*.com/*Asiaweek*/intelligence/2000/07/25/index.html, as of 03 January 2001).
57 Estanislao 2000: 37.
58 Zainal Abidin Sulong, quoted from Korhonen 1998: 178.
59 Yamakage 1995: 123.
60 Soesatro 1991: 82.
61 *New Straits Times*, 19 January 1991: 10.
62 *Asiaweek*, 1 September 2000, 'We Must Stick Together. ASEAN's top minds consider how to keep the organization relevant.' (http://www.*Asiaweek*.com/*Asiaweek*/magazine/2000/0901/asean.roundtable.html, as of 03 January 2001).
63 The coastal areas facing the Yellow Sea of North and Northeast China, North and South Korea, and Japan.
64 Hong Kong and China's Guangdong and Fujian provinces.
65 Thailand, Laos, Cambodia and the Indo-Chinese Peninsula.
66 Taga 1994: 228. Other examples are the 'Brunei, Indonesia, Malaysia, Philippines-East ASEAN Growth Area' (BIMP-EAGA) or the 'Japan Sea Economic Zone' including the coastal areas of Northeast China, the Russian Far East, South and North Korea, and Japan
67 Yamazawa 1994: 262.
68 Xiangming Chen 1995.
69 Ohmae 1995: 81.
70 See for example: Lee Tsao Yuan 1992; Toh Mun Heng/Low 1993; Krumar/Siddique 1994.
71 Ohmae 1995: 21.
72 Thambipillai 1998: 251.
73 Xiangming Chen 1995: 594.
74 Islam/Chowdhury 1997: 25.
75 Rocamora 1994: 33.
76 Asia–Pacific and Pacific Rim are used here synonymously. Both refer to the sum of states bordering the Pacific Ocean, i.e. the Pacific states of Southeast and Northeast Asia, North and South America.
77 See Japan Center for International Exchange 1980, 1982 for an summery of early proposals and Kohona 1996 and Yamaoka 1996 and Yamazawa 1998 for critical evaluations.
78 Habib 1995: 307. For one of the most comprehensive discussions of the region concept in the context of Asia–Pacific see Buzan 1998.
79 See Acharya 1997 for a good summary of these elements. He uses the term soft regionalism instead of soft institutions, which I consider more suitable to distinguish this principle from the concept of open regionalism. See Dosch 1998 for more details and references.
80 See for example: Soesastro 1998 a, b; APEC 1994: 3–4; and many others.
81 Acharya 1997: 326.

82 However, the current controversy on 'constructive engagement' (see below) challenges this norm.
83 *Straits Times,* 13 November 1994: 17.
84 Acharya 1997: 329.
85 See for example Satoh 1998; Seki 1996; Nakasone 1996; Funabashi 1996–97; Chan Heng Chee 1997; Chia 1994; various issues of the Indonesian Quarterly; the annual proceedings of the Asia–Pacific Roundtable, organised by the Institute of Strategic and International Studies (ISIS), Kuala Lumpur etc.
86 See the volumes Aggarwal/Morrison 1998 and Bergsten 1997.
87 See Islam/Chowdhury 1997: 20–25 for an overview.
88 Kamiya 1996: 107.
89 See for example Nakasone 1997; Koh 1998.
90 It goes without saying that this is not solely an East Asian but a universal phenomenon. The arguments holds true for anyone connected with neo-realism, for example, which is as much a theory as a policy strategy in international relations. Therefore it is most difficult if not impossible to clearly differentiate between the concept's analytical from and strategic elements. Would anyone really want to classify Henry Kissinger in this respect?
91 See for example Olds *et. al.* 1999; Maull/Segal/Wanandi 1998; Krause/Umbach 1998; Gipoloux 1994; Fukasaku 1995.

3   Economic cooperation in East Asia

Revisiting regional concepts and the subregional case of ASEAN

Philippe Régnier

Introduction

This chapter reviews how East Asian theoretical and empirical literature has envisaged and covered the concept of economic regionalism since the late 1960s and 1970s. Economic cooperation *per se* was not high on the regional agenda in East Asia until the late 1970s. By then it had come to be only a mild policy preoccupation of local governments and remained so throughout the 1980s, albeit under the shadow of rapid domestic and regional growth. In fact, little change in this state of affairs had been perceived until the outbreak of the East Asian financial crisis in mid-1997. It is therefore fair to conclude that the development of formal regional cooperation has been scarce compared to the dynamic expansion of *de facto* economic integration.

Within this context, the focus of this chapter is constrained to a limited range of regional economic issues of possible relevance to the region. Each of these issues will be initially discussed in a more general sense, and then tentatively examined under the framework of the subregional case of ASEAN economic cooperation.

Over the past two decades, and according to the so-called new regionalism school of thought, the intensification of regionalism has centred around three major geographical areas where domestic, regional and global economic activity has traditionally been most developed. Within the so-called triad of the three dominant macro-economic regions (Northern America/NAFTA, Western Europe/EU, and East Asia), East Asia emerged as one of the three poles of regionalism and inter-regionalism, in addition to Western Europe and Northern America, at least until the outbreak of the East Asian financial crisis.[1]

Compared with the two other regional entities, East Asian regionalism has been the most difficult to summarize and conceptualize.[2] There has been a lack of focused dynamics both in real and institutional terms, and in order to correctly perceive the constraints and limited achievements of East Asian cooperation over the past few decades, it is necessary to draw on the theories of regionalization developed economies and among developing nations. Japan is of course the key economic powerhouse and, together with the four newly industrialized economies (Hong Kong, South Korea, Singapore, Taiwan), it has constituted the economic inner core of East Asia. However, the economic re-emergence of China and the spill-over potential of an enlarged ASEAN also have to be taken into account. Finally, developments with respect to APEC since 1989 have complicated the overall regional/inter-regional picture, since they are in stark contrast with Prime Minister Mahathir's plea for an East Asian Economic Caucus (EAEC).[3]

In reviewing the literature, this contribution seeks to answer both why and how East Asians have come to envisage economic regionalism (versus globalism), regional economic cooperation (versus integration), and regional economic functionalism in sectoral areas of extra- and intra-regional cooperation.

The central hypothesis is to propose that East Asian literature has been both initially and also increasingly influenced by Western neoliberal theories. As also outlined in Dosch's chapter, this phenomenon began within the context of the old regional school of integration theories, and has continued into the 1980s and 1990s with the new regional school preaching open economic regionalism. Against the very slow progress of East Asian *de jure* economic cooperation, numerous empirical works by both East Asian and Western authors have demonstrated in the late 1980s and early 1990s the rapid emergence of a *de facto* economic regionalization, based on the sharp increase of intra-regional transactions in goods and services. While the 1997 to 1998 crisis may have downsized such transactions in the short term, this trend will remain valid in the medium and long term.

Controversies in regional theories and their interpretations in East Asia

Neither overall regionalization nor economic regionalization more specifically have been high priorities on the agenda of post-World War II China, Japan, and the newly emerging independent nations of Northeast and Southeast Asia. The first tentative efforts such as SEATO (1954) and ASEAN (1967) were primarily inspired by Cold War geo-strategic considerations supported by the USA, and had only minor economic content. This had remained globally valid until the 1980s, yet with some inflections from the late 1980s onward as a direct consequence of the rapid economic take-off and development of most East Asian nations.

What is a region in economic terms?

In long-term geographical and historical terms, the concept of an East Asian region remains very loose and fluctuating. The very concept of Asia has never been fully clarified and universally accepted, and the situation is much more confusing when it comes to sub-Asian concepts such as the Far East, East Asia, Southeast Asia, and so on.[4]

For example, the 1944 British geo-strategic concept of Southeast Asia has risen and declined in the study of international relations since then, as has been well documented in a 1996 study published by Tim Huxley.[5] This confusion over the concept of Southeast Asia has further increased due to the challenges arising from more recent phenomema such as the subregional creation of ASEAN (1967), which has led to a gradual submerging of the totality of Southeast Asia by the step-by-step enlargement of ASEAN up until 1999 (with the admission of Cambodia as the last non-member state belonging to Southeast Asia).

A further example is the concept of East Asia, which as a separate regional entity in its own right has gained ground along the rapid growth and so-called 'economic miracle' of most East Asian developing economies during the 1980s and early 1990s. The Malaysian proposal of an East Asian Economic Caucus (EAEC) has given further but also controverted support to the concept of East Asian emerging economic autonomy. However, Mahathir's proposal for an EAEC was at the time far more politically and anti-American/anti-Western oriented than purely economically motivated. This observation shows that any pertinent, if not comprehensive definition of a region cannot be restricted to an economic content.

Karl Deutsch, one of the fathers of modern integration theories, and many authors and practitioners dealing with regionalism after him, has come to the conclusion that sustainable regionalization can rely only on a wide plurality of ingredients. A central factor is the existence of a relative convergence of cultural, economic, social and political regimes among member-states of any given region or subregion. In its radical forms, such convergence may lead to transfers of national competences to a supranational authority, which may eventually contribute to confederal and federal states (as experienced in the nineteenth and twentieth centuries) or to more original regional organizations (such as the European Common Market, leading to the later EEC and then the EU until now).[6]

When applied to the pure economic sphere, this type of analysis tends to suggest that those regions potentially sustainable in economic terms are those which over time have experienced a rather strong density of diversified economic transactions, especially in trade and services. These criteria may suggest that East Asia has evolved in this direction, but only recently (1980s and 1990s). It encompasses a few dominant economies and many marginal contributors, meaning a sharp and unequal convergence in intraregional economic transactions. When applied to one subregion of East Asia such as ASEAN, most member-states do not meet these criteria of strong economic convergence, with the exception of Singapore and possibly Malaysia. In the post-East Asian crisis, many observers note a deepening divide between Northeast and Southeast Asian economies.

Regionalism versus globalism?

Since the early confederal and regional economic theories and their empirical implementations, fears of intra- and/or extra-regional discrimination, exclusion or isolation have prevailed both among the national economies directly involved, and among the nations of the rest of the world. As a matter of fact, all East Asian nations have remained extremely pragmatic and have observed a low profile on this issue. This common attitude, even in the case of ASEAN, is in sharp contrast to the highly ambitious regional schemes initiated in Africa, Central America and South America since the late 1950s and 1960s. In retrospect, most of these schemes have dramatically failed for non-economic but also economic reasons.[7] More recent initiatives, such as the Mercosur in South America, for example, have yet to prove their sustainable viability. Even with these strong trends towards economic regionalism, due to its encompassing nature it can cause concern both to outsiders and to those insider economies at a less or least level of development.

First, it may be perceived, both internally and externally, as a second best alternative to global efforts aiming at open economic multilateralism. Most East Asian economies have traditionally established more dense links with the extra-regional world economy than with each other. The most advanced and open economies are worried by protectionist tendencies from within the region, generally supported by the least developing nations or by different sectoral lobbyists in each member-state. Small advanced or less developed economies fear any inward-looking regional arrangements, which may be encouraged by the giant economies of the region. Least developed economies tend to refuse open competition from Japan and the East Asian newly industrialized economies.

Second, many insiders and outsiders refuse to face the risk of diverting instead of creating intra- and extra-regional economic transactions, even if modest regional schemes are envisaged such as preferential trade arrangements or free trade areas. This argument may be demonstrated by the failure or marginal success of some subregional initiatives such as the ASEAN preferential trade agreement (PTA, 1979) and the ASEAN Free Trade Area (AFTA, 1994) respectively.

Third, depending on controverted geopolitical and geoeconomic viewpoints, economic regionalism may be used by insiders as a bargaining tool in global/multilateral economic negotiations. A case in point is the use by the USA of the inter-regional APEC forum, encompassing East Asia, as a bargaining chip for the multilateral trade negotiations on services under the GATT/WTO Uruguay Round.

Open economic regionalism versus functional and sectoral integration?

Functional theories, as applied in the construction of federal states or in the specific case of the European Union, imply that regional economic cooperation can bypass the early stage of a free trade area, and lead to sectoral or across-the-board integration. The following stages may be a customs union (overall or excluding certain products), a common market (overall or excluding certain sectors), and finally and economic and financial union (with or without sectoral exceptions).

Until the 1997 to 1998 financial crisis, and considering the wide economic and social heterogeneity of the region, there has been a strong consensus among most East Asian intellectuals and practitioners for rejecting the notion of institutionalized economic integration proceeding from self-imposed supranational objectives, rules and regulations.[8] Their preference has favoured the notion of 'open regionalism'. In other words, the regional structure of transactions among East Asian nations is desirable up to the point of not affecting or discriminating the relations of East Asia *vis-à-vis* the rest of the world.

At the inter-regional level, APEC has remained a consultative body and at best a kind of multilateral discussion forum between the two sides of the Pacific Rim. APEC-style open economic regionalism has not even transformed itself into a loose free trade area, considering the numerous countries involved and especially the too-wide disparities among them. Furthermore, the East Asian financial crisis may have eroded inter-regionalism, as illustrated in the respective context of the most recent ASEM and APEC Summit meetings in 2000.[9]

At the regional level, some kind of *de facto* EAEC has gradually emerged within APEC, especially to counterbalance the economic superpower of USA, and to meet or resist US liberalization pressures. However, the emerging convergence among East Asian economies has been seriously challenged by the various implications of the financial crisis. On the other hand, they could be encouraged to develop some kind of common front to cope with raising globalization pressures in the near future.

At the subregional level, the creation of AFTA by ASEAN in 1992 has been more of a hasty reaction to the negative perception of fortress EU (and possibly of NAFTA as well) than a deep commitment to a free trade area by both old and new member-states. Even before the financial crisis, many observers from both inside and outside ASEAN were questioning the feasibility of AFTA by 2005 or 2010. How far does AFTA remain at all or is it a remote if not illusive objective?[10]

Economic integration and state sovereignty?

Contrary to intergovernmental organizations of regional cooperation, where member-states fully retain their identity and sovereignty, both federalist and functionalist theories of regional integration are aimed at transcending the nation-state. They imply various supranational transfers of competence.

Since the 1960s, all East Asian governments and most authors have continuously held to their newly conquered independence and to priorities of constructing their national identities. The option of institutionalized integration has therefore been firmly rejected. The preference for traditional forms of diplomatic consensus and cooperation, or the so-called 'Asian way' of implementing regionalization, has been maintained up to the 1990s. In any case, the experience of EU institutions has shown that the supposed and complete decline of state powers, including their economic and financial powers, are far from confirmed even in the case of the European integration process.

The extreme heterogeneity of East Asia has constantly challenged two key aspects of regional theories. It is questionable whether any goal of advanced regional economic cooperation (yet of the intergovernmental type) can be separated from the aims of a certain political and social convergence among the states concerned. The ASEAN experience between the mid-1970s and the mid-1990s is probably a case in point. It is also necessary to ask whether regional economic integration (*de facto* and/or *de jure*) leads to some forms of segmented or overall socio-political integration.[11] A subregional illustration of a *de facto* but controverted integration among two states refers to the close and interdependent relationship between Malaysia and Singapore.

Instability of regional schemes among developing countries

Derived in the 1950s and 1960s from early regional theories after the European model and from various United Nations' attempts to organize international negotiation platforms for newly independent Third World countries, a number of rather ambitious regional schemes were initiated for economic and/or political reasons, particularly in Africa and Latin America. Some were even targeting a certain degree of integration (in Eastern Africa, Central America, Andean countries in South America and so on). A few decades later, if not before, most of these early attempts had failed, often rather dramatically. Economic disparities, political changes and tensions, historical rivalries and old, unsolved conflicts were always the key problem.[12] Asia has remained at the margin of this first wave of regionalism, with the exceptions of ASEAN in Southeast Asia and SAARC in South Asia.[13] Yet, even in the case of ASEAN, often praised for its pragmatic approach, the profile and implementation of regional cooperation have remained extremely modest.

In the 1990s, there was a second and a wider wave of regionalization reacting to or combined with newly emerging trends of globalization within the OECD zone (EU and NAFTA), among Third World countries (Mercosur), and also between OECD and developing states (APEC and lately ASEM). Within the triad of the three major poles of global economic activity (North America, East Asia and Western Europe), East Asia is the only region that is dominated by emerging and developing economies, with the exception of Japan.

Subregional economic cooperation revisited in East Asia: the case of ASEAN

Following on from the discussion of the five theoretical issues mentioned in the first part of this chapter, the same issues are tentatively examined below in the subregional case of ASEAN economic cooperation.

What is economic region: ASEAN, Southeast Asia and beyond?

Southeast Asia as an economic region

As mentioned above, Western recognition of Southeast Asia as a distinct entity is relatively recent, dating back to only the 1940s.[14]

On the one hand, the phenomena of Southeast Asia being gradually recognized as a region comprises a specific element, primarily of a postcolonial geopolitical, human, cultural, linguistic and environmental nature. However, on the other hand, the emergence of that region as a distinct part of the world economy may be traced back to the 1920s, when the natural resources and potential markets of Southeast Asia (with Singapore and Malaysia at its centre) became the focus of rising rivalry between the USA and Japan. After the Second World War and especially since the 1960s, decolonized Southeast Asia as a regional division was more and more an external product of new economic internationalization and division of labour initiated by the OECD nation. Regions and regional subdivisons as relics of colonial imperialism have often continued to be used in a completely new world economic setting. Southeast Asia/enlarged ASEAN is no exception.[15]

In the wider context of the world economy, Southeast Asia has never been a unified region until today. In addition to the pre-colonial and colonial distinctions between vast agriculture-based and commodity/sea-based territories, both decolonization and the Cold War promoted the divisions between pro-Western capitalist economies and anti-Western planned economies at least until the 1980s, particularly as regards Burma. During the same period, the extremely rapid industrialization of Singapore, Malaysia and Thailand introduced new economic and social dichotomies within ASEAN and especially enlarged ASEAN, including the poor states of Indochina and Myanmar. Finally, the question has been raised in the 1980s and 1990s, and especially since the respective launching of APEC and AFTA, whether the pure regional economic content and unity of Southeast Asia alone is relevant enough by international standards, or whether enlarged ASEAN is increasingly a part of East Asia (primarily dominated by Japan and possibly Greater China) or of the wide Pacific Rim (with North America and possibly Japan as the co-leading house).

ASEAN economic cooperation: some main issues revisited

Even when economic cooperation was hurried along after 1975, the main impetus came from regional and global developments, which were thought to convey important political and strategic messages and implications.[16]

From the early days of ASEAN, economic cooperation was not high on the agenda, simply because priorities essentially lay elsewhere in the political and security spheres. Singapore and Indonesia have occupied opposite ends of the potential economic cooperation spectrum, with the Philippines and Thailand closer to the positive position of Singapore, and with Malaysia closer to the more tenuous position of Indonesia.

Even the first ASEAN Summit in 1976 to take action in the economic field was commonly assumed to be a political response to Indochinese events. The agreement to give each other priority in sales of rice and oil during the 1979 oil crisis was primarily a low-cost expression of ASEAN solidarity. In other words, economic goals have been used by ASEAN as a tool of veiled politics, sometimes as an instrument of apolitical image, and as an additional expression of political unity. From the early days of ASEAN industrial projects, PTA and other modest economic cooperation instruments envisaged in the late 1970s until the launching of AFTA in the 1990s, concern that divergences in economic policies and levels of development might damage the image of solidarity may partly explain why ASEAN has not taken on more projects or begun to move towards economic integration.[17]

Both ASEAN and non-ASEAN authors tend to share a common view that the economies of the region do not stand in practical complementary relationship to each other compared to what they can obtain from bilateral or multilateral arrangements with major economic powerhouses such as Japan, the USA or the EU. Therefore, proposals for a free trade zone and customs union have either been unacceptable to some member-states or impossible to implement in reality.[18] AFTA has been precisely facing such difficulties, even before the East Asian financial crisis of 1997 to 1998. On the eve of the financial crisis, confidence in ASEAN economic cooperation was growing. Due to continued growth and rapid market liberalization both domestically and internationally, most ASEAN member-states had started to view more positively the costs and benefits of AFTA-related economic cooperation. The adoption of liberalization policies, the turn to growth strategies based on attracting FDI, and the emergence of potential economic blocs in Europe and North America had been their primary motives.[19]

Obviously the deepening of ASEAN economic cooperation depends to a large extend on the further industrialization and diversification of each member's economy, and therefore on increasing transactions of both a complementary or competitive nature. First, it remains to be seen how far this process had been developing until the 1997 to 1998 crisis as a Southeast Asian autonomous phenomenon or as largely interdependent with the Northeast Asian economies (especially Japan, Korea and Greater China).

Second, as is well shown in Bustello's contribution, the 1997 to 1998 crisis has at least temporarily called into question the weaknesses of ASEAN economic cooperation, including AFTA. The incapacity of ASEAN to face the crisis as a strongly united regional grouping has been demonstrated by Bustello, but this deficiency may also be traced throughout the whole history of ASEAN economic cooperation. ASEAN has never considered adopting provisions to help member-states when their economies are in trouble. For example, when the Philippines faced serious difficulties in the 1980s, ASEAN did not rescue Manila in any way. 'If ASEAN cannot come to the rescue of a member-state that is economically hobbled, what's the organization for?'[20]

Regionalism versus globalism

As was shown in the above section, economics has never been the driving force behind ASEAN. Consequently, Southeast Asian authors have dealt even less than their Western counterparts with the economic fundamentals necessary for ASEAN construction. Only a few exceptions may be traced among individual economists (such as Narongchai Akranasee, Mohamed Ariff, Chia Siow Yue, Suthiphand Chirativat, Joseph Tan, John Wong), or research institutions such as the ASEAN Economic Research Unit, based at the Institute of Southeast Asian Studies in Singapore.

Intraregional economic cooperation has never been a high priority. Though very modest in profile, the first ASEAN projects adopted in the late 1970s have failed, such as the PTA (Preferential Trade Arrangement) or the mega-industrial projects.[21] Second-generation projects such as AFTA are still in the making. So far, the flow of intraregional economic and financial information has been accelerated thanks to increasingly regular meetings not only among ASEAN career diplomats, but also among ASEAN senior officials in charge of industry, finance and other services.

However, extra-regional economic cooperation has somehow been more successful. ASEAN external diplomacy has been rather active *vis-à-vis* major trading and financial partners of the OECD (EU, USA, Japan, Canada, Australia, New Zealand, South Korea). The ASEAN–EU dialogue even led to the first historical agreement linking two regional groupings in 1980. This agreement has been renewed several times since.[22]

Considering a relative convergence among member-states of inter-regional and global economic interests, another aspect also high on their respective external relations' agenda, ASEAN has been able to harmonize its position and speak with only one voice in some of the most influential multilateral economic forums. ASEAN economic diplomacy has been able to play a role within the Bretton-Woods and United Nations specialized agencies concerned. Since the late 1980s, it has also emerged as a player in inter-regional forums such as APEC or more recently ASEM. In practice, the ASEAN spokesman's role has quite often been attributed either to one member-state, whose economy is more internationalized than the others in certain sectors, or to one high-profile senior official or minister held in particularly high regard by the world community.[23]

This type of economic diplomacy has produced tangible results: the ASEAN region has been perceived as a group of countries that is open to the rest of the world and to global interests, attracting and generating more economic transactions than any other developing region of comparable size (with the possible exception of neighbouring Greater China).[24] This image has somehow suffered since the financial crisis of 1997 to 1998, and several ASEAN economies have yet to completely recover.

Open regionalism versus functional integration

Contrary to most other groupings among developing nations emerging in the 1960s and 1970s, ASEAN has opted since its very beginning for 'open self-reliant regionalism'.[25] During the first phase of economic cooperation formally launched between 1976 and 1979, all the initial instruments such as the PTA or the later AIJV scheme (ASEAN Investment Joint Ventures) have respected this principle. Only the ASEAN industrial projects were possibly more inward thinking and import-substitution oriented, and therefore of a tentative functional nature, but their dismal failure has proven once again the small collective size of ASEAN markets and their necessary exposure to the world economy.

Particularly during the 1980s and 1990s, due to rapid growth of most member-states and rising global competition pressures, a sudden surge of regional and extra-regional publications has praised the merits of open regionalism and wide liberalization *vis-à-vis* foreign economic players. Even the most protectionist member-state, namely Indonesia, has gradually joined this regional trend (described by Jörn Dosch as the new regionalism), whereas the Malaysian proposal for an East Asian Economic Group or East Asian Economic Caucus (EAEC) has been more political than economically oriented in nature.[26]

Functionalist integration of the ASEAN economies, after the model of the EU, for instance, has been constantly rejected by a majority of member-states including both their officials and their intellectual community. The very notion of formal integration has been rejected as a threat to the economic sovereignty and the central interests of individual member-states. The first stage of functionalist integration, namely a free trade zone, had not been envisaged until 1992, and its second and third stages, namely a customs union and a common market, have always been opposed.

> The Fourth ASEAN Summit in Singapore in 1992 cleared the doubts about ASEAN's stand on regional integration. The leaders made it clear that AFTA is not so much about integrating among members, but it is the way in which ASEAN members can get together to increase their competitiveness in the world.[27]

On the eve of summer 1997, it was generally assumed that ASEAN was moving towards the necessary deepening and broadening of its economic cooperation, which could be gradually met thanks to continued growth and production diversification. The sudden financial crisis of July 1997 and its wide spill-over effects have swept away the feasibility of such objectives in the immediate future.

The debate opposing regional functionalism to open regionalism might yet refer to shifting paradigms in the current period of economic globalization. On the one hand, one prevailing regional grouping such as the EU seems to combine several instruments of functionalism with global economic diplomacy and action. On the other hand, at least until the crisis, the ASEAN economies have been increasingly integrated both globally and regionally, making possibly classical regional functionalism less necessary, especially at intergovernmental and institutional levels.[28]

Regional economic integration and state sovereignty?

The vast majority of Southeast Asian authors and practitioners have considered the concepts of overall integration – and economic integration in particular – as non-relevant in the case of ASEAN. However, the concept of economic sovereignty has been poorly defined and confused with wider considerations related to prevailing concepts of political and legal sovereignty. Some have tried to reconcile respect for economic sovereignty with the necessity of classical but effective means of intergovernmental cooperation in some limited sectoral or subsectoral areas.

There has been some enduring confusion between *de jure* and *de facto* economic integration. It is only since the 1980s that *de facto* integration of ASEAN has been progressively acknowledged, with the rapid growth of transactions in goods and services within both Southeast Asia and Northeast Asia.

When adopting the so-called new regionalism approach illustrated by initiatives such as APEC or AFTA, most ASEAN governments have decided to rely much more than in the past on open trade and investment promotion mechanisms. Therefore, the main players of *de facto* economic integration have been major economic agents, both in the public and private, and both domestic and foreign sectors. The role of transnational actors such as foreign investors (mainly multinational corporations) and East Asian investors (overseas Chinese, and other investors from Japan, Taiwan, South Korea, Hong Kong, Singapore, Malaysia, Thailand) has also been underlined.[29]

In addition to historical integration links such as between the economies of Singapore and Malaysia, new concepts of bilateral or trilateral integration frameworks have been initiated by some ASEAN member-states. *De facto* integration between Singapore and the Malaysian state of Johor on the one hand, and the newly established complementarity between Singapore and the Indonesian Riau archipelago (neighbouring Batam and Bintan islands in particular) on the other, have led to the proposal of the growth triangle concept. The first proposed triangle was the Johor–Singapore–Batam triangle. Then, more recently, other triangles of growth have been proposed such as Southern Thailand/Northern Peninsular Malaysia/Penang, Eastern Malaysia/Brunei/ Southern Philippines and so on, not to mention Northern Thailand/Northern Laos/Northern Myanmar.[30]

During the 1990s, the main issue of unity versus division among ASEAN member-states has centred on the debate dealing with enlargement and/or strengthening of ASEAN. The political option of favouring enlargement first, namely to the Indochinese states and Myanmar, has widen the gap and disparities among the economic and social regimes of all member-states. Until the East Asian financial crisis of 1997 to 1998, ASEAN had not been able to significantly strengthen its economic cooperation, apart from through the reaffirmation of the rather loose AFTA concept.[31] As demonstrated by Pablo Bustelo (Chapter 8), the financial crisis has shown that the ASEAN economies have so far been incapable of producing either a common front or mutual assistance mechanisms in favour of the most affected member economies (despite early declarations back in the late 1970s).

Instability of regional schemes among developing countries?

Many Southeast Asian authors (and also foreign ones) have long praised the performance of ASEAN in terms of having been able to create a zone of peace, stability and development, with no interruption since 1967.[32] In most respects, ASEAN has apparently been a success story, at least when compared with most other regional groupings among developing nations. This success story is more political than economic in nature, but it does also apply to the economic sphere, even though ASEAN economic cooperation proper is not primarily responsible for the rapid development and *de facto* gradual integration of the region.

Looking at the current situation, and beyond the immediate crisis, the picture is very uneven.[33] On the one hand, and compared to other Third World groupings, it may be argued that cohesion versus division among ASEAN economies is not standing at one extreme or the other. Even if quite weak, there is a certain convergence of economic and social interests among ASEAN member-states, and one single economy does not dominate the others, such as India in the case of SAARC. Singapore's economy is strong both regionally and internationally, but within the spatial limits of a city-state. The economic situation of Indonesia, as the biggest member-state, stands between the three newly industrialized economies of ASEAN (Singapore, Malaysia, Thailand) and the poorest developing ones (Indochina and Myanmar). There is thus some room for enlarging and, indeed strengthening, ASEAN economic cooperation.

On the other hand, ASEAN cohesion is challenged by the recent financial crisis, and its severe and often unexpected economic, social and even political implications in some key member-states. A wider question is focused on the capacity of ASEAN to digest or resist global competition. Furthermore, the concept of regional economic cooperation among developing countries alone might appear somehow out of date. Real economic transactions now place Southeast Asia in a vacuum, yet have to include the heavyweight of Northeast Asian economies and the role of key extra-regional trading and investment partners.

Therefore, ASEAN has perhaps become too narrow a regional concept when applied to Southeast Asia. Whether or not merged with wider regional or inter-regional concepts such as East Asia/EAEC or APEC/Pacific Rim, the ASEAN economies are becoming increasingly linked to *de facto* or *de jure* groupings, which associate both developing and developed nations. This evolution is not specific to economics, but applies to other fields of cooperation such as security matters, dealt with in the ASEAN Regional Forum.

Conclusion

Looking back at the arguments put forward in this chapter, three conclusions may be tentatively drawn.

First, there are more elements of convergence than a profound divide between the first theoretical part of this chapter and the empirical review of ASEAN economic cooperation as a case study.

Second, East Asian and Southeast Asian literature dealing with ASEAN economic cooperation was somewhat slender up until the late 1980s and early 1990s. This may be a sign that after the initial decisions in the mid-1970s to give it a boost, economic cooperation has not been high on the regional agenda for very long. It also indicates, as often commented in both East Asian and Western literature that the relative success story of ASEAN has had little to do with economic affairs. It may also tentatively demonstrate that the sustainable political legacy of ASEAN may lead to increased economic cooperation in the long term (as in the case of AFTA 2005).

Third, this chapter has reviewed some of the reasons behind as well as the means through which East Asians have combined economic regionalism and global commitments, and the ways in which low profile intergovernmental economic cooperation and high-profile *de facto* economic integration have constantly overlapped, especially during the 1980s and 1990s.

Notes

1 Kavi Chongkittavorn, 'East Asian Regionalism: So Close and yet so Far', *South East Asian Affairs,*1998, pp. 45–50; A. Hurrell, 'Regionalism in Theoretical Perspective', in L. Fawcett and A. Hurrell, eds, *Regionalism in World Politics: Regional Organization and International Order* (Oxford: Oxford University Press, 1995).

2 James A. Caporaso, 'Regional Integration Theory and East Asia ', in Chae-Han Kim, ed., *Domestic Politics, Trade Negotiations and Regional Integration: The US, Japan and Korea* (Seoul: The Hallym Academy of Sciences, Sowha Publishing, 1998).

3 Kriwat Phamorabutra, 'Mahathir's Proposal for East Asian Economic Caucus (EAEC)', MA Thesis (International University of Japan, 1997).

4 Arnfinn Jorgensen-Dahl, *Regional Organization and Order in South-East Asia* (London: Macmillan, 1982).

5 Tim Huxley, 'Southeast Asia in the Study of International Relations: The Rise and Decline of a Region', *The Pacific Review*, Vol. 9, No. 2 (1996), pp. 199–228.

6 Karl Deutsch, Richard Merritt and Bruce M. Russett, eds. *Political Community and the North Atlantic Area* (Princeton, NJ: Princeton University Press, 1957); eds, *From National Development to Global Community: Essays in Honor of Karl Deutsch* (London: G. Allen & Unwin, 1981).

7 E.B. Hass, 'Turbulent Fields in the Theory of Regional Organizations', *International Organization*, Vol. 31, No. 1 (1977), pp. 73–82.

8 Ross Garnaut, *Open Regionalism and Trade Liberalization* (Singapore: Institute of South East Asian Studies, 1996).

9 Narongchai Akrasanee and David Stifel, 'The Political Economy of the ASEAN Free Trade Area', in Pearl Imada and Seiji Naya, eds, *AFTA: The Way Ahead* (Singapore: ISEAS, 1992); Jayant Menon, *Adjusting Towards AFTA: The Dynamics of Trade in ASEAN* (Singapore: ISEAS, 1996); Andrew Tan, *Intra-ASEAN Tensions* (London: Royal Institute of International Affairs, 2000); Joseph L.H. Tan, 'AFTA in the Changing International Economy', in Joseph L.H. Tan, ed, *AFTA in the Changing International Economy* (Singapore: ISEAS, 1996).

10 Jacques Pelkmans, 'Institutional Requirements of ASEAN with Special Reference to AFTA', in Imada and Naya, *AFTA: The Way Ahead*.

11 Andrew W. Axline, 'Underdevelopment, Dependence and Integration: The Politics of Regionalism in the Third World', *International Organization*, Vol. 31, No. 1 (1977) pp. 83–105; C. Vaitsos, 'Crisis in Regional Economic Cooperation (Integration) among Developing Countries: A Survey', *World Development*, No. 6, (1978), pp. 744–749.

12 Jorgensen-Dahl, *Regional Organization*, pp. 9–44.

13 Donald K. Emmerson, '"South East Asia": What's in a Name?', *Journal of South East Asian Studies*, Vol. 15, No. 1 (1984), pp. 1–21.

14 Chris Dixon, *South East Asia in the World-Economy: A Regional Geography* (London: Cambridge University Press, 1991).

15 Jorgensen-Dahl, *Regional Organization*, p. 134.

16 Michael Antolik, *ASEAN and the Diplomacy of Accommodation* (London: Sharpe, 1990); Harold Crouch, *Domestic Political Structures and Regional Economic Co-operation* (Singapore: ISEAS, 1984).

17 Michael Leifer, *Dilemmas of Statehood in Southeast Asia* (Vancouver: University of British Columbia Press, 1972); Hassan S. Kartadjoemena, *The Politics of External Economic Relations: Indonesia's Options* (Singapore: ISEAS, 1975); Ryokichi Hirono, 'Towards Increased Intra-ASEAN Economic Cooperation', *Asia–Pacific Community*, No. 3 (1978–79), pp. 92–118; Chung-Si Ahn, 'Forces of Nationalism and Economics in Asian Regional Cooperation', *Asia Pacific Community*, No. 7 (1980), pp. 106–118; Chia Siow Yue, 'SEAN Economic Cooperation: Singapore's Dilemma', *Contemporary Southeast Asia*, Vol. 2, No. 2 (1980), pp. 113–134.

18 Narongchai Akrasanee, 'The Political Economy of the ASEAN Free Trade Area', in Imada and Naya, *AFTA: The Way Ahead*, pp. 27–47; Suthiphand Chirathivat, 'ASEAN Economic Integration with the World through AFTA', in *AFTA in the Changing International Economy* (Institute of Southeast Asian Studies, Singapore: ISEAS, 1996).

19 *Business Day* (Manila), 14 June 1984.

20 Gerald Tan, *ASEAN Economic Development and Cooperation* (Singapore: Times Academic Press, 1996), pp. 170–196; Guat Tin Ooi, 'ASEAN PTA: An Assessment'; Gerald Tan, 'ASEAN PTA: An Overview', and Chee Peng Lim, 'ASEAN Co-operation in Industry: Looking Back and Looking Forward', in Noordin Sopiee *et. al.* eds, *ASEAN at the Crossroads: Obstacles, Options, and Opportunities in Economic Co-operation* (Kuala Lumpur: Institute of Strategic and International Studies, 1987); H. W. Arndt and Ross Garnaut, 'ASEAN and the Industrialization of East Asia', *Journal of Common Market Studies*, Vol. 17, No. 3 (1979), pp. 189–211.

21 'Cooperation within a Wider Framework: ASEAN External Relations', in ASEAN Secretariat, *ASEAN Economic Co-operation: Transition and Transformation* (Singapore: Institute of Southeast Asian Studies, 1997); see also *ASEAN Economic Cooperation Handbook*, compiled by Hans Christoph Rieger (Singapore: ISEAS, 1991).

22 Ross Garnaut, *Open Regionalism and Trade Liberalization* (Singapore: ISEAS, 1996); Chee Peng Lim, 'ASEAN's Policies Towards the EU', in Chia Siow Yue and Joseph Tan, eds, *ASEAN and EU: Forging New Linkages and Strategic Alliances* (Singapore: ISEAS, 1997); Djisman S. Simanjuntak, 'EU–ASEAN Relationship: Trends and

Issues', in Chia Siow Yue and Marcello Pacini, eds, *ASEAN in the New Asia: Issues and Trends* (Singapore: ISEAS, 1997); J. Soedjati Djiwandono, 'The Role of ASEAN in the Asia–Pacific Region', in Dalchoong Kim and Noordin Sopiee, eds, *Regional Cooperation in the Pacific Era* (Seoul: Institute of East and West Studies, Yonsei University Press, 1988).

23 Dewi Fortuna Anwar, 'Indonesia and ASEAN Extra-Regional Economic Co-operation', in *Indonesia in ASEAN: Foreign Policy and Regionalism* (Singapore: St Martin's Press and ISEAS, 1995).

24 ASEAN Secretariat, *ASEAN Economic Co-operation*, pp. 196–198; 'External Economic Relations', in *ASEAN Economic Cooperation for the 1990s: A Report*, published by ASEAN Standing Committee (Manila: Philippine Institute for Development Studies, 1992); J. Saravamamuttu, 'ASEAN Postures and Performances in North–South Negotiations', in Pushpa Thambillai and J. Saravamamuttu, eds, *ASEAN Negotiations: Two Insights* (Singapore: ISEAS, 1985).

25 Chong Li Choy, 'Open Self-Reliant Regionalism: Power for ASEAN's Development' (Singapore: ISEAS, 1981).

26 Anwar, *Indonesia in ASEAN*, Chapter 3, 'Economic, Functional and Structural Aspects of ASEAN Co-operation for Indonesia (1967–87)'.

27 Suthiphand Chirathivat, 'A Step Towards Intensified Economic Integration', in Wolfgang Moellers and Rohana Mahmood, eds, *ASEAN Future Economic and Political Cooperation* (Kuala Lumpur: ISIS, 1993).

28 Suthiphand Chirathivat, 'What Can ASEAN Learn from the Experience of European Integration?', in Chia and Tan, *ASEAN and EU,* pp. 208–210.

29 hia Siow Yue and Wendy Dobson, 'Harnessing Diversity', in Chia and Dobson, eds, *Multinationals and East Asian Integration* (Singapore: ISEAS and International Development Research Centre, Canada, 1998); see also OECD, *Foreign Direct Investment, OECD Countries and Dynamic Economies of Asia and Latin America: Regional and Global Gains from Liberalization* (Paris: OECD, 1995); World Bank, *East Asia's Trade and Investment* (Washington, DC: World Bank, 1994); H. Jansson, *Transnational Corporations in Southeast Asia* (Cambridge: Cambridge University Press, 1994); K. Ohno and Y. Okamoto, 'Multinational Firms in Market-led Integration in Asia', in *Regional Integration and Foreign Direct Investment: Implications for Developing Countries* (Tokyo: Institute of Developing Economies, 1998).

30 Myo Thant, Ming Tang and Hiroshi Kakazu, *Growth Triangles in Asia: A New Approach to Regional Economic Cooperation* (Oxford: Oxford University Press, 1994); Tsao Yuan, ed., *Growth Triangle: The Johor-Singapore-Riau Experience* (Singapore: ISEAS and IPS, 1991); see also Arthur Andersen Co, *The Growth Triangle: A Guide to Business* (Singapore, 1991).

31 Chia Siow Yue, 'The Deepening and Widening of ASEAN', *Journal of the Asia Pacific Economy* (1996), pp. 59–78; Chin Kin Wah, 'ASEAN: The Long Road to One Southeast Asia', *Asian Journal of Political Science,* No. 5 (1997), pp. 1–19; Ajit Singh, 'Towards One Southeast Asia', *ASEAN Economic Bulletin,* Vol. 4, No. 2 (1997), pp. 126–131; Barry Wain, 'ASEAN is Facing its Keenest Challenges to Date', *Asian Wall Street Journal Weekly* (23 February 1998), p. 17; see also Sukhumphand Paribatra, 'From ASEAN Six to ASEAN Ten: Issues and Prospects', *Contemporary Southeast Asia,* Vol. 16, No. 3 (1994), p. 250.

32 Hans C. Blomqvist, 'SEAN as a Model to Third World Cooperation?', *ASEAN Economic Bulletin,* Vol. 9, No. 2 (July 1993), p. 58. Jörn Dosch and Manfred Mols, 'Why ASEAN Cooperation Cannot Work as a Model for Regionalism Elsewhere: A Reply', *ASEAN Economic Bulletin,* Vol. 11, No. 2 (1994), pp. 212–222.

33 UNCTAD, *Rapidly Emerging Regional Integration Systems: Implications for the Asian Developing Countries and Possible Policy Responses* (Geneva: UNCTAD, 1995); Ezra Vogel and Uchida Ichiro, *East Asia Towards the Year 2000: What the*

Region Should, Can and Will Do (Kuala Lumpur: ISIS, 1996); Yoshinobu Yamamoto, 'Regionalism in Contemporary International Relations', in *Regionalism in the World Economy: NAFTA, the Americas and Asia Pacific* (San Diego: Whiting Jr, 1996); Rüdiger Machetzki, 'ASEAN – Politics and Economic Development', in Wolfgang Pape, ed., *Shaping Factors in East Asia by the Year 2000* (Hamburg: Institute of Asian Affairs, 1996); Ross Garnaut and Peter Drysdale, eds, *Asia Pacific Regionalism: Readings in International Relations* (Pymble: Harper Educational, 1994); R. Lawrence, *The Global Environment for the East Asian Model* (Cambridge, MA: Harvard University, John F. Kennedy School of Government, 1994); R. Lawrence, *Integrating National Economies, Regionalism, Multilateralism and Deeper Integration* (Washington, DC: The Brookings Institution, 1996); Hadi Soesastro, 'ASEAN and APEC: Do Concentric Circles Work?', *The Pacific Review,* Vol. 8, No. 3 (1995), pp. 475–493.

Part II

Regional cooperation in practice in East Asia and encountering regional theories

4 East Asian regionalism and the evolution of a fragmented region

A conceptual approach towards the political sector of security

Fu-Kuo Liu

Introduction

Regionalism, which has taken place in East Asia for decades, may be regarded as an evolution of the regionalization of economic development. Through the learning process of economic development, economic growth has flourished throughout the region, while interactions among regional countries have further enhanced the process of regional economic integration. This phenomenon of regional economic cooperation that embraces an outward-looking economic policy has been characterized as Asian 'new regionalism'.[1] It encourages not only increasing regional but also inter-regional economic interaction. Over the years, through trade, investment and the industrial division of labour, economies have together moved towards closer interdependence and have thus established regional commercial networks. The economic effects of regional cooperation have largely contributed to bringing about a regional identity upon which regionalism would have to depend. Along the liberalist line, with its vision of growing regional cooperation, one might expect that both indigenous and international interest-driven players, including states, could be seen to drive the region towards a course of market integration and should in turn motivate further cooperation.

In the real world however, economic cooperation does not necessarily result in political harmonization in the region, contrary to what theorists of integration had presumed. In East Asia, this is especially the case. A general lack of consensus among regional countries on most regional political issues is clearly reflected in the absence of regional political mechanisms, although considerable regional collective efforts at promoting cooperation have been made in non-political fields, mainly in the economic realm. Without common political understanding in the region, the 'community' in East Asia is yet to be proven a full-fledged one. Rather, political differences in the levels of international cooperation among regional countries may have become a centrifugal force against the trend of regional economic integration. To some extent, it is this political dissension that accelerates the development of fragmented regionalism at the opposite end of regional cooperation. As a result, fragmented regionalism has constantly increased general security concerns. In addition, the emergence of regionalism and regional identities has rigidly challenged the traditional belief of states in self-fulfilment of nationalism and national identities. From a political perspective, security issues which countries generally centre on are *domestic disarray* (political unrest), *violation of territorial integrity* (expression of hostility), *encroachment on sovereignty of individual states* (the effects of interdependence) and *identity confusion* (policy contest).[2] All the above security concerns might similarly, through different means, undermine the 'organizational stability of the state'[3] and thus lead to progressive disintegration in the region. In spite of a strong momentum for economic interactions playing a vital part in enhancing economic integration in East Asia, the nature of regional cooperation continues to be in contradiction to state-dominant agenda.

Under the broader understanding of comprehensive security, the political sector aims to deal mainly with threats to state sovereignty.[4] Unlike the traditional definition of security, the political sector will focus on non-military threats to sovereignty. Its referent objects will be analysed through multi-level approaches including regional systems, states and subnational groups. The scope of this chapter will therefore be focused on referent objects at regional and national level.

This chapter seeks to explore the implications of a progressive regionalism for national security in East Asia. It intends to develop an understanding of the political sector of security and to explore the assumption that increased regional political fragmentation would jeopardize regional stability and thus result in greater security concerns. Since such fragmentation in this region would likely eliminate any opportunity of promoting cooperation at the international level, and may even make related states vulnerable to threats, its effects would give rise to security threats to individual states. Some regional practices have shown a corresponding impact upon the political fragmentation of regional security; recent domestic unrest in Indonesia and Malaysia, the rivalry between China and Taiwan over legitimacy and sovereignty, the sovereign disputes of the South China Sea, are all examples of such outcomes. Major questions to be asked are: As regionalism based on economic cooperation develops, what exactly has it put forward in the form of any conceived threat to the integrity of national sovereignty in East Asia? How does political fragmentation in the region impact on regional security structures? To what extent does the political sector of security serve the complementary dimension of studying East Asian security?

The nature of Asian regionalism and increasing political disintegration

The emerging community in the Asia Pacific region stems from the effects of market integration and a common understanding over the need to strive for economic growth. Countries in the region have for decades followed similar experiences of high-growth economic development and even of nation-building processes. At the regional level, apart from national governments, the private sector, especially enterprises, has played a critical role in intensifying transactions, and more importantly has brought about business networking, which has become the foundation of growing regionalism and economic integration. Indeed, increasing external and intra-regional trade as well as progressive economic development has not only raised the desire of states and enterprises for cooperation, but it has also directly encouraged further economic integration. Once the trade pattern and economic development of individual economy has become more regionalized, there will be increased economic incentive to arouse further interactions as well as cooperation.

As has been shown many times in previous research, according to a historical analysis of trade patterns in East Asia, there was a definite intensification of interdependence in the region over the period between 1930s to the 1990s, and in turn intra-regional trade expanded rapidly.[5] Nevertheless, this does not imply that regionalism in East Asia would in any way develop towards a European direction of institutional integration;[6] nor would it lead to political integration. Instead, progress in this area remains driven mainly by the private sector rather than intergovernmental efforts, let alone transnational political attempts. When referring to the East Asian context and its general diversifying trade patterns, 'soft regionalism' with its loosening features of regional cooperation creates the most satisfactory portrait of regional resilience among regional countries.

In theory, without any regional political mechanism in place, to assure further progress in cooperation or at least a continuation of the current course of regional cooperation in East Asia, one should not be too optimistic about what can be made out of economic cooperation in the end. On the contrary, economic integration in East Asia is in reality far from feasible at present, since the region has for so long suffered from a high degree of political, societal and cultural heterogeneity. Although East Asia has shown a progressive form of regionalism, the driving force of increasing interdependence has come largely from profit-driven private sectors in their quest to gain better access to regional markets. It may be fair to say that the emergence of Asian regionalism has not been deliberately planned beforehand, but rather has been driven on the basis of economic demand. This understanding is revealing with regard to the inclination for pragmatism among most East Asian countries. Since Asian regionalism has been the evolving outcome of a regional cooperation process, its effects in enhancing regional stability have also been derived from an increase in general economic well-being.

In terms of the overall development of Asian regionalism, its momentum remains anchored in low politics of transnational interactions, though some countries are inclined to step up the involvement of high politics in regional establishments (e.g. the USA's intention to upgrade the annual dialogue levels at the Asia Pacific Economic Conference (APEC)). It will not become geopolitically or economically significant until regional governments are able actively to engage in the process of regional cooperation.

Although regional cooperation in East Asia has, by nature, reflected international connections through various activating referent objects, this cooperation does not unconditionally result in the best national interests of an individual state. The process of further regional cooperation or integration among states would steadily lead to encroachment of national sovereignty into some policy fields. States thus tend to reserve further commitment to the progress of regional integration (transnational establishment), once it is perceived that the move may be contradictory to their national interests. For example, since the outbreak of the Asian financial crisis in the summer of 1997, even the Association of Southeast Asian Nations (ASEAN), the most advanced model of regional integration in East Asia, has encountered a potential challenge from the newcomers, namely Vietnam, Laos and Myanmar. As has been felt at the various levels of recent ASEAN meetings, members have gradually expressed a deep sense of suspicion as to whether it would be wise, to press ahead further with the process of integration.[7] Due to problems over original differences in political systems, economic policy, and the development levels between the new comers and the long term ASEAN members, the credibility of ASEAN as a regional cooperation mechanism has recently been in doubt. Economically, while each member of ASEAN was similarly battered by the economic crisis, there is little chance that members will stand firm together in their varying regional interests. Politically, neither could they uniformly side with an individual member to cope with China on the South China Sea issues. These outcomes have clearly appeared as a crack inside the regional mechanism. Political differences within ASEAN and the internal difficulties of individual members may also have played a large part.

On the surface of developing Asian regionalism, it looks as if growing economic transactions across the region might soon inspire regional coherence from one field to another. The post-Cold War euphoria of accelerating regional stability and prosperity has undoubtedly been one of the main ingredients of the developing new regionalism which is currently appearing in East Asia. Nevertheless, regional economic coherence does not automatically enhance the resolution of political differences between states. As the involvement of individual states in regional or international affairs continues to follow along the lines of national interests, in this regard it reflects a true story of ferocious power struggles behind genuine regional economic cooperation. China, for instance, has tried very hard to engage in international community in the hope of advancing its fledgling economic development, and this has resulted in its gradual integration into the international system. However, China's advancement in political outreach and military buildup has heightened the security worries of its neighbouring countries. Following an earlier American strategy of containment and lately of constructive engagement, for various political reasons regional countries will wish to remain in line with China, but most, particularly ASEAN countries, in consideration of domestic political complications, will keep China at arm's length. In 1995, ASEAN's hasty expansion to include those countries (Laos, Myanmar, Vietnam and Cambodia), which for many do not yet fully qualify for its institutional standards, has been regarded as designedly making a strategic attempt to balance China's threat.[8] By nature, political discord in the region has directed cooperation momentum away from a peaceful course of economic integration and towards disintegration.

In terms of regional cooperation, it is obvious that there has been an asymmetric picture in the development of East Asian regionalism. This is why Asian regionalism, with its two opposing features, is not convinced that rationalization effects would link to further integration already in place.[9] In fact, regional economic cooperation has been going on for decades. For advocators of regional integration, the true effect of this cooperation has been to stimulate hope for an evolving regional identity from the cooperative ground of individual national identities. On the other hand, in spite of closer economic cooperation in the region, one can still easily spot various political flashpoints threatening stability and peace throughout the region. Political antagonism in the region operates as an undercurrent running beneath the tranquil sea's surface, which has the power to dismantle emerging regional establishments and dissolve common regional understanding brought about by economic cooperation. This is partly why major regional countries (e.g. the USA, China and Japan) have been very reluctant to take on the proposition of combining economic and security cooperation within the context and the framework of APEC.

To sum up, the current development trend of Asian regionalism could best be illustrated as the complex of 'economic centripetal' and 'political centrifugal' effects. The first decade of the post-Cold War era in East Asia has witnessed fresh chances and a number of new issues flourishing in the international arena, which may have given rise to demands for a new agenda and energy from both international practitioners and students alike. For many, increasing concerns over the future of East Asia have come to a critical juncture where it is believed that more emphasis should be given to political discord and its profound implication for long-term security development.

Political fragmentation and regional security concerns

While successful economic development has contributed to the emergence of regionalism and, in turn, is leading towards a course that precipitates the formation of an Asia Pacific community both in a multilateral setting and in bilateral relations, significant political fragmentation remains. Less governmental commitment to regional political cooperation has partly characterized the actual features of East Asian regionalism. This would certainly diminish any efforts to step up the utility and ability of regional mechanisms. The political reluctance of regional countries to join forces in promoting regional integration reflects the fact that, for individual states, their national agenda is always far more important than their international agenda. In other words, political survival is the most crucial element of national security in East Asia. Since there has always been a lack of experience with regard to political cooperation region-wide in East Asia, persistent discord among regional countries has contributed much to the emergence of security concerns.

Apart from the apparent progress in the economic development realm, most East Asian countries do not have much in common. Regional diversity among states is obvious, ranging from religion, ethnicity, political systems, sociocultural values and military strength. Centred on those diversities, the progress of making regional efforts to push forward cooperation has been constrained under the need to tow the political line. Therefore, while ASEAN should in fact be seeking to advance its progress in economic cooperation, there remains a major barrier, which is deeply rooted in domestic difficulties and political differences between member-states. ASEAN as a whole has been playing an active role in regional economic and security cooperation, but its strength has unfortunately been offset by its own internal political limitations.

China, too, has been embroiled in the same kind of political constraints with neighbouring countries. Since its reformation in 1979, many have gained opportunities of access to China's huge markets. China has thus accelerated its pace of integration into the outside world. At the same time, while gradually converging with the regional trend of economic rationalization, China has posed a constant military and political threat to the entire East Asian region by continuing her military buildup. Politically, self-reliance in countering foreign oppression has long been considered as one of the main policy-making factors in China. In the past, such a policy had arisen out of historical necessity. Nowadays, China has instead inclined towards increasing her military buildup and keeping an eye on the East Asian balance of power structure, which has, not surprisingly, become inevitable.[10] As a consequence, China's bilateral relations with Japan, the two Koreas and the United States, Southeast Asian countries and especially with Taiwan have been constantly problematic and worrisome.

In the Northeast Asian setting, North Korean self-segregation from the outside world, as described by most Western scholars,[11] remains the most volatile and dangerous state in the region and has posed a serious all-out security threat to South Korea and Japan as well as the whole region. Following North Korea's recent attempts to demonstrate its military intention and capability by penetrating South Korea's border and testing newly developing ballistic missiles, Taepodong, serious regional security concerns have re-emerged over Japan. The immediate effect has been to raise Japanese anxiety over the security threat from North Korea and thus stir up their demand for accelerating national defence buildup.[12] The political tension building up between Pyongyang and Seoul has once again eliminated any possible hope of maintaining a harmonious position in the Peninsula and has caused the further drifting apart of related countries. Since the beginning of its division, the two Koreas have engaged in physical zero-sum contention for unification of the Korean nation. Over the decades, each side has treated the other as its number one national security threat. Apart from the two Koreas, this regionalization of political issues is further reflected at the level of the great powers, in particular with regard to the interests of the four superpowers (Japan, China, Russia and the USA), and the ensuing conflict over their political insistence. Clearly, the main source of fragmented region in East Asia can be found at both levels.

In general, fragmented regionalism appears to stem from the political overstretch of individual states as a direct effect of internal and regional issues. It shows that the state is still the most critical actor in dominating the scene of

East Asian international relations. To a large extent, conflicting national interests have been fundamental to international politics. Competing for individual national interests has become a major task of regional foreign policy. Based on incompatibility of different national interests, one cannot forecast that the effect of regionalism will finally overcome everything including conflicting national interests and lead to political coherence in East Asia. How do we identify fragmented regionalism? From what aspects might one link a fragmented region with regional security? Although economic integration in East Asia has advanced somewhat, further progress to bring about political cooperation remains far from feasibly for the moment. Several analytical variables in studying regional disintegration are examined below, which could well be used as basic indices of fragmented regionalism. In general, there are five variables to be explored (1) individual differences of policy preference; (2) internal chaos with regional implications; (3) international competition to maximize the share of regional advantage; (4) conflict of national and regional development; and (5) lack of leadership.

Individual differences of policy preference

Regional countries, no matter what their size and level of economic development, act according to their own national interest. Apart from a high degree of heterogeneity in East Asia, the disagreement over individual state policy preferences, which derives from differing national agendas and political aims within the region, is inevitable within the context of fragmented regionalism. For instance, in confronting the Asian economic crisis on 1 September 1998, Malaysian government in an undated policy shift decided to fix the exchange rate between the ringgit and the US dollar in order to damp down its overheating economy by imposing direct national control over money flow.[13] This decision to close the currency market has plunged ASEAN into internal disharmony. Although the policy option taken has little to do with right or wrong, it has substantially crippled the effectiveness of ASEAN as a regional architect to act in time of necessity.

Internal chaos with regional implications

Asian regionalism has taken shape as a result of cross-border economic cooperation. Domestic turmoil caused by political struggle, market failure, ethnic conflict, social unrest or religious antagonism in one country will normally carry weight through the rest of the region. While turmoil contains specific regional implications, it can easily stir up regional tension and even open old wounds between groups of countries. In this regard, it serves as a centrifugal force against regionalism, which may eventually destroy the original consciousness that fostered regional cooperation in the first place. The riot that broke out in Indonesia in May 1998 was attributed to a combination of domestic political struggle, multi-ethnic conflict and large-scale social unrest. It is claimed that anti-ethnic Chinese crime was intentionally instigated by the military, which is something that has become of great concern to all Chinese communities around the world. Although the effects of the domestic turmoil in Indonesia have alerted the region to security threats in comprehensive manner, it has in effect not only hampered Indonesia in carrying on its role of leading ASEAN forward, but also the momentum of regional cooperation of which Indonesia intended to be the core.

International competition for maximizing the share of regional advantage

In the case of the South China Sea, while there has not yet been a regional consensus on how regional countries should settle the issue, every claimant to the disputed territory has so far tried to bid secretly for an increased share of limited regional resources. This is a prototype of realist power politics playing a major role in the region, which shows that states may compete for their own interest and later challenge one another. Many believe that in countering the growing diversified issues of the post-Cold War era, the region requires persistent peace and stability. In truth, no one country can afford to change the current course of mutual engagement and regional dialogue arrangements.[14] By contrast, states always attempt to make further advancements either on a legal or illegal basis before toeing the line with others. This reality in East Asia has shown that any established problem-solving regional mechanism may serve only as a starting point for testing one another's policy baseline. A subtle mix of competition/confrontation would be a more accurate depiction of East Asian regional politics. Furthermore, cooperation may have less relevance in the realm of high politics.

Conflict of national and regional development

National interest is not necessarily in compliance with regional interest. Once defined, the national interest of a state is often in direct conflict with the progress of regional cooperation; hence states are likely to withdraw from further involvement in regional cooperation. It may yet appear to be a case of worrying about encroachment on national sovereignty in most parts of East Asia. National interest will undoubtedly remain at the top of the national agenda for many years to come. In spite of encouraging further policy coherence among members in the APEC process and its decidedly market-led approach, APEC's policy domains continue to be relatively limited to low politics (e.g. trade liberalization in specified sectors).[15] The APEC process has not yet led to institutional development, nor has individual national sovereignty been challenged. However, APEC processes respect the differences of individual countries and are by nature a consensus-seeking establishment. It is fair to say that in time of difficulty, APEC's impetus to develop will be alleviated, as has been shown in the progress made during the Asian economic crisis.

Lack of leadership in East Asian regionalism

As pointed out by many researchers of Asia Pacific economic cooperation, one of the crucial issues in East Asian regionalism has been political and structural difficulty.[16] Strong leadership in the formation of an East Asian trade bloc may be critical to its success. Since the end of the Second World War, the USA has continued to be the only hegemon in East Asia, though it has declined lately. Regional countries have never experienced, and may not be ready to accept, any regional leadership of their own. Currently, all three potential regional powers – Japan, China and ASEAN – do not seem feasible to take the lead at present for various reasons. It seems that regional powers are much more concerned with any shift occurring in the balance of power structure than any progress in regional cooperation. Regionalism in East Asia thus represents a somewhat haphazard yet closely knit trade and industrial development pattern. In other words, without political leadership, regional effort does not carry with it any obvious goal and may point to nothing more than a consensus-building process.

These variables of fragmented regionalism suggest that national political intention may turn out to be the most critical issue in improving regional cooperation. Above all else in East Asia, the private sectors have contributed significantly to the emergence of regionalism and regional integration over the past few decades. From the realist perspective, the state still dominates much of the international arena, which leaves little room for other players. The fact that there is a tendency to persistently fall short of political leadership and political commitment in the development of East Asian regionalism indicates that the region will remain fragmented for some years to come. More importantly, political discord in the region may bring about a greater threat to the future of regional cooperation and thus raise security concerns.

Because East Asia is a fragmented region, there has not been a region-wide consensus on what, how and who should be working along with let alone making up the general mutual trust among regional countries. While many are optimistically looking forward to the development of regionalism, others have had to come to terms with the reality that East Asia is still one of the most dangerous regions in the world, a view constantly reflected by its own constituents. The multilateral establishments as well as bilateral relations have also been problematic in a political sense.

The political sector of security in a fragmented East Asian setting

By nature, since the end of the Cold War security threats have become very diversified in East Asia. Fragmented regionalism will be one of the major trends that will steadily contribute to the intensification of political tension in the region. The risk brought about by this structural deficiency could destabilize the region and so arouse security concerns. As part of a comprehensive concept of security, students have for years attempted to categorize it into several individual sectors.[17] To be distinguished from and not to be confused with other sectors of security, the heart of the political sector of security refers mainly to non-military threats to sovereignty.[18] In the East Asian context, this definition would only be applicable with extended ideas.

The basic assumption of comprehensive security suggests that the concept of security might contain multi-faceted approaches to East Asia, namely multi-dimensional and multi-levelled security of analysis. Whereas in the past security issues had been largely external in nature, the new focus will be more on internal (regional and national) security issues than was traditionally the case. Bearing in mind the definition of security that has been specified above, when considering the purpose behind the study of the political sector of security in East Asia, several crucial questions need to be explored: Is there any security threat posed to the sovereignty of an individual state in East Asia as a result of the development of regionalism? What security concerns would be brought about by the enduring trend of fragmented regionalism? What does fragmented regionalism imply for future security cooperation in the region?

From the theoretical practice of fragmented regionalism, five variables have been identified as critical to regional security. It has been suggested that bilateral and multilateral political relations should be a focal point for the political sector of security, despite the fact that economic interdependence encourages leeway for political cooperation at the regional level. Therefore, according to the East Asian security setting, 'political security' could be further categorized into a two-level analysis: relations between individual states, and involvement of individual states in regional arrangements. The former would focus more on security issues resulting from the domestic position of a state. Internal problems with their wider effects upon a state and any external hostility brought about against a state would be included. The latter would consider security threats at the regional level. It would concentrate on the general trends of progressive regionalism and their impact upon a state.

Domestic disarray (political unrest)

Asian regionalism has been formulated according to the progress of economic interdependence. The structure of Asian security has to a large extent been delicately balanced on the principle of 'regional resilience' or 'comprehensive security.'[19] The premise of maintaining regional security is that all parties concerned would be in relatively good shape before being admitted to it. Once political unrest erupts in one country, the immediate effect would be to cause tremors and perhaps later result in changes to the balance of the security structure. Regional countries would then have to rebuild their security structures and risk greater security threats following on from settling down into a new order. To individual states, domestic political unrest may, in theory, step up the hope of external powers intervening and could mean that its chances of becoming a regional member improve. Recent cases of Indonesia and Malaysia have revealed that, in the aftermath of economic crisis, political unrest has not only decreased their influence in international politics, but has also crippled the normal operation of regional arrangements (e.g. ASEAN and APEC).

Violation of territorial integrity (expression of hostility)

Apart from military advancement in the region, any political conduct with reference to disputed territories that regional governments may carry through could cause further political tension. Until international law gives the verdict of territorial dispute to the South China Sea issues, substantial obstacles will remain to reaching an acceptable settlement. The present regional ethos of dealing with security issues has largely relied on the successful practice of confidence-building measures (e.g. the ASEAN Regional Forum (ARF) continues to emphasise the importance of confidence-building measures (CMBs) as the first step leading to its success).[20] It has been discovered that insufficient mutual trust established so far in the region could hamper any effort to bring about security cooperation. Actions instigated to build up a feeling of trust among East Asian countries are critical to its future. China's intention to enlarge its practical presence in the South China Sea by issuing domestic legal documents and constructing fishing/military bases around the disputed areas has been interpreted by many in ASEAN as extremely provocative. In addition, in declaring its right to use force against any attempt to divide the country, China has repeatedly threatened to attack Taiwan, which has not only seriously challenged the balance of power in East Asia and destroyed regional harmony, but has also greatly threatened Taiwan's security and people's survival. If any disagreement over bilateral relationships were to endanger regional stability, surely the whole region would have no choice but to give the matter due attention. It may lead to a regional security structure for all.

Encroachment on the sovereignty of individual states
(the effects of interdependence)

The more economic interdependence takes place in a region, the more harmonious regional effects throughout societies could reap benefits. Nevertheless, it could also at times bring about national security concerns, as states may gradually feel exploited by the force of regionalism. In the process of regional integration, individual states may face growing demands for sharing sovereignty in some policy issue areas. Fearing that too much may be gained by the progress of regional movement, states would take the initiative to halt the process. It is common practice that in pooling sovereignty, states can only tolerate a limited degree of shared sovereignty. This outcome suggests that in a strong, state-led region it will be more difficult to agree on the concept of transferring and sharing sovereignty. In East Asia, national resistance on shifting sovereignty to a regional level is even more obvious, while there is not yet a credible regional establishment firmly in charge. This may partly explain why in East Asia the building of a security cooperation structure has so far been less than productive.

Since the onset of establishing ASEAN, the principle of 'non-intervention' in any state's domestic affairs together with 'national resilience' has been well respected in the wider regional context. It has thus left little room for strengthening regional integration efforts.

Identity confusion (policy confrontation)

In theory, with the progress of regional integration, there will emerge from the grass-roots level of regional societies an effect of identity transformation from a national level to a regional one. In the case of East Asian regional cooperation, since most regional countries are either still continuing or have just completed the nation-building process, most of them are experiencing a newly established national identity. While the emergence of regionalism driven by a strong desire for economic interdependence has introduced most people to a vague regional identity, national governments are struggling to reinforce uniformity of national identity. At present, political enthusiasm does not seem to match the expectation of economic momentum and could frustrate the whole regional cooperation momentum. At worst, the introduction of regional identity would clash with those who are still seeking a distinct and harmonious national identity. To them, the push towards a regional identity would be seen as something different from their individual identities and thus would result in severe security concerns.

What then does political security mainly refer to, and should it perhaps be the subject of a separate detailed study? Analysis would suggest that political security is the most dominant source of research focus under the wider context of East Asian security, if the most controversial and sensitive one. While current military and economic security may dictate the major course of security concerns in East Asia, political security would have to be regarded as the most critical.

Conclusion

For decades, many have observed the progressive economic growth and the emergence of regionalism in East Asia. One may wonder why the prescriptions of economic interdependence advocates and the assumed necessity for wider cooperation in regional integration as suggested by theorists of regional integration have shown no sign of materializing. Still, there are a number of simmering security issues, cross-Taiwan Strait issues, the South China Sea issue, the Korean Peninsula,[21] the future role of China, and continuing US engagement in East Asia,[22] that continue to challenge regional stability. It may, as I have argued, reveal that this fragmented region will be derived from five variables: individual differences of policy preference, internal chaos with regional implications, competition for regional advantage, conflict of national and regional development, and a lack of leadership in regionalism. All of these could, to some extent, engender bilateral or regional conflict, which would turn out to be generative of new security threats to the region.

In the political field, a fragmented East Asian region has become an obvious reality. Unfortunately, elites in the region have not yet turned their attention to building an understanding of fragmented regionalism. The emergence of regionalism, driven by strong economic interactions, may have blurred the reality of political disintegration. This is not to suggest that one should be pessimistic about the future of security cooperation in the region. Instead, we should understand that with the realization of political security in practice, regional countries would no longer be so reactionary in promoting economic and security cooperation. Moreover, any concerted attempt to categorize the study of political security may lead to closer links between policy and reality, which would certainly be conducive to an increased understanding of security.

Finally, from the political perspective of security, nationalism in East Asia may be playing an active role in driving individual states into conflict with one another. It seems that beyond this analysis, fragmented regionalism will in future be directed by the ensuing development of nationalism in China, the two Koreas, Japan, as well as that of some others in the region.[23] Nationalism may become an important variable of security threats.

Notes

1 With the emergence of transregional links, since the 1980s Asian 'new regionalism' and later 'open regionalism' has been defined by scholars as differing from more inward-looking establishments in the previous understanding of regionalism elsewhere. See e.g. Norman Palmer, *The New Regionalism in Asia and the Pacific* (Lexington, MA: Lexington Books, 1991); also Ross Garnaut and Peter Drysdale, eds, *Asia Pacific Regionalism: Readings in International Economic Relations* (Pymble, Australia: Harper Educational, 1994).

2 This differs from Buzan's categories of political threats, which focused on organizing ideologies and traditions, national identity, intentional and structural threats, and political systems. Barry Buzan, *People, States, and Fear: An Agenda for International Security Studies in the Post-Cold War Era* (London: Harvester Wheatsheaf, 1991), pp. 118–122 and 369.

3 Ibid., p. 118.

4 Barry Buzan, Ole Waever and Jaap de Wilde, *Security: A New Framework for Analysis* (Boulder, CO: Lynne Rienner, 1998), p. 141.

5 Peter A. Petri, 'The East Asian Trading Bloc: An Analytical History', in Garnaut and Drysdale, eds, *Asia Pacific Regionalism*, p. 119.

6 As has been widely discussed in previous literatures, theoretical argument of regional integration tends to classify the difference between various regional efforts by using the terms 'market integration' or 'economic cooperation' and 'institutional integration' or 'discriminatory integration'. See Peter Drysdale and Ross Garnaut, 'Principles of Pacific Economic Integration', in Drysdale and Garnaut, eds, *Asia Pacific Regionalism*, p. 52.

7 This tendency towards suspicion which has gruadually grown significant in the meetings within ASEAN has been verified by a recent meeting discussion on 14 August 1999 between myself and members of the Centre of Strategic and International Studies at Jakarta.

8 As described by Carolina Hernandez, ASEAN enlargement was driven by strategic considerations. Hernandez, 'Peace and Security in the Taiwan Strait and the South China Sea: Implication for Regional Stability in ASEAN', paper delivered at the

International Forum on Peace and Security in the Taiwan Strait, on 26–27 July 1999, Taipei, Taiwan, organized by the 21st Century Foundation, Taipei and American Enterprise Institute, Washington, DC.

9 Kay Moller quite rightly earlier challenged this point that economic interdependence in East Asia leading to less conflict would be a myth. Moller, 'East Asian Security: Lessons from Europe?', *Contemporary Southeast Asia*, Vol. 17, No. 4 (March 1996), p. 363.

10 This point has been well elaborated by Wu Xinbo, 'China: Security Practice of a Modernizing and Ascending Power', in Muthiah Alagappa, ed., *Asian Security Practice: Material and Ideational Influences* (Stanford, CA: Stanford University Press, 1998), p. 135.

11 All these descriptions have been discussed by David Kang, 'North Korea: Deterrence Through Danger', in Alagappa, ed., *Asian Security Practice*, pp. 234–235.

12 *The Economist*, 21 August 1999, pp. 21–22.

13 As a way of preventing attack from money speculators, the ringgit rate was fixed at 1:3.80 against the US dollar. It is said that the move has contributed greatly to Malaysia's economic recovery in 1999. Chen May Yee, 'Malaysian Sees Curbs as Social Stabilizer', *The Asian Wall Street Journal* (30 August 1999), p. 5.

14 Sujit Dutta, 'In Search of New Security Concepts', *Strategic Analysis*, Vol. 20, No. 1 (April 1997), p. 15.

15 Richard Higgot, 'APEC: A Sceptical View', in Andrew Mack and John Ravenhill, eds, *Pacific Cooperation: Building Economic and Security Regimes in the Asia–Pacific Region* (Boulder, CO: Westview Press, 1995), p. 78.

16 Soogil Young, 'Globalism and Regionalism: Complements or Competitors?', in Garnaut and Drysdale, eds, *Asia Pacific Regionalism*, p. 189.

17 Buzan *et. al.*, *Security*, pp. 7–8 and 21–47.

18 For detailed discussion on what would be considered in the study of the political sector of security, please refer to Buzan, *et. al.*, *Security*, pp. 141–145.

19 Referring to the comments made by J. Soedjati Djiwandono, 'Process of Comprehensive Security: An Indonesian Perspective', *The Indonesian Quarterly*, Vol. 23, No. 3 (1995), p. 232.

20 Chairman's Statement, the Sixth Meeting of the ASEAN Regional Forum, Singapore, 26 July 1999.

21 Recently the North–South Summit in Pyongyang in June 2000 stimulated euphoria in the Peninsula's future. Although the future is still fraught with uncertainty and practical difficulties, it has increased the likelihood of reconciliation between the two. There have been many analyses on the development. To name just a few: Calvin Sims, 'Summit Glow Fades as Koreans Face Obstacles to Unity,' *New York Times*, 22 June 2000; 'Canada Applauds Successful S-N Korea Summit', *Korean Times*, 30 June 2000; Cho Yang Uk, 'Future of Korea depends on willingness to change', *Asahi Evening News* (Tokyo), 3 July 2000.

22 According to a recent survey by *PacNet*, these five issues have been recognized as the top five security threats to East Asia. *PacNet* (Pacific Forum/CSIS), No. 32, 20 August 1999.

23 Hisahiko Okazaki, 'A Half-Century of Peace in East Asia As Well', paper delivered at the International Forum on 'Peace and Security in the Taiwan Strait' on 26–27 July 1999, Taipei, Taiwan, organized by the 21st Century Foundation, Taipei, and the American Enterprise Institute, Washington, DC.

5 Regionalism and subregional cooperation

The ASEAN experience

Nadhavathna Krishnamra

Introduction

This work examines the contribution to regional cooperation in the Asia–Pacific of the Association of Southeast Asian Nations (ASEAN) through an analysis of its past experience and future prospects. ASEAN was founded in 1967 as a vehicle for cooperation among states in Southeast Asia, and has widely been recognized as a successful, if indeed not the most successful, manifestation of regionalism in the developing world. Most notably, ASEAN is identified with its own brand of regionalism: one involving loose and voluntary cooperation among the states concerned on the basis of consensus and dialogue, rather than through formal instruments and legal obligations.

ASEAN now comprises all ten countries of Southeast Asia, and has thus firmly established itself as the representative of the region as a whole. Probably for the first time, ASEAN can be considered a true expression of regionalism. While technical organizations exist alongside ASEAN, most of the crucial interactions at the regional level by Southeast Asian countries are now undertaken within the scope of ASEAN. At the time of its founding, however, ASEAN was perceived in more controversial terms. Then, the conservative political affiliations of its founding countries, Indonesia, Malaysia, Singapore, Thailand and the Philippines, gave rise to accusations that it was an anti-communist bloc, and that its very existence would serve to divide rather than unite the region. However, though the countries concerned were ideologically similar, they possessed very different political and administrative structures. Moreover, their economic systems were radically different, e.g. the free trading Singapore and the relatively protectionist Indonesia. Thus the homogeneity within ASEAN often referred to by present-day commentators did not exist at the time of its founding. The ASEAN founding countries did nevertheless agree on one common priority: to ensure regional stability through establishment of a framework for cooperative relations. To this day, commitment to ASEAN is an avowed objective of each Southeast Asian government upon taking office.

In reviewing the contribution to regionalism of ASEAN, a central hypothesis is that political imperatives have driven regional cooperation within Southeast Asia, at least until recent years. However, the uncertainties raised by the recent challenges posed to the region's economic accomplishments, and the political repercussions there from, have served to demonstrate that the political consensus behind ASEAN is increasingly predicated on the promotion of economic growth. Hence the importance of enhanced economic cooperation and coordination is recognized by regional policy-makers, and will be the major driving force for cooperation in the next stage of Southeast Asian regionalism.

Politics sets the tone: regionalism in Southeast Asia through the eyes of policy makers and regional and international commentators

Before looking at the evolution of cooperation within ASEAN, it is appropriate to review what policy-makers as well as regional and international scholars have said and written *vis-à-vis* regional organization in Southeast Asia since the origins of ASEAN. The starting point of any examination must in fact be the evolution of the concept of Southeast Asia itself, which is a relatively modern phenomenon. Southeast Asia was first referred to as such during the 1930s, with the concept being consolidated during the Second World War and the subsequent decolonization. However, with the absence of local scholarship during the initial post-war period, foreign scholars dominated regional studies in the 1950s and 1960s, and in so doing perpetuated their theories and preconceptions of Southeast Asian politics.

The policy-makers of the time emphasized the theme that the priority among the emergent states of Southeast Asia was national development and national independence, and the various country studies which were produced during this early period confirmed this line of thinking. Neither policy-makers nor scholars paid much interest to prospects for regional cooperation within Southeast Asia, which was not regarded as a priority. At the same time, the preponderant political role of the United States within the region in fact reinforced national linkages with the United States on a bilateral basis, with the founding of the Southeast Asia Treaty Organization (SEATO) only formalizing the alignment at a multilateral level.[1] Much of the early scholarship on the region in fact originated from the United States, which with its growing engagement in Southeast Asia required intellectual inputs for its policy initiatives.[2] This led to a certain prescriptive perspective in the literature of the period, as the various academics sought to influence decision-makers' thinking regarding Southeast Asia. Even as the first generation of local scholars were emerging by the early 1970s, they were heavily influenced by Western political science concepts, in particular realism, having received their education in the United States and in Europe. Local scholarship was handicapped by the fact that no regional institutions possessed courses on Southeast Asian Studies. Local scholars also tended to focus their research on their respective countries, and it was only in 1968 that the Institute of Southeast Asian Studies (ISEAS) was established in Singapore, and it was not to be until the 1970s that Southeast Asia studies was to be made available in Thailand and Malaysia.[3]

Regionalism therefore did not feature prominently in the national policies of regional states, although functionalist theories did play a role in the establishment of technical regional bodies. It was not to be until the late 1960s that regional cooperation was first significantly discussed within the framework of consolidating peace and stability in Southeast Asia in the late 1960s. While policy-makers such as Thanat Khoman of Thailand, Tunku Abdul Rahman of Malaysia and Adam Malik of Malaysia talked of uniting to consolidate the regional reconciliation between Indonesia, Malaysia and Singapore, authors such as Bernard Gordon sought to find ways and means of ensuring a constructive role for Indonesia's energies, including through regional consolidation, while cooperation was also seen as a means to ensure stability and national development.[4] Thus international scholars have been at the forefront of the idea of regional organization in Southeast Asia from the beginning. At this initial period, various attempts at regional organization were made with differing formats, namely the Asian and Pacific Council (ASPAC), the Association of Southeast Asia (ASA) and MAPHILINDO. What was characteristic in these bodies was that the concept of the 'region' in question remained ill-defined. At the time, regional cooperation as defined by Southeast Asian leaders did not encompass exclusively the geographical scope of Southeast Asia. With important externalities such as the role of the United States, the economic strength of Japan and ideological concerns, a purely Southeast Asian body did not seem to hold great future. As Philippine Foreign Minister Narciso Ramos put it 'We should not be deluded into adopting solutions only on the basis of geography or race. What unites people is their identity of political convictions and economic interests.'[5] However, what is significant was that after the demise of ASPAC by the early 1970s, Southeast Asian regionalism had little linkage with the rest of East Asia until the genesis of the dialogues under the auspices of the Pacific Economic Cooperation Council (PECC) which had blossomed by the 1980s.

ASEAN, it is argued here, was the first organization, which specifically aspired to cover all the states of the Southeast Asian region. Yet there was little academic interest paid to ASEAN in its initial years, as it was not considered to offer particular promise. It was not to be until the mid-1970s with the collapse of the regimes in Indochina that ASEAN received noteworthy attention. Policy-makers agreed to comprehensively enhance ASEAN cooperation to improve its capability for acting as unifying point. It was then that ASEAN was first perceived by regional and international commentators as a source of regional order. By this time, regional scholars were emerging, with the writings of Lau Teck Soon and Chin Kin Wah of Singapore, Jusuf Wanandi and Ali Murtopo of Indonesia, Noordin Sopiee of Malaysia, as well as various Thais, being notable in supporting such perspectives. In particular, the economic initiatives launched at the 1st ASEAN Summit in Bali in 1976 seemed to lend credibility to the organization as a worthy vehicle for economic cooperation.[6] At the same time, the ASEAN Secretariat was perceived to be a possible nucleus for further advances in regional organization.[7]

Interest in ASEAN was further stimulated by the Vietnamese invasion of Cambodia in late 1978, which consolidated ASEAN's regional role. While the incident led to a situation whereby, for over 20 years, the regionalism of ASEAN was pitched against that of Indochina and alongside the relative detachment of Myanmar, ASEAN's contribution and credibility were greatly enhanced in the eyes of many international commentators. For many scholars, diplomatic initiatives characterized ASEAN's main course over much of the 1980s, and ASEAN was primarily seen as an instrument of foreign policy of individual states rather than of economic or development policy.[8]

As we have seen, the commitments made at the 1st ASEAN Summit in Bali in 1976 to upgrade economic cooperation, helped to elevate interest in ASEAN. And yet the Preferential Tariff Arrangements (PTA) launched in the aftermath of the Bali Summit and the subsequent Kuala Lumpur Summit proved unattractive to private investors, and a number of efforts were made to increase their coverage as well as the preferences offered. This led to efforts in the run-up to the 3rd ASEAN Summit in Manila in 1987 to brainstorm on ways and means of enhancing economic cooperation, which fed through into the literature of this time. It was also not surprising that, given Singapore's interest in promoting liberalization of trade within ASEAN, Singaporeans and academics associated with ISEAS should have been behind much of the literature and academic initiatives.[9]

The theme of renewal continued through much of the literature of the late 1980s, and was given real substance by the 4th ASEAN Summit in Singapore in 1992. In a similar manner to the Manila Summit, this event was associated with a great deal of academic activity at the regional level, which helped to drum up support for a free trade agreement within ASEAN. The result was the elevation of cooperation not only in the economic sphere, with the launch of the ASEAN Free Trade Area (AFTA), but also in the formal adoption of political and security cooperation by ASEAN for the first time. The writings of regional policy-makers and commentators from this time reflect the mood of optimism within ASEAN, one born out of political and economic confidence. The double-digit growth rates in the ASEAN economies in the late 1980s and early 1990s gave ASEAN an international stature it had never before attained. ASEAN was even envisaged in one contemporary study as playing a full role as a regional organization to assist the United Nations: 'ASEAN ... with its economic dynamism and political track record in resolving the Cambodia question, is ideally positioned to enter into such a cooperative arrangement with the increasingly overstretched and under funded United Nations.'[10]

Given the regional divisions of the 1980s, the 5th ASEAN Summit in Bangkok in 1995 was a landmark event. It saw the first meeting of all ten leaders of Southeast Asia, and laid the foundations for an expansion of ASEAN membership. However, membership seemed to have been a source of some debate among commentators. Many regional scholars saw it as being a positive contribution to consolidating regionalism in Southeast Asia and realizing ASEAN's original objectives, while helping to bridge the ideological divide by bringing Cambodia, Laos, Myanmar and Vietnam into the mainstream of Southeast Asia.[11] Others were more circumspect, pointing to potential impacts on traditional ASEAN modes and ASEAN solidarity. Few would have foreseen the disruptive effect of the Asian economic crisis, which would follow within a few year's on the moral authority of the original ASEAN members.

The membership issue once again raised the question of similarities of the ASEAN experience with the European example, for Europe was undergoing the same process of expansion and renewal at this time. Nevertheless, while much of the language of some of the founding fathers was set in a very conventional functionalist mould, possibly inspired by contemporary Europe, and implied that ASEAN would progress through a free trade area to a customs union and onto a common market, the structures that were established in 1967 were quite distinctive in form.[12] However, the picture was not a static one, and recent scholars have pointed out that the changing fortunes of European cooperation have in turn affected ASEAN considerations of Europe.[13] In fact, the major differences between ASEAN and Europe did not lie in form, they lay instead in the modes of procedure: consensus was adopted as the principal mode of conduct which has sustained ASEAN for over 30 years and more. In fact, there have been very few votes taken by ASEAN officials, ministers and leaders, even on economic questions. Consensus and accommodation were particularly crucial in the initial years when residual suspicions remained among the key members, namely Indonesia, Malaysia and Singapore, and this point has been noted by commentators as a factor contributing to ASEAN's distinctive character.[14] Forging consensus will gain even more attention in the next few years as the work of integrating the new members continues to proceed apace. Arguably, any form of regional cooperation in the Asia–Pacific involving ASEAN will have to be based on the all-important basis of consensus. With this in mind, many regional authors continue to refer to ASEAN's distinctiveness. Others, while accepting the distinctive nature of ASEAN cooperation, tend to maintain that it is temporary, particular when considering wider trends in international affairs towards the blurring of distinctions.[15]

An important trend in the recent literature on ASEAN is to place emphasis on the idea of community, whether in the political, economic or functional spheres. While such an idea had already been discussed by earlier commentators in the 1970s, including Arfinn Jorgensen-Dahl and Michael Haas, it has been given greater immediacy in the post-Cold War period.[16] Commentaries in this vein assume that ASEAN is at an advanced stage of regional integration, having progressed from cooperation to integration and moving towards an integrated community. Such a concept also reflects the thinking that now that ASEAN has reached a level of maturity in its external relations, it should concentrate more on deepening its internal integrative processes.

In the political field, the idea of ASEAN as a security community assumes the development of norms and principles to govern interaction by members, the most important being that force is ruled out as a means to settle disputes. The fact that ASEAN has been referred to as a possible example of a security community is demonstrative of the perceived advance made in regional organization in Southeast Asia, for such a concept had been originally developed from the perspective of post-war Europe by Karl Deutsch and colleagues such as Amitai Etzioni.[17] The discourse on ASEAN as a security community has been developed in detail by Amitav Acharya, Sheldon W. Simon, Barry Buzan, Muthiah Alagappa and others. For example, Muthiah Alagappa refers to ASEAN's success as a 'partial pluralistic security community', given the increasing predictability in the interactions.[18] At the same time, this process of community-building is not seen as being confined to ASEAN alone, but is projected into broader scope within the ASEAN Regional Forum (ARF). The ARF, which was founded in 1994 but has yet to reach full maturity, is seen as having the potential to move into a security community in the future with its emphasis on confidence-building and promoting predictability. Meanwhile, in the economic sphere the reference to community is made with respect to enlarging the scope of cooperation beyond AFTA, such as in AFTA-Plus. Community is also being discussed with respect to making ASEAN more meaningful to its citizens. At the same, the conflicting demands of sovereignty and the imperatives of cooperation have reinforced tendencies towards looking at present requirements, particularly when they relate to wider frameworks such as the Asia–Pacific, in terms of complex interdependence.[19]

The foregoing discussion has demonstrated that, conceptually, regionalism may be seen to have progressed substantially within Southeast Asia during the first three decades of ASEAN's existence. Nevertheless, ASEAN's regionalism is marked by a strong element of pragmatism rather than following predetermined routes, with ideology playing a minor role. The literature on ASEAN also provides some revealing insights into how the writings of regional and international commentators related to ASEAN cooperation. For example, as the evolution of ASEAN has been strongly influenced by policy shifts and realignments, reflecting more the convergence of national interests of the ASEAN member countries rather than adherence to models of regional cooperation, the increase in attention paid by scholars and commentators to ASEAN at specific points in time correlate to periods of activism in ASEAN cooperation. These challenge the assertions that cooperation in Southeast Asia has had a 'minimal impact' on wider theoretical debates on regional cooperation.[20]

The lessons from recent experience: developments from 1995

Having reviewed the evolution of thinking on ASEAN, it may be noted that some of the recent developments within ASEAN tend to give the impression that ASEAN is moving towards some convergence with traditional notions of integration theory. Indeed, many of those currently involved in ASEAN decision-making now come from academic backgrounds, including the Foreign Ministers of Thailand and Indonesia, a development which may suggest a greater receptiveness to conceptual approaches to cooperation. ASEAN's cooperation during the first 20 or so years was very much based on voluntary mechanisms in the form of declarations or limited agreements. However, the developments since the 4th ASEAN Summit in Singapore would seem to suggest that a more predictable and rule-based pattern of political and economic relations is emerging, although very much in the tentative stage. Certainly, the cooperation mechanisms have broadened to a significant degree, so as to involve regular meetings of the Economic Ministers and more recently Finance Ministers, such that the annual Ministerial Meeting has lost a certain aura. The key policy body responsible for setting broad directions for ASEAN is now the ASEAN Summit, which is being held every three years at a formal level, and informally in between, and whose role is continuing to be reviewed with a view to making it more effective.

The intensification of economic cooperation is led by efforts in realizing AFTA. The launch of AFTA in 1992, after intense lobbying by Singapore and Thailand and with important concessions given by Indonesia, was followed by a flurry of activity in the economic sphere.[21] AFTA may be set alongside the failure of its predecessor, the PTA, which depended on voluntary offers of tariff reductions. By contrast, AFTA works through coordinated tariff reduction schemes which provide a definite timetable with which to push through the trade liberalization agenda. Moreover, to complement AFTA, new initiatives such as the ASEAN Investment Area (AIA) and ASEAN Industrial Cooperation Scheme (AICO) have been launched. Again these have replaced older initiatives such as the ASEAN Industrial Joint Ventures (AIJV) and ASEAN Industrial Projects (AIP), which failed to attract sustained private sector interest and suffered further due to the unwillingness of the ASEAN governments to make significant investments.[22] Apart from the new economic cooperation schemes, ASEAN is also enhancing its cooperation and coordination on international economic issues. Recently, ASEAN has projected greater solidarity in trade negotiations through the Uruguay Round leading up to the establishment of the World Trade Organization (WTO) by 1995 and election of the new WTO Director-General to succeed Renato Ruggiero in 1999, a fact that has not gone unnoticed by regional leaders.[23]

Political activities have received less publicity since the elections in Cambodia in 1999. ASEAN has concentrated on building the conditions for a more predictable set of regional relations, such as through realization of the Zone of Peace, Freedom and Neutrality (ZOPFAN), which had its origins in the Kuala Lumpur Declaration of 1971, but which had remained rather dormant since. With this in mind, a plan of action for achieving ZOPFAN was drawn up in 1993, a result of which was the founding of the ARF in 1994 and the signing of the Southeast Asia Nuclear Weapon Zone Treaty in 1995. However, the activities of the ASEAN Troika on Cambodia between 1997 and 1998, comprising Indonesia, the Philippines and Thailand, in tandem with the so-called 'Friends of Cambodia', to re-establish peace and stability in Cambodia following the July 1997 political crisis in that country has served to demonstrate that the ASEAN methods could continue to play a role in promoting peace and stability in the Asia–Pacific as a whole. However, it is frequently neglected that such activities are conducted with regard to situations outside ASEAN proper. ASEAN traditionally abides by the principle of non-interference in the internal affairs of member states and studiously avoids commenting on situations in member countries, except with the consent of the states concerned. Notwithstanding the greater degree of openness elicited by the moves taken since 1999, notably by Thai Foreign Minister Surin Pitsuwan, and supported by the Philippines, to promote an 'enhanced interaction' between members, ASEAN still maintains that this principle, as enshrined in the TAC, is sacrosanct. Indeed, such a principle is claimed by new members as one of the main incentives for their joining. However, now that ASEAN has encompassed all states of Southeast Asia, and ASEAN is formulating rules of procedure for the High Council, a ministerial-level body envisaged under the TAC as a dispute settlement mechanism, there are pressures, internal and external, for ASEAN to play a greater role in the management of situations within the territories of ASEAN member countries. The call for the establishment of an ASEAN Troika on an ongoing basis, as endorsed by the ASEAN leaders at the 3rd ASEAN Informal Summit in November 1999, is a manifestation of ASEAN's response to such pressures.

This activism has been accompanied by another contemporary development, the expansion of ASEAN's role in other regional bodies. The early 1990s saw the consolidation of Asia Pacific Economic Cooperation (APEC) and the ARF, which are seen by commentators as being indicative of the 'new regionalism', within which the distinctions between Southeast Asian, East Asian and Global exchanges are being blurred. Whatever the rationale behind such impulses, this outward-looking development will help determine ASEAN's role in the Asia–Pacific in the years ahead.

ASEAN and the ARF: a seeming paradox?

Another outcome of the decision taken at the 4th ASEAN Summit to upgrade ASEAN's political and security cooperation, and to seriously engage external powers in the security of the Asia–Pacific Region, may be seen in the founding of the ARF. In the early 1990s, ASEAN was at the height of its economic success. The end of the Cold War and elections in Cambodia had fostered conditions that seemed propitious for the enhancement of peace and stability in Southeast Asia, but which challenged ASEAN's ability to play a leading role. As the 1995 ARF Concept Paper put it: 'The centre of the world's economic gravity is shifting into the region. The main challenge of the ARF is to sustain and enhance this peace and prosperity.' With this in mind, ASEAN and its dialogue partners together forged a forum for security discussions and cooperation out of the existing Post-Ministerial Conferences (PMC).

The ARF may be seen as an apparent paradox as it represents ASEAN's attempt to maintain regional order, but by involving the major powers with stakes in the region. ASEAN commentators have insisted that ASEAN inputs have contributed to the ARF's distinctiveness, which distinguishes it from regional security organizations such as the Organization for Security and Cooperation in Europe (OSCE).[24] However, given ASEAN's relative weakness in security terms, ASEAN has found it difficult to maintain the leading role that it set for itself.[25] The dialogue partners have invested substantial political capital into the ARF, but have demanded some control over its direction in exchange. Indeed, the fact that the ARF has prospered due to the dialogue partners' active involvement and that the Forum has quickly moved on to discuss the overlap between confidence-building and preventive diplomacy has been a development which has caused some ambivalence within ASEAN circles.

The ARF is now an extremely diverse body comprising the ten ASEAN countries, ASEAN's ten Dialogue Partners, as well as Papua New Guinea and Mongolia. However, the ASEAN countries have consistently maintained that they wish to remain in the driving seat of the ARF. To a certain extent, the adoption of ASEAN modes of operation has ensured that the pace of the ARF can be controlled by ASEAN countries. This is facilitated by the fact that decision-making within the ARF is based on the ASEAN practice of consensus and dialogue, with little institutionalization of the process despite the multiplication of activities. Moreover, while inter-sessional activities may be co-chaired by non-ASEAN countries, the annual ARF Ministerial Meeting is always chaired by ASEAN by the current chairman of the ASEAN Standing Committee. The recent example provided by ASEAN participation in APEC has also provided food for thought on the evolution of regionalism in the Asia–Pacific. The ASEAN countries remain wary of seeing the ARF develop in the institutionalized direction of APEC, for while the APEC Secretariat is located in Singapore, the overall direction of APEC is to a large extent out of ASEAN's control.

At the same time, pressures will nevertheless continue for the ARF to progress further from confidence-building to preventive diplomacy and on to conflict resolution. A number of important policy issues face ASEAN within the ARF: of further developing the process and broadening the scope of coverage of issues to maximize the ARF's relevance and effectiveness, but at the same time to keep the interest of major players such as China and the United States by ensuring a pace of development that is comfortable to all.[26] In fact, the search to capture the initiative is basic to ASEAN's position within the ARF, for it was ASEAN interest in controlling the direction of security cooperation in the Asia–Pacific which led to its advocacy of the ARF in the first instance. Nevertheless, while ASEAN seeks to be in the driving seat of the ARF, the Forum's process-driven dynamics have also in turn forced ASEAN to engage itself more actively in all aspects of the ARF's development.

Prospects for ASEAN into the twentieth-first century

As the only regional organization in Southeast Asia, ASEAN continues to be judged and assessed constantly. In terms of achievement, it may be said that ASEAN has laid the basis for political dialogue and cooperation, and has made advances towards building a community in Southeast Asia. It has provided the base for power projection to enhance the bargaining power of its members, in particular of the smaller Southeast Asian states. At the same time, flexibility is maintained for its member states to act in accordance with their national priorities through keeping the subjects of cooperation relevant to hard-headed national interests.

However, until recently the Association has been less successful in promoting its economic cooperation. Its interest in promoting a social or human dialogue has also not kept pace with its political and economic achievements. Yet conceptually, functional cooperation in various fields such as science and technology, social development, and culture holds a greater formal importance than political cooperation, which is not specifically mentioned in the initial documents. On the surface, therefore, ASEAN has yet to live up to certain important benchmarks, but it has established a solid basis for progress in various areas.

Cambodia's admission into ASEAN in April 1999 has fulfilled the dream of ASEAN's founding fathers that the organization should encompass the whole of Southeast Asia. With the likelihood that the regional role of East Timor would probably not be decided in the near future, the situation of East Timor *vis-à-vis* ASEAN remains to be resolved. With that in mind, the entry of Cambodia marked the realization of the concept of ASEAN Ten, which had been enshrined in ASEAN terminology since the 5th ASEAN Summit in 1995. However, despite the completion of the expansion process, many within ASEAN still believe that the task of realizing ASEAN Ten still continues and that enlargement of membership is only one dimension. In this perspective, ASEAN Ten also implies the consolidation of ASEAN unity and solidarity, for ASEAN's traditional practices had been greatly transformed during the enlargement process to encompass the mainland countries.

In future, the major accomplishments towards region-building will likely be more economic in nature. Although there is substantial work to be done in realizing political blueprints such as the Southeast Asia Nuclear Weapon-Free Zone and advancing ASEAN's role in the ARF, the most urgent tasks no longer lie in the political sphere. Moreover, settling domestic and bilateral political questions is not an area traditional to ASEAN endeavour, and will therefore require time before an appropriate comfort level is achieved.

ASEAN continues to find it difficult to grasp political issues not of concern to all countries, particular when they concern the major powers. Outstanding issues of sovereignty continue to pose problems not only between the ASEAN member countries, but also between ASEAN and China. The Philippines has expressed its disappointment that ASEAN support for its dispute with China over the Spratlys islands as from 1998 has not been as forthcoming as it might have expected, although efforts to reach an agreement between ASEAN and China on a Regional Code of Conduct on the South China Sea are still continuing. Another major issue is the question of political succession: observers have talked constantly of the challenge of leadership in the next generation on from that of the founding fathers. Certain of ASEAN's dialogue partners are particularly concerned with the implications for regional stability and with the long-term prospects for ASEAN. For example, one recent US study has pointed out that 'the critical security threat remains the prospect of prolonged destabilization in Indonesia and the implications for cooperation and leadership in the region ... Indonesia's political weakness may undermine the effectiveness and major accomplishments of ASEAN.'[27] Such views are shared within the region, and while political changes in Indonesia have not so far had significant implications for ASEAN, they have resulted in major disruptions to Indonesian politics.[28] Nevertheless, a new Indonesia may be seeking to extend the scope of its interaction beyond the immediate framework of ASEAN. President Abdurrahman Wahid has complained 'We have been too passive in our foreign relations', and has lately paid a great deal of attention to cooperation between Indonesia, India and China, and increasing the interaction with these large regional powers, which seem to echo sentiments from the Sukarno days.[29] What is certain is that increased activism in Indonesian foreign policy will be followed with great interest among its ASEAN partners, for ASEAN was founded on the premise of Indonesia's self-restraint in regional and international terms.

Buffeted as they have recently been by the globalization process, and in particular by the Asian financial crisis, the ASEAN countries will nevertheless continue to look outwards in terms of economic development. However, in their perspective they have become more cynical with respect to the opportunities and challenges of globalization. The challenge of globalization was a major theme of the first ASEAN-UN Summit held in Bangkok on 12 February 2000 on the sidelines of the Tenth Session of the United Nations Conference on Trade and Development (UNCTAD X), with ASEAN countries demanding a more level playing field. As an indicator of sentiment among many ASEAN policy-makers, the Permanent Representative of Thailand to the United Nations has likened the Asian financial crisis to a tango in which all players must carry out their parts, namely the afflicted economies as well as the developed economies: 'So far, our story of this tango debacle shows that it has been the case of opportunities for the strong and challenges for the weak.'[30] Instead of pragmatically embracing the economic and financial liberalization with open arms, they are more likely to weigh carefully the costs and benefits involved. Moreover, while their field of action continues to be the world market, they have embraced with greater enthusiasm the opportunity to create more profound linkages within East Asia.

Certainly, while the idea of the supremacy of 'Asian Values' has receded with the economic crisis, a new impetus has been found for East Asian cooperation within the scope of ASEAN+3, namely the ASEAN countries and China, Japan and South Korea which has *de facto* represented the implementation of the Malaysian-proposed East Asia Economic Caucus (EAEC) in all but name. The first ASEAN+3 Summit took place during the 2nd ASEAN Informal Summit in Kuala Lumpur in December 1997, while the second meeting was held during the 6th ASEAN Summit in Hanoi in December 1998. At the third ASEAN+3 Summit held in Manila in November 1999, the East Asian leaders for the first time agreed upon a common document, the Joint Statement on East Asia Cooperation, which consolidates this emerging framework and sets the tone for its activities in the coming years. In addition to the Summits, lower-level and more specialized activities are also being organized. Such confluence within East Asia has not gone unnoticed by others, including in the United States and Australia. As a US study has proposed, in order to shore up its influence in Southeast Asia in the aftermath of the financial crisis: 'The United States should bolster weakened regional cooperation through more political support for ASEAN and the ARF.'

Enhancing the effectiveness of decision-making will be another challenge for ASEAN in the future. With the increasing participation of academics and Non-Governmental Organizations (NGOs) in various aspects of ASEAN cooperation, it will become more essential for ASEAN to enhance its responsiveness to national constituencies. Recent episodes such as response to the Haze issue in 1997–1998 have led commentators to highlight the need to enhance the effectiveness of the decision-making structure to accommodate emerging issues.

So far ASEAN has seemed to handle the succession of leadership well. However, a more substantial change in political culture may be seen in the absorption of new members. Institutional memory so much lacking in the Association will become a greater asset in maintaining ASEAN on its past course and ensuring that new members abide by the basic ground rules. Indeed, it may be said that expansion of membership will take ASEAN back to its roots on certain issues, with a more intensive process of consensus-building being required and renewed emphasis being placed on developmental issues in addition to trade. Indeed, themes such as social safety nets, human resource development and Mekong Basin development have become ASEAN's keynote programmes over the last couple of years, promoted by Thailand with the active support of Cambodia, Laos, Myanmar and Vietnam. This 'back to basics' approach is likely to dominate ASEAN endeavours for some years to come.

Conclusion

The examination of the ASEAN experience leads to a number of findings which are relevant to regionalism in the Asia–Pacific as a whole.

The story of ASEAN's evolution has not broken any paradigm. Conceptually, ASEAN continues to realize the objectives set in its founding charter. Through its various mechanisms, it has united the Southeast Asian region in a web of cooperative endeavours in a wide variety of fields. Through the cooperation among member states and through its dialogue relationships with its external partners, it has also promoted greater coherence and predictability in inter-state relations in the Asia–Pacific. At the same time, in doing so it has expanded on initial objectives in an innovative manner. Indeed, long before the concept of comprehensive security was fully developed, Southeast Asian policy-makers translated national priorities of development and security into their conception of regional organization as expressed through ASEAN.

Regionalism has become an essential part of the external interaction of ASEAN member states, whether in the political, economic and functional spheres. ASEAN is often considered by Southeast Asian leaders as forming the core of a concentric circle of cooperation, which expands outwards to involve bodies such as APEC and ARF before reaching the global arena.

Accordingly, Southeast Asia continues to project itself outwards rather than inwards as part of its attempt to retain the initiative in the region's interactions with the outside world. Recent examples are seen in the inception of APEC in the economic sphere and ARF in the political sphere, and new forms of interaction may emerge in the future, including a clearer development of East Asian cooperation involving ASEAN, China, Japan and South Korea. At the same time, the Southeast Asian countries remain attached to ASEAN as the primary mechanism. In this perspective, commitments to AFTA, ARF, ASEM and EAEC are merely extensions of cooperation within ASEAN and are not likely to supersede it in priority.

At the same time, Southeast Asian regionalism has always been fluid and will keep on transforming its emphases. Thus, the initial emphasis on political order will make way for a broader-based cooperation. In so doing, ASEAN is likely to adopt a more rule-based and formalized approach to cooperation more typical of economic bodies. This move, however, will be controlled, and the original diplomatic modes of interaction will continue to hold sway for some time to come, particularly as the new members stress the importance of the principle of consensus as enshrined in the original ASEAN political documents. At least until it has fully integrated the new members in all aspects of activities, ASEAN will draw greater inspiration from the basic documents than from new policy frameworks.

Commitment to ASEAN through the recent financial crisis suggests that the traditional paradigm involving state-to-state relations will remain predominant within Southeast Asia for some time into the future. While the short-term response was national solutions in the absence of significant and timely international support, there is a consensus on the need for enhanced regional cooperation among the states concerned. Expansion of membership to encompass countries such as Vietnam and Myanmar with a long history of nationalism and self-reliance will further ensure that ASEAN will retain its faith in national sovereignty. As a building block for East Asian regionalism, the ASEAN experience suggests that East Asian regionalism will be based on voluntarism and pragmatism rather than a predetermined evolution. Particularly when considering competing national priorities in Southeast Asia, sub-regional development, including growth triangles, will continue to play a subsidiary role and will be unlikely to develop into a new paradigm in the near future.

From the examination of the literature, country studies analyzing the policy-making frameworks of countries such as Singapore, Indonesia and Thailand have also provided important insights to ASEAN decision-making. For countries such as Thailand, an active role in ASEAN served to demonstrate the Thai Government's commitment to the region and to cooperation with neighbouring countries. Clearly, work needs to be done on further defining and studying the priorities in the new ASEAN members' approaches to regional cooperation. At the same time, more work is still required in assessing the roles of certain of the older member states, such as Brunei and even Malaysia, and the contribution of individual think tanks within the various countries. With the increasing interaction between Track I and Track II discussions, the greater interplay between academic and bureaucratic circles will be worthy of future attention.

Finally, some of the writings and academic discussions reviewed reflect real policy issues during the course of ASEAN's development, from the establishment of an appropriate framework for cooperation in the 1970s to community building in the 1990s and beyond.

Notes

1 See George Modelski, *SEATO: Six Studies* (Melbourne: ANU, 1962).

2 See Russell H. Fifield, *Americans in Southeast Asia: The Roots of Commitment* (New York: Thomas Y. Crowell & Co., 1973).

3 See Charnvit Kasetsiri, 'Overview of Research and Studies on Southeast Asia in Thailand: Where do we come from? Where are we? Where are we going?' *Thammasat Review*, Vol. 3, No. 1 (June 1998), p. 28; Mohamed Habib and Tim Huxley 'Introduction' in Mohamed Habib and Tim Huxley, eds, *An Introduction to Southeast Asian Studies. Collection* (Singapore: ISEAS, 1996), pp. 2–4.

4 See Bernard K. Gordon, *The Dimensions of Conflict in Southeast Asia* (Englewood Cliffs N.J.: Prentice-Hall Inc., 1966), pp. 121–122.

5 Speech by Narciso Ramos at the 1st ASPAC Ministerial Meeting, Seoul, 1966. Documents of the 1st Ministerial Meeting for Asian and Pacific Cooperation (Seoul, Ministry of Foreign Affairs, 1966), p. 29.

6 See, for example, Arnfinn Jorgensen-Dahl, *Regional Organization and Order in Southeast Asia* (New York: St. Martin's Press, 1980); Hans H. Indorf, 'ASEAN, Problems and Prospects', *ISEAS Occasional Paper,* No. 38 (Singapore: ISEAS, 1975).

7 Michael Haas, 'The ASEANization of Asian International Relations', *Asia Pacific Community,* No. 6, (Fall 1979), p. 80.

8 See, for example, Donald E. Weatherbee, ed., *Southeast Asia Divided: The ASEAN-Indochina Crisis* (Boulder: Westview Press, 1985); M. Rajendran, *ASEAN's Foreign Relations – The Shift to Collective Action* (Kuala Lumpur: Arenabuku Sdn. Bhd., 1985); William S. Turley, ed., *Confrontation or Coexistence: The Future of ASEAN-Vietnam Relations* (Bangkok: ISIS, 1985).

9 See Marjorie L. Suriyamongkol, *Politics of ASEAN Economic Cooperation: The Case of the ASEAN Industrial Projects* (Singapore: OUP/ISEAS, 1988); Noordin Sopiee, Chew Lay See and Lim Siang Jin, eds, *ASEAN at the Crossroads: Obstacles, Options and Opportunities in Economic Cooperation* (Kuala Lumpur: ISIS (Group of 14), 1987); *The First ASEAN Roundtable: New Directions for ASEAN Economic Cooperation* (Bangkok: ISEAS, 1986).

10 Sarasin Viraphol, 'Forward' in Sarasin Viraphol and Werner Pfennig, eds, *ASEAN-UN Cooperation in Preventive Diplomacy* (Bangkok: International Studies Centre, Ministry of Foreign Affairs of Thailand, 1995), p. 1

11 See, for example, Sukhumbhand Paribatra, 'From ASEAN Six to ASEAN Ten: Issues and Prospects' *Contemporary Southeast Asia,* Vol. 16, No. 3 (December 1994), pp. 243–258.

12 Bela Balassa, *The Theory of Economic Integration* (London: George Allen & Unwin Ltd., 1962), p. 2.

13 Christoph Rieger, 'The Treaty of Rome and its Relevance for ASEAN', *ASEAN Economic Bulletin,* Vol. 8, No. 2 (November 1991), pp. 160–161.

14 Michael Antolik, *ASEAN and the Diplomacy of Accommodation* (New York: M.E. Sharpe Inc., 1990).

15 Muthiah Alagappa, 'Asian Practice of Security: Key Features and Explanations' in Muthiah Alagappa, *Asian Security Practice* (Palo Alto: Stanford University Press, 1998), pp. 644–647.

16 Haas, op. cit., pp. 72–86.

17 Karl Deutsch *et. al., Political Community and the North Atlantic Area. International Organization in the Light of Historical Experience* (Princeton, Princeton University Press, 1957).

18 Alagappa, p. 635. See also Amitav Acharya, 'A Regional Security Community for Southeast Asia?' *The Journal of Strategic Studies,* Vol. 18, No. 3 (September 1995), pp. 175–200.

19 See, for example, Muthiah Alagappa, 'Systemic Change, Security and Governance in the Asia–Pacific.' in Chan Heng Chee, *The New Asia–Pacific Order* (Singapore: ISEAS, 1997), p. 80.

20 Habib and Huxley, p. 7.

21 Dewi Fortuna Anwar, *Indonesia in ASEAN: Foreign Policy and Regionalism* (Singapore, ISEAS, 1994); Kanishka Jayasuriya, 'Singapore: The Politics of Regional Definition' *Pacific Review,* Vol. 7, No. 4, 1994.

22 See Marjorie Suriyamongkol, *The Politics of ASEAN Economic Cooperation. The Case of the ASEAN Industrial Projects* (Singapore, OUP/ISEAS, 1988).

23 While campaigning for election as WTO Director-General, Thai Deputy Prime Minister Supachai Panitchpakdi observed 'What we have learned is economic and political interests are inseparable … we have also learned that ASEAN is the most important and staunchest supporter of Thailand.' *Bangkok Post* (9 May 1999).

24 The ARF Concept Paper of 1995 specifically mentions that 'the ARF must be accepted as a sui generis organization. It has no established precedents to follow.'

25 Amitav Acharya, 'Background and Application to the Asia–Pacific Region' in Desmond Ball and Amitav Acharya, *The Next Stage: Preventive Diplomacy and Security Cooperation in the Asia–Pacific Region,* Canberra Papers on Strategy and Defence No. 31 (Canberra: ANU, 1999), p. 28.

26 See Rosemary Foot, 'The Present and Future of the ARF: China's Role and Attitude' in Khoo How San, ed., *The Future of the ARF* (Singapore: Institute of Defence and Strategic Studies, 1999), pp. 130–132.

27 Beyond the Asian Financial Crisis: Challenges and Opportunities for US Leadership. A Special Report of the US Institute of Peace (Washington DC: US Institute of Peace, 1998), p. 12.

28 See Zakaria Haji Ahmad and Baladas Ghoshal, 'The Political future of ASEAN after the Asian crisis' *International Affairs,* No. 75 (April 1999), pp. 776–778.

29 See interview in *The Nation* (30 April 1999).

30 Statement by H.E. Mr. Asda Jayanama, Permanent Representative of Thailand to the United Nations before the High Level dialogue on the theme of the social and economic impact of globalization and interdependence and their policy implications, 53rd UNGA, New York (17 September 1998), New York: Permanent Mission of Thailand, September 1998, p. 2.

6 Regionalism and regional governance in Northeast Asia

Tsutomu Kikuchi

Introduction

The purpose of this chapter is to analyze the past records and prospects of establishing a stable structure of regional governance in Northeast Asia. Although many experts have described the region as inherently conflictual in nature (noting the continued prevalence of geopolitical thinking in the state apparatus of Northeast Asian countries),[1] this chapter argues that there exists a possibility of Northeast Asia evolving into multilayered nested regimes based upon existing (global) multilateralism, regionalism, minilateralism, bilateralism and domestic political changes.

Given the complexity of regional relations, it is desirable but quite difficult to establish a region-wide comprehensive multilateral mechanism that is both able to be inclusive of all relevant countries and at the same time could be utilized as a body to regulate politico-military, economic and social transactions. This being the case, we have to look for other ways to ensure regional governance.

In this chapter, first, after examining the various characteristics of international relations in the region, I will go on to analyze the characteristics of (global) regulatory regimes that presently cover Northeast Asia, in terms of regionalism, bilateralism and the domestic political changes taking place in the respective countries. Second, I would like to examine the relationships between them, and third, to point out the importance of developing multilayered nested regimes to regulate interactions among the countries of the region and put mutual constraints on them. In conclusion, I argue the conditions that are necessary in terms of forging a stable regional governance structure.

Characteristics of international relations in Asia

There are many problems and obstacles that have prevented a regional governance structure from emerging in Asia in general and Northeast Asia in particular. Several characteristics of the region should be noted.

Post-Cold War issues

Asia is now in a transitional era. The end of the Cold War changed a basic structure of international relations in the region, but the future structure has not yet been seen. The relationships among the major powers, for example, are still unstable and uncertain, although there are some positive developments recently. The distribution of power is unstable as industrialization changes relative capabilities among them. Most of the states have territorial and/or historical disputes with their neighbors. Two unresolved problems of divided countries left over from the Cold War are the focus of armed confrontation.

Post-Colonial issues

The nation-building process is still underway in this region. Most of the Asian nations still carry a post-colonial character. Many countries in the region have made great efforts to enhance state structure and national cohesion among the peoples, but there still remain countries that face internal instability originating from the weakness of the governing regimes. Weakness of the governing regimes causes many regional problems.

Most of the countries in the region are in the modernist stage of development, which is defined by strong government control over society and a restrictive attitude toward openness and pluralist concepts of the world. Some of the regional countries are facing insecurity in their governing regimes, which results from domestic instability and external environmental factors such as economic globalization. The absence of viable states (both in terms of effective state apparatus and mutually accepted territorial boundaries) makes the process of region-building difficult, if not impossible. These problems already stand as major obstacles to the development of effective regionalism in Northeast Asia. The instability of regimes, their intolerance of all opposition, and the erosion of projects of state-dominated economic development work powerfully to undermine sustained interstate cooperation in Northeast Asia.[2]

In the post-colonial modernization process, 'national autonomy' and 'national independence' are highly regarded by political leaderships. Many Asians still stick to a quite traditional or 'collectively-(mis)conceived' concept of national sovereignty and the principle of non-intervention in internal affairs. They have strong concerns about ceding national sovereignty in the name of economic integration and cooperation.

Post-Imperial issues

China occupies a special place in the Asian security environment, given its historical record and today's rising power. We can discern three different tiers of historical problems coexisting in today's international relations in Asia, which could be described as (1) Post-Cold War, (2) Post-Colonial, and (3) Post-Imperial, respectively. By 'post-imperial' I mean problems originating from, or accompanied by, the breakdown of a China-centered imperial system that began in the middle of the last century with the arrival of the Western powers. Most of today's 'hot spots' in Asia, actual or potential, are located along the periphery of the old China-centered system. This fact attests to the longevity of what we call the 'post-imperial' problems. These are not necessarily old stories. The geopolitical reality of the situation still remains basically unchanged as far as China is concerned.

Weakness of the governing regime

The extent to which regional cooperation can develop is likely to depend very heavily on the coherence and viability of the states and state structures within a given region. The instability of political regimes, their intolerance of all opposition, and the erosion of state-led economic projects all work to undermine sustained interstate cooperation. Essentially, states remain as the essential building-blocks on which regional cooperative exercises are built.[3]

Post-territorial issues: economic globalization

Economic globalization is posing serious challenges to nation states, especially to developing states that are still in the process of nation-building. Increasingly economic/trade negotiators are concerned about what is taking place within national boundaries in terms of competition policy and industrial policy, both of which are closely linked with a state's governing structures. Much discussion is now taking place over the absence or presence of a 'level playing field.'[4] The cumulative effect of these transnational forces clearly leads to an erosion of national sovereignty.

As wealth and power are increasingly generated by private transactions that take place across the borders of states rather than within them, it has become harder to sustain the image of states as the preeminent actors at the global level. In the current global society the unique political status of states must be balanced against the fact that the most economically powerful actors of the international arena are multinational enterprises (MNEs).[5] Actually, commodities are produced through the integration of production processes performed in a multiplicity of national territories. Whether any given nation is included in global production networks or excluded from them depends upon the decisions of private actors such as MNEs. In an ever evolving international economy, MNEs are increasingly becoming independent actors. In fact it would not be far-fetched to state that MNEs are now engaged in their own 'foreign policy.'[6] The era of happy marriages between firms and states is long gone. States can try to make their territories attractive, but they cannot dictate the structure of global production networks. In a world of global production networks, access to capital and technology depends upon strategic alliances with those who control the global production networks, rather than on the control of any particular territory. In a global economy where there is a surplus of labor, control over large amounts of territory and population can be more of a burden than an asset.

In order to adjust the trend of economic globalization and obtain an economic opportunity, all countries are forced to change internal regulatory systems. In fact, these changes are quite often directly related to the governing regimes of the countries concerned. They are carrying out the difficult task of strengthening state structures, while simultaneously making them compatible with the rest of the world in rapidly changing national, regional and international environments. This puts the countries in a serious dilemma.

Security dilemma

If security dilemma theory is applied to Northeast Asia, the risk of 'spirals of tensions' developing in the future may still be worth serious consideration. It is a well-known fact that the presence of historically deep-seated mistrust has further exacerbated the security dilemma in the region.[7]

One possible approach to ameliorate security dilemmas and to enable the prevention of spirals of tensions is to have an outside arbiter play a policing (mediating or balancing) role to reduce the perceived need for regional countries to begin destabilizing security competitions. For this reason, most of the security experts seem to agree to the proposition that a major factor in containing potential tensions in Northeast Asia (and East Asia as a whole) is the continuing military presence of the US.

However, the form of the engagement of the US in the region has potentially important implications for regional security. The recent disputes over the US–Japan alliance demonstrate this clearly. According to security dilemma theory, defensive systems and missions, such as the new defensive roles of Japan and the introduction of new defensive systems like TMD, will not provoke arms races and spirals of tensions. The build-up of defensive weapons and the adoption of defensive postures and doctrines should not fuel the security dilemma and spirals of tensions, because such capabilities and methods are not useful for aggression. Even more importantly, such defensive weapons serve to stabilize the regional environment, since they tend to shore up the territorial status quo by deterring aggressors from achieving revisionist goals, whereas offensive weapons are destabilizing because they threaten the status quo.[8]

However, this logic is not applicable in the case of contemporary Northeast Asia, This has been clearly demonstrated by the fact that Beijing, together with Russia and North Korea, has expressed deep concerns about the new developments in the US–Japan alliance. China's main security goal (and the most important issue for the existing political regime to legitimate its government) is to prevent Taiwan from moving towards independence. In other words, the main threat to China is a political change in cross-strait relations that would legalize and freeze the territorial status quo.[9]

This implies that without mutual recognition of the territorial status quo and with a prevalence of deep concerns about the shifting relative power on one side against the others, a defensive defence posture will not serve to ameliorate suspicion and vulnerabilities and therefore the security dilemma.

Positive developments

In spite of various shortcomings and the obvious defects acting against efforts to forge regional regimes /institutions, there have been a number of positive developments in the region.

Economics, politics and security

Economics (economic cooperation) and security are closely connected concepts in terms of regime making in the region. There are several basic mechanisms for economic cooperation that act to promote security cooperation: transforming the structure of interstate relations from zero-sum game to a game; making the interstate relations more negotiable; providing the scope of economy; promoting an on-going process of socialization and enmeshment through which definitions of interests and identities may shift; changing the values of members and the ways in which costs/benefits and rational actions are constructed; affecting the ways in which security interests are defined and understood, etc.

The main way in which the economic situation is closely connected to that of regime is through the inter-linkages of security and stability. Russia's internal economic turmoil, China's expected slowdown in economic development and the rising income gap between the rich and the poor in China, as well as North Korea's serious economic difficulties are all examples where economics has had grave impacts on regime security. Furthermore, some of the Northeast Asian countries are now in an era of power transition. Weakness in their domestic power bases has made it difficult for these governments to take conciliatory steps towards ameliorating tensions.

Economics and security issues are closely connected in another way. KEDO (Korean Peninsula Energy Development Organization) is one such instance. KEDO has demonstrated the linkage of the issue of proliferation of weaponry and the technology of mass destruction with economic assistance. Close linkages between the suspension of the transfer of missiles and related technology and the 'inspection' or 'visit' to the suspected nuclear sites with economic assistance ('compensation') is another example. Even for China, its agreement to subscribe to CTBT and MTCR was closely connected with its desire to maintain its trade relations with the US, the continued provision of MFN status from the US and accession to GATT/WTO which are so important for China.

Comprehensive security

Clearly, what has been described up to this point demonstrates that it is far too limited to restrict the consideration of security issues to military affairs. Rather, we have to conceive of security from a broader perspective. Of course, military measures are still quite important for security in the region. However, in the present day, there are numerous security-related problems that would, at the very least, be ineffectively resolved through military measures and, at the worst, could be severely aggravated through such means. Therefore it is apparent that we need a broader approach to the issue of security.

A recent example of the need for a more comprehensive security conceptualization is the Asian financial crisis. It has proven that economic phenomena such as the dramatic decline of a currency can cause even greater damage to a country's security than that of what might be caused through armed conflicts with neighbouring countries.

One of the most serious security threats in this part of the world is, in fact, not a militarily derived one. In terms of this region it would be fair to say that the gravest security issues lie both in domestic politics (domestic instability) and in the effects of the rapidly changing global political economy. Even in Northeast Asia where a highly competitive security framework has dominated relations among the participating countries, the fundamental problem is not a military one, but rather tends to be an internal one, for instance there are the problems of unstable governing regimes, lack of national cohesion and so forth.

Security complex: from competitive to cooperative one

In terms of security relations, Northeast Asia is one example of what Barry Buzan calls 'regional security complexes.' Buzan describes a regional security complex as a set of states with significant and distinctive networks of security relations that ensure that the members have a high level of interdependence in the realm of security: a group of states whose primary security concerns link them together sufficiently closely that their individual national security cannot realistically be considered apart from one another.[10]

The overall Cold War pattern of security in Northeast Asia has been substantially determined externally. The security complex in Northeast Asia today includes a competitive security system, a common security system, and some cooperative security systems. A cooperative security system has been extending to Northeast Asia recently, albeit a thin and weak one.

Changing role of the states and regionalism: 'competition states'[11]

With the progress of economic globalization, those traditionally domestic political concerns such as education, transportation, energy, law and order as well as fiscal policy are increasingly needing to be understood in the context of comparative international competitiveness.[12] The rapid expansion of economic interdependence has changed international competitiveness among the states constantly and rapidly, inducing the states to share the costs of the ensuing huge structural adjustments.

Changes in the operation of global markets and the growth of a global production system, together with those in technology and communications, have had a grave impact on the ways in which governments defined their most important policy goals – economic development and political autonomy. As far as most nations are concerned, it is essential that internationally competitive enterprises flourish within their territories, in order to maintain and develop their economies and to provide economic welfare to their people. In this context, traditional national economies have become too small in scale.

In addition, as economic activities become globalized and economic exchanges beyond national borders are rapidly expanding, nations and corporations, in order to achieve economic prosperity, have to compete worldwide for the sale of their products and, in turn, must seek efficient combinations of factors of production such as labor, capital and technology throughout the world. They have to locate themselves in the global economic networks in which they will seek market access to the maximum possible extent, or alternatively, they have to construct such networks for themselves. Multinational corporations are constantly seeking new markets and production bases. The competition to attract foreign direct investment intensifies as global investors seek better places to do business.

Thus, the nature of competition encourages the formation of larger units, both to enhance economic efficiency and to ensure the political power necessary to bargain effectively over the rules and institutions that govern the regional and global economy. In this regard, economic regionalism may be driven jointly by governments and transnational enterprises, and the politics of regionalism can be understood in terms of a convergence of interests between the ruling state elite and firms.

Globalization, nation-states and regionalism

With the progress of globalization, all countries face what we may call mega-competiton. It is not certain that states and societies can stand the continuing pressure and high pace of adaptation, disruption and humiliation that are placed on them by intense competition in a global economy. Nor is it clear that existing political and economic frameworks can handle either the global consequences of economic liberalization, or the domestic consequences of de-industrialization, rising unemployment, and decreasing levels of social welfare.

If some of these ills are insurmountable, or if there is a scramble to try to secure their places, then the pressure to organize regionally may become quite strong. Regions will offer some compromise between the excessive competition of the global economy and the diseconomies of scale. Within a region there are some economies of scale and some possibilities of protection against the more merciless aspects of global mega-competition. Regionalism can also provide a strong base for operating within it, and some convergence of policy preference in economic management between developed and developing countries will facilitate the formation of regionalism.[13]

Multilateralism, regionalism and bilateralism in Northeast Asia

Asia in the global regulatory regimes

First, what political/security and economic regulatory mechanisms cover Asia today? Various types of international regulatory regimes have been expanding to include Asia. All states (except Taiwan) are members of the United Nations. Regional and international regimes provide common rules, principles and norms to regulate interaction among the various entities in a specific issue area. NPT/IAEA covers the whole region. If China and Taiwan succeed in obtaining the WTO membership, most of the countries in Northeast Asia are under the rules of GATT/WTO. The GATT/WTO provides member economies with clearly specified obligations, legally-binding commitments, dispute-settlement mechanisms and nondiscrimination and universal application among more than 130 member economies. Given the fact that the GATT/WTO is touching upon various internal regulatory systems of the member economies, the involvement of these countries in the WTO process will make a contribution to making their economic systems more transparent and compatible with the rest of the world, thereby placing their economic relations with the outside world on a more stable regulatory foundation.

In addition, most of the countries have already joined CTBT and MTCR or expressed their promise to subscribe to the norms and rules of MTCR. 'The Chiang Mai Initiative' for currency swap among the ASEAN+3 countries (agreed to in June 2000) will make a further contribution to enhancing financial discipline and transparency among the countries. If Taiwan and Hong Kong also join the initiative, the regional architecture for financial stability will be even further strengthened.

Transregional regimes

Northeast Asia has been witnessing the emergence of many region-wide transregional regimes to manage politico-security interactions and economic exchanges.

APEC has developed principles and rules of trade/investment liberalization and encouraged its members to subscribe to them through 'peer pressure.' China and Taiwan joined the APEC forum in 1992. Even Russia has become a full member. Thus, except for North Korea, all the countries of the region are now members of APEC. The ARF was also established as a formal mechanism to promote politico-security dialogues among the countries in the region.

In addition, we have recently witnessed another region-wide forum made up of three East Asian countries: the so-called 'ASEAN+3' which consists of Japan, China and South Korea. This forum is likely to become further institutionalized in the coming years, adding yet another regulatory mechanism to the region.

KEDO is a unique organization in the sense that it includes a diverse group of countries as members in terms of geographical locations. KEDO also has a transregional character in the different sense that the KEDO regime is tightly nested into the global NPT/IAEA regime. Put differently, NPT/IAEA is a supportive transregional arrangement to regulate the operation of KEDO. Furthermore, KEDO has been making a great contribution to non-proliferation by establishing a mechanism to provide energy resources to North Korea.

In spite of the criticisms by pessimists, a regional dialogue forum could play an important role in encouraging more intensive and extensive interactions between states. Regional organization can shape state practices by establishing, articulating, and transmitting norms that define what constitutes acceptable and legitimate behavior. States as actors abide by these norms not only because of the effects of coercive power but also because of the desire to be viewed as operating legitimately; that is, they need to justify and bring their policies in line with accepted practices of state action.[14] Regional regimes can encourage states and societies to imagine themselves as part of a region.[15] They can play an important role in providing socializing mechanisms.[16]

Regionalism in Northeast Asia

Many ideas for promoting regionalism specifically focusing on Northeast Asia have been explored so far. Among them, the Four Parties Talk was finally launched as a formal multilateral process.

Other ideas such as a Six Parties Dialogue Forum and a Northeast Asian Security Dialogue Forum have failed to obtain regional agreement. To be noted in this context is that subregional multilateral dialogues and consultation among all or some of the regional countries such as US-Japan-Russia, US-China-Japan, Japan-China-South Korea, the US-Russia-China-Japan-South Korea (North Korea) have been so far conducted at the second track level. Economic forums to promote sub-regional economic cooperation among the areas surrounding the Sea of Japan have also been conducted at semi-official levels.[17]

Informal summit meetings among Japan, China and South Korea have been established recently to discuss the matters of common concern, although institutional arrangements have not well developed.

The surge of bilateralism

In Northeast Asia the competitive security system that dominated the region during the Cold War era has almost disappeared among the major powers. A competitive security system is now localized between the two Koreas. Today, no persistent divisions exist among the major powers. We have been witnessing the emergence of a cooperative security system within which potential enemies are 'internalized.' While it is true to say alliance mechanisms exist to prevent and respond to emergencies within a cooperative security system, unlike those in a competitive security system, alliances within a cooperative security system do not presuppose any specific enemies.[18]

Even so, the old bilateral tensions have remained and, in fact, new tensions have also emerged. US–China, Japan–Russia, and Japan–China relations were rather unstable until quite recently. However, for the last few years, the major powers have gradually engaged in defining their respective relations on a bilateral basis. This is clearly demonstrated in the recent surge of bilateral summit meetings between the major powers.[19]

As can be seen from the above analysis, the recent surge of bilateralism has some distinguishing characteristics which are quite different from those seen during the Cold War era. The essence of which can be outlined as follows;

Firstly, the major powers mutually confirm that they are partners in establishing a new regional (global) order, and that they will not neglect each other. They recognize differences existing between them, but promise not to return to a confrontational relationship and, more importantly, to continue to consult each other. They give mutual reassurances that they will not return to hostile relations such as US–Soviet confrontation during the Cold War. The term 'strategic partnership' has underlined such relationships.

Secondly, while the major powers enhance their bilateral relations, they are quite careful not to create concerns on the part of third countries that enhanced bilateralism is targeted at excluding the third parties. During the Cold War era strategic partnership meant that the partners enhanced their unity and cooperation against the outside third countries. It was quite competitive and confrontational in nature. However, today's strategic partnership is not targeted at specific outside enemies. For example, the China–Russia strategic partnership is not confrontational against such outside powers as the US and Japan. The US–China strategic partnership does not carry any connotations of intending to antagonize the outside powers.

Although balance of power tactics will continue to be utilized as a means of enhancing the power and interests among the major powers, the development of non-hostile bilateralism may serve to act as a kind of counterbalance to this, since it can contribute to putting mutual constraints on state behavior by developing common rules and practices.

Other bilateral relations have also either been enhanced or at least placed back on track. The historic summit that was held between North and South Korea is one such example. Despite the fact that the opening of the North Korean society to the outside world is still to be seen, it is undoubtedly a major advance forward in the sense that North Korea has normalized its bilateral relations with various countries. In fact, relations between Japan and South Korea have been developing considerably well ever since the Korean financial crisis. Furthermore, one of the more positive after-effects of the crisis has been the further promotion of bilateral consultation and cooperation between Japan and South Korea. Both governments have agreed to explore the possibility of working towards concluding a bilateral free trade agreement.[20] The successful conclusion of a bilateral FTA between Japan and South Korea will make a great contribution not only to strengthening the foundation of their respective economic diplomacy at multilateral forums such as GATT/WTO and APEC, but also to enhancing the political foundations between the two countries.[21] In this regard, the regional implications of the recent changes of Japan's trade policy, together with the new proposals of forming a regional FTA in East Asia, should definitely be further explored.

Business and second track linkages: bridging missing links

Up to the present, the 'missing' forms of bilateralism have been mainly taken care of by the private sector. As a result, quite a considerable amount of 'Private diplomacy' has been conducted. Yet another important and relevant turn of events is the recent expansion of business links between the South and the North. The respective governments have also encouraged closer economic links, even if from different political motivations.

However, this surge of bilateralism has not extended to trilateral or mini-lateral arrangements in Northeast Asia except for those among the allies (US, Japan and South Korea) and for those arising out of the Four Party Talks on the Korean Peninsula. So far, trilateral dialogues have been mainly taken care of in terms of second track solutions. These second track channels have provided senior government officials (in their private capacities) with informal dialogue forums to discuss sensitive political issues, without the official commitments of the governments concerned. Regional multilateral dialogue frameworks have also been provided for in the form of transregional bodies such as APEC, ARF and CSCAP.

Domestic change: emerging liberal internationalist coalitions

Economic globalization and interdependence, along with the effects of mega-competition, have produced many major consequences. One such outcome is the convergence of policy preferences between the developed and developing countries over their development strategies. Until the 1980s, the relations between the developed and developing countries had been decidedly confrontational in nature. The basic strategy historically adopted by developing countries has been one of protective import-substitution policies, which are inward-looking in nature.

Since the early 1980s, however, developing countries have begun to move toward economic liberalization and reform. They have even aggressively sought market access to and investment from developed countries. China's changing economic relations with the developed countries have been one such demonstration of this fundamental change in economic management.

Both a greater sense of economic vulnerability and the growing fear of marginalization, brought about mainly with the ending of the Cold War as well as through the effects of economic globalization, have further forced developing countries to introduce external and internal reform measures to obtain the confidence of foreign investors. Developing countries have lost their value as bargaining chips in a world where the US and the Soviet Union had once courted them for their favors. Neither aid, nor trade, nor security is assured in the post-Cold War environment.

Correspondingly, the increased economic interdependence with the outside world has produced powerful liberal internationalist coalitions that have a strong commitment to maintaining better economic relations with the outside. It has become a kind of universal truth that economic welfare is increasingly dependent upon exchanges with the outside.

An active participation of state and private actors in the economic globalization process has had a grave impact on the allocation of power among the interest groups in the respective countries. In most countries throughout the globe, the power of the liberal internationalist coalitions has been enhanced in domestic politics and so has come to a strong position in favoring further integration with the international economy.

Internationalist groups have begun to look for new markets for their foreign direct investments in their never-ending quest to enhance the international competitiveness of their industries by combining comparative advantages beyond the national boundaries (labor, capital, technology and so forth). This movement has been further pushed, by the constant strengthening of influence and power of internationalist groups in their respective countries. They have demanded that the government change regulations that had prevented the firms from operating beyond national boundaries. Surprisingly, the logic of these internationalist groups has become more powerful than the logic of real politics. This has been clearly demonstrated in the active business operations by Taiwanese firms in the mainland and in respect of South Korean firms' further engagements in business in North Korea.

In turn, since liberal coalitions opting for vigorous participation in the international economic order have been supportive to cooperative regional security arrangements, there is a linkage with regionalist trends as well. Liberal internationalists are more likely to embrace regional cooperation than their political adversaries (inward-looking and protectionist forces).

China is a case in point. The expansion of economic relations with the outside world has resulted in the formation of new interest groups that strongly favour further integration into the regional and global economy.

With the introduction of economic reform measures in China since the late 1970s (even North Korea in the early 1990s to some extent), the definition of interests and the understanding of appropriate economic policy have shifted to a large extent. The shift towards market liberalization and the move towards integration into the global economy may even have brought about a profound impact on the way Northeast Asia states (especially China) have defined their core goals of foreign policy (military security, economic prosperity and political autonomy) and the range of acceptable trade-offs between them.

China's membership in APEC and its continued attachment to economic reform, together with the more recent strenuous efforts to obtain WTO membership, serve to demonstrate the strength of the liberal internationalist coalitions in China. I think that, the trends toward economic liberalization and a deeper integration with the global economy will be extremely difficult to reverse.

Since the economic globalization process has had a grave impact on the power allocation among the interest groups in the respective countries, it is quite important to pay due attention to the impact of globalization on the emerging liberal coalitions favouring integration with the international economy and to watch their influence on domestic decision-making processes in the Northeast especially in China.

It may be true that the kinds of ties binding different actors (institutions, economic sectors, groups, bureaucracies) to global economic and other international processes do affect their conceptions of interests, and that these conceptions are expressed domestically and regionally.

Even North Korea had come to show its willingness to participate in deeper economic exchanges with the outside world in the early 1990s. This shows that there exists a mindset that recognizes the importance of engaging in economic interactions with outside countries as a means of maintaining economic and political survival. It should also be noted that North Korea's new economic policies were accompanied by more cooperative policies toward the South, resulting in the historic Basic Agreement between the two in the early 1990s. In this context, it is still to be seen whether North Korea's recent active diplomacy will evolve to show some changes in its previous isolated and 'independent' policy.

If economic growth continues in China, a broader constituency in favor of economic interdependence is likely to develop, albeit very slowly. The existing consensus – which at a minimum supports most reforms that have occurred thus far and at least a few further steps – is strong enough to make an outright policy reversal extremely unlikely.

Thus, future developments in the domestic politics of the relevant countries will be crucial in terms of forging stable regional governance. If outward-oriented liberal coalitions, supported by international community and institutions, become a dominant political power in the domestic politics of the respective countries, a cooperative regional order may be the most efficient for both their domestic political and global implications.

Tentative conclusions

Theoretically, there may be three scenarios of a future regional security complex in Northeast Asia: a security community, a security regime, and a conflict-ridden region. Which of these scenarios is most likely to eventuate in the years to come?

One fundamental change that has been discussed is that we have been witnessing a surge of non-hostile bilateralism among the major powers in the region. Will this lead to a more stable power structure among the major powers based upon the principle of multilateralism? Or rather, will this lead to a more 'concerted' bilateralism, while retaining the unique characteristics of the respective bilateralisms intact, but with gradually developing common codes of conduct, norms and rules among themselves through bilateral dealings?

An effective mechanism has to have the following features at least: (1) reliance on multilateral consultations among the major powers to manage critical situations, (2) a commitment to protect all essential members, and (3) a mutual recognition that all the major powers must have equal status and that none should be humiliated. For a stable regional order to be established, the region has to develop its own mechanism to regulate strategic interactions among the major powers. The region has to develop a mechanism that is flexible enough to allow the major powers to adjust their relationships in accordance with changing situations. The mechanism also has to be resilient enough for the major powers to jointly engage in such activities as tension reduction and conflict management. It must simultaneously engage and deter a potential hegemonic power.

Given the different perceptions among the major powers in terms of political and economic values and the future shape of the regional and global order, it is highly unlikely that the major powers will succeed in establishing a multilateral mechanism for mutual constraint and consultation through which they may regulate their strategic interactions based upon commonly acceptable norms, principles and codes of conduct. In the foreseeable future it should be very difficult for them to develop such multilateral mechanisms as 'balance of powers' or 'concert of powers' that could be flexible enough to adjust the changing power relations among themselves and that would be resilient enough to allow them to deal jointly with tensions and conflicts that may emerge in the region. Rather, we should take a more multifaceted 'nested' approach to regional order making.

More probably, in the foreseeable future, Northeast Asia will only succeed in creating security regimes in the context of a supportive transregional international environment.[22] The establishment of APEC, ARF, and KEDO reflects this process. Therefore the first task will be to develop bilateralism at an even pace, then to combine the respective bilateral relationships with each other and to forge a loose mechanism of mutual restraints and cooperation. Furthermore, it is important for bilateralism to be nested into broader regional and global cooperative frameworks.

On the one hand, multifaceted non-competitive bilateralisms, if they develop at an even pace, will promote a more regulated form of strategic interactions among the major powers. 'Concerted bilateralism,'[23] if successful, will greatly contribute to putting mutual restraints on the powers not to engage in deviant behavior that is against the vital interests of the others, and should in turn lead to mutually coordinated cooperative actions.

At the same time, given the existing institutional arrangements to deal with politico-security and economic issues dealt with under bodies such as APEC, ARF, KEDO and so forth, we could point out that if Northeast Asia is to build a successful regional regime, it will only be able to do so in the context of a supportive transregional international environment.[24]

Transregional institutions, on the other hand, will make a contribution to developing regionally acceptable rules and norms, codes of conduct, rules for decision-making and so forth, which will collectively put constraints on the deviant behavior of members. Regional institutions can do this by providing mechanisms that fit the specific conditions relating to the issues concerned. Regional institutions may also serve to encourage cooperative actions among the countries by reducing transaction costs as well as the detrimental effects of mutual suspicion. In fact, despite their many limitations and defects, multilateral regional institutions are useful in terms of imposing greater political costs for non-participation and non-compliance on countries acting against the collectively-formulated rules and norms. These transregional institutions and economic relations, however shallow and weak they may be, do tend to represent a willingness on the parts of states in the region to begin talks on a regular basis, in terms of their regional security and economic relations. Such global mechanisms as the UN, NPT, WTO, and IMF will also serve as an additional form of transregional organizations that may provide a mechanism to put institutional constraints on states' behavior and to help states learn regionally and internationally recognized norms and rules of conduct.

The sum total of such multilayered nested regimes (based upon domestic changes, bilateralism, minilateralism, regionalism and global multilateralism) will forge a governance structure that may collectively regulate strategic interactions among the nations concerned. Such regimes may also become engines for further cooperation and give rise to the expectation that states will act with restraint when disputes occur.[25]

In summary, the following conditions should be noted in terms of forging a stable regional governance structure in Asia in general and Northeast Asia in particular.

(a) Emerging bilateralism among the major powers (the USA, Japan, China and Russia) has to be enhanced, thereby forging regulated patterns of interactions which will contribute to the emergence of what we may call (loose) 'concerted bilateralism'.[26]

(b) Given the differences in basic values among the major powers, it is not expected that the various bilateralisms will develop into a tightly structured 'concert of powers' mechanism that may regulate their respective interactions and put mutual binding constraints on them against deviant behavior. Thus, bilateralism should be supplemented by and nested into broader sub-regional and transregional politico-security and economic regimes.

(c) Given the differences in basic values, mutual distrust among the countries in Northeast Asia and the disagreement on the territorial status quo, transregional supportive arrangements to forge regional cooperative mechanisms are an essential element. That is, regionalism in Northeast Asia will be forged, by nesting it into the existing broader transregional (and global) regimes. Transregional regimes will provide common norms and rules around which regionalism is forged, without causing serious political tensions among the countries concerned.

(d) Regional regimes, on the other hand, could make a great contribution to 'injecting' global and transregional rules, practices and norms into the region by successfully establishing regional mechanisms that could respond to the specific situations of the regional issues concerned. APEC, ARF and KEDO are few among these regional regimes. APEC has contributed to 'injecting' the global rules and norms into the Asia–Pacific by providing various instruments such as the provision of economic and technical assistance to the countries in the region. (The global regimes such as the GATT/WTO cannot provide such assistance.) KEDO includes a mechanism to provide light-water nuclear reactors and heavy-oil to North Korea as a 'compensation' for the suspension of developing their previous nuclear program. (Global regimes such as NPT/IAEA do not have any instrument to provide energy to North Korea and, therefore, could not solve the crisis that was caused by the North Korean nuclear program.) While the ARF has concentrated its efforts on encouraging the member countries.

(e) A lack of official linkages will have to be supplemented by informal second track and business linkages. The establishment of informal dialogue channels and business links should serve as useful instruments to establish a habit of dialogue and to strengthen liberal (internationalist) coalitions in the respective countries that may be seeking to cultivate closer economic relations with outside countries (therefore seeking a more peaceful regional environment).

(f) Thus, one way in which to establish sub-regional regimes would be to nest the regional relationships into the existing regional and global regimes. Northeast Asia can then develop various regulatory regimes by using the existing regimes. Transregional regimes can be seen to play supportive roles to promote sub-regional cooperation.

(g) Transregional institutions such as ARF, APEC, NPT/IAEA and GATT/WTO could play an important role not only in introducing mutually binding rules but also in developing a habit of dialogue, norms and principles for state behavior. Furthermore, there is a role for them in ameliorating mutual suspicion and security dilemmas as well as in providing a (sub)regional shield to protect the region and to win the global economic competition.

(h) Liberal internationalist coalitions (coalitions comprised of firms, business organizations, government agencies and intellectuals), which place a high priority on strengthening economic ties with the outside world, are emerging in various parts of Northeast Asia. Their political influence is constantly increasing in domestic politics. They play an important role in promoting cooperative foreign policies, because a peaceful environment is essential to maintaining economic linkages with the outside world. It would not be too far-fetched to imagine that these coalitions may become linchpins to prevent relations with the neighbours from further deteriorating.

(i) The changing roles and functions of states ('Competition State') in this age of a more globalized economy have strengthened the political foundation of liberal internationalist coalitions, and in turn these coalitions have been playing a key role in facilitating economic growth through promoting and enhancing relations with the outside.

Notes

1 See, for example, Paul Dibb, David D. Hale and Peter Prince, 'The Strategic Implications of Asia's Economic Crisis', *Survival*, Vol. 40, No. 2 (Summer 1998), pp. 5–26; Barry Buzan and Gerald Segal, 'Rethinking East Asian Security,' *Survival*, Vol. 36, No. 2, pp. 3–21.

2 Thus, it is no coincidence that the most elaborate examples of regionalism (the EC, NAFTA, ASEAN, Mercosur) have occurred in regions where state structures remain relatively strong and where the legitimacy of both frontiers and regimes is not widely called into question (although territorial disputes might continue to exist). In this context, regionalism and state strength do not stand in opposition to each other. States remain the essential building blocks with which regionalist arrangements are constructed. As ASEAN demonstrates, regional cooperation will contribute to strengthening (not weakening) the national resilience of the member countries.

3 Andrew Hurrell, 'Regionalism in Theoretical Perspective', in Louise Fawcett and Andrew Hurrell, eds, *Regionalism in World Politics* (Oxford University Press, 1996), pp. 67–68.

4 Arguments for creating a level playing field are troublesome. International trade takes place precisely because of differences among nations. In a fundamental sense, cross-border trade is valuable because the playing field is not level. Miles Kahler, *International Institutions and the Political Economy of Integration* (Washington, The Brookings Institution, 1995), p. xvii.

5 See Robert B. Reich, *The Work of Nations* (New York: Vintage Books, 1992).

6 See Susan Strange's various pioneering works, including 'States, Firms and Diplomacy', *International Affairs*, Vol. 68, No. 1 (January 1992), pp. 2–16. Also see *The Retreat of State: The Diffusion of Power in the World Economy* (Cambridge: Cambridge University Press, 1996).

7 The theory points out that, in an uncertain and anarchic international system, mistrust between two or more adversaries can lead each side to take precautionary and defensively motivated measures that are perceived as offensive threats by others. This can lead to countermeasures by the other sides, thereby escalating regional tensions, reducing security, and creating self-fulfilling prophecies about the danger of one's security environment. Robert Jervis, *Perception and Misperception in International Politics* (Princeton UP, 1976), ch.3.

8 I owe this part to Thomas J. Christensen, 'China, the US-Japan Alliance, and the Security Dilemma in East Asia,' *International Security*, Vol. 23, No. 2 (Spring 1999), pp. 49–80.

9 Christensen, *ibid.*

10 Barry Buzan, *People, States, and Fear: An Agenda for International Security Studies in the Post-Cold War Era*, 2nd ed. (Boulder: Lynne Rienner, 1991). See also various articles included in David A. Lake and Patrick Morgan, eds, *Regional Orders: Building Security in a New World* (PA: Pennsylvania University Press, 1998).

11 On the concept of 'competition state,' refer to Philip G. Cerny, 'Paradoxes of Competition State: The Dynamics of Political Globalization,' *Government and Opposition*, Vol. 32, No. 2, 1997, pp. 251–274.

12 R. Palan and J. Abbott, *State Strategies in Global Political Economy* (London: Pinter, 1999), chapter 3.

13 On political and economic factors behind contemporary regionalism, see Andrew Hurrel and Louise Fawcett, eds, *Regionalism in World Politics* (New York: Oxford University Press, 1995); Edward Mansfield and Helen Milner, eds, *The Political Economy of Regionalism* (New York: Columbia University Press, 1997).

14 In fact, this is an important function of ASEAN.

15 As was shown in such cases as ASEAN, regional organizations deliberately encouraged their members to imagine themselves in a new social space bound by some common characteristics. Regional institutions can be a site of identity and interest formation. To begin, organizations are just talk shops. However, increasingly they rely upon face-to-face encounters like 'seminar diplomacy' to instill in the participants a sense of common purpose. It is easy to dismiss these forums as talk and little else. However, many experiences in various parts of the world provide compelling evidence that from such dialogues come new self-understandings.

16 The way interactions and institutions affect the processes of mutual cooperation and identity formations also hints to the role that learning and knowledge-sharing play in these processes. In fact, the ASEAN case demonstrates that learning and knowledge-sharing may help create a common identity and interests. The rapprochement between Brazil and Argentina in the 1990s also demonstrates the importance of the learning process in the sense that both countries came to recognize the importance of regional economic liberalization and cooperation for their well-being and security.

17 Taking one example, the annual conference of Northeast Asian economic cooperation (which is held in Niigata, Japan) has been strongly pushed by local and central governments, with the participation (from both the official and private sectors) of the neighboring countries, including Russia, China, Mongolia, and North and South Korea.

18 Yoshinobu Yamamoto, 'Security Cooperation in Northeast Asia,' paper presented to the *12th Asia Pacific Roundtable*, May 31–June 4 1998, Kuala Lumpur.

19 For a more comprehensive analysis of the bilateral relationships between the major powers, see Yoshinobu Yamamoto, 'Quadruple Relations and Japan' paper presented at the conference 'Russia and Asia' co-organized by JIIA and SIPRI, February 20–21, 1999 in Tokyo, Japan.

20 First of all, a bilateral FTA will provide an overall framework for the two countries to consult each other on various bilateral economic issues such as industrial coordination and dispute settlements as well as regional and global issues such as APEC and GATT/WTO. A bilateral FTA will place bilateral economic transactions on a more stable political foundation. This will also make a great contribution to peace and prosperity in Northeast Asia. Closer economic integration underlined by a FTA between Japan and Korea will create more stable economic circumstances, especially for Korea, without being affected by the fluctuation of the yen-dollar exchange rate. If further economic integration takes place between the two countries, Korea will participate in the production network led by Japanese multinational corporations and find better market penetration worldwide (especially in East Asia). For example, Korea's overseas business in the region will be backed by Japan's financial support. Korean exports to ASEAN will also be covered by Japan's trade credit with ASEAN. A free trade agreement with Korea will also provide Japan, which has been suffering economic difficulties and facing a sudden collapse of its business network extending to other parts of Asia, with new business opportunities. Japan can have easy access to capable and highly skilled workers in Korea. If both economies fail to tackle deeper integration issues, already troubled Korean industries such as the petrochemical, semiconductor, and liquid crystal industries will face an over-capacity problem and a deflationary spiral, thereby further delaying economic recovery. Both governments have already agreed to explore the possibility of concluding a bilateral FTA and commissioned a joint research project to be carried out by research institutes of both countries. If this idea is received positively by the Korean side, the momentum for further integration will be created. The internationalization of the Japanese currency (yen) will further promote the integration process.

21 It should be noted that worldwide only the Northeast Asia economies are not members of any formal regional economic integration arrangements. This weakens their respective positions in an era of 'inter-regional economic diplomacy' as well as in multilateral forums such as APEC and GATT/WTO.

22 Barry Buzan, 'International Security in East Asia in the 21st Century: Options for Japan', *Dokkyo International Review*, Vol. 9, 1996, pp. 281–314.

23 I came to know the term 'concerted bilateralism' in my communications with Professor Brian Job of the University of British Columbia, Canada. I express my sincere thanks to Brian.

24 In one sense, this is simply another way of pointing out that the necessary condition for this scenario is that the US must stay engaged in Northeast Asia (and East Asia as a whole). In fact, most of these organizations can be seen as designed primarily to help bind the US to Northeast Asia by creating an Asia–Pacific super-region.

25 Today, the US, Japan and China each have enough economic power to destabilize the global economy. Put differently, there has been informally established an economic relationship similar to that symbolized in MAD (Mutually Assured Destruction) among the US, Japan and China in the Asia–Pacific region. Each has the economic capability to 'destroy' the others. Economic 'MAD' has to be stabilized through intensive dialogues and developing mechanisms to regulate interactions. However, although various frameworks for policy coordination such as G5/G7 have been developed among the Western developed countries, China has not yet become fully involved in intensive dialogues for policy coordination with the Western developed economies. That is, no framework for policy dialogues to stabilize 'Economic MAD' has been developed so far.

26 On theoretical arguments of 'nesting', see Vind Aggarwal, *Liberal Protectionism: The International Politics of Organized Textile Trade* (Berkeley: University of California Press, 1995); Vinod Aggarwal and Charles Morrison, eds, *Asia–Pacific Crossroads: Regime Creation and the Future of APEC* (New York: St. Martin, 1998).

7 Northeast Asia

Developmental political economy and the prospects for regional economic integration

Christopher M. Dent

Introduction

Northeast Asia remains the only major region in the world not to have embarked on a regional economic integration (REI) project. Various political, economic and historical factors are usually attributed to this, including salient nationalism, territorial disputation, inter-civilizational tensions, contesting regional hegemony and low intra-regional economic exchange. However, recent linked changes in the domestic political economies of Northeast Asian states, especially since the 1997–98 financial crisis, should provide greater conductivity towards new regionalist initiatives. In exploring the prospects for REI in Northeast Asia, this chapter makes a number of propositions.

First, for any substantive REI arrangement or project to be viable in Northeast Asia, membership should be, at least currently, restricted to Japan, South Korea, Taiwan and China (including Hong Kong SAR). Only on these economies in geographic Northeast Asia can a robust inter-state REI arrangement work (Table 7.1). Significant economic and political impediments make both the Russian Far East (RFE) and North Korea's participation extremely problematic.[1] Second, the political economies of Japan, China, South Korea and Taiwan possess strong developmental characteristics, inferring that their respective national economic development has in various guises been strategised by the state as understood in a Gerschenkronian 'late industrialisation' sense. It is further proposed that to talk of their developmental political economies captures the embedded nature of the 'domestic' in both its historic and international contexts. To elaborate further, the contemporary economic development of the Northeast Asian four has been both spurred and shaped by the perceived necessity to catch-up with the advanced industrial nations of the West. In Northeast Asia, state economic policy and economic society have to varying degrees been honed towards achieving this end. However, the pressures of globalisation and neo-liberal advocacy have brought new developmental challenges to Northeast Asia, particularly with respect to managing economic 'openness'.

The above last point links to the third proposition, namely that recent changes in the developmental political economies of Northeast Asian states have predisposed them to new regionalist possibilities. For Japan, South Korea and

Table 7.1 Northeast Asian economies: Comparative profile (1997)

	Population (m)	GDP ($bn)	GDP per capita ($)	Ave. ann. growth in real GDP 1990–97 (%)	Trade as % of GDP	Trade balance ($bn)	Origins of GDP (agri)	industry	services	Ave. ann. rates (1990–97) of unemp.	inflation
Japan	126.0	4,812.1	38,160	1.5	10.5	+101.6	1.7	37.1	61.2	2.7	1.2
China	1,244.2	1,055.4	860	11.2	22.7	+46.2	18.7	49.2	32.1	2.7	9.2
S. Korea	45.7	485.2	10,550	7.1	38.5	−3.2	5.7	42.9	51.4	2.3	6.0
Taiwan	21.7	283.4	13,060	6.7	48.1	+13.9	2.7	35.0	62.3	1.9	3.1
Hong Kong	6.5	163.8	25,200	5.3	131.8	−21.1	0.1	15.4	84.5	2.2	7.6

Source: Economist Intelligence Unit

Taiwan this particularly concerns the evolving nature of developmental statism and the shift from national to regional economic management. For China and to a lesser extent Taiwan, the compliance to WTO membership will make an important impact on domestic economic and political processes, integrating them into wider regional and international frameworks. It is proposed that these two broad developments will make the Northeast Asian group more conducive to regional economic integration in general. Fourth and lastly, the creation of a Northeast Asian Regional Economic Association (NEAREA) is proposed as a flexible yet purpose-driven REI arrangement for the region that could serve many important functions. These relate not only to helping Northeast Asian states come to common terms with the new developmental challenges later identified, but also to Northeast Asia's positive contributions it can make toward broader regional, transregional and multilateral economic orders.

Northeast Asia: a region without regionalism?

It may appear odd to many that a region of such geoeconomic importance which contains highly internationalised economies should be unique in not having established any REI arrangement in the contemporary period. There is no modern historical precedent of regional economic integration in Northeast Asia bar Japan's Greater East Asian Co-Prosperity Sphere, whereby the wider region was incorporated into a imperial division of labour during the 1930s and 1940s. For many decades if not centuries, inter-state suspicion and tension have prevailed in the region, and it is only since the Cold War thaw that relations between Northeast Asian states began to effectively normalise. While, then, the process of mutual trust-building is relatively young, promoting Northeast Asian regionalism is generally critical to the future stability and security of the region itself, and also to that of East Asia and possibly beyond.

To establish the extent to which Northeast Asia is a region without any manifest regionalism, we must first make the distinction between regional economic co-operation (REC) and regional economic integration (REI). The former typically refers to measures that link up infrastructures, improve the management of common resources and so on, while the latter normally refers to an institutionalised convergence or congruence of the economic policies (especially trade but also in other areas such as finance) of countries within the same regional location. Hence, REI can range from basic free trade agreements in selected industrial sectors to the comprehensive integration forged by economic and monetary union, as currently undertaken by the European Union (EU). It therefore follows that REC entails less political commitment to, and political 'community' with, regional neighbours than REI, and hence less of a compromise to national sovereignty.

Northeast Asian states began to experiment with REC initiatives from the early 1990s as part of normalising 'great power' (i.e. China, Russia, Japan) relations in the post-Cold War era.[2] In this transition from adversarial geopolitics to exploratory economic co-operation, the most important REC project to emerge has been the Tumen River Area Development Programme (TRADP), the main focus of which is large-scale transport and energy infrastructure projects. Indeed, this is the only existing inter-governmental endeavour aimed at specifically promoting regional economic development in Northeast Asia.[3] The Tumen River Area sub-regional zone specifically relates to the North Korea's Rajin-Sonbong Economic and Trade Zone, Eastern Mongolia, China's Yanbian Korean Autonomous Prefecture in the Jilin Province, the RFE's Primorsky Territory and South Korea, which provides key technical and financial support.[4] In terms of economic geography, this represents a small sub-regional territory construed primarily on the need to enhance *de facto*, business-driven integrational linkages. Moreover, the involvement of public policy officialdom draws mainly from sub-national political authorities, with most central government bodies remaining wary of such localised transnational developments that could potentially challenge their own national authority. Although transborder economic exchange within Tumen River area sub-region continues to intensify, the TRADP itself has experienced considerable difficulties in progressing towards its set objectives.[5] This is not least because of 1997–98 crisis-induced financial problems experienced by South Korea, the TRADP's main capital supplier.

The failure of albeit a somewhat problematic set of Northeast Asian participants to effectively develop REC initiatives appears to question the wisdom of proceeding with any REI project, as these generally carry more ambitious political and economic objectives. Moreover, promoting and developing both forms of economic regionalism in Northeast Asia face significant constraints. These principally concern:

- **Salient nationalism**: various forms of nationalistic sentiment remain strong in Northeast Asia, and any regionalist initiative that significantly compromises national sovereignty is likely to encounter considerable resistance at the domestic constituency level.[6]
- **Territorial disputation**: although the North–South Korea border remains the last Cold War frontier in the region, other inter-state tensions persist. A number of territorial disputes continue to impede the trust-building process between Northeast Asian states after decades of adversarial geopolitics. China–Taiwan relations pose a more specific challenge.
- **Inter-civilizational tensions**: there prevails a deep and historic mistrust at the civil level between the different peoples of Northeast Asia, with Japan–China–Korea rivalries especially long established. The hegemonic struggle between Japan and China has a deep history, and Korea's geographic position between these two regional giants is a continued source of perplexity.
- **Contesting hegemony**: as hinted above, Japan and China have long remained uneasy regional bedfellows. Progress made in Northeast Asian regionalism largely depends on resolving the regional hegemonic question between the two great powers.

- *Underdeveloped intra-regional economic exchange*: a rising trend in Northeast Asian intra-regional economic exchange is evident (Table 7.2). However, current levels of mutual trade and FDI may still not convince the region's states that a critical economic interdependence between them exists, and hence the need to co-manage it via regional-level mechanisms. This particularly applies to Japan, whose relatively much lower intra-regional trade coefficient reflects the wider internationalisation of Japanese corporate activities.

The above point to a limited basis on which a Northeast Asian regional consciousness or regional community-building could be developed. In addition, there has been a historic lack of externalised pressures upon Northeast Asian states to form a distinct regional grouping. This, of course, contrasts with the contemporary experience of Southeast Asia, where the creation of the Association of Southeast Asian Nations (ASEAN) in 1967 was principally intended as a capitalist bulwark against the advance of communism in the region. However, all Northeast Asian states with the exception of North Korea and Mongolia currently participate in the Asia–Pacific Economic Co-operation (APEC) forum, which (as other chapters have detailed) consists of a trans-Pacific arrangement aimed at enhancing economic co-operation and integration between its 21 member economies.

Indeed, Northeast Asia's engagement in transregional initiatives can be traced back to APEC's antecedents. As Chapter 6 discusses, Japan's contribution to the intellectual and practical development of Asia–Pacific regionalism is notable. The notion of a Pacific Free Trade Area (PAFTA) was first proposed at the Japan Economic Research Centre's (JERC) first international conference in November 1965 by a paper presented by two leading Japanese economists, Kiyoshi Kojima and Hiroshi Kurimoto.[7] Although PAFTA never transpired, Japan provided the impetus for two other key regional initiatives during the late 1960s, namely the Pacific Basin Economic Council (PBEC) and the Pacific Trade and Development (PAFTAD) conferences. The former was an extension of an original Japan–Australia private sector forum which came to include the US, New Zealand and Canada, and whose aim was to enhance commercial co-operation across the Asia–Pacific. The latter was devised as a parallel forum for academic debate on regional economic co-operation. Japan was also a major driving force behind the development of the Pacific Economic Co-operation Conferences (PECC) which was established by another Japan–Australia initiative in 1978. However, it generally failed in its aim to promote economic co-operation across its expanding transregional membership[8] during the 1980s. In part, APEC was conceived out of PECC's frustrations and failures as a new route to hopefully more substantive outcomes. Japan and South Korea were the only Northeast Asian participants in attendance at APEC's inaugural ministerial meeting held at Canberra in November 1989,[9] with China, Taiwan and Hong Kong joining two years later in 1991.

Table 7.2 Northeast Asia: Trends in intra-regional trade (1960–1998)

	1960		1970		1980		1990		1997		1998	
	EAsia	NEA-5	EAsia	NEA-5	EAsia	NEA-5	EAsia	NEA-5	EAsia	NEA-5	EAsia	NEA-5
Japan	22.2	5.7	20.8	9.5	22.7	10.5	28.6	16.6	38.1	22.9	34.3	21.6
China	11.5	6.0	42.6	41.9	47.2	40.7	58.6	47.0	55.5	47.8	53.8	44.8
S. Korea	33.3	28.0	43.1	40.1	31.1	25.6	35.0	28.9	43.7	30.6	39.5	32.3
Taiwan	53.7	43.0	45.6	36.3	35.4*	27.7*	42.9	33.4	48.2	37.1	47.6	36.2
Hong Kong	43.2	27.9	36.3	29.0	38.8	32.6	59.3	51.7	62.3	54.8	64.0	54.6
Total	**8.9**	**9.9**	**11.3**	**16.5**	**13.9**	**17.8**	**21.7**	**28.9**	**26.5**	**36.0**	**25.8**	**35.6**

Source: IMF Direction of Trade Statistics, various editions
Note: * 1978 data

The Northeast Asian states' involvement in the APEC process is revealing as it has demonstrated many of the reasons why a separate Northeast Asian regional grouping has not emerged. From a geo-strategic perspective, both Japan and China see APEC as a means to neutralise the regional hegemonic ambitions of the other. The mutual participation in a regime that encompasses the US and a wide transregional membership negates the ability of either power to achieve superiority, as may transpire in a distinct Northeast Asian or even East Asian grouping.[10] Most Northeast Asian states have also been wary of APEC's trade liberalisation programme, preferring instead to promote its original regime objectives of trade facilitation and economic and technical co-operation, or ecotech (Ravenhill 2000).[11] This programme, which aims to create a free trade and investment zone across the Asia–Pacific by phased 2010 and 2020 deadlines, had became the centrepiece of APEC from 1993 onwards.[12] Its main advocates comprise APEC's 'Anglo-Saxon' members (i.e. US, Canada, Australia and New Zealand) yet many Asian members remain suspicious of a hidden agenda, this being the former using APEC trade liberalisation to resolve its trade deficit problems with the latter.[13]

Japan has never shown real interest in utilising APEC as a forum for trade liberalisation, preferring instead recourse to WTO channels.[14] Meanwhile, both China and Taiwan's recent trade liberalisation owes more to the implementation of concession and compliance measures required by their respective WTO accessions rather than APEC-inspired 'concerted unilateral liberalisation', the principle by which APEC members are to meet the regime's liberalisation objectives.[15] Furthermore, recent trade liberalisation in South Korea can be primarily attributed to IMF-induced structural reforms undertaken in the wake of its 1997–98 economic crisis. Northeast Asian states were also at the centre of APEC's 1998 debacle over its Early Voluntary Sectoral Liberalisation (EVSL) scheme, where Japan in particular resisted Anglo-Saxon members' pressure to extend liberalisation into forestry and marine product sectors. Unable to resolve the dispute at APEC's 1998 Kuala Lumpur summit, its members were compelled to transfer the issue to WTO arbitration.

Similar future conflicts within APEC may become increasingly regularised as members leave the tricky task of liberalising 'sensitive' sector trade till last before the 2010/2020 deadlines. Japan especially has proved reluctant to liberalise its trade regime in 'sensitive' industry sectors beyond its Uruguay Round commitments. China can be expected to focus more on complying to the WTO's 'transition schedule' of implementing trade liberalisation measures up to the mid-2000s rather than draw inspiration from APEC-driven processes, although the former may serve the latter if only by circumstance. Taiwan's own WTO 'transition schedule' is far less onerous than China's and therefore requires less attention. However, given the political importance of securing WTO membership, Taipei is likely to concentrate its resources of economic diplomacy towards this new multilateral channel rather than any regional counterpart. South Korea, which shares a similar tradition of economic nationalism with Japan, may also be anticipated to resist moves to liberalise trade in 'sensitive' sectors such as agriculture and heavy industry.

As REI arrangements usually begin with some form of free or preferential trade agreement, Northeast Asia's experience with APEC's trade liberalisation agenda may seem to provide little hope any forthcoming REI initiatives. Northeast Asian states participation in other regional economic fora are also revealing. Within the Asia-Europe Meeting (ASEM) framework – established with the EU in 1996 – Japan, China, South Korea and ASEAN states are engaged in a process of enhancing trade facilitation and not brokering trade liberalisation deals.[16] At recent 'ASEAN Plus' summits, the same Northeast Asia three have joined Southeast Asian states in post-crisis explorations to improve capacities of regional economic governance. However, this has concentrated almost exclusively on matters of finance rather than trade, an issue deserving of some concern.

To summarise this section, we have noted that Northeast Asia remains the only major economic region not to have embarked on its own REI project, and even attempts at developing sub-regional economic co-operation has proven problematic, as demonstrated by the Tumen River Area Development Programme. Where Northeast Asian states have participated in wider regional and transregional economic fora, such as APEC, ASEM and the new 'ASEAN Plus' summits, they have demonstrated a general preference for lower key regional collaboration and concession, e.g. trade facilitation over trade liberalisation. Yet recent changes in the political economies of Northeast Asian states could make them more conducive to future regionalist proposals, as we shall now discuss.

Developmental political economies in transition

In the contemporary era, the interface between the domestic and international has become increasingly important. Globalising forces continue to break down national boundaries between states and create new transnational phenomena. Consequently, the domestic political economies of Northeast Asian states are caught in a two-way causality of adaptation and change, being shaped by external pressures but with internal factors simultaneously influencing the foreign economic policies of each state. As argued in the introduction, the political economies of Japan, China, South Korea and Taiwan possess strong developmental characteristics which have recently undergone a process of considerable change, and much can be understood in the above context. The once relatively 'closed' economies of Northeast Asia have increasingly had to open themselves up to meet the challenges posed by globalisation.

Two branches of developmental political economy are considered here. One of these concerns the developmental statism of Japan, South Korea and Taiwan, and the other the developmental challenges that integrating into WTO membership poses to both China and Taiwan. In general terms, the rationale of developmental statism draws much from Gerschenkron's (1962) work on 'late industrialisation.' In his historical study on economic backwardness, Gerschenkron stressed the key developmental role of the state in mobilising the necessary resources to reduce the techno-industrial gap between 'late industrialisers' and the advanced industrial powers. Drawing mainly upon the experiences of nineteenth-century continental Europe and the early twentieth-century Soviet Union, Gerschenkron demonstrated the importance of the state's industrial and mercantile policies in gradually strengthening an initially weak domestic business sector in the pursuit of techno-industrial catch up. Gerschenkron's typology also strongly suggested that the market will eventually supersede the role of the state as industrialisation proceeds, a consequence being that mercantilism will gradually give way to liberalism. This was due to the domestic business sector gradually weaning itself from the state as a result of its evolving independent strength. The eventually redundant developmental role of the state in Gerschenkron's thesis is resonant for twenty-first century studies of late industrialisation as it predicts that the developmental state is essentially a 'transitional phenomenon'.[17]

The origins of developmental statism in Japan date back to the Meiji restoration of the 1860s, when the country's vulnerability to the expansionary commercial ambitions of Western industrial powers first became apparent. Japan's more robust developmental state framework implemented after the Second World War became the paradigm emulated by other aspiring East Asian industrialisers, most notably South Korea and Taiwan. The expansion and upgrading of export-based industrial capacity has been central to the transformative projects of Northeast Asia's developmental states, and owed much to the pursuit of neo-mercantilist policies. Strategic trade policies form the 'promotive' aspect of neo-mercantilism, whereby the state provides a raft of competitiveness-enhancing measures, e.g. export subsidies, R&D grants, infrastructural support for new technology development. Meanwhile, neo-mercantilism's 'protectionist' aspect insulated domestic producers from injurious foreign competition, especially where it may compromise export capacity in new technology sectors.

Developmental statism is buttressed by economic nationalism, which is often propagated by the state to create popular support for its neo-mercantilist policies. Economic nationalism can be generally defined as the proclivity of the state, firms and individuals for economic actions, decisions or alliance-formation that seek to advance the nation's international position at the potential expense of foreign national or international interests.[18] Hence, it forms part of neo-mercantilist ideology whereby import restriction and export promotion policies are prescribed with the aim of increasing a nation-state's power and security within the international economic system. In Northeast Asia, economic nationalism is particularly strong in Japan and South Korea. For example, in both of these countries a consumer preference for foreign products over their domestic counterparts is generally considered disloyal to the national developmental cause. In the past, Japanese and Koreans have also traditionally preferred to work for home companies rather than foreign inward investor firms for similar reasons.

The interwoven combination of state-strategised national economic development, neo-mercantilist policies and economic nationalism in Northeast Asia's developmental statism created relatively closed economies. However, developmental states like all others had to adapt to new realities, and in particular the twin imperatives of globalisation and neo-liberal advocacy. Partly in response to the broad paradigm shift in the West to 'new right' ideology and policy, as embodied by Thatcherism and Reagonomics, Northeast Asian states began to liberalise their commercial regimes (i.e. trade, foreign investment, finance) from the early 1980s onwards. Subsequently, the sources of neo-liberal advocacy strengthened both domestically and externally with the effect of eroding the basis of developmental statism.

Domestic sources of neo-liberal advocacy derive from two main factors. The first of these relate to what Woo-Cumings (1991) refers to as 'ideological osmosis', whereby the domination of Japanese-trained technocrats in Northeast Asia's economic bureaucracies and policy think tanks, imbued with neo-mercantilist values, have been gradually replaced by US-trained economics graduates that are invariably inculcated with neo-liberal values. This process is most evident in South Korea, the Northeast Asian state to have moved furthest in recent years to embracing the neo-liberal paradigm, at least in terms of rhetorical politics.[19] The second concerns the democratisation process in which the emergence of a more pluralistic society and the polycentric distribution of power has undermined the authoritarian basis of the developmental state. This can be partly explained by the so called 'grave-digger' hypothesis of the developmental state, in which the state's nurturing of the business sector creates an increasingly empowered bourgeoisie that in turn seeks greater political power and a more liberal policy agenda. In both Taiwan and South Korea, the onset of democratisation from the late 1980s onwards saw the empowerment of their respective business sector's political influence over policy formation. While admittedly many constituents of the business community have pressured the state into maintaining protectionist barriers in certain sectors, as noted earlier regarding APEC-driven liberalisation, broader pressures have centred on liberalising policy regimes to enable greater freedom of business activity. In addition, democratisation has also to a lesser degree strengthened the political influence of Northeast Asian civil society, although this has often proved a counter-pressure to neo-liberalism as events during and since the WTO's 1999 Seattle Ministerial Meeting demonstrated.

External sources of neo-liberal advocacy have also softened the neo-mercantilist practices of Northeast Asian states. A deepening participation in international economic organisations (IEOs), such as the WTO, IMF, OECD and World Bank, has further conditioned them to neo-liberal norms and values – the implicit core ideological basis of these institutions. For example, concessions made by South Korea in order to enter the OECD and by Taiwan in its accession into WTO membership required both to liberalise their commercial regimes during the 1990s. Furthermore, greater engagement in IEOs has fortified the channels by which proponents of the so called 'Washington consensus' (especially the US) can assert their own neo-liberal advocacy.[20] The US's active utilisation of the WTO's disputes settlement mechanism and its influence in shaping the new trade agenda testify to this. Moreover globalising forces, as with democratisation at the domestic level, have provided additional compelling pressures upon Northeast Asia's developmental states to liberalise. This has particularly occurred in the finance sector where the region's governments have removed controls that hindered home firms' access to new global sources of capital. The growing engagement of these same firms in transnational business activity has further required the opening up of trade and FDI regimes in order to reduce the associated costs of such activity. In Taiwan, liberalism and internationalisation were the twin slogans of government used to push through its neo-liberal policy reforms from the early 1980s onwards. In the 1990s, the Korean Government deployed its *segyehwa* (globalisation) programme to achieve similar ends, whilst the Japanese Government's 'deregulation' programme has been the centrepiece of its economic diplomacy with both the US and EU for over a decade.

It is not suggested here that globalisation will bring eventual neo-liberal normalisation across the international system, or that increasing degrees of globalisation lead to corresponding diminishments of state power. As Evans (1997) and Weiss (1998, 2000) have contended, states may seek to harness globalising forces to suit its own policy objectives: in other words, 'globalisation is able to make of the state only what the state is able to make of globalisation'.[21] For example, the Singapore Government works in close collaboration with hosted foreign multinationals within the framework of the its competitiveness strategy. Furthermore, neo-mercantilism in Japan, Taiwan and South Korea is to some extent 'embedded', inferring that untangling it from the complex socio-cultural and institutional fabric of economic society will in certain instances prove extremely difficult.[22] The depth of economic nationalism in Japan and South Korea is a case in point, as is the 'export or die' mentality of many Northeast Asian foreign economic policy-makers.

Notwithstanding an apparent resilience of the Northeast Asian developmental state in the global era, recent events and developments surrounding the 1997–1998 East Asian financial crisis lent new force to both domestic and external sources of neo-liberal advocacy. This was especially manifest in South Korea, the region's most crisis-bound economy in over 1997–1998. The country's own neo-liberal constituency gained the upper hand by laying the blame for the crisis on the technocratic managers of the developmental state. South Korea's new President Kim Dae-jung, who was inaugurated at the height of the crisis, intended to introduce sweeping economic, political and social reforms under the slogan of 'market democratisation'. Under the terms of the IMF 'bailout' programme, the Korean Government were compelled to significantly liberalise its commercial regimes, including the termination of its euphemistically phrased 'Import Diversification Programme' that was essentially a panoply of trade barriers specifically imposed on Japanese products.

Further similar changes in Northeast Asian trade and other commercial policies are required if REI is to make any progress in the region. The problem thus far has been that neo-mercantilists make awkward bedfellows. However,

Japan and Taiwan are also moving towards greater commercial openness in their own post-crisis search for a new developmental paradigm. Partly in response to persistent *gaiatsu* (foreign pressure), Japan has made sustained efforts to remove various non-tariff or 'structural' barriers that impede its import trade, and has proved an active supporter of the WTO. Taiwan, like China, accelerated the pace of its trade liberalisation as part of the WTO accession process, with both set to join the Organisation in early 2001 after concluding a lengthy and protracted series of bilateral negotiations with incumbent members. Of the four Northeast Asian economies, Taiwan has been arguably the most open and thus compliance to WTO norms and rules should not prove too difficult a challenge. Nevertheless, the Taiwanese developmental political economy is yet to be tested by the rigours that accompany full multilateral trade citizenship. The potential domestic backlash from having to phase out protectionist insulation in key sectors such as autos, services, alcohol and agriculture may be considerable, especially where its may pose a threat to Taiwan's somewhat precarious economic security.[23] Yet to most of Taiwan's domestic business and societal constituencies, the costs incurred by WTO membership are more than offset by the conferred economic and political benefits. It remains difficult to predict the extent to which WTO membership will lend political legitimacy to Taiwan's statehood. However, domestic support of WTO participation will remain strong whilst it provides more secure international market access for Taiwanese firms, a robust disputes settlement mechanism with major trade partners and a substantial expansion of Taiwan's 'international space'.

The impact on China's developmental political economy is expected to be even more profound. Whilst the vigorous capitalist development in its coastal regions continues unabated, the country's interior economy remains dominated by a lethargic state-owned enterprise (SOE) sector. Moreover, most of China's SOEs have long been protected by state-trading arrangements that are to be gradually dismantled in compliance to WTO rules. At a general level, WTO membership will force the pace of China's transition to a more open, market-based economy and thus have significant developmental consequences. These are likely to broaden given the potential for the WTO to extend multilateral norms into traditionally domestic policy realms, such as state aids, competition policy, environmental and labour standards. China's future integration into the multilateral trade order may well prove problematic for various reasons. Firstly, the strong nationalist sentiment in Chinese society could react adversely to WTO rulings and agenda-setting perceived as 'foreign meddling', and China is likely to champion the developing country cause against developed country advocacy of 'new' trade issues (e.g. labour standards) on the WTO agenda. Secondly, the albeit gradual dismantling of protectionist barriers could generate mass unemployment in China's interior provinces, thus testing both the structural flexibility of the economy and the patience of domestic economic constituencies. Thirdly, key sectors of the Chinese economy (e.g. low-tech manufactures, fuels, telecoms) are to be liberalised in accordance to the demands of incumbent WTO members. The subsequent impact on China's enterprise managers and workers will hence be considerable, making the WTO a byword for globalisation in the more insulated corners of Chinese economic society. But like Taiwan, China will also value highly the economic benefits from WTO membership (e.g. international market access, dispute settlement), especially after having being victim itself to extensive protectionism from its major trading partners, for instance in the form of anti-dumping duties.

How, though, will the above changes to Northeast Asia's developmental political economies affect their disposition to regional economic integration? The growing economic openness evident in Japan, China, South Korea and Taiwan does suggest a possible conductivity towards new regional trade arrangements. The progressive softening of neo-mercantilism and the firmer embrace of globalisation by the millennial eve has certainly prepared their respective economic societies for a more comprehensive integration into the international economic system. New proposals for Northeast or East Asian regional economic integration could be promoted as a parallel and complementary process to this. Indeed, it could prove a more palatable route to economic openness by circumscribing the perceived excesses of external neo-liberal advocacy, e.g. bilateral pressure from the US. In the section that follows, the notion of a Northeast Asian Regional Economic Association is explored as a potentially viable regionalist response to light of preceding discussions.

Towards a Northeast Asia regional economic association?

It has been acknowledged that significant constraints face Northeast Asian REI, yet its promotion would offer Japan, China, South Korea and Taiwan the opportunity to meet the new developmental challenges previously identified. The positive spillover effects outside the region could also be substantial for reasons discussed below. Like all proto-regional groupings, Northeast Asia would need to start with a relatively flexible arrangement with the capability of adapting to new developments in the regional and global political economy. The value of forming a Northeast Asian economic grouping may already be fermenting in the minds of key stakeholders. As noted earlier, Japan, China and South Korea have meet with ASEAN as a quasi-collective in recent 'ASEAN Plus' summits, and to a lesser extent in the ASEM framework. Admittedly, there exists the dilemma of Taiwan's full representation in such a small sub-group where close interaction with mainland Chinese officials is unavoidable. However, this has been managed within APEC since 1991 with Taiwan adopting a China-user friendly designation (e.g. 'Chinese Taipei'), and moreover they are now fellow WTO members which will bring more regularised economic diplomacy contact.

As footnoted earlier, a Northeast Asian Economic Forum (NEAEF) already exists but this is more sub-regionally and sub-nationally focused on the TRADP, hence omitting Taiwan altogether whilst including North Korea, Mongolia and the RFE. It is proposed here that a new alternative – the Northeast Asian Regional Economic Association (NEAREA) – could be created that incorporates up to national level representation and which provides a viable institutional basis for developing a more substantive Northeast Asian economic regionalism. Like APEC and the WTO, NEAREA would be overtly economic in nature, therefore negating nationhood as a prerequisite of membership and hence permitting Taiwan greater latitude to defend its rights of participation. As a fellow 'economic state', Hong Kong SAR could also join on a separate basis to mainland China if deemed beneficial. In addition, North Korea, the RFE and Mongolia could acquire a lower level affiliation if so desired with the possibility of the TRADP and other sub-regional economic initiatives placed under the broader NEAREA's umbrella.

Furthermore, like ASEAN the new NEAREA arrangement would be an association rather than a 'community' or 'union', thus avoiding any explicit or implicit future commitment to pool national sovereignty. In addition, the concentric circle trend in regionalism is becoming an important trend in the global political economy, as illustrated by ASEAN and its free trade area (AFTA) within the broader APEC framework. There is no reason in principle why NEAREA could not co-exist with ASEAN, or for that matter with NAFTA, in the APEC environment and make similar contributions towards creating a free trade and investment zone in the Asia Pacific. More specifically, NEAREA could serve various important functions, as proposed below:

A regional forum

For Northeast Asia's business community, civil society and economic policy-makers, discussing common issues relating to changes in the respective developmental political economies of Japan, China, South Korea and Taiwan. For the business community this may concern adjustment strategies in the context of domestic market opening and the impact of other neo-liberal reforms. In addition, business representatives could explore the opportunities for Northeast Asian intra-regional trade facilitation in joint discussion with economic policy-makers. Representations from an emerging Northeast Asian civil society also have much to discuss given post-Seattle developments and their new found empowerment, as well as the encroachment of social issues on trade policy agendas worldwide. Meanwhile, economic policy-makers would be preoccupied with exchanging views on how to manage the changes to the Northeast Asian developmental political economy outlined above. This tri-dimensional forum could also serve as a Northeast Asian collective entity that external representations may approach with a view to establishing a dialogue. Furthermore, its 'low politics' formula rather than one apexed by summitry helps avoid the 'high politics' predicament of Taiwan–China relations.

A regional consensus-builder

In which common positions in key regional and global economic issues may be reached within NEAREA and presented both domestically and externally. Together, the Northeast Asian states could command a potentially powerful voice in international affairs, and exploiting this potential may yield significant national benefits to each. By concentrating on economic affairs, and thus lowest common denominator issues, NEAREA could also make a significant contribution towards building inter-state trust in Northeast Asia, complementing endeavours made in security-based regional fora such as CSCAP and ARF. Consensus-building would not necessarily require summitry, with meetings convened between economic ministers from Japan, China, South Korea and Taiwan sufficing, albeit with a mandate and guidance supplied by premierial offices. This follows the early APEC model and again helps negate Taiwan–China problematics.

A supra-regime enhancer

Whereby a prime function of NEAREA is to strengthen the capacity of Northeast Asian states to realise 'higher' regime objectives. In this context, we are referring to economic regimes deemed above (i.e. supra) NEAREA itself in which Northeast Asian states already participate, most importantly the WTO and APEC. For example, NEAREA could galvanise the Northeast Asian contribution towards sectoral trade liberalisation, particularly in those sectors under WTO scrutiny, although for reasons stated earlier progress in 'sensitive' industry trade will prove difficult (see next section). It could also support other aspects of supra-regimes by providing the collectively focused means to enhance trade facilitation, economic and technical co-operation, investment promotion, the effective implementation of accords and other agreements, and the general compliance to supra-regime rules and norms. The motivations of Northeast Asian states for doing so based on two main factors. Firstly, to legitimise the formation of NEAREA and accrue its benefits, its members must demonstrate its regime-compatibility with the WTO and APEC in particular. More especially, REI arrangements must increasingly prove their congruity with the multilateral economic order. Secondly, NEAREA provides a vehicle to fortify the general Northeast Asian position *vis a vis* that of APEC's Anglo-Saxon members. Both NAFTA and AFTA proclaim their own supra-regime enhancement credentials, so why in principle should not a NEAREA arrangement, and moreover bestow the Northeast Asian states a firmer collective stake in shaping the APEC process. In more general terms, the NEAREA concentric circle could prove a useful sub-regional counterbalance in the APEC political economy. Moreover, with the expanding diversity of APEC membership may come the need for sub-grouping based on common economic-geographic factors, with these groups acting as sub-regional building blocks contributing to the greater regional whole.

A catalyst for regional free trade arrangements

In both Northeast Asia itself and the APEC zone, as hinted above. NEAREA could emulate Singapore which has recently pursued a strategy of building free trade coalitions between itself and other APEC members, including New Zealand

and Chile, the idea being of moving forward the APEC trade liberalisation process by brokering sub-group concessional agreements. Either collectively or partially, NEAREA may provide a useful link in such a chain, and both Japan and South Korea have already been approached by Singapore to join it own. However, establishing a separate Northeast Asian Free Trade Area has unpredictable spillover effects in the wider international system (e.g. trade diversion and a consequent 'third' country backlash), and could prove too ambitious a regionalist objective. Nevertheless, NEAREA could concentrate on establishing sectoral free trade agreements within its own core membership with other APEC or even WTO members given the option to participate. In accordance with its supra-regime enhancement function, NEAREA agreements would not want to distract from the WTO or APEC's work but rather progress it. Like other APEC members, Northeast Asian states have been signatories to recent WTO liberalisation accords on IT, telecoms, financial services and e-commerce trade. However, other sectors such as audio-visual products may be viable for NEAREA to explore as an initial experiment with region-based sectoral free trade with radial arrangements with other economies subsequently promoted. Admittedly, though, Northeast Asia's long standing preference for trade facilitation over trade liberalisation may narrow the options here.

A regional hub for financial co-operation and integration

As has already been debated in recent 'ASEAN Plus' summits. Northeast Asia possesses the world's top three foreign exchange reserve-holders (i.e. Japan, China and Taiwan) and maintains formidable financial strength. While the creation of a yen bloc remains problematic, Northeast Asia holds the key to cultivating regional monetary or financial co-operation in East Asia. At the November 1999 'ASEAN Plus' summit in Manila, Southeast and Northeast Asian members (Taiwan not invited) even considered the possibility of establishing a future unified regional market and common currency. However, the structural economic and political profile of East Asia makes these objectives rather utopian,[24] although Japan's Premier Obuchi's idea establishing a permanent East Asian financial and economic aid fund is viable and NEAREA could perform the inter-governmental mechanism required to provide the necessary substance from Northeast Asia. Japan has already undertaken various measures of financial support and co-operation aimed at assisting troubled East Asian economies through the New Miyazawa Initiative and Asian Development Bank, and could perform this role singularly.[25] As a demonstration of regional solidarity, other Northeast Asian states could also assist Japan's post-crisis endeavours to strengthen regional financial governance and support mechanisms in East Asia.

Of course, any Northeast Asian regionalist initiative that aspires to embrace Japan and China into a coalitional relationship must confront both significant domestic political barriers and external 'third country' circumspection. The US would prove particularly wary of any Sino-Japanese development that potentially compromised its strategic position in the Asia–Pacific both economically and politically. Yet the formation of a Northeast Asian sub-group may be more preferable to the US, EU and others than a larger consolidated East Asian bloc. Many observers are already predicting such an outcome in the next decade or so, especially if the recent 'ASEAN Plus' summits evolve into something more tangible. Moreover, American and other neo-liberal advocates may welcome a NEAREA-type arrangement if it accelerates the opening up of the once relatively hermetical Northeast Asian economies. For the Northeast Asian states, NEAREA could help them come to terms with the globalisation-liberalisation pressure nexus whilst satisfying foreign demands for their greater commercial openness. As previously stressed, this does not imply the demise of Northeast Asian developmentalism but rather its adaptation to new global, multilateral and post-crisis circumstances.

Notes

1 Given its relative underdevelopment and peripherality, the case for Mongolia's inclusion in such an arrangement is also tenuous.
2 G. Rozman, 'A Regional Approach to Northeast Asia', *Orbis*, Vol. 39, No. 1 (1995), pp. 65–80; Rozman, 'Northeast Asia: Regionalism, a Clash of Civilisations or Strategic Quadrangle?', *Asia–Pacific Review*, Vol. 5, No. 1 (1998), pp. 105–126; Rozman, 'Flawed Regionalism: Reconceptualising Northeast Asia in the 1990s', *The Pacific Review*, Vol. 11, No. 1 (1998), pp. 1–27.
3 The original idea for the TRADP arose through Northeast Asian Economic Forum (NEAEF) which has over time proposed other sub-regionalist initiatives, including a Northeast Asian development bank, a centralised database for firms on markets, finance and technology opportunities, and a regional energy consortium (Valencia 1999). However, most are yet to be initialised.
4 D. Aldrich, 'If You Build It, They Will Come: A Cautionary Tale About the Tumen River Projects', *Journal of East Asian Affairs*, Vol. 11, No. 1 (1997), pp. 299–326; L.J. Cho, 'Regional Economic Co-operation and Integration in Northeast Asia for the Twenty-First Century', paper presented at the Eighth Northeast Asian Economic Forum Conference, 28–30 July 1998, Yonago, Japan; A. Marton, T. McGee, and D.G. Paterson, 'Northeast Asian Economic Cooperation and the Tumen River Area Development Project', *Pacific Affairs*, Vol. 68, No. 1 (1995), pp. 9–33.
5 Aldrich, op. cit.
6 T. Akaha, ed., *Politics and Economics in Northeast Asia: Nationalism and Regionalism in Contention* (London: Macmillan, 1999).
7 JERC, 'Measures for Trade Expansion of Developing Countries', *Japan Economic Research Centre*, October 1996, pp. 93–134; P. Korhonen, *Japan and the Pacific Free Trade Area* (London: Routledge, 1994).
8 By the late 1980s, PECC members had come to comprise the current APEC membership plus the Pacific islands.
9 The ten other original members were the US, Canada, Australia, New Zealand and the ASEAN-6.
10 This largely explains the failure of Malaysian Prime Minister Mahathir's attempts to forge an East Asian Economic Caucus (EAEC) as a rival to APEC. However, the reluctance of Northeast Asian states to entertain such an idea also stems from not wanting to antagonise the US.
11 J. Ravenhill, 'APEC Adrift: Implications for Economic Regionalism in Asia and the Pacific', *The Pacific Review*, Vol. 13, No. 2 (2000), pp. 319–333.

12 The 2010 deadline is set for developed economy members and the 2020 deadline for APEC's developing countries. APEC's trade liberalisation programme originally derived from recommendations embodied within reports submitted by its Eminent Persons Group (EPG) during 1993–1995.

13 Japan and China being the most obvious targets here.

14 Y. Funabashi, *Asia Pacific Fusion: Japan's Role in APEC* (Washington, DC: Institute for International Economics, 1995); Y. Yakamoto, and T. Kikuchi, 'Japan's Approach to APEC and Regime Creation in the Asia–Pacific', in V.K. Aggarwal and C.E. Morrison, eds, *Asia–Pacific Crossroads: Regime Creation and the Future of APEC* (New York: St. Martin's Press, 1998); J. Ravenhill, 'APEC Adrift: Implications for Economic Regionalism in Asia and the Pacific', *The Pacific Review*, Vol. 13, No. 2 (2000), pp. 319–333.

15 Indeed, according to Ravenhill (2000), only New Zealand and the Philippines have liberalised substantially beyond Uruguay Round commitments as part of their own APEC Individual Action Plans.

16 A 2000 report submitted by the ASEM Vision Group, itself modelled on APEC's EPG, recommended that an Eurasian free trade area be created by 2025. However, the proposal met a cold response from both EU and most East Asian ministerial representatives.

17 C.I. Moon, 'Political Economy of East Asian Development and Pacific Economic Co-operation', *The Pacific Review*, Vol. 12, No. 2 (1999), pp. 199–224.

18 See Baughn and Yaprak (1996), Crane (1998) and LeviFaur (1997) for a wider discussion on economic nationalism.

19 Y.T. Kim, 'Neoliberalism and the Decline of the Developmental State', *Journal of Contemporary Asia*, Vol. 29, No. 4 (1999), pp. 441–461; C.I. Moon, and S.Y. Rhyu, 'The State, Structural Rigidity, and the End of Asian Capitalism: A Comparative Study of Japan and Korea', in R. Robison, M. Beeson, K. Jayasuriya and H.R. Kim, eds, *Politics and Markets in the Wake of the Asian Crisis* (London: Routledge, 2000).

20 In a much quoted comment, Bhagwati (1998: 11) made the observation that, 'Wall Street's financial firms have obvious self-interest in a world of free capital mobility since it only enlarges the arena in which to make money. It is not surprising therefore that Wall Street put its powerful oar into the turbulent waters of Washington political lobbying ... [Moreover] ... Wall Street has exceptional clout in Washington for the simple reason that there is a definite network of like minded luminaries among the powerful institutions – Wall Street, The Treasury Department, the State Department, the IMF and the World Bank. ... This powerful network ... is unable is unable to look much beyond the interest of Wall Street, which it equates with the good of the world. Thus the IMF has been relentlessly propelled toward embracing the goal of capital account convertibility'.

21 L. Weiss, *The Myth of the Powerless State: Governing the Economy in a Global Era* (London: Polity, 1998), p. 338.

22 C.M. Dent, 'What Difference a Crisis? Continuity and Change in South Korea's Foreign Economic Policy', *Journal of the Asia Pacific Economy*, Vol. 5, No. 3 (2000); C.I. Moon, and H. Yoo, 'Embedded Mercantilism and Regional Integration in East Asia', paper presented at the 17th World Congress, International Political Science Association, 1997. T.J. Pempel, 'Regime Shift: Japanese Politics in a Changing World Economy', *Journal of Japanese Studies*, Vol. 23, No. 2 (1997).

23 C. Lee, 'On Economic Security', in G. Wilson-Roberts, ed., *An Asia–Pacific Security Crisis?: New Challenges to Regional Stability* (Wellington, New Zealand: Centre for Strategic Studies, 1999).

24 This has not stopped the Japanese Institute for International Monetary Affairs, as well as Thai and Korean research organisations, conducting feasibility studies into Asian monetary union.

25 Moreover, Japan's motives for providing substantial financial support to other East
    Asian economies is partially driven by a broader strategy of internationalising the yen,
    The Economist, 12.02.2000; C.W. Hughes, 'Japanese Policy and the East Asian
    Currency Crisis: Abject Defeat or Quiet Victory?', *Review of International Political
    Economy*, Vol. 7, No. 2 (2000), pp. 219–253.

Part III

The new direction of East Asia regionalism

8 The impact of the financial crises on East Asian regionalism

Pablo Bustelo

Introduction

The novelty of the East Asian financial crises lies in the fact that they were related to non-conventional adverse macroeconomic fundamentals: imprudent financial liberalization, over-indebtness in short-term liabilities, and excessive domestic investment in manufacturing sectors with excess capacity and in non-tradables sectors. Of course, herd-like behaviour in international capital markets also played a prominent role in the onset of the crises.

Since they might be defined as crises due to excessive liberalization (including both domestic deregulation and external opening), the crises may have two long-term implications: contrary to conventional wisdom, reinforcement of the East Asian developmental and state-led model of capitalism; and enhancement of the prospects for an 'East Asian' (as opposed to a 'Pacific') understanding of the region.

As closer economic ties between countries in the area have greatly expanded over the past decade, economic regionalization in East Asia has proceeded in a much more dynamic fashion than have regionalist projects. The latter have been restricted by their 'informal' character, for example, their limitation to economic issues (and their focus on 'open regionalism' and subregional zones) and their strict respect, in interstate relations, of non-interference (although non-interference is beginning to be replaced by 'constructive engagement').

The crises might perfectly reduce the speed of regional economic integration on a short- and medium-term basis and also bring about, among East Asian political leaders, a much reduced interest in the informal and 'open' regionalist project. If these trends result in a 'pure' East Asia, increased political regionalism is a question that is certainly open to debate.

Financial crises: features, origins and implications for East Asia

Main features

The East Asian financial crises between 1997 and 1999 were, to an extent which is difficult to understand today, unanimously unpredicted. Academic specialists on currency crises, debt-rating agencies, and even the Asian Development Bank (ADB) and the International Monetary Fund (IMF), failed to predict not only the crises but also any kind of major economic or financial disturbance (1996).[1] In fact, the background in 1990 to 1996 of the later distressed East Asian economies featured generally sound, conventional macroeconomic fundamentals (ADB, 1999): high savings and investment rates, robust growth, moderate inflation, fiscal surpluses or balances, limited public debts, substantial foreign exchange reserves and high and apparently sustainable net capital inflows. The international economic and financial environment was also buoyant: low interest rates in developed countries (especially in Japan), reasonable growth of GDP in the USA and the EU and of world merchandise trade, and stability in world commodity markets. The crises thus came as a total surprise. Also unanticipated were their deep impact and their prolonged duration.

The East Asian financial turmoils were also heterogeneous. Southeast Asia suffered from a balance-of-payments crisis, albeit with distinctive features respective to similar episodes in the past, such as the Exchange Rate Mechanism (ERM)'s crisis in Western Europe during 1992 to 1993[2] and the Mexican crisis in 1994 to 1995,[3] and also exhibiting several important differences between each of the countries concerned.[4] In Northeast Asia, on the contrary, South Korea suffered initially only from liquidity problems of domestic banks and companies (and not from a severe currency overvaluation and/or a high current account deficit). These problems were associated with domestic over-investment and excessive external debt accumulation, but Korea finally also had to face sharp international solvency difficulties.

Besides, the East Asian crises have been tremendously controversial, both in respect to the explanations offered by analysts and specialists and the solutions implemented by the IMF in Thailand, Indonesia and South Korea and, against the tide, by Malaysia.

Moreover, due to the importance of East Asia in the world economy, the global impact of its crises was very significant in 1997 to 1998. For instance, the world was on the brink of a global recession in mid-1998, while several other developing and transitional regions (Latin America – especially Brazil, Argentina and Chile – and Russia) were affected, and most of the developed economies continue to suffer from the trade impact of the Asian crises, which is detrimental to their growth.

Main factors

Although there are several schools of thought on the issue,[5] a combined explanation of the crises is surely appropriate.[6] An analytical distinction between common and specific factors is outlined below.

All East Asian economies (except Japan and, partially, China and Taiwan) displayed four main weaknesses in 1996 to 1997.

First, the later troubled East Asian economies pursued, albeit to different degrees, premature and indiscriminate financial liberalization in the 1990s,

involving both domestic deregulation and external opening. Financial liberalization included measures directed at increasing the number of financial
institutions and the scope of their activities, to allow the entry of foreign banks,
and to authorize greater access of banks and non-bank financial institutions to
international capital markets. Interest rate controls and restrictions on corporate
debt financing and cross-border borrowing were lifted. A prominent feature was
that liberalization proceeded without adequate prudential supervision and
regulation of financial activities. Moreover, governments simultaneously
abandoned policy coordination of investments and borrowings. Therefore, the
crises might well be characterized as 'crises of under-regulation.'[7] Under-
regulation allowed banks and non-bank financial institutions to overlend to
private firms, to overborrow from abroad, to engage in risky activities, and to
present a growing maturity and currency mismatch between assets and liabilities.

Second, a salient feature was overindebtedness in foreign liabilities (mainly
private, denominated in foreign currencies, short term and unhedged).
According to the World Bank's data, the total foreign debt (respective to
GNP) amounted in 1996 to 64 per cent in Indonesia, 56 per cent in Thailand,
52 per cent in Malaysia, and 51 per cent in the Philippines and in South Korea;
that is, higher proportions than the respective figures for Argentina, Brazil and
Mexico in 1982, when the Latin American debt crises unfolded. Bank lending,
financed to a great extent by foreign borrowings (since borrowing abroad at low
rates to relend domestically at high rates was profitable), to the private sector
increased between 1990 and 1996, by more than 30 points of GDP in Thailand
and the Philippines and more than 20 points in Malaysia, and reached sizeable
levels in Thailand and Malaysia (102 per cent and 93 per cent of GDP in 1996).
The debt structure displayed a high proportion of liabilities in Japanese yen and
US dollars, since borrowing in Japan and the USA, at low interest rates to lend in
developing East Asia, which had substantially higher rates, was obviously a very
lucrative operation. Moreover, in mid-1997, short-term foreign debt, as a
percentage of total foreign liabilities, reached high levels in South Korea
(67.8 per cent), Thailand (65.5 per cent) and the Philippines (65.6 per cent).

Furthermore, most of the debt exposures were unhedged, as a result of the
underdevelopment of domestic hedging products, because purchasing them
offshore would have increased the cost of borrowing abroad, and as a
consequence of the perceived insurance of the currency pegs with respect to
the exchange rate risk. Therefore, the East Asian economies featured increased
vulnerability to liquidity problems and balance of payments crises: the ratio of
short-term foreign debt to official foreign exchange reserves was very high in
Korea (204 per cent in the second quarter of 1997), Indonesia (170 per cent)
and Thailand (145 per cent), while the ratio of narrow money (M2) to reserves
surpassed 400 per cent (the level attained in Mexico in 1994) in the all five
economies.

Third, another weakness was overinvestment, especially in manufacturing
sectors with excess capacity, inflated real estate and booming stock-markets. In
the mid-1990s investment rates surpassed 40 per cent of GDP in Thailand and

Malaysia, and 35 per cent in Indonesia and South Korea. The incremental capital–output ratio (ICOR) displayed an upward tendency in the early 1990s in South Korea, Thailand and Malaysia, indicating a process of declining investment efficiency and falling capital profitability. An increased share of bank lending was directed to speculative investment in real estate, equities, and other financial assets. For instance, real estate exposure of domestic banks was very high (30 to 40 per cent of total bank lending) in Malaysia and Thailand.

Fourth, herding behaviour in the global financial markets (e.g. financial panics) prompted massive currency depreciations and a tremendous fall in stock indexes. According to the Institute of International Finance, net private capital inflows to the five troubled East Asian economies (Indonesia, Malaysia, the Philippines, South Korea and Thailand) increased from US$37.9 billion in 1994 to US$102.3 billion in 1996, but registered a figure of only US$0.2 billion in 1997 and of *minus* US$27.6 billion in 1998 (IIF, 1999).[8] The bulk of this reversal (amounting to more than 10 per cent of their combined GDP) was related to swings in commercial bank lending and portfolio investments. The ensuing liquidity squeeze – since foreign creditors were less willing to roll-over their loans – was intensified by domestic residents' reluctance to hold deposits in domestic currencies. Meanwhile, manufacturing companies presented a high financial leverage (high ratios of borrowing to investments and of debt to equity), and many financial institutions (both banks and non-bank financial institutions) were undercapitalized, and had few liquid assets and a high level of collateralized lending. In a context of persistent speculative attacks a vicious circle appeared, as hikes in interest rates created defaults and credit crunches and as falling asset prices reduced collateralized lending, prompting companies to sell land and other assets, which further depressed their prices.

Specific factors in Southeast Asia, on the one hand, and in South Korea, on the other, were the following. First, sharp currency real appreciation and/or high current account deficits in Southeast Asia. Massive capital inflows and pegged nominal exchange rates to the US dollar (which provoked an important swing in real effective exchange rates following the sharp appreciation of the US dollar since mid-1995) led to currency real overvaluation. Between December 1990 and March 1997, currency real appreciation amounted to 47 per cent in the Philippines, 28 per cent in Malaysia, 25 per cent in Indonesia and Thailand, and 6 per cent in South Korea.[9] On the other side, slowing exports, due to overproduction in semiconductors, the stagnation of Japan and the shift of trade advantages towards China, led to high current account deficits (an average, in 1995 to 1996, of 8 per cent of GDP in Thailand and Malaysia, 5 per cent in the Philippines and 3 per cent in Indonesia). Therefore, only Thailand and the Philippines featured both weaknesses, while Indonesia did not present a high external deficit and Malaysia did not experience a severe overvaluation. Second, a high proportion of portfolio investments in total foreign capital inflows in South Korea (54 per cent versus 41 per cent in Thailand and 18 per cent in Indonesia in 1996). As mentioned earlier, Korea's problems were not related to a sharp currency appreciation or associated to a high current account deficit.

In the two years preceding the crises, currency real appreciation amounted to 4.4 per cent in South Korea. (It surpassed 15 per cent in the Philippines and Thailand, and 12 per cent in Malaysia and Indonesia.[10] In 1996 and 1997 the Korean current account deficit was low and declining (4.7 per cent and 2 per cent of GDP, respectively.).

Main implications

The East Asian crises seem to have had two main implications for the political economy of the region.

First, and contrary to mainstream assertions, the crises did not represent the demise of the East Asian developmental and state-led model of capitalism. For instance, Alan Greenspan, chairman of the US Federal Reserve, argued at the time that the Asian crises would have the (allegedly beneficial) effect of moving East Asian economic practices closer to those associated with the US or Anglo-Saxon model. Michel Camdessus, managing director of the IMF, saw in the crises a 'blessing in disguise'. In fact, the crises were not due to a specifically Asian 'crony capitalism'; in fact, quite the opposite. Conventional approaches contend that in the past the East Asian political economy certainly rendered higher growth and fewer social ills than did the Anglo-Saxon political economy, but that it was also plagued with 'cronyism' (collusive state–private relations), limited political competition and staunch nationalism. The time should now be right, it is argued, for a total reassessment of state-led models, 'Asian values' theories and exclusive Asian regionalism tendencies. Contrary to this view, the Asian recent experience in fact represents a crisis of the Western low-growth and market-led (or liberal) model of capitalism (and also of globalization).

The post-crises intellectual environment is exhibiting two distinct, although related, tendencies: (1) on a general level, we are witnessing the first post-Cold War serious and widespread questioning of the current model of globalization and, more specifically, of the wisdom of unregulated financial markets;[11] (2) in East Asia, renewed scepticism over the Anglo-Saxon model of capitalist development is underway. The latter is surely related to a growing dissatisfaction with mainstream Western explanations of the Asian crises (as epitomized in most IMF publications, from *Finance & Development* to the *World Economic Outlook*), whose central tenet has been to blame excessive state interference. Most Asian (and some Western) scholars would instead emphasize, as the main culprits of the crises, premature and imprudent financial liberalization and the abandonment of the traditional institutional structure of collaboration between governments, banks and firms and, more precisely, of borrowing and investment coordination by the state.[12]

Moreover, there is growing resentment in East Asia over the IMF's handling of the crises, which is perceived (in a rather simplistic but not totally incorrect manner) as having aggravated the recession, and as having been designed to allow more Western banking investments and trade inroads and to protect foreign creditors at local expense. Although, as a result of the crises, governmental practices in Asia will surely (and they should) become leaner, more transparent and less receptive to rent-seeking behaviour, 'it is unlikely that all elements of the 'developmental' statist model will be torn up in the interests of a purer Anglo-American neo-liberalism.'[13] Rather, the recent experience of turmoil in Asia may reinforce the attractiveness of the East Asian style of regulated capitalism in its historical mould of the 1970s and 1980s (before the global economic environment distorted it for the benefit of more liberalized practices).

Second, the crises may enhance the prospects for the continued development of an 'East Asian' (as opposed to a 'Pacific') understanding of the region. Policy responses to the crises have already led to more regional economic and political coordination. For instance, the Association of South East Asian Nations (ASEAN) has developed mutual surveillance mechanisms and has abandoned its traditional non-interference policy in order to adopt 'constructive engagement' or 'involvement' in other members' economic and even political internal affairs. Moreover, IMF's prescriptions, although swallowed in the short term, will not be appreciated in the long term. Furthermore, the crises have rendered irrelevant the Asia–Pacific Economic Cooperation (APEC) 'consensus' on creating a liberal free trade area across the Pacific in 2020. However, as explained below, some perceptions may go against a new effort geared at a 'pure' East Asian regionalism (such as giving birth to an East Asian Economic Caucus – EAEC – instead of pursuing current APEC's objectives). Regional integration (or regionalization) has intensified crisis contagion between national economies. ASEAN (and also APEC, by the way) was unable to deliver a quick and effective response to the crises in Southeast Asia. Regional trade and investment integration is now regarded as reducing the domestic effects of national expansionary policies, as the case of Malaysia in 1998 to 1999 suggests. In the post-crises environment, East Asian governments may have second thoughts on the benefits of trade and financial liberalization (both regional and global), which they vigorously (and imprudently) pursued between 1990 and 1996.

In short, the Asian crises not only highlighted the dangers associated with unfettered global financial markets but also the shortcomings of spreading the Western type of liberal capitalism into a radically different context. Moreover, while it may be fair to conclude that the crises have also rendered APEC irrelevant, whether they will benefit or harm the East Asian process of regionalization and projects of regionalism is something that remains to be seen.

East Asian economic regionalization and regionalism

Regionalization and regionalism

Regionalization represents a process involving mainly non-state actors (private companies exporting to, importing from and investing in neighbouring economies). Regionalism is related to a project calculated by states in order to promote a political framework for regionalization.[14]

In East Asia, economic regionalization (or integration) has been pursued in a very dynamic fashion over past decades. But East Asian regionalism (excluding the ASEAN process) remains informal, in stark contrast with formal regionalism in Western Europe through the Economic and Monetary Union (EMU) and, to a lesser extent, in Northern America through the North American Free Trade Area (NAFTA).[15] As a consequence of the legacy of European and Japanese imperialism in the area prior to the Second World War and of the central role of the USA in shaping East Asia during the Cold War, many regional states remain concerned that institutionalization will lead APEC (and also an eventual EAEC) to domination by the big powers: the USA and Japan in the former case; Japan in the latter.[16] The main implication of this informal or 'loose' regionalism is that there are no clear spill-overs from economic aspects to other functional areas, even in ASEAN.

Economic regionalization in East Asia

The growth of intra-East Asian trade and investment has been a salient feature of the world economy since the early 1980s.[17] For instance, the share of intra-East Asian exports in total East Asian exports increased from 21.1 per cent in 1980 to 24.4 per cent in 1985, to 31.1 per cent in 1990 and to 40.5 per cent in 1994. The share of intra-East Asian imports increased from 17.8 per cent in 1980 to 20.1 per cent in 1985, to 28.8 per cent in 1990, and to 34.2 per cent in 1994.[18] For Japan, the share of its exports to East Asia rose from 21.9 per cent in 1980 to 22.3 per cent in 1985, to 24.3 per cent in 1990, and to 38.9 per cent in 1994. The share of its imports from East Asia increased from 20.8 per cent in 1980 to 23.0 per cent in 1985, to 23.2 per cent in 1990, and to 37.2 per cent in 1994.[19]

In fact, intra-regional export shares have grown faster in Asia between 1984 and 1994 (from 26 per cent to 39 per cent) than in the EU (54 per cent and 56 per cent) and in North America (42 per cent and 48 per cent).[20]

As far as cross-border investments are concerned, foreign direct investment (FDI) from Japan and the ANIEs in narrowly defined East Asia represented 30 per cent of their total outward investments in 1982. The figure for 1993 was a high 50 per cent.[21]

East Asian regionalism

Regionalism in East Asia[22] has been mainly informal and 'elusive' (Ojendal, 1997),[23] except in the case of ASEAN (which, after the Hanoi Sixth Summit in 1998, already includes the ten countries in Southeast Asia). Regionalism in the area has been much more a *de facto* than a *de jure* process.

First, East Asian regionalism has been limited to economic issues, with no effective projects on political and security matters – except, in the latter case, for the ASEAN Regional Forum (ARF). Moreover, this economic regionalist stance has featured two important aspects. On the one hand, it seeks an 'open regionalism' or a 'regional multilateralism', since it rejects discrimination against the rest of the world; that is, it is opposed to a 'closed' trading bloc. On the other hand, it has proceeded mainly in Southeast Asia – through the project of creating an ASEAN Free Trade Area (AFTA) – and in subregional economic zones (Pomfret, 1996):[24] the Johor–Singapore–Riau (JSR) growth triangle, between Malaysia, Singapore and Indonesia; the Indonesia–Malaysia–Thailand growth triangle; the Brunei–Indonesia–Malaysia-Philippines area (also called East ASEAN Growth Area (EAGA)); the South China Growth Triangle (Taiwan, Hong Kong, and the southern provinces of China); and the Tumen River Area Development Project (China, North Korea, Russia, Mongolia, South Korea and Japan). Second, East Asian regionalism has been especially scrupulous in respecting states' sovereignty. Up until the present, it has been based on the adherence, in interstate relations, to the principle of non-interference in political and even economic affairs, in stark contrast with, for instance, the European Union.

Both features reflect a choice for a pragmatic regionalism, since East Asian leaders decided to reject political decisions encompassing the entire region or creating external common borders, and also to respect ongoing economic processes and flows across nation-states, without even thinking of dismantling or blurring the latter.[25] This had several a priori advantages: East Asian informal regionalism had in fact more ambition than NAFTA (limited to trade issues) and more political consistency than the EU (which has difficulties in harmonizing domestic economic policies).

The decision to pursue regionalism (though following rather than preceding economic processes) was surely intended to articulate an effective response to the increased globalization and deregulation of world markets (and the consequent erosion of national economic control), to the 'Western' or liberal form economic globalization was adopting, and to 'closed' regionalism in other parts of the world (mainly NAFTA and EMU, which involve dangers of mercantilist economic rivalry).

'Open' regionalism, as embedded, for instance, in the 'APEC vision', was intended to secure access to the US market for East Asian exporters. For instance, in 1995 the share of the US market in total exports was 35.8 per cent in the Philippines, 23.7 per cent in Taiwan, 21.8 per cent in Hong Kong, 20.7 per cent in Malaysia, 19.3 per cent in South Korea, 18.3 per cent in Singapore, 17.8 per cent in Thailand, 16.7 per cent in Indonesia, and 16.6 per cent in China.[26] Only China and Indonesia exported more to Japan than to the USA. Moreover, 'open' regionalism also reflected the East Asian desire to maintain US military presence in the area, in order to defuse tensions between Japan and China (over regional hegemony), Russia and Japan (over the Kuril islands/ Northern Territories), South Korea and North Korea (over the reunification issue), Japan and South Korea (over the Tokto islands), Taiwan and China (over respective political identities), Japan and China (over the Senkaku/Diaoyu islands), the Spratlys dispute, and other regional rivalries.

However, while most observers have lauded this pragmatic regionalist project, some have highlighted its shortcomings. For instance, a larger normative project may be needed in order to transform East Asia into a region with more cohesion, a more distinctive identity, greater capacity for autonomous action in the world scene, and more effective institutions. The main limitations of the East Asian current 'loose' regionalism are associated with the difficulty in separating economics from politics and with the desirability of subordinating economic activity to socially and regionally defined objectives. Moreover, a more formal kind of regionalist project might also help in overcoming the logic of geopolitical rivalries and thus in creating a more effective programme of comprehensive regional security, beyond the actual consultations in the ARF framework.

In short, while 'open' regionalism might be ineffective in a world of increasingly inward-oriented trading blocs, some kind of strictly East Asian formal integration might be also desirable. For instance, the proposal of creating an EAEC has recently been receiving more and more support among East Asian social, economic and political actors.

Financial crises and the regional process and project in East Asia[27]

Before the crises erupted in mid-1997, economic integration in the region was perceived as having strong synergistic effects, since it spurred industrial growth and exports through intra-regional trade, investment and technology flows. After July 1997, the crisis spread rapidly from Southeast Asia (Thailand, Indonesia, Malaysia and the Philippines) to Northeast Asia (initially Taiwan and Hong Kong, and finally South Korea) in a contagion which also aggravated Japan's recession.

Regional economic integration was then beginning to be perceived as harmful for the eventual recovery of the battered economies. Four main reasons may be given for this changing attitude.

First, regional integration has clearly intensified crisis contagion. Pure contagion may be distinguished from spill-over effects.[28] Pure contagion refers to the fact that institutional investors, such as mutual funds, insurance companies, pension funds and hedge funds, tend to lump together subregions and countries in emerging markets, regardless of the specific economic soundness of those respective subregions and countries. There are mainly three spill-over effects: (1) some countries have to apply competitive devaluations to remain competitive with regard to similarly exporting and currency-battered countries; (2) intra-regional trade and investment interdependencies mean that crises are transmitted through fewer exports, more imports and fewer investments to and from the region; and (3) foreign investors tend to make portfolio adjustments due to the fact that losses in one market lead funds to liquidate investments in other regional markets.

Second, regional responses to the crises have been dismal at best. Japan's early proposal for an Asian Monetary Fund (AMF) was dismissed due to strong resistance from the USA and the IMF. ASEAN was unable to deliver a quick and effective response to the crisis in Thailand and Indonesia.[29] The 1997 Summit of APEC in Vancouver, besides including US President Clinton's assessment that the crises were simply 'a few glitches on the road', endorsed plans to support further financial deregulation in the area and approved a controversial proposal for an Early Voluntary Sectoral Liberalization (EVSL) scheme in nine sectors: environmental goods and services, fish and fish products, forest products, medical equipment and instruments, energy, toys, gems and jewellery, chemicals, and telecommunications. The 1998 Summit of APEC in Kuala Lumpur simply transferred responsibilities in trade liberalization to the World Trade Organization (WTO), due to strong opposition from Japan and Malaysia, and awarded the management of the crises to the IMF and the Group of Twenty-two (G22). The 1999 Summit of APEC in Auckland emphasized even more liberalization as a contribution to the East Asian recovery. Direct initiatives from APEC to confront the crises should have been contemplated, although it is true that the Forum was not planned for crisis management. Japan's and Japan-USA's initiatives in late 1998 also featured excessive delay and involved insufficient amounts of financial assistance.

Third, regional economic integration, in the context of a general slump, strictly limits the domestic effects of national expansionary macroeconomic policies. For instance, since Malaysia departed from the IMF prescriptions, while Thailand and Indonesia did not, its expansionary fiscal and monetary policies tended to translate themselves into increased imports from neighbouring economies, into a higher trade deficit and therefore into additional restrictions on economic recovery. A viable alternative should have been a regional concerted effort to decrease interest rates and to provide fiscal stimuli, as suggested by the World Bank (1998).

Fourth, the post-crises scenario might be one of national governments having second thoughts on further trade and financial liberalization, since its premature and indiscriminate implementation between 1990 and 1996 was a major factor in the turmoils. This may deal a fatal blow not only to the opening trend respective to the global economy but also to the ongoing process of trade barriers dismantling and financial opening in ASEAN (and, of course, in APEC).

To conclude, while the short- and medium-term effects of the financial crises might involve a backlash against regional and trans-Pacific economic integration, it remains to be seen whether these forces will counterbalance one of the long-term effects of the turmoil: an enhanced prospect for a pure 'East Asian' (as opposed to a 'Pacific') understanding of the region; that is, a real East Asian regionalism.

Notes

1   However, a praiseworthy exception was Korean economist Park Yung-chul; see Park, 'East Asian Liberalization, Bubbles and the Challenges from China', *Brookings Papers on Economic Activity*, No. 2 (1996), pp. 357–371.

2   The ERM episode in 1992 to 1993 was related to previous restrictive monetary policies, first in the European periphery and later in Germany, while interest rates were considerably lower, in 1994 to 1996, in the troubled East Asian economies and also in Japan and the USA.

3 The Mexican crisis of 1994 to 1995 was the consequence of a sharp decline in the private savings rate (that is, of over consumption), while the Asian episodes were related to excessive investment and overproduction. See a comparative analysis of the Mexican and Asian crises in Gabriel Palma, 'Three and a Half Cycles of "Mania, Panic and [Asymmetric] Crash": East Asia and Latin America Compared', *Cambridge Journal of Economics*, Vol. 22, No. 6 (1998), pp. 780–808.

4 Malaysia and the Philippines presented both high current account deficits and currency over valuations, but Indonesia did not feature a large current account deficit, while Thailand did not experience a large appreciation of its currency.

5 See a survey in Bustelo, 'The East Asian Financial Crises: An Analytical Survey', *ICEI Working Paper*, No. 10/98 (ICEI, Complutense University of Madrid, October 1998). A similar view of the following discussion may be found in Abdur R. Chowdury, 'The Asian Currency Crisis: Origins, Lessons and Future Outlook', *Research for Action*, No. 47 (Helsinki: UNU/WIDER, 1999); Reuven Glick, 'Thoughts on the Origins of the Asian Crisis: Impulses and Propagation Mechanisms', *Pacific Basin Working Paper*, No. 98/07 (Federal Reserve Bank of San Francisco, September 1998); For country-by-country analyses, see Ross H. McLeod and Ross Garnaut, eds, *East Asia in Crisis: From Being a Miracle to Needing One?* (London: Routledge, 1998); Heinz W. Arndt and Hal Hill, eds, *Southeast Asia's Economic Crisis: Origins, Lessons, and the Way Forward* (Singapore: ISEAS, 1999); Karl D. Jackson, ed., *Asian Contagion: The Causes and Consequences of a Financial Crisis* (Boulder, CO: Westview Press, 1999); K.S. Jomo, ed., *Tigers in Trouble: Financial Governance, Liberalisation and Crises in East Asia* (London: Zed Books, 1998); Pierre-Richard Agénor, Marcus Miller, David Vines and Andrew Weber, eds, *The Asian Financial Crisis: Causes, Contagion and Consequences* (Cambridge: Cambridge University Press, 1999).

6 Pablo Bustelo, Clara García and Iliana Olivié, 'Global and Domestic Factors of Financial Crises in Emerging Economies: Lessons from the East Asian Episodes (1997–1999)', *ICEI Working Paper*, No. 16/99 (ICEI, Complutense University of Madrid, November 1999).

7 Chang, Ha-joon, 'Korea: The Misunderstood Crisis', *World Development*, Vol. 26, No. 8 (August 1998), pp. 1555–1561, repr. in Jomo, ed., *Tigers in Trouble*, pp. 222–231.

8 IIF, *Capital Flows to Emerging Market Economies* (Washington, DC: Institute of International Finance), 24 April 1999.

9 Steven Radelet and Jeffrey Sachs, 'The Onset of the Asian Financial Crisis', *Brookings Papers on Economic Activity*, No. 1 (1998), pp. 1–90.

10 Gerardo Esquivel and Felipe Larraín, 'Latin America Confronting the Asian Crisis', *HIID Development Discussion Paper*, No. 681.

11 Richard Higgott and Nicola Phillips, 'The Limits of Global Liberalisation: Lessons from Asia and Latin America', *CSGR Working Paper*, No. 23/99 (University of Warwick, January 1999); Pablo Bustelo and Iliana Olivié, 'Economic Globalisation and Financial Crisis: Some Lessons from East Asia', *The Indian Journal of Quantitative Economics* (Punjab School of Economics, Amritsar, 1999).

12 Chang, Ha-joon, 'Korea: The Misunderstood Crisis'; K.S. Jomo, ed., *Tigers in Trouble: Financial Governance, Liberalisation and Crises in East Asia* (London: Zed Books, 1998); Robert Wade, 'The Asian Debt-and-Development Crisis of 1997–?: Causes and Consequences', *World Development*, Vol. 26, No. 8 (August 1998), pp. 1534–1554.

13 Richard Higgott, 'The Politics of Economic Crisis in East Asia: Some Longer Term Implications', *CSGR Working Paper*, No. 02/98 (University of Warwick, March 1998).

14 Andrew Gamble, and Anthony Payne, eds, *Regionalism and World Order* (Basingstoke: Macmillan, 1996); Louise Fawcett and Andrew Hurrell, eds, *Regionalism in World Politics: Regional Organization and International Order* (Oxford: Oxford University Press, 1995).

15 For a review of regionalism in the world economy, see Takatoshi Ito and Anne O. Krueger, eds, *Regionalism versus Multilateral Trade Arrangements* (Chicago, IL: University of Chicago Press, 1997); Jeffrey A. Frankel, ed., *The Regionalization of the World Economy* (Chicago, IL: University of Chicago Press, 1998).

16 Bernard Mitchell, 'Regions in the Global Political Economy: Beyond the Local–Global Divide in the Formation of the Eastern Asia Region', *New Political Economy*, Vol. 1, No. 3 1996), pp. 335–354.

17 Gavin Boyd and Alan Rugman, eds, *Economic Integration in the Pacific* (Aldershot: Edward Elgar, 1998).

18 East Asia is here narrowly defined and comprises Southeast Asia, the Asian Newly Industrializing Economies (ANIEs) (Hong Kong, Singapore, South Korea and Taiwan) and China.

19 ADB, *Asian Development Outlook 1996 and 1997* (New York: Oxford University Press-Asian Development Bank, 1996), Tables 3.1 and 3.2.

20 Ibid., Figure 3.4.

21 Ibid., Figure 3.5.

22 General studies on East Asian regionalism prior to the crises are Palmer (1991); Garnaut and Drysdale, eds (1994); Ross, ed. (1994); Mack and Ravenhill, eds (1995); Bora and Findlay, eds (1996); and Herman and Pyle, eds (1997).

23 Joakim Ojendal, *Regionalization in East Asia and the Pacific: An Elusive Process?* (Helsinki: UNU/WIDER World Development Studies 11, 1997).

24 Richard Pomfret, 'Sub-regional Economic Zones', in Bora and Findlay, eds, *Regional Integration and the Asia–Pacific*, pp. 207–222.

25 Jean-Luc Domenach, *L'Asie en danger* (Paris: Fayard, 1998), p. 158.

26 ADB, *Asian Development Outlook 1997 and 1998*, Table A12.

27 For further information and analyses, see the papers on East Asia presented at the CSGR 3rd Annual Conference, 'After the Global Crises "What Next for Regionalism"' (University of Warwick, September 1999).

28 Paul Masson, 'Contagion: Moonsoonal Effects, Spillovers, and Jumps between Multiple Equilibria', *IMF Working Paper*, No. 98/142 (September 1998).

29 Chang Li Lin and Ramkishen S. Rajan, 'Regional Responses to the Southeast Asian Financial Crisis: A Case of Self-help or No Help?', *Australian Journal of International Affairs*, Vol. 53, No. 3 (1999), pp. 261–281; Hadi.Soesastro, 'ASEAN During the Crisis', *ASEAN Economic Bulletin*, Vol. 15, No. 3 (December 1998), pp. 373–382.

9 The concept of 'Greater China' and East Asia

Wei-Wei Zhang

Since the 1980s, the world has witnessed a growing economic integration of diverse Chinese communities, as demonstrated in the expanding worldwide business network of traders and financiers of Chinese origin and in the increased economic cooperation between Hong Kong, Taiwan and the Chinese mainland. This has generated a strong curiosity about the emergence of the so-called 'Greater China,' a concept defying easy definition. For understandable reasons, the intellectual and political elite in various Chinese communities have demonstrated a special interest in studying the idea of 'Greater China.' This chapter represents an initial attempt to survey and assess, essentially but not exclusively, this diversified 'Chinese' understanding and interpretation of 'Greater China' as well as to examine the evolution and implications of this formative grouping in the economic and political context of East Asia. 'Greater China' is used here as a generic term covering concepts with specific reference to 'Greater China' as well as those without such reference, yet in the judgment of the author, falling into the category of 'Greater China' in its neutral and apolitical sense, i.e. a term depicting a growing coherent pattern of regional co-operation among the Chinese communities, rather than a pejorative term reminding one of political and military expansionism.

The origin of the concept

The origin of the concept of 'Greater China' can be traced to the traditional distinction between *China Proper* and *Outer China*.[1] Most China scholars agree that China's long history was characterized by a distinction of *China Proper* and *Outer China,* and the central government's control over *Outer China* was considered as loose, and more cultural than territorial. Yet these terms also implied the acknowledgment of a large and coherent sphere of Chinese political and cultural influence.

The usage of 'Greater China' in its present meaning, however, did not come until the late 1970s when China adopted a policy of reform and opening to the outside world. Since then, Beijing's trade with Hong Kong expanded rapidly and Hong Kong became the bridge between China and the outside world. Beijing modified its policy towards Taiwan since the late 1970s, from 'liberating

Taiwan' to 'striving for peaceful reunification' and 'welcoming Taiwanese investors.' In this context, demonstrating their foresight, some Taiwan and Hong Kong scholars began to explore possible regional cooperation among Chinese communities. The first idea in this connection may be attributable to a Taiwanese journal called *Changqiao* (*Long Bridge*). An article in the 1979 June issue of *Changqiao* raised the idea of a *Chinese Common Market* (*Zhonghua gongtong shichang*) that 'would link Taiwan, Hong Kong, Macao, Singapore and the Chinese mainland.'[2] It is generally agreed, however, that the first scholar who made an in-depth study of the prospects of 'Greater China' was Huang Zhilian, a Hong Kong futurologist. As early as November 1980, Huang advanced two concepts: *Zhongguoren Gongtongti* (*Chinese Community*) and *Zhongguoren Jingji Jituan* (*Chinese Economic Grouping*). In contrast to the article in *Zhongqiao*, Huang confined his concepts to covering only Hong Kong, Taiwan and the Chinese mainland, and he predicted:

> The relationship between the political economic systems of the Chinese mainland, Hong Kong and Taiwan will become ever closer. Eight to ten years from now, i.e. in the late 1980s, there may well emerge a Chinese Community or Chinese Economic Grouping in the Asia–Pacific.[3]

Huang's prediction, visionary as it was, however, failed to arouse sufficient attention then, partly due to the fact that at that point, there had been little contact between Taiwan and the Chinese mainland. It was not until the late 1980s when economic and other exchanges multiplied between Taiwan and the mainland that there began an outpouring of similar concepts on economic, cultural and even political integration of different Chinese communities. Since the early 1990s, even international institutions like OECD, IMF and the World Bank began to group Hong Kong, Macao, Taiwan and the PRC under the heading of 'Greater China' in their reports. With Hong Kong on its way to returning to China in 1997, the concept began to gain further credence, for it was widely perceived that Hong Kong, China and to a certain extent, Taiwan, had been economically integrated. 'Greater China' has thus become, in Harry Harding's words, 'part of the trendiest vocabulary used in discussions of contemporary global affairs.'[4]

Indeed, the term 'Greater China' is now increasingly employed beyond the academic circles, for instance, by multinational corporations with business operations in the region. Many companies have treated Hong Kong, Taiwan and the Chinese mainland as a single market. Multinational corporations such as Nestle and ABB have set up branches in Hong Kong or Shanghai for coordinating their businesses in the 'Greater China Region.' Lufthansa established its information service for all its operations in 'Greater China.' Mutual funds have used the term for their operations in this part of the world, such as 'Greater China Opportunity Fund' and 'Greater China Fund.' Now the term 'Greater China' is used for virtually all discussions covering Hong Kong, Taiwan, Macao and the PRC. For instance, Chinese dissidents used the term to discuss democracy and human rights issues in these areas.[5] The term is also employed by some websites (e.g. Greater China Kaleidoscope) exclusively devoted to the Chinese world.

Boundaries of 'Greater China'

Boundaries of 'Greater China' are, like the meaning of the concept, confusing and controversial, but some broad contours can be discerned if one examines the evolution of academic and political discourse on the issue. Five major boundaries are outlined below, and they are different from each other, yet to varying degrees overlapping.

The first is a zone of Hong Kong plus southern China, i.e. Hong Kong and its immediate neighbour Guangdong province. This view was espoused by those who focused on Hong Kong's economic integration with southern part of China (e.g. American scholar E. Vogel's idea of *Hong Kong-Guangdong Economic Zone*[6]). This view was widely shared by Chinese officials and scholars in the mid-1980s when Hong Kong had become increasingly integrated with Guangdong province, well before Taiwanese investment had poured into the mainland. This boundary could be seen as initial attempts at perceiving long-term cooperation of different Chinese communities beyond their administrative borders. The concept is still used widely now to describe a sub-regional integration within some form of 'Greater China.'

The second is Hong Kong, Taiwan, Macao plus southern China. This boundary began to emerge with the rapid expansion of Taiwanese investment in southern China, especially Fujian Province since the late 1980s. Jin Hongfan's *South China Economic Circle* (*Nan zhongguo jingji quan*) was delineated in this way.[7] This boundary also incorporates sub-regional zones like the proposed *Taiwan Straits Economic Circle* (*Haixia liang-an jingji quan*),[8] which includes Taiwan and Fujian province in cooperation with other regions of southern China.

The third one consists of Hong Kong, Taiwan, Macao and the whole of the Chinese mainland. This is currently the most widely accepted boundary. It is a fairly realistic assessment of the on-going process of economic integration of these Chinese communities, which has certainly moved beyond southern China. Furthermore, this boundary is politically less sensitive, as it does not include ethnic Chinese in other countries. This boundary is now accepted by international institutions like the World Bank and the IMF.

The fourth includes Hong Kong, Taiwan, Macao, the Chinese mainland and Singapore. Adding Singapore to 'Greater China' is a view shared by some overseas Chinese scholars, as Singapore has a large ethnic Chinese population, active in exploring China and the Chinese market, and Singapore has played a role in trying to bridge the political gap between Beijing and Taipei. This boundary is used for instance, by Zhen Zuyuan, a Chinese American scholar, who devised the concept of *Greater China Common Market* (*Dazhonghua gongtong shichang*).[9]

The fifth covers Hong Kong, Taiwan, Macao, the Chinese mainland, Singapore and ethnic Chinese communities in Southeast Asia. According to Lu Shipeng, a Taiwanese scholar, who elaborated Zhen Zuyuan's concept of

Greater China Common Market, 'Greater China' should include ethnic Chinese in Southeast China, in view of their close business ties with China, Hong Kong and Taiwan.[10] Gao Xijun, another Taiwanese scholar, proposed to establish *Asian Chinese Common Market* (*Yazhou huaren gongtong shichang*), which included all ethnic Chinese in Asia.[11]

Of the above five descriptions, which largely reflect the evolving, confusing and overlapping boundaries of 'Greater China,' the third one is the most widely accepted. It designates a formative Chinese-based economy composed of Hong Kong, Taiwan, Macao and the Chinese mainland. This process has been shaped by common economic interests and shared culture. It is still largely informal and constantly evolving, with little institutional framework, yet it has generated and may continue to generate significant implications for the parties involved and for the region and beyond.

Three major meanings of 'Greater China'

What does the concept of 'Greater China' mean? Like other political concepts, it is difficult to provide a precise definition for it. The author's attempt here is to focus on three major meanings of the concept. These meanings are broadly outlined as (a) economic 'Greater China', (b) cultural 'Greater China' and (c) political 'Greater China'. This division does not imply that 'Greater China' is a simple concept fit for easy compartmentalisation. On the contrary, it is a concept loaded with geographical, economic and political referents. Confusing and complex as it may appear, the concept is, however, analytically distinguishable for the purpose of a more focussed examination here.

Economic 'Greater China'

The economic sense of 'Greater China' is arguably the most fundamental meaning of the concept as reflected in virtually all intellectual and political discourse in this regard. In China's pre-reform years, Hong Kong, Taiwan and the People's Republic had little commercial interaction with each other. But since Beijing decided to open its door to foreign trade and investment in 1978, the situation has changed dramatically. Hong Kong has long established itself as a bridge between China and the outside world. Hong Kong's trade with the mainland grew 25 times between 1980 and 1993. The Chinese mainland is now Hong Kong's largest trading partner, accounting for 35 per cent of Hong Kong's total trade value. The mainland is also the largest market for Hong Kong's re-exports as well as the second largest investor in Hong Kong. Hong Kong is already the largest external investor in the Chinese mainland. Such a high degree of integration serves to explain why various ideas concerning 'Greater China' first centered on the interactions between Hong Kong and the Chinese mainland. A similar process of economic integration between Macao and the Chinese mainland has occurred over the same period of time, although Macao's economy is much smaller than Hong Kong's.[12]

In comparison, Taiwan is a latecomer. Taiwan had continued its policy of 'no contact' with its communist enemy until 1986, and then shifted the policy under a combination of economic and political forces: the rising cost of labour and manufacturing in Taiwan, the pull of China's huge domestic market, international commercial competition, Beijing's preferential policies for attracting Taiwan's capital and technology, and more relaxed political climate in both Taiwan and the mainland. It is amazing that despite formal political animosity between Beijing and Taipei, in less than a decade, Taiwan has become the second largest external investor in the mainland, next to Hong Kong. Merchandise exports from Taiwan to the mainland grew in double digits since 1987. Accumulated Taiwan's direct investment in the Chinese mainland exceeded US$41.3 billion in contract terms, of which US$21.4 billion had been actually committed by the end of 1998.[13] The bilateral indirect trade reached US$120 billion in accumulative terms from 1988 to 1998, an average annual growth rate of 36.13 per cent.[14]

As a result, a Chinese-based economy composed mainly of Hong Kong, Taiwan, Macao and the Chinese mainland began to take shape since mid-1980s. It has become a new epicentre for industry, commerce and finance. This area possesses a significant amount of technology and manufacturing capability (Taiwan and coastal China), first-class marketing and services skills and networks and fine communication (Hong Kong and Taiwan) and a huge pool of financial resources (Hong Kong, Taiwan and the Chinese mainland) and enormous supply of natural resources and labour and huge market potentials (China). From Hong Kong to Guangdong, from Taipei to Shanghai, this influential network is often based on extensions of the traditional clans and family ties. Each of the three areas is already an important trading power in its own right, combined they were creating a new global economic force. No major policymakers or businessmen can look at the three pieces of 'Greater China' without considering the growing links among them. For instance, any US attempt to revoke China's Most Favoured Nation status will inevitably undermine the economies of Hong Kong and Taiwan. The immediate impact of this integration is the talk of the rise of 'Greater China.' The following concepts are often employed in the discourse of an economic 'Greater China.'

Firstly, *the Chinese Economic Area* or CEA (*Zhonghua jingji qu*). This is undoubtedly the most used term now in analyzing the economic integration of various Chinese economies. This politically neutral term is widely used in the writings of Chinese scholars and reports of World Bank, IMF and OECD. The fact that the concept includes only four Chinese-dominated economies makes it more politically acceptable to both Chinese and non-Chinese. The adoption of this term by international financial institutions has provided added authority to the legitimacy of the concept. Huang, the first author of a detailed study of *Chinese Economic Community*, also accepted this term in his discussions on Chinese economic integration. He pointed to the need for the establishment of a *Coordinating System for the Chinese Economic Area* (*Zhonghua jingji xiezuo xitong*), because CEA's four components differed from each other in both economic and political systems. Huang proposed some sub-regional cooperation or '*4 plus 3*' formula within the System, notably cooperation between China's four coastal provinces (Guangdong, Guangxi, Fujian and Hainan) and their three neighbours Hong Kong, Macao and Taiwan. Huang argued that the '*4 plus 3*' subregional cooperation should include a series of mutually accommodating industrial policies and strategies for shaping up an economy of scale in the Greater China region.[15] In the context of CEA, this author presented the idea of an *Informal Integration of CEA* (*Zhonghua jingji qu de feizhengshi zhenghe*) and argued that expanding such informal integration, with a set of institutional mechanisms, may go a long way in ensuring more fruitful economic integration of the Chinese communities and even lead to a shift of paradigm for the whole issue of political reunification, including transcending the sovereignty dispute and developing new forms of close partnership.[16]

Secondly, as for the *Greater China Common Market* (*Dazhonghua gongtong shichang*), this concept was in fact, put forward by Chinese American scholar Zhen Zuyuan in 1988.[17] The concept was initially conceived of within the context of aiming for eventual political reunification. It emphasizes the growing international trends towards regional groupings, and suggested that Chinese economies should form their own institution of cooperation, i.e. the *Greater China Common Market,* in which there will be less trade barriers, easy flow of capital resources and more business networking. Like the process of European integration, the *Greater China Common Market*, according to Zhen, should facilitate economic integration so as to create necessary conditions for eventual political reunification. Zhen proposed to set up the headquarters of this common market in Hong Kong or Singapore and hold annual meetings of the common market regularly in the major cities of the Chinese world, such as Beijing, Hong Kong, Taipei or Singapore. He suggested the two sides of the Taiwan Straits to recognize each other as a political entity so as to pave the way for the 'revival of the Chinese nation' in the new millennium.

Thirdly, in terms of *the Chinese Economic Circle* (*Zhonghua jingji quan*), this idea was put forward by Chinese scholar Chen Yichun in 1988.[18] It analyzes not only the internal structure of this circle, but also the intra-relations among its components as well as the circle's relations with the outside world. According to Chen, the *Chinese Economic Circle* should entail two parallel levels of '*circulation*': namely, an '*internal circulation*' (*Neixunhuan*), i.e. the integration of the three Chinese economies (Hong Kong, Taiwan and the Chinese mainland) in the field of natural resources, labour and market, and an '*external circulation*' (*Waixunhuan*), i.e. the three parties' continued participation in their respective international business networks, while simultaneously joining their efforts in exploring the international market.

Fourthly, with respect to the *Greater China Economic Integration* (*Dazhonghua jingji zhenghe*), this concept was advanced by Chinese American economist Gregory Chow in 1993.[19] Chow tackled the issue from an economist perspective and presented a de facto feasibility study for this formative Chinese-based economy. He concluded that there were five common features in these economies in favour of *Greater China Economic Integration*: (i) reduced government intervention; (ii) emphasis on agriculture in the case of Taiwan and the Chinese mainland; (iii) export-driven development strategy; (iv) emphasis on price stability; and (v) gradually liberalizing import control and introducing realistic exchange rates. Chow advocated economic integration of Hong Kong, Taiwan and the Chinese mainland in the field of capital, technology, management, finance, banking and international market sharing.

Fifthly, *Quadripartite Economic Cooperation* (*Liangan sifang jingji hezuo*). This concept refers to economic integration between the Chinese mainland, Taiwan, Hong Kong and Macao. It is the officially sanctioned term in China and widely used in the Chinese official literature.[20] The term 'Greater China' is deemed too politically sensitive, given China's desire to resist the image of a rising China as a threat to the international community. The boundary envisaged in this concept is identical to the concept of the *Chinese Economic Area (CEA)*. It is oriented towards achieving the dual goal of China's modernization and reunification under *One Country, Two Systems*. Beijing has formulated a series of policies to promote such quadripartite economic cooperation partly to promote China's modernization, and partly to achieve its ultimate reunification with Taiwan. The return of Hong Kong and Macao has made Beijing more anxious to embrace Taiwan through expanding economic integration and political negotiations. Some Chinese scholars such as Cui Dianchao and Zhao Baoxu also elaborated their understanding of 'Greater China' as a transitional process from economic integration to political reunification with Taiwan under the model of *one country, two systems*.[21]

Sixthly, there are a group of concepts put forward by Taiwanese officials and scholars. For instance, *Chinese-Hong Kong Economic Circle* (*Zhonghuagang jingji quan*) and *Chinese Community* (*Zhonghua gongtongti*) put forward by Qiu Changhuan, a senior Taiwanese official in 1991, referred to the economic integration of Hong Kong, Taiwan and the Chinese mainland, leading to an eventual peaceful reunification. Taiwan's former prime minister Li Huan observed on various concepts of 'Greater China:' 'No matter it is the *Chinese Economic Common Market* or *Greater Chinese Commonwealth*, these ideas are based on the common interests and ideals of all Chinese.' Vincent Siew, Taiwan's former economic minister and present prime minister, was also reported to have proposed in 1991 to set up a *Chinese Common Market*.[22] Even Lee Tenghui himself observed in 1995, 'Taiwan's economy must be developed with the mainland as its hinterland.'[23] On different occasions, senior Taiwanese officials like Ma Yinjiu and Hao Bochun all commented positively on such concepts as *Chinese Economic Circle* or *Greater China Economic Community*.[24] It is generally believed that the major obstacle to greater economic integration remains political. Dispute between Beijing and Taipei over sovereignty has sometimes caused the other side to panic, and the two sides are frequently on a collision course on the international arena. All this has made the cross-Strait relations less stable, thus affecting the pace and scope of economic integration, let alone a formal Chinese reunification.

There are also economic challenges to such integration. Although the momentum for greater economic integration has been strong, there have been structural problems affecting such integration. For instance, Hong Kong's status as a free port makes it difficult to envisage its inclusion into a Chinese free trade area, unless China is ready to turn itself into a huge free trade entity.[25] Furthermore, while labour-intensive products from the mainland have replaced made-in-Taiwan goods over the recent years, China's medium-technology products are beginning to compete with Taiwan-made products. Many Taiwan-invested companies have begun to localize their purchases of raw materials and semi-finished products in the mainland. China's growing concern for environment protection has also set limits to a variety of Hong Kong and Taiwanese investments. Taiwan investors are further handicapped by Taipei's policy of restricting large and high-tech investment in the mainland. Taiwan is still unwilling to accept the direct links of post, air and shipping between the two sides, although informal integration has developed to such a degree that some kind of breakthrough in these areas seems to be inevitable (especially if both sides join the WTO in a not too distant future). Taipei fears that excessive dependence on the mainland market would give Beijing undue leverage in its dealings with Taiwan. Taipei is trying to toe the difficult line of maintaining the island's economic competitiveness while not allowing it to be dependent on the mainland.

Despite various political obstacles and economic challenges, many Chinese economists are cautiously optimistic about the long-term prospect of an economic 'Greater China'. The economies of Hong Kong, Taiwan, Macao and the Chinese mainland are by far more complementary than competitive. With intensified economic integration, there may well emerge new forces for peaceful solution to the political problems between Beijing and Taipei. The rapidly growing 'three-way economic integration (of Hong Kong, Taiwan and the Chinese mainland),' as claimed in an article in *Business Week*, may well be a more 'comfortable' and 'apolitical' path to unification than any formal political settlement.[26] However, the political disputes between Beijing and Taipei, if mismanaged, could be most costly for the further growth of this Chinese-based economic integration.

Cultural 'Greater China'

Since 1978, there has been an increased cultural exchange among the people of Chinese descent from different parts of the world. This trend has been facilitated by modern means of transport and communications. Over 3 million people from Taiwan already visited the mainland by 1998 and there were 160,000 visits from the mainland to Taiwan by 1997. The flow of mails across the Taiwan Straits reached over 50 million pieces in 1997, and telephone calls between the two sides amounted to 60 million in the same period.[27] Exchanges of visits between Hong Kong and the mainland are even more frequent. In 1998, mainland visitors became the largest tourist population in Hong Kong, followed by the Taiwanese.

With the increase of people-to-people exchange is the increased cultural contact, reflecting the natural desire of various Chinese communities sharing a common culture.

At the level of popular culture, the inflow of pop culture from Hong Kong and Taiwan to the Chinese mainland had literally caused a 'cultural revolution,' leading the way to de-politicize the once heavily politicized Chinese culture on the mainland. Artists and performers from Hong Kong and Taiwan found larger audience in the mainland. Chinese novels, plays and music pieces are now borderless and appreciated by all Chinese, inside or outside China.

At the level of high culture, intellectuals and scholars from different Chinese communities now visit each other more frequently than ever. They discuss wide-ranging issues of their mutual interests. Linguists from the two sides are working on joint projects of compiling dictionaries to bridge the linguistic gaps created by decades of separation. The discourse on the so-called neo-Confucianism (*Xinrujiao*) has attracted attention across the Chinese communities, partly due to the unique experience of modernization in several Confucian societies. Interestingly, rather than weakening the Chinese identity, globalization of world economy and fast improvement of communication and technology have made it, as Wang Gongwu, a leading historian, argued, 'both convenient and imperative for overseas Chinese to maintain at least a partial identity as members of a global Chinese culture.'[28]

Cultural China (*Wenhua zhongguo*) put forward by Tu Wei-ming, a Chinese American professor at Harvard, may be the most significant concept in capturing this trend towards Chinese cultural identity. Tu suggested a global 'cultural China,' including not only those of Chinese descent, but also those non-Chinese with a personal or professional interest in China. Tu in fact 'defines the membership of a global Chinese culture culturally, rather than ethnically: it consists of all of those, from whatever ethnic background, who participate in the "international discourse of cultural China" and who thereby join in the creation of a modern Chinese identity.'[29]

Tu also discussed the issues concerning the capital of Cultural China. Rather than seeing Beijing or Shanghai as its capital, Tu argued the periphery as the center, implying that peripheries like Hong Kong and Taipei may 'set the cultural agenda for the center,' partly because, as Tu believed, many Chinese intellectuals preferred to see several centres of cultural life that are autonomous from the political capital. Tu also tried to define the content of Cultural China: it ranged from neo-authoritarian political culture prevailing in the mainland and Singapore, to growing democratic culture in Taiwan to a transnational popular culture shaped by commercial artists, musicians and writers.

The content of Cultural China includes the afore-mentioned neo-Confucianism. Tu himself is a leading scholar of this school of thought, which emphasizes the compatibility of Confucianism and Western liberalism and suggests that Confucian ideas and institutions may prove to be capable of providing China with a solid foundation on which constitutional democracy can be established. This school partly reflects the desire of many overseas Chinese to reform

China's political system by drawing both on Confucian ideals and Western liberalism.

The rise of Cultural China was also parallel with the rise of the so-called Asian model of development and Asian values, following the relative economic success of some Asian economies. Even with the Asian financial crisis, it was still argued that Confucian values or Asian values had played an important role in the economic progress these economies had experienced prior to the crisis and will continue to have its relevance in the post-crisis era. Asian values were supposed to stress diligence, education, high saving and social harmony. Like Max Weber's argument about the Protestant and the spirit of capitalism, Asian values, controversial as they were, were attributed by many as capable of explaining the relative success of some Asian economies over the past decades. The Asian financial crisis may have dampened the enthusiasm of some pundits of Asian values, but this sense of cultural uniqueness is still very much behind the concept of a cultural 'Greater China.'

Another important concept, which is arguably more political than cultural, was called *Reunification Based on Chinese Culture* (*Zhongguo wenhua wei jichu de tongyi*). It was advanced by Chen Lifu, a senior KMT leader and Confucian scholar, at the 13th Congress of the KMT in July 1988. Inspired by the prospect of so-called *Chinese century* (*zhongguoren siji*), Chen suggested Taiwan to abandon its 'three no's' policy and provide long-term concessional loans to the mainland to help build up the Chinese economy in the next millennium under the condition that Beijing abandon the use of force against Taiwan and abolish the Four Cardinal Principles.[30] Chen believed that the basis of China's national reunification should be the Chinese culture shared by the people of the two sides of the Taiwan Straits. Chen's argument was controversial, and Beijing long rejected his political demand. Yet both Beijing and Taipei also stressed the importance of Chinese culture in the eventual reunification.

In his famous eight-point proposal on reunification announced in 1995, Jiang Zemin claimed:

> The splendid culture of five thousand years created by the sons and daughters of all ethnic groups in China has become ties keeping the entire Chinese people close at heart and constitutes an important basis for the peaceful reunification of the motherland. People on both sides of the Taiwan Straits should inherit and carry forward the fine traditions of the Chinese culture.[31]

In his reply to Jiang's proposal, Lee Teng-hui also highlighted the role of Chinese culture, as Lee stated:

> Chinese culture, known for its comprehensive and profundity, has the pride and spiritual support of all Chinese. In Taiwan, we have long taken upon ourselves the responsibility for safeguarding and furthering traditional Chinese culture, and advocate that culture be the basis for exchanges

between both sides to help promote the nationalist sentiment for living together in prosperity and to foster a strong sense of brotherliness. In the immense field of cultural activities, both sides should improve the breadth and depth of various exchange programs, and further advance media, academic, scientific, and sports exchanges and cooperation.[32]

One of the four principles in Taiwan's official Guidelines for National Unification set out in 1991 was: China's unification should aim at promoting Chinese culture, safeguarding human dignity, guaranteeing fundamental human rights, and practicing democracy and the rule of law.[33]

Along with this primacy of Chinese culture is the supposedly cohesive and integrative function of the Chinese language in promoting the integration of Chinese communities. *The Chinese Characters Circle (Hanzi quan)* was a concept raised by Chinese scholars in late 1980s and early 1990s. Chinese characters had been long criticized as a disservice to China's modernization, for they were perceived as hard to learn and difficult to adapt in the technology age. Yet, thanks to the economic dynamism demonstrated in various Chinese communities and technological breakthroughs in computer-processing Chinese characters, scholars started to reassess the role and function of the Chinese language. For instance, An Zijian, an influential Hong Kong scholar and politician, wrote extensively on supposed advantages of Chinese characters. He argued that Chinese language, with its same written form for different dialects, helped sustain China's unification throughout the past two thousand years. Compared with the Latin alphabetical system, An Zijian argued, Chinese characters are equally expressive, yet far more compact. Chinese characters are also said to be more capable of generating new expressions than European languages, with 3,600 common characters capable of generating any new words, while the English language alone has over 100,000 different words by now.[34]

Controversial as his arguments may be, most Chinese scholars agree that the fact that 93 per cent of Chinese share the same written language is a major factor contributing to China's continued unity and will facilitate China's eventual reunification. There is no effort on the part of the Chinese government to establish institutions like the Francophone. Yet both Beijing and Taipei are promoting Chinese culture abroad in part to bring overseas Chinese to their respective side. Beijing already started a 24-hour satellite Chinese TV channel devoted to promoting China and Chinese culture around the world. The network claims to cover 95 per cent of the earth's surface. Taipei offers many scholarships to overseas Chinese students to study in Taiwan and plans to launch a similar global TV network in the millennium year to compete with Beijing. Both sides have sponsored numerous newspapers and journals catering to the overseas Chinese communities. Beijing refurbished in 1995 the mausoleum reputedly for the Yellow Emperor, the legendary founder of the Chinese race. The renovation included large amount of donations from overseas Chinese. The cite was to provide 'a place for all Chinese people to worship their ancestors.'[35]

Whatever political intentions on the part of Beijing or Taipei, a cultural 'Greater China,' with all its variants, reflects a widely-shared view among Chinese communities that Chinese culture seems to have a potent cohesive power, which is certainly extolled by politicians and scholars alike, though often with different purposes. Politicians tend to stress the shared Chinese culture as a tool for a political cause, while scholars are more concerned with the intrinsic values of Chinese culture and its relationship with other cultures and with modernization. It is also true that an ultimate reunification of the mainland and Taiwan based on the shared culture enjoys considerable support from the overseas Chinese. All advocates of a cultural 'Greater China' share a confidence in the time-honoured Chinese civilization. The economic successes of various Chinese communities have generated a sustained interest in the role of Chinese values in promoting modernization. This interest has been demonstrated in the regularly held World Conference of Ethnic Chinese Entrepreneurs, which extols the shared entrepreneurial spirit as well as the business networks based on the shared culture. In China, this mood was reflected in the so-called 'fever of Chinese learning' (*guoxuere*) in the early and mid-1990s. Public mood may change over time, yet Chinese culture is still likely to generate its strong influence on the gradual integration of the Chinese communities, irrespective of its final political shape.

Political 'Greater China'

The discourse of 'Greater China' and its variants generally reflect a widely shared desire for some form of eventual integration of the Chinese world composed of Hong Kong, Macao, Taiwan and the Chinese mainland. With China's reunification with Hong Kong and Macao, many are exploring new initiatives at reunifying Taiwan and the Chinese mainland. Indeed, ideas of economic and cultural 'Greater China' often contain political messages concerning China's eventual reunification. For instance, most advocates of various formulas of economic 'Greater China' argued that economic integration was the best way leading to unification. Chinese leaders certainly hoped that the 'trade and economic exchanges (between Taiwan and the Chinese mainland) ... will help check' the pro-independence trend in Taiwan and promote Taiwan's 'peaceful unification with the motherland.'[36] Jin Hongfan's concept of *the Taiwan Straits Economic Circle* had been conceived as something that would eventually create reunification based on *One Country, Two Systems*.[37] This political desire for reunification has its historical root. In the past two millennium, China was divided many times, but the driving force behind most governments had always been to reunify the country.

Some scholars have put forward the concepts along the lines of federalism and confederation such as *Greater China Confederation* (*Dazhonghua banglian*) by Fei Xiping and *Chinese Federal Republic* (*Zhonghua lianbang gongheguo*) by Zhu Gaozheng or *Chinese Confederation* (*Zhonghua banglian*) by Wang Zuorong.[38] The most notable idea in this connection was advanced by Yan Jiaqi, a mainland scholar in exile living in the United States. Yan proposed transforming the present Chinese polity into a federal structure, and then creating an even looser confederate structure to incorporate Taiwan, Macao and Hong Kong.[39] China's historical experience of *China Proper* and *Outer China* was an inspiration to Yan's line of thinking. Many of China's problems resulting from Beijing's excessive power were another reason for Yan to conceive a federal structure as a way to reform China's present polity.

China's reunification with Hong Kong and Macao has provided additional impetus to those who advocate a politically unified China. The model of *One Country, Two Systems* put forward by Deng Xiaoping, as applied in Hong Kong and Macao, is meant to persuade the Taiwanese leaders to reunify with Beijing. For over three decades after 1949, both Beijing and Taipei hoped to reunify the country under a single government and with a common political, social and economic system. Each side claimed that it was the sole legitimate government of China. In the late 1970s, Beijing took the initiative to modify its policy for reunification, abandon the slogan of 'liberating Taiwan' and claimed to pursue the policy of *One Country, Two Systems*. Within this conceptual framework, Hong Kong, Macao and Taiwan would become special administrative regions of the People's Republic. They would be allowed to retain their social and economic system and enjoy a high degree of autonomy. Beijing would not impose tax on them or send officials to administer these regions. They could preserve their own currencies and judicial independence. As a special gesture to Taiwan, Beijing claimed that Taipei could even maintain its own armed forces and enjoy certain degree of foreign policy autonomy. But under the formula of *One country, Two Systems*, all the polities other than Beijing would be considered as local governments.

Declining this initiative, Taipei put forward a range of different formulas, including *One country, Two Governments* (*Yiguo liangfu*), *One Country, Two Political Entities* (*Yiguo liangge zhengzhi shiti*), *Transitional Two Chinas Leading to One China* (*Yige zhongguo wei zhixiang de jieduanxing de liangge zhongguo*), *One Divided and Separately Ruled China* (*Yige fenzhi de zhongguo*).[40] The essential theme of these formulas is to request Beijing to recognize Taipei as an equal and sovereign government, enjoying equal status in international arena. Taipei held that there is one Chinese nation, but that nation has been divided and run by two equal governments, similar to the case of German nation divided into East and West Germanys. In July 1999, Lee Teng-hui even claimed that his government intended to deal with Beijing on a 'special state-to-state' basis. Beijing rejected this furiously as an attempt to create 'two Chinas,' fearing that any official recognition of China's separate rule would perpetuate China's status of division. Lee's statement has caused new tensions between Beijing and Taipei, which, if mismanaged, could spin the crisis out of control, creating dangerous implications for both sides and for regional peace and stability.

Taipei claims that it has not changed its policy of seeking eventual unification with Beijing. But the difference between Beijing and Taipei over the content of

China's reunification runs deep. Beijing expressed the view that the two sides should keep their separate political systems: the mainland being socialist, and Taiwan remaining capitalist, and two sides co-exist peacefully under one unified China. In contrast, Taipei held that China should be unified under a good political system (*Yiguo liangzhi*). 'China should be united at such a time and in such a manner', as one of the Taiwanese official statements claimed, 'that the rights and interests of the people in the Taiwan area are respected and their security and welfare protected. Unification should be achieved in gradual phases on the principles of reason, peace, parity and reciprocity,' and there should be a 'unification under freedom, democracy, and equitable distribution of wealth.'[41]

Critiques of China's unification stress the gaps in the standards of living, economic institutions, political system and legal system between the Chinese mainland and Taiwan.[42] The counter-argument goes that such gaps are gradually narrowing, with Beijing's effort for economic liberalization and loosening up its political control. Most Taiwanese apparently prefer to maintain the status quo, i.e. neither immediate reunification with the mainland, nor immediate declaration of independence, which would inevitably provoke a military confrontation, as Beijing repeatedly claims that it will have to resort to force if Taiwan declares independence.

If political unification seems to be far away, the economic integration across the Taiwan Straits has created considerable mutual dependency and vulnerability, some kind of institutional mechanism had become necessary for coordinating the exchanges between Beijing and Taipei. In 1991, the two sides finally established semi-official institutions for dialogue with each other: the Straits Exchange Foundation (SEF) for Taiwan and the Association for Relations across the Taiwan Straits (ARATS) for the mainland. This marked a major breakthrough in the bilateral relations. Such direct semi-official contacts culminated in 1993 when Wang Daohan and Koo Chen-fu, the respective heads of the ARATS and SEF met each other in Singapore, and signed a few technical agreements. But the road towards a peaceful co-existence is not plain sailing. The second round of Wang-Koo talks had been cancelled by Beijing in protest of Lee Teng-hui's visit to the United States. After a new round of meetings between Wang Daohan and Koo Chen-fu in October 1998, there seemed to be positive momentum to improve the bilateral ties. Yet since the 'state-to-state' formula was announced in July 1999, Beijing-Taipei relations were once again plunged into a period of instability.

It is still difficult to predict the future of a political 'Greater China.' Lee Teng-hui himself is not optimistic about the idea. In a meeting with him in 1996, Lee made his point clear:

> As for the integration of the mainland, Hong Kong and Taiwan, I think it is a question for the future, a question to be resolved by our future generations. In Europe, integration covers political, economic and security dimensions, whereas in Asia, the Cold War is not yet over, and there are still communist countries and very many political and security problems.[43]

But the picture is not all-grim. In addition to the continued momentum of economic integration, which is the driving force for improved political ties between the two sides, some of Beijing's leaders also demonstrated greater flexibility concerning China's reunification. One option in the air is that both Beijing and Taipei consider changing their 'national titles' in order to accommodate their eventual reunification. Wang Daohan raised another interesting concept of *A Unifying China* (*Yige zouxiang tongyi de zhongguo*):

> One does not need to use 'past tense' or 'future tense' to describe 'one China.' 'One China' can be in 'progressive tense,' that is, a unifying China, and the Chinese on either side of the Taiwan Straits are engaged in creating one unified China.[44]

Reformulating the Taiwanese formula of *One Divided and Separately Ruled China* (*Yige fenzhi de zhongguo*) in 1999, Wang Daohan proposed another interesting concept of *One China to be Ruled Separately* (*Yige zhongguo de fenzhi*). Apparently, Taipei's concept emphasizes separation over unification while Wang's reformulation stresses unification over separation. Wang's idea is a sign of flexibility on the part of Beijing's moderate leaders. Mutual political distrust, however, remains deep in both Taipei and Beijing. While Beijing is strongly suspicious of Taiwan's possible move towards independence, Taipei does not trust Beijing's expressed goodwill for peaceful unification. All signs suggest that it will require enormous political wisdom, courage and patience to build mutual trust before a political 'Greater China' can ever be achieved.

'Greater China' and East Asia

The above examination of various interpretations of 'Greater China' suggests that three aspects of 'Greater China' enjoy a high degree of consensus: (a) 'Greater China' is widely perceived as a growing informal economic epicenter, (b) the most widely accepted expression in this regard is the Chinese Economic Area (CEA), and (c) it is composed essentially of Hong Kong, Taiwan, Macao and the Chinese mainland.

The evolution of 'Greater China' in this sense has been an open process, inextricably linked to the economic development in the region. It is the result of regional economic restructuring since the late 1960s. The so-called 'flying geese theory' or 'multiple catching-up' has reflected this pattern of economic restructuring in East Asia: the Little Dragons first overtook Japan in competitiveness in textile and other labour-intensive manufactured goods in the late 1960s and early 1970s, and by the mid-1980s, the comparative advantage in such production shifted to ASEAN's emerging economies and then China. By the early 1990s, most labour-intensive industries in Hong Kong and Taiwan had been transferred to the Chinese mainland. This has propelled the growth of intra-regional trade between Hong Kong, Taiwan and the mainland

and inflow of capital from Hong Kong and Taiwan to the mainland, thus laying the foundation of a formative 'Greater China'.

'Greater China' as a process of open regionalism has been particularly evident in its evolving relations with Japan. If Japan was still trying to retain knowledge-intensive, value-added production at home in the 1980s, the continuous appreciation of the *yen*, however, forced Japan to shift its value-added industries elsewhere, notably the Greater China region since the late 1980s. Only a decade ago, most Japanese-invested companies in China still sourced components from Japan. By the 1990s, however, they increasingly shifted the whole integrated production from upstream to downstream to China in order to cut costs. It is striking to note how Japanese firms are now reorganising their production bases and supply networking in the Greater China region. For instance, Japanese appliance manufacturers in China now typically secure components from China, Hong Kong and Taiwan. At the same time, many small and medium-sized firms in Japan, which had lost orders when Japanese appliance manufacturers moved overseas, started to invest in China in order to save their markets. In this context, many firms in China, Hong Kong and Taiwan have grown in close association with Japanese firms and markets.[45]

This open regionalism of 'Greater China' has been largely shaped by the open nature of its 'members'. Hong Kong has been one of the freest economies in the world. Taiwan has long been dependent on foreign trade for generating over 90 per cent of its GDP. China has, over the past twenty years, changed from a closed country to an increasingly open economy. The way in which China has pursued its policy of decentralisation and opening to the outside world serves to illustrate this point. Thanks to its policy of decentralisation, a hallmark of Beijing's economic reform programme, China has encouraged all its provinces to work out its own strategy for an open-door policy. Consequently, many border provinces have initiated vigorous border (both land and sea) trade with China's neighbours: Heilongjiang with Russia; Yunnan with Burma; Guangxi with Vietnam; Liaoning and Shandong with South Korea and Japan, Guangdong with Hong Kong and Fujian with Taiwan. As a result, the Chinese economy has been unprecedentedly intertwined with that of other economies in East Asia.

The open nature of 'Greater China' is also reflected in its capacity to propel the regional economic growth, as it has become a new epicentre for industry, commerce and finance in the region. Most neighbours have benefited from their dynamic business ties with the loose and informal 'Greater China'. China's relations with other sub-regional groupings are also a case in point. For instance, the proposed Tumen Development Zone (around the Tumen River Delta) offers enormous potential for co-operation among China, Russia, North Korea, Mongolia, South Korea and Japan. Beijing is a keen supporter of the Zone idea. The Chinese side has proposed to build up the Zone so as to expedite the development of the Chinese northeast, the Russian Far East and North Korea. Beijing even suggested to set up a single zone extending over territorial borders, in which products, people and capital would be able to move freely, and the Zone should be managed by an international organisation that will co-ordinate the various national interests involved.[46]

China's altitude towards the Japan Sea Rim Economic Sphere offers another interesting example. China does not openly endorse the idea, partly due to China's suspicion of Japan's intention to dominate the region, yet Beijing allowed and even encouraged its coastal provinces like Jilin and Shandong to develop special ties with Japan. China also helped build the so-called Eastern Maritime Silk Road from Sakata Port in Yamagata Prefecture to China's Harbin via the Amur River, cutting the time for travel from China's northern Heilongjiang Province to Japan in half and the cost to a third compared to the conventional route through Dalian.[47]

The depth and scope of Greater China's engagement with the region has been highlighted by the Asian financial crisis. While individual economies of 'Greater China' have become more interdependent of each other during the crisis, they have also developed shared interest in resisting the crisis and assisting the region's recovery from the crisis. Beijing, Taipei and Hong Kong have all offered assistance to the recession-torn countries. They have all participated in a 'regional rescue fund.' As the fortune of 'Greater China' is already linked with that of other economies in the region, it needs continued regional prosperity for its own growth.

Prior to the crisis, this growth of intra-regional trade and interdependency in East Asia were widely interpreted as a trend towards East Asian regionalism. It was often described as a counter current against the growing regionalism in Europe and North America or as a symbol of East Asia's rise in the international arena. Malaysian Prime Minister Mahathir's concept of creating an East Asian Economic Caucus (EAEC) epitomised this tendency. The Asian financial crisis has, however, revealed the structural weakness of many Asian economies and dealt a heavy blow to the idea of East Asian regionalism, for the crisis has shown the extent to which many East Asian economies still rely on external help for their recovery. While recognising the importance of intra-regional trade in East Asia, Beijing, Taipei and Hong Kong have never endorsed an exclusive economic arrangement for East Asia. China understands its needs for funding, technology and the market from developed countries. Hong Kong can not survive if it loses its status as a most free economy in the world. Taiwan's largest trading partner remains the United States. The political distrust between China and Japan is another reason why Beijing is not in favour of any exclusive economic arrangements for East Asia, as it fears the revival of Japan's pre-war Co-Prosperity Sphere.

However, the Asian financial crisis also highlighted the importance of regional Cupertino. There is a general appreciation of China's policy to keep its currency stable and stimulate its domestic consumption and Japan's commitment to provide more assistance and stimulate its domestic demand. With ever increasing intra-regional interdependency and growing suspicions about unrestrained globalisation, some form of open regionalism in East Asia is still held by many as a viable idea.

While the evolution of 'Greater China' is largely an open process, it has also increased competition between 'Greater China' and other economies in the region. Such competition is manifested, for instance, in the flows of FDIs. China has become the second largest recipient of FDIs in the world (next to the United States) since the early 1990s. Hong Kong and Taiwan are the two largest sources of FDIs for China. Furthermore, it is not always easy to identify clearly the sources of FDIs. They may come from mixed overseas Chinese sources: an investment may come from a Hong Kong company created by an ethnic Chinese tycoon from Malaysia, with large family networks in Indonesia. But it can also be argued that much of the profit these companies gain in China also go back to the investors' countries, though it has been difficult to compile empirical evidence in this regard.

'Greater China' also means a heightened competition with some developing countries of the region, including its Southeast Asian neighbours, in both labour-intensive and knowledge-intensive industries. China is now world's largest manufacturing base for labour-intensive products. Thanks to investors from Hong Kong and Taiwan, the Chinese mainland has significantly upgraded its manufacturing capacity for international trade. China's foreign trade has grown fast over the past two decades. Hong Kong and Taiwan have also supplied institutional substitutes for a viable market economy, such as laws, regulations, business culture and management to help bridge the gap between China and the world market. Furthermore, China enjoys comparative advantages not only in labour-intensive industries, but also in many sectors of modern industries and scientific research, compared with developing countries at a similar level of development. Investors from Hong Kong and Taiwan are now inspiring China to link its research with industry and the market. Beijing and Taipei are vigorously promoting their respective technology-intensive industries, while Hong Kong is building almost from scratch, with some help from the mainland, its high-tech research and industry. In other words, many countries are feeling the competition from 'Greater China' in both labour-intensive and knowledge-intensive industries. This competition may intensify as the process of globalisation continues. However, such competition may well be inevitable, as this is largely entrenched in the current international economic structure. In other words, even if the Southeast Asian economies were not competing with 'Greater China', they would be competing with others like India or Mexico. In the age of globalisation, developing countries may have to seek their own niches through market competition, while keeping their doors open for possible dialogues and co-operation.

The political consequence of 'Greater China' for its 'members' and for the region is more complicated. Will it lead to China's reunification with Taiwan as Beijing desires? Will political problems across the Taiwan Straits lead to increased mutual suspicion, confrontation and even disruption of regional peace and prosperity? Will 'Greater China' be the new hegemon in the region when such integration becomes more institutionalised? It is indeed amazing that in the absence of mutual recognition of sovereignty and government's co-ordination, there has been a fast movement of information, finance, goods and capital that binds together the two sides of the Taiwan Straits. This informal integration may create more incentives for the two sides to eventually overcome their political differences. However, political distrust between Beijing and Taipei is deep, and any military conflict arising from this distrust may engulf not only the two sides, destroying the prospects of an economic 'Greater China', not also the whole region, thus undermining East Asia's peace and prosperity. East Asia, barely over the worst of an economic crisis, cannot afford a major regional conflict. A peaceful solution to the political differences between Beijing and Taipei would be in the interest of the two sides across the Taiwan Strait as well as the whole region.

Political suspicion about the rise of 'Greater China' still runs deep at the regional level, just as many countries in the region fear China's excessive predominance may change forever the balance of power in East Asia. In order to alleviate such concerns, Beijing rarely uses the concept of 'Greater China'. Beijing spares no effort to resist the image of a rising China as a threat to regional or international peace. Beijing also has a genuine concern that the sensitive ethnic relations in Southeast Asia may be greatly complicated by any talk of 'Greater China' that includes overseas Chinese living in Southeast Asia.

As mentioned earlier, Beijing endorses the concept *Liang'an Sidi Jingji Hezuo (Quadriparitite economic cooperation)*[48] and encourages economic co-operation and political reunification among the People's Republic, Taiwan, Hong Kong and Macao. For China's neighbours, while the strained relations between Beijing and Taipei are viewed as destabilising, they also worry that a politically unified 'Greater China' may represent a resurgent China and an upsurge in Chinese nationalism, which may also threaten the peace and prosperity in East Asia.

In the study of international relations, it is a functionalist view that economic exchanges lead to more peaceful inter-state relations. China's recent experience seems to have proved this. But the realist school argues that with power augmentation, a country has a tendency to discover new interests and more places to apply that power. It was the case with virtually all former European empires. While modernisation has significantly expanded China's incentives in engaging itself with the outside world, a modernised China will have to prove in the future that it can be an exception to this rule.

China's concept of its historic empire was, however, different from the Romans or the British, for whom, the empires were built by conquest over long distances. For most of its two thousand years of history as a unified country, this was not the case with the so-called Chinese empire. With the exception of the early Mongol period of 90 years and the early Qing dynasty, when China was itself part of the world empire of the non-Chinese, most Chinese emperors preferred to control China's traditional lands adhering to a belief in China's centrality and invulnerability. Chinese empire was based more on China's supposedly cultural superiority than military conquest. If two thousand years of history is a guide for future, it does not seem likely that China will necessarily strive to build an imperialist empire in the region at the expense of the country's already extensive engagement with the outside world. Yet, the Chinese historic empire, different from other empires, has, for its own reasons, left unpleasant memories on many of China's neighbours. Conditions for this kind of empire no longer exist and are unlikely to reemerge in the future. Regional institutional frameworks should be developed, in which a modernised China will be an important member, subjected to the same rules of the game like others, so that no country in the region will ever attempt to build an empire. In this context, most Asian countries hope to see a stable and healthy China as the key to their regional prosperity. Greater efforts and political wisdom are still required to make the rise of 'Greater China' or the CEA an open and smooth process in parallel with China's engagement with other countries and institutions in the region and beyond. It should be a peaceful process that will serve the interest of regional stability and prosperity in the new millennium.

Conclusion

There is a diverse range of concepts depicting the framework for integrating various Chinese communities. Of these concepts, 'Greater China' seems to be inclusive enough to cover most variants. While the idea originates from the early time of *China Proper* and *Outer China*, its more recent meaning reflects the increased interactions among diverse Chinese communities. Indeed, entrepreneurs and traders from various Chinese communities have pioneered an informal integration through their innumerable personal ties and business networks. This informal integration may be compared to building a house without a blueprint: in the absence of a chief architect and master blueprint (i.e. without government's coordination), builders (entrepreneurs, traders, artists, scholars, etc.) have already, often without their own knowledge, gone a long way in building the foundation of this house, seemingly oblivious of its future shape.

The above discussion of different interpretation of 'Greater China' seems to reveal that despite the controversial nature of the concept, there is already a broadly shared consensus on some major aspects of such an informal integration between the Chinese communities. The consensus includes:

(a) 'Greater China' refers essentially to the integration of Hong Kong, Taiwan, and the Chinese mainland;
(b) Such integration is largely economic and informal, driven in part by the shared culture;
(c) The frequently used term in this connection is the Chinese Economic Area;
(d) 'Greater China' has reflected an open regionalism that has been shaped by the economic restructuring in East Asia and may continue to operate as a dynamic epicentre for regional economy, and
(e) A political 'Greater China' is still difficult to achieve, due to the disputes between Beijing and Taipei. The concept is also politically sensitive in the region, given many people's fear of Chinese predominance in the region.

From a long-term perspective, some formal form of economic 'Greater China' may occur, as increased mutual dependency and vulnerability require more institutional building, and the economies of Hong Kong, Taiwan, Macao and the mainland are far more complementary than competitive and the potential gains from cooperation are so huge. This process will be further strengthened by the shared Chinese culture. However, this process is unlikely to be smooth, and some tricky problems within 'Greater China', especially the political disputes between Beijing and Taipei, may slow down or even derail this process. The ultimate success of 'Greater China' or Chinese Economic Area still depends on whether Beijing and Taipei can resolve their political differences and whether this 'entity' can evolve its own norms and institutional frameworks. It is a widely shared hope among the Chinese communities that the on-going informal economic integration between Taiwan and the Chinese mainland will create new momentum and conditions for resolving peacefully the political problems between them.

The open regionalism as represented by 'Greater China' seems to be in the economic interest of the region, as it has generated and may continue to generate growth for all. If China is on its way to become the world's largest economy in the first half of the new millennium, as many economists have predicted, an open 'Greater China' is bound to create wide range of new opportunities for expanding trade and co-operation in the region and beyond. For understandable reasons, this process also increases economic competition between 'Greater China' and other economies, though such competition may not necessarily be unhealthy to the competitors involved.

It is true that a political 'Greater China' is difficult to achieve, primarily because of the Beijing-Taipei disputes. Such an 'entity' is also viewed with suspicion and fear in the region. While China's historic legacy does not suggest an intention to build an imperialistic empire, much still remains to be done to enmesh this huge country into the mainstream of regional affairs and institutional frameworks. Leaders from various Chinese communities still have to demonstrate their vision, wisdom and courage to make the rise of 'Greater China' a smooth and transparent process, with benefits not only for China and the Chinese but also for other countries and peoples in the region and beyond.

Notes

1. Harry Harding, 'The Concept of Greater China: Themes, Variations and Reservations,' *The China Quarterly*, 1993, pp. 661–663.
2. Cited in *Far Eastern Economic Review* (20 July 1979), p. 24.
3. Huang Zhilian, *Meiguo 203 nian: dui meiguo tixi yu weilaixue de fenxi* (*America at 203 Years: an Analysis of the Historiography and Futurology of the American System*) (Hong Kong: Zhongliu Press, 1980), pp. 915–929.
4. Harry Harding, p. 660.
5. For instance, China's leading dissident Wei Jingsheng and Hong Kong's democracy advocate Martin Lee held a briefing at the Palais des Nations, Geneva, on *Democratic Development in Greater China* on 14 April 1999.

6　E. Vogel, *One Step Ahead in China – Guangdong under Reform* (Cambridge, Mass.: Harvard University Press, 1989).

7　Jin Hongfan, Zhen Zeqing and Liu Yishen, *Mingtai Jingji Guanxi: Lishi Xianzhuang Weilai* (Fujian-Taiwan Economic Relations: Past, Present and Future) (Xiamen: Lujiang Press, 1992), p. 160.

8　Ibid., pp. 156–164.

9　Zhen Zuyuan, *Dazhonghua Jingji Gongtongti de Gouxiang* (The Idea of Greater China Economic Community), *China Times* (27 June 1988).

10　Cited in *Taiwan Times* (22 September 1988).

11　Gao made this proposal in at a symposium on China's external economic relations held at University of California, Berkeley in August 1998.

12　For example, Macao's contracted investment in China reached over 9 billion US dollars and actual investment was 3.3 billion US dollars by the end of 1998. See *Renmin Ribao* (24 May 1999).

13　'China says 1998 trade gap with Taiwan $12.76 billion,' Reuters News, *Infoseek* (29 January 1999).

14　*Renmin Ribao* (overseas edition) (9 April 1998).

15　See Liu Rong (ed.) *Zhonghua Jingji Xiezuo Xitong Lun* (On Coordinating System for the Chinese Economy) (Hong Kong: Sanlian Press, 1993), p. 52.

16　Wei-Wei Zhang, 'Beijing and Taipei: Building a Framework and Mechanism for Informal Integration', presented at the 13th Sino-European Conference held in Taipei in 1996. See also *Asian Review* (*Yazhou Pinglun*), (Spring–Summer 1998), No. 7, pp. 94–109.

17　Zhen Zuyuan, *Dazhonghua Jingji Gongtongti de Gouxiang* (The Idea of Greater China Economic Community), *China Times* (27 June 1988).

18　Chen presented his view at a symposium on China's external economic relations held at University of California, Berkeley in August 1998.

19　See Tian Zhili, *21shiji Zhonghua Jingjiqu* (Chinese Economic Area in the 21st Century), (Taipei: Lixu Press, 1998), pp. 71–73.

20　See, for instance, Ji Chongwei (ed.) *Zhongguo Dalu yu Gang Ao Tai Diqu Jingji Hezuo Qianjing* (the Prospects of Economic Co-operation between the Chinese Mainland and Hong Kong, Macao and Taiwan) (Beijing: People's Daily Press, 1995). This is one of the most authoritative books on the subject published in China.

21　See Wu An-Chia, *Taihai Liang-an Guanxi De Huigu Yu Zhanwang* (Cross-Taiwan Strait Relations: Retrospect and Prospect) (Taipei: Lifework Press, 1996), pp. 167–168.

22　See Tian Zhili, pp. 79–80.

23　Lee Teng-hui, Statement at the 10th Plenary Session of the National Reunification Council, 8 April 1995.

24　See Tian Zhili, pp. 79–80.

25　This point was made by Yun-wing Sung, cited in Harding, p. 669.

26　'Asia's New Fire-breather,' *Business Week* (10 October 1988), pp. 54–55.

27　*Renmin Ribao* (overseas edition), 10 October 1998.

28　Wang Gongwu, 'Among non-Chinese,' *Daedalus*, Vol. 120, No. 2 (1991), p. 136, and Harding, p. 677.

29　Harding, p. 674.

30　The Four Cardinal Principles are adherence to (1) Marxism-Leninism and Mao Zedong Thought; (2) socialism; (3) the leadership of the Communist Party of China; and (4) the people's democratic dictatorship.

31　*Renmin Ribao*, 31 January 1995.

32　Lee Teng-hui, Statement at the 10th Plenary Session of the National Reunification Council, 8 April 1995.

33　Ibid.

34　See Tian Zhili, pp. 242–243.

35 'The New Nationalism,' *Far Eastern Economic Review,* November 9, 1995.
36 Yang Shangkun's remark in 1990, cited in Wu An-chia, p. 214.
37 Jin, Zhen and Liu (1992), p. 164.
38 Zhang Zanhe, *Liang-an guanxi bianqian shi* (A History of the Cross-Strait Relations) (Taipei: Zhouzhiwenhua Press, 1996), pp. 435–439.
39 Yan Jiaqi, *Lianbangzhi zhongguo gouxiang* (*The Concept of a Federal China*), *Ming Bao* (Hong Kong, 1992).
40 See Wu An-chia, pp. 143–146.
41 *Guidelines for National Reunification,* quoted in Wu An-chia, p. 226.
42 See, for example, Gao Chang, *Haixia liangan jingji zhenghe kexingxing fenxi* (An analysis of the feasibility of cross-Strait economic integration), *Taiwan jingji yanjiu yuekan* (Taiwan Economic Research Monthly), Vol. 14, No.6 (June 1991), pp. 67–74.
43 Personal notes, 25 September 1996.
44 Wang Daohan's conservation with the author on 5 October 1996.
45 Robert Taylor, *Greater China and Japan* (Routledge: London and New York, 1996), pp. 138–140.
46 Robert Taylor, p. 166.
47 Robert Taylor, p. 164.
48 The literal translation of this term should be 'Cross-Straits and Quadripartite Economic Co-operation.'

10 Sovereignty at bay?

Business networking and democratic politics of informal integration between Taiwan and Mainland China in the 1990s

Tse-Kang Leng

Cooperation and conflicts between Taiwan and Mainland China provide a unique case for East Asian regionalism and integration. Three factors entangle this unique case of East Asia regionalism: economic globalization, national sovereignty, and democratic politics. The case of Taiwan and Mainland China indicates that in terms of the various dimensions of East Asia regionalism such as economic, political, security, and socio-cultural perspectives, political factors still play a dominant role in regional cooperation and regime formation. Policies of major power, especially policies of the United States, have also influenced autonomous actions within the framework of East Asia regionalism. In the case of cross-Taiwan Straits interaction, the ultimate goal of the United States is to maintain status quo within the framework of stability in East Asia.

From an optimistic perspective, economic complementarity and the division of labor between these two economies will lead to a de facto integration in the economic realm. In reality, the dynamic alliances among multinational corporations, Taiwanese firms, and mainland China's coastal areas create a 'networking economy' parallel to that of nation states. Furthermore it could be argued that economic, social and cultural interactions may eventually lay a solid foundation for future political integration.

From a pessimistic point of view, political antagonism and concerns for national sovereignty on both sides of Taiwan Straits are still dominant forces controlling the direction and tempo of economic interaction. In reviewing the development of cross-Straits relations in the 1990s, economic integration and political hostility has come to coexist within the context of economic globalization. The networking economy across the Taiwan Straits has neither lead to the demise of nation state nor to the rise of a 'greater China'.

One key reason for the ascendance of political factors in cross-Straits relations is the democratic transition that has taken place in Taiwan. While it may hold that global trends of democratization can lead to a 'democratic peace', it is also fair to say that democratic regimes' attempts at protecting democratic norms and spreading democratic culture may just as likely lead to the 'democratic crusading' of provocative actions towards non-democratic countries. Scholars have also argued that some internal characteristics of democracy, such as irrational public opinion and electoral cycles, may in fact make the external policies of liberal regimes more war-prone and volatile. Differing from 'mature democracies', these 'democratizing regimes' lack a coherent mechanism of regularized leadership changes, institutional stability, stability of preferences, and consensus on core national interests. Without these crucial factors of a liberal democratic regime, 'democratizing' regimes may play destabilizing roles in the international system.[1] In other words, 'democracy' per se is a double-edged sword. The rising global trend of democratization tends to link domestic political change with the management of external relations. Peace and conflicts across the Taiwan Straits are a reflection of this democratic dilemma.[2]

By juxtaposing these cooperative and conflicting trends of cross-Taiwan Straits relations, this chapter aims to analyze the political factors impeding the institutionalization of economic integration and regional cooperation in the 1990s. This chapter argues that economic interdependence, especially asymmetric interdependence, does not necessarily lead to regional cooperation and regional integration. Rather with respect to East Asia, the linkages between domestic and external relations greatly influence the scope and content of regionalism. In this case, it is clear that nation states adjust, rather than retreat, their roles in the market economy in the era of global capitalism. However, state actions in the framework of East Asia regionalism are still constrained by the major powers in the region especially the United States. Economic cooperation and integration are crucial political, rather than economic, issues in the regional and international settings.

'Civilian governance' of economic relations between Taiwan and Mainland China

In the early stage of cross-Straits economic interaction, most Taiwanese firms in Mainland China were small and medium size enterprises. These firms have concentrated their investments on China's booming coastal areas. Due to policy restrictions and risk evaluation, larger enterprises have taken a more conservative approach in their policies towards investment projects in Mainland China. In addition, big scale investment projects were not realized until the mid-1990s. In 1993, about 41.68 per cent of Taiwan's large enterprises invested in mainland China; whereas in 1998, the percentage rose to 56.63, a growing factor of 35.86 per cent.[3]

The Taiwanese government has adopted relatively constrained policies on promoting cross-Straits trade and investment. The main reason for this containment is the concerns over political side effects stemming from Taiwan's economic dependence on Mainland China. However, on the other hand the state efforts to compete with the market mechanism have not been too successful either. Even though the Taiwanese government set up a general framework geared to provide 'indirect economic transaction' with Mainland China, the Taiwanese business community has still managed to find its own way to march into the booming mainland market. In other words, the real dynamism of cross-Straits trade and investment relies on the energetic Taiwanese business community, not the ambitious policies promoted by the state.[4] There are practicalities behind this since high labor and land costs have made labor-intensive industries in Taiwan no longer profitable. For Taiwan's small and medium-sized enterprises, moving their businesses to Mainland China is the only way for survival. According to various surveys, these small and medium sized firms do not intend to create any kind of 'vertical division of labor' between Taiwan and Mainland China; on the contrary, more than half of these firms move their production lines completely to Mainland China. Investment value is accelerated once they are embedded in the huge mainland market. The real investment amount is always triple that originally planned.[5]

Big Taiwanese enterprises adopt different strategies to develop the mainland market. In the past decades, Taiwan's export-led growth was conducted by the endeavors of small and medium size firms. Traditionally Taiwan's big enterprises and enterprise groups have focused on Taiwan's own domestic market. China's gradual opening of its domestic market thus provides strong incentives for Taiwanese large sized enterprises to launch new projects on Mainland China.

Taiwan's big enterprises differ from solely owned, short-term oriented investment strategies adopted by small firms, which tend to establish joint ventures with mainland partners. Joint ventures help to create a network with mainland's down-stream industries. This networking capacity could also improve marketing capacities of Taiwanese firms in Mainland China. The investment project of Hua-Hsin-Li-Hua (HHLH), a big Taiwanese electronics company, illustrates a case of such division of labor. Through its controlling company in Hong Kong, HHLH moved to establish joint ventures with Shanghai Telecom in 1993. HHLH has established its network in mainland China via three different channels: (1) by investing in the existing equipment of mainland partners; (2) by transferring components from Taiwan to update mainland factories; (3) by setting up totally new factories on mainland China. HHLH also establishes cooperative relationship with other smaller mainland as well as Taiwanese firms to guarantee the supply of crucial parts. Currently all the seven branch companies of HHLH sell for the domestic market of Mainland China only. According to HHLH's own estimation, the total production value of its mainland branches will reach 600 million US dollars in the year 2000.[6]

To sum up, the recent trend of Taiwanese investment to Mainland China could be outlined as follows:

1 Taiwanese investment in Mainland China in the early stages has been mainly export-oriented. Taiwanese firms reprocess products in Mainland China and sell to the world market. Since the mid-1990s, as the mainland's domestic market has further opened up, so has Taiwanese investment gradually shifted its focus.

2 In addition to manufacturing industries, big enterprises from Taiwan put more emphasis on the booming service sectors in Mainland China such as banking, stock markets, and real estate markets. This trend may accelerate after mainland and Taiwan both join the WTO.

3 According to various surveys, about 60 per cent of Taiwanese firms in Mainland China are profitable. Due to tax and other concerns, it is believed that reported profit rate is underestimated.

4 Taiwan's regulatory policies have little, if any, impacts on existing Taiwanese enterprises on Mainland China. Considering political factors and their close connections with the state, big enterprises in Taiwan keep a low profile about their mainland projects. Instead, they utilize their international networks to escape governmental regulations from the home country.

5 As Taiwanese investment deepens, Taiwanese capital will become a more integral part with mainland's local development. Taiwanese investment creates jobs, brings know-how technologies, and improves living standards of the host areas. In reality, this trend creates a de facto economic integration across the Taiwan Straits.

Another factor for consideration is that the 'civilian governance' in the economic realm tends to create a bottom-up force for cross-Straits cooperation. It also lays a foundation for economic integration in the Taiwan Straits region. Although empirical proof on the 'spill-over' effects to the political realm are still to be observed, it is clearly apparent that economic relations are serving as a catalyst to link the social dynamics of the two sides of Taiwan Straits. The social and economic impacts of Taiwan's democracy are a pre-condition for positive interaction between Taiwan and Mainland China.

Business networking and Taiwanese investment in Mainland China

As the preceding analysis shows, big Taiwanese firms began rushing into the mainland market from the mid-1990s. In addition to their focus on the Mainland's domestic market, these bigger firms have sought to adopt strategies of internationalization in order to escape from the regulatory policies in Taiwan. This move has also served to decrease political risks for their projects in Mainland China. In other words, the globalization of firms has made it more difficult for both sides of the Taiwan Straits to effectively control capital and trade flows between them. Traditional mercantilist thought presumes that states can control private firms, and thus use economic relations as a leverage to protect national interests. Nowadays however, globalized firms cannot be easily 'used' by any single country. Therefore, internationalization may, in fact, twist or alleviate the political effects of economic dependence because firms have gradually become more independent.

Taiwanese investment in Mainland China is also a part of the global network of economic internationalization. For instance, the Taiwan government prohibits the investment of high-tech and infrastructure industries in Mainland China. However, Taiwanese firms have adopted strategies of international operation to escape from government regulations. Taiwanese capital can be found in the

Nanjing-Wenzhou railway project on Mainland China. The Acer group has also utilized its subsidiaries in Malaysia to invest in CD-ROM factories in Suzhou through technology transfers.[7] Since technology transfers through a third country are not clearly prohibited by current Taiwanese policies, firms seeking to internationalize have followed a similar strategy in taking advantage of the gray areas in legal restrictions.

Another strategy for the Taiwanese enterprises has been to obtain capital in the international capital market to support their mainland projects. The favorite places for Taiwanese business communities are Singapore and Hong Kong. Wong-Wong Cookies Company, the biggest Taiwanese company of this kind in Mainland China, has accumulated more than US$63 million from the Singaporean stock market. Even though Hong Kong has been an integral part of China since July 1, 1997, many Taiwanese companies are optimistic about its highly liberalized capital market and are utilizing Hong Kong as a base of financial management.[8] Other multinational corporations such as Formosa Plastics have used their branch companies or subsidiaries in a third country to undertake projects in Mainland China. Moreover, Taiwanese investors can bring their capital out of Taiwan by transferring the foreign exchange earned from exports. Exporters sometimes retain their foreign exchange to invest in Mainland China, and a large portion of these flow directly into China, with Taiwan being unable to control the capital outflow.[9] In practice, if the investors are endowed with dual nationality and do not have Taiwan residence status; their investment activities are outside legal restrictions.[10]

Another example of internationalized firm behavior is Formosa's power plant project in Zhangzhou, Fujian Province. When Formosa's Y.C. Wang announced the project in mid-1996, it caused a major shock to Taiwan's mainland economic policies. However, even so, in this US$3 billion investment, the Mother Company would only contribute US$400 million, or approximately 14 per cent of the total. Indeed, Formosa's overseas subsidiaries will play a major role in terms of investors, while international banks, including Japan's Mitsubishi and Sumitomo and several German banks, had expressed interest in loaning more than US$2 billion.[11] In other words, major financial support would have been from international, rather than domestic, sources. According to the reviewing rules of the Economic Screening Committee, Taiwanese companies' foreign subsidiaries can freely invest in mainland China without reporting to the government if the mother companies' stock share does not exceed 20 per cent. In the Formosa case, the Mother Company holds only 10.6 per cent of the stock.[12] In other words, in legal terms, the government would have found it difficult to block the project.

Although Wang finally submitted the investment project to the government for review, he himself withdrew the proposal afterwards under the pressure of the MOEA. However, as in the Haicang case, this project has not come to a stop; Wang has made it clear that the Zhangzhou project will not be used to 'support the bandit', claiming that he intends to support more Taiwanese companies in mainland China, to import more equipment from Taiwan, and enhance Taiwan's international competitiveness through economic division of labor with mainland China. In March 1998, Wang declared that Formosa planned to sell the ownership of the Zhangzhou factory to foreign companies. Once the restrictions of the Taiwan government are lifted, Formosa will buy back the factory. According to the Minister of Economic Affairs, such moves 'do not go against the current policy'.[13]

Another recent trend of cooperation among firms has been the forming of strategic alliances. In this new world of economic globalization, boundaries of individual firms have become fuzzier as their spheres of influence over the management of resources has been extended to embrace a variety of cooperative arrangements and network agreements. This new constellation of strategic alliances is a loosely coupled system characterized by coordinate specialization in the production of goods and services, as informal contracts govern the behavior of individual members, without any one dominant member, and negotiation and consensus-building take place before collective action.[14]

Rather than competing with Multinational Corporations (MNCs), some Taiwanese firms have played the role of a bridge between foreign firms and Mainland China's domestic companies. Due to cultural and linguistic differences, MNCs sometimes have had difficulties in utilizing Mainland China's resources.[15] Allying with Taiwanese firms has helped to resolve these difficulties and has enhanced their bargaining power through collective actions. Furthermore, Mainland China's 'investment protection agreement' with foreign countries can also serve as an indirect umbrella for strategic alliances.

According to various surveys, most Taiwanese strategic alliances tend to concentrate on transportation tools and food industries. As stated earlier, these industries are domestic rather than export oriented. The natural choice for an investment site for the domestic market is Shanghai, which offers a huge consumer population in the Yangtze River delta.[16] A typical alliance would involve a situation whereby Taiwanese firms provide marketing and production capacities while MNCs would offer the necessary technologies and capital. Furthermore, since strategic alliances focus on Mainland China's domestic market, foreign brand names are crucial for success. Taiwanese marketing and production techniques have thus successfully transferred these brands with 'Chinese characteristics.'

In addition to the role of Taiwan firms' as a bridge between MNCs and the mainland market, MNCs can also play a role in integrating enterprises on both sides of the Taiwan Strait. These MNCs have investment projects on both sides, and thus have indirectly created a vertical and horizontal division of labor between Taiwan and Mainland China. For example, pharmaceutical industries in Japan initiate a joint project with Taiwanese and mainland partners to develop global herb medicine market. About thirty Taiwanese pharmaceutical enterprises begin to merge into an integrated company. This newly integrated company then forms a strategic alliance with Tsumura group in Japan. The strategic alliance combines Taiwan's manufacturing capacities with Japan's technology and international marketing advantages. This new alliance cooperates with the mainland's existing herb industries to guarantee the supply of raw herb materials. Production lines in Taiwan produce high-quality herb medicine and on-sell to the international market.[17] With the multinational corporations serving as a bridge, integration of the two sides of the Taiwan Straits into the global economy is realized.

Economic globalization and business networking more or less constrain the capacities of the state to participate in economic activities. In the case of Taiwan and Mainland China, an optimistic outlook points to the real dynamism of cross-Straits economic interaction, which is vested in individual firms or alliances of firms.[18] The phenomena of 'global capitalism' may further deter the use of economic statecraft by individual states. On the other hand, in terms of firm behavior scholars also indicate that even highly internationalized multinational corporations retain their national characteristics. These firms are a reflection of the interaction of state efforts and the domestic constellation of social and cultural forces.[19] State structures and political perceptions within the nation state have a great impact on regional integration. From a synthetic perspective, the state and market mechanism collectively determines the degree of integration both in the economic and political sphere.

Both Taiwan and Mainland China intend to utilize these economic interactions as a useful tool to achieve political purposes. Conversely though, the essence of this trend towards economic liberalization and globalization is that it sets up a major challenge to a more traditional wisdom advocating this kind of 'economic statecraft'. In the past decades, both Taiwan and Mainland China have adjusted themselves in order to adapt to the global trend of globalization. These two Chinese political entities have also experienced tremendous changes in domestic politics and cross-Taiwan Straits relations. Coping with economic globalization while at the same time promoting the national interest has become an international and domestic concern for both Taiwan and Mainland China.

As the world economy becomes more globalized, internationalized firms will come to further challenge state intervention in the market mechanism. In other words, the business community has emerged to play a major role somehow parallel to governments on both sides of the Taiwan straits. The effectiveness of economic statecraft is then clearly dependent on the balance of the bargaining power between the states and firms. Through various alliances of business networking, pure 'Taiwanese investment' becomes more difficult to be identified. Mainland China's potential 'economic sanctions' on Taiwanese investment may hurt international investment in Mainland China as a whole.

Hence, the 'de facto' integration between Taiwan and Mainland China in fact complicates the utilization of economic statecraft. Economic globalization and international strategic alliances impose major challenges of regulatory policies on both sides of the Taiwan Straits. The interaction between the international-oriented Taiwanese firms and mainland's local economies may serve as a catalyst of economic interdependence, rather than unilateral dependence, across the Taiwan Straits. From this perspective, the political and economic entanglements between Taiwan and Mainland China should be reconsidered under the broader context of international politics of economic globalization.

Political forces behind regional integration and disintegration

From a purely economic perspective, Taiwan and Mainland China are mutually complementary. In terms of a 'Greater China Economic Circle' which includes Taiwan, Hong Kong, and Mainland China's coastal areas, it seems to be a natural trend of integration. However, reviewing the development across the Taiwan Straits since 1989, economic cooperation has not come to the political sphere. While economic interactions have quite naturally become closer and closer, political differences still exist, and have even widened. In 1996, political tensions were escalated to a point of crisis with Mainland China's launching of missile tests near Taiwan's northern and southern ports. Such tendencies can be seen to derive from two major factors that will continue to contribute to the 'disintegration' of these two Chinese political entities regardless of de facto economic integration: political distrust toward political integration, and the differences between the regime types across the Taiwan Straits. In other words, Taiwan's democratic transition in the 1990s has lead to political uncertainty regardless of economic determinants.

The traditional wisdom of democratic peace argues that democratic norms and processes restrain domestic ambition to provoke international wars. Under the institutional constraints of democratic processes democratic leaders would find it difficult to move their countries into war. Hence, democracies rarely fight each other.[20] Moreover, political liberalization and democratization creates a strong civil society. Forces within the civil society help promote transnational economic, cultural, and technological cooperation. These transnational efforts reduce the importance of national sovereignty and lead to international peace.

While entirely plausible this 'democratic peace' argument is in fact, still subject to empirical test.[21] In the real world of the state system, this sense of insecurity has clearly originated from the structural constraints of international anarchy, not from a domestic constellation of power shifts. Facing an 'imperfect world' within which democratic and authoritarian regimes coexist under the international system, democracies perceive an even stronger challenge from undemocratic regimes. In other words, the sense of distrust within democratic regimes toward non-democratic regimes may introduce more uncertain factors other than peace and cooperation in the international system.

Taiwan's democracy and political distrust toward regional integration

The major source of Taiwan's distrust towards regional integration across the Taiwan Straits, stems from the asymmetry of power between Taiwan and Mainland China. Considering the size of China, the mainland market, it is as a big 'sponge' to act to attract Taiwanese investment. Along with Taiwan's economic dependence on Mainland China there is the decidedly unpalatable situation of Beijing's continuous diplomatic blockade and the threat of use of force toward Taiwan. From Taiwan's perspective, the asymmetric distribution of power between Taiwan and Mainland China cannot help but lead to Taiwan's 'vulnerability' and 'sensitivity' within this unique relationship.[22]

In addition, since the political systems of Taiwan and Mainland China are showing a widening gap, this serves to further deepen distrust over any arrangement to move towards immediate political integration as proposed by Mainland China. From the liberal democratic standard, Taiwanese people enjoy full protection of civil rights and civil liberties under the rule of law. Major political posts from the central to the local governments, including the president, are elected directly by the citizens. Public trust toward Mainland China's 'one-country, two systems' formula of unification is relatively low even as economic integration has deepened.

Prior to Mainland China's opening up to the world in the late 1970s, Taiwan's economic prosperity had already come to show sharp contrasts to the mainland's economic system. However with the launching of Deng Xiaoping's economic reforms, Mainland China has since proved itself to be the most dynamic economy in the world. With these developments, Taiwan has found it more problematic to utilize economic performance or Taiwan's 'economic miracle' as an effective mechanism with which to alleviate the pressure of China's unification proposals, or even as an excuse to avoid the same. More recently then, Taiwan's western-style plural democracy has thus in turn become a useful tool to demonstrate it's differences with Mainland China.

In an important speech delivered at the National Unification Council, Taiwanese President Lee Teng-hui clearly indicated that China's unification must be under the guidelines of democracy, freedom and equitable prosperity. Such 'democratic unification' will safeguard the rights and interests of all Chinese, and is in keeping with global trends. The nation should, by no means, neither be reunified under the proven failure of communism nor the so-called 'one country, two systems' formula.[23] Furthermore, he went on to elaborate Taiwan's position on the issue of China's unification as follows:

First, neither reunification under communism nor the 'one country, two systems' formula will help to bring about democracy to the whole of China. Instead, it will send the people of the mainland even further from their aspirations to enjoy a democratic way of life.

Second, only if China is reunified under a democratic system can the strengths of Taiwan, Hong Kong, and the Chinese mainland be forged together as a source of regional stability. A reunified China that is closed and autocratic would necessarily provoke anxiety in neighboring countries, upset the power balance in Asia and threaten the peace and stability of the Asia–Pacific region.

Third, only through the implementation of a comprehensive democratic system, under the rule of law along with transparent political processes, will mutual trust be enhanced between the two sides. And only democracy will ensure that both sides in fact honor their agreements and guarantee a new win–win situation.[24]

In other words, Taiwan has put forward the formation of a Taiwanese, western style of democracy as the precondition for China's unification. This 'democratic precondition' is also linked together with the international skepticism of the rise of an undemocratic and hegemonic China. The political logic of Taiwan's 'democracy card' is to put Taiwan's security in the broader context of democratic peace in the post-cold war world. The argument follows that an authoritarian and communist China may be a major source of regional instability. Further to this, forcing a democratic Taiwan to accept a unification arrangement initiated by a potential hegemon is against moral justice and political reality. The two sides of the Taiwan straits may only realize 'constructive dialogues' under a situation of democracy and peace.[25] The hidden agenda of this democratic argument is that if China does not democratize, political integration between Taiwan and Mainland China will be long delayed.

Another impediment of political integration is the development of a unique political identity in Taiwan. According to the interdependence school of thought, cooperation in 'low politics' will 'spill over' to the sphere of 'high politics' and lead to further integration. Through the creation of a common culture and economic interdependence, mechanisms for further integration will gradually become institutionalized.

However, the political entanglements between Taiwan and Mainland China provide an alternative for this rather optimistic view of integration. With fifty years of 'de facto separation', Taiwan has continued to build up its own political identity totally separate from the PRC's control. This process has been further accelerated since the regime on Taiwan began to democratize.

While the quest to build up a Taiwanese identity has been initiated by the ruling KMT party in Taiwan, the evolution of this process does not have its origins in the initial rulership. After being defeated by the Chinese communists on Mainland China, Generalissimo Chiang Kai-shek withdrew his government to Taiwan in 1949. To Chiang, the Republic of China on Taiwan was the legitimate Chinese government in exile. In fact, at that time, the ultimate purpose of developing Taiwan was to 'recover' the mainland and to overthrow the so-called rebellious regime in Beijing. To the ordinary Taiwanese person then, the KMT government was not seen as indigenous, and moreover was seen to lack a legitimate power to rule. Even, during Taiwan's authoritarian era, there was no such thing as a 'Taiwanese identity'. Political socialization emphasized only the identity of China, not Taiwan. This trend was not reversed until the fading away of leaders from Mainland China and the liberalization of Taiwan's authoritarian governance. As the KMT gradually became more grass-roots in nature, concern switched to simply sustaining the status of the ruling party in Taiwan. To maximize its votes and to incorporate pro-independence voices as advocated by the opposition party, the KMT had no choice but to diminish its 'Chineseness' and transfer itself from an 'external force' into an 'indigenous party'. Building the Taiwanese identity has since been a useful tool for the KMT to mobilize support in the electoral campaigns.

Not surprisingly then, democratization has been accompanied with the rise of a new Taiwanese culture. The quest for Taiwanese autonomy has mushroomed after more than thirty years of economic prosperity in Taiwan. While a strong middle class pushes the state for deepening political liberalization, a new 'Taiwanese culture' has also developed within the general public. This new 'Taiwanese culture' is based on a Chinese heritage, but adds new ingredients to accommodate the capitalist society and a fast-changing world–pragmatism, incrementalism, and compromise. As democratization progresses, Taiwan's dynamic civil society and it's drive to be recognized as a dignified and autonomous entity will continue to rise. This is a natural development, which stems from economic growth, but is still different from taking the road to 'Taiwan independence'.

The quest to define the 'New Taiwanese', is similarly a realization of Taiwanese identity. The gist of the New Taiwanese ideology is in fact a concerted effort to diminish the potential conflicts emanating from the differing provincial origins among the Taiwanese residents. It is also a direct challenge to the conspiracy of dividing the Taiwanese inhabitants into the 'Chinese' and 'Taiwanese'. Regardless of whether one is an 'aboriginal', 'mainlander', or 'Taiwanese' on Taiwan, the only criteria to distinguish the 'New Taiwanese' is the we-group feeling to develop a common future.[26] In other words, the quest of building a 'New Taiwanese' is not ethno-centric. Although the instrumentalism of the 'New Taiwanese' in the election campaigns is obvious, the ultimate goal is to escape the status of 'periphery' under the illusion of a 'greater China' conceptualisation, and to reaffirm Taiwan's identity as the first given priority.[27]

Taiwan's response toward Mainland China's 'one China principle' under the 'one country, two systems' formula is that the 'one China principle' is the future goal. There is no 'one China' at the current stage. President Lee confirmed this policy line even before the release of 'special state-to-state' announcement. The major difference is the break up of the 'one China' myth. In an interview conducted in 1998, Lee argued that today there is only 'one divided China', with Taiwan and the mainland each being a part of China. Because neither has jurisdiction over the other, neither can represent the other, much less all of China.[28] The 'one China' principle refers to a geographic and historical concept. From a political perspective, China has been divided since 1949. The 'special state-to-state' argument further elaborates the 'one (political) divided China' thesis, and has put cross-straits relations into the international rather than a domestic context. However, Taiwan still does not deny the possibility of a reunified China in the future.[29] The Republic of China has existed in the world for almost ninety years. After it's defeat in the Chinese civil war, the ROC's territory has up to the present time always been limited to that of Taiwan, and has thus created two separate jurisdictions of China. Taiwan argues that before any meaningful dialogues can resume, both sides of the Taiwan Straits must recognize this reality. Otherwise, Taiwan's acceptance of Mainland China's 'one China' principle means nothing but the demise of ROC's sovereignty.

Multiple factors explain Taiwan's policy shifts. As indicated in the preceding analysis, the sharp differences in regime types across the Taiwan Straits and the development of Taiwan's separate identity after democratization provides the groundwork of this policy change. In addition, the shrinking of Taiwan's bargaining status after the release of Clinton's 'three no's' arouses the anxiety of being forced to negotiate under mainland China's 'one country, two systems' formula. This anxiety over the possible loss of a hard-earned democratic autonomy has been further escalated as Mainland China has come to intensify pressure on Taiwan in the international arena. This is in fact, a reaction to Mainland China's continued regard for Taiwan as a 'renegade province' and it's blockade on Taiwan's participation in the international arena as a full sovereign state. Taiwan argues that only under a situation of equality and mutual respect could an effective form of peaceful interaction and talks between Taiwan and Mainland China be realized.[30] In other words, from Taiwan's perspective, future talks about political integration must be based on an equal footing. By no means is political integration between Taiwan and Mainland China seen as a process of incorporating PRC's Taiwan province into the 'motherland'.

Mainland China's unification initiatives and responses to regional conflict

The basic logic behind the mainland's 'one China Principle' of national unification in fact differs from the main arguments stemming from the integration schools of thought. From PRC's perspective, China and Taiwan have historically been an integrated part; while Taiwan's emphasis on its own autonomy is seen as an attempt to 'separate' or to defy China's integration. In other words, national integration, under the so called 'one China principle', is the sole premise for any kind of meaningful interactions to resume. Beijing would never abandon the use of force to protect the integrity of China's territory. By contrast, as the preceding analysis illustrates, Taiwan's position is to urge mainland face the reality of a 'divided China' at the current stage. For Taiwan, China's unification is an open-ended question, depending on the future developments across the Taiwan Straits.

The essence of Beijing's political logic can be seen in examining PRC Premier Zhu Rongji's remarks during his official visit to the United States. In a joint press conference with US president Bill Clinton, Zhu used the example of the American Civil War to demonstrate Beijing's resolution to use force against Taiwan if necessary. He said that Beijing should learn from Abraham Lincoln's spirit to launch a war to maintain national integrity.[31] In other words, the political momentum behind the PRC's 'one China' principle is to fight against separatism, not just to promote national integration. National integration is the pre-condition, not the ultimate goal, of managing cross-Straits relations.

The 'one-China' premises have been an official policy for Beijing to deal with Taiwan. In his famous 'Eight Points Talk', PRC president Jiang Zemin indicates:

Adherence to the principle of one China is the basis and premise for peaceful reunification. China's sovereignty and territory must never be allowed to suffer split. We must firmly oppose any words or actions aimed at creating an 'independent Taiwan', and the propositions 'split the country and rule under separate regimes', 'two China over a certain period of time', etc., which are in contravention of the principle of one China.[32]

However, the real connotation of the 'one China' principle may at times alternate, depending on the degree of political intensity across the Taiwan Straits. After the much opposed visit by Lee Teng-hui's to Cornell in 1995, Mainland China launched a series of unprecedented harsh attacks on Taiwan's efforts to promote international exposure. Beijing then began to stress a strict definition to define the 'one China' principle: 'There is only one China in the world; Taiwan is a part of China; the People's Republic of China is the sole legitimate government representing the whole China'. Any attempts other than this 'one China principle' equals to Taiwan independence.[33] This strict interpretation of the one China principle was again resumed after the announcement of Taiwan's 'special state-to-state' policy. In addition to denying the existence and legitimacy of the Republic of China, the Mainland has also gone even further to equate the Republic of China to the Wang Jingwei regime during the Second World War.[34] Under this trilogy of 'one China' and the denial of the existence of a democratic Taiwan, there is little room for Taiwan to resume talks on unification.

In any other 'normal situation', the third part of the trilogy (the PRC is the sole legal government of China) is intentionally omitted by Beijing, especially on occasions to resume bilateral talks. However, in the international arena, the three-part definition of one China is firmly adhered to by the Mainland. In the regular bilateral cross-Straits talks, Mainland China has put more emphasis on the first two parts of the definition. On various occasions, mainland China has used testing balloons to show the flexibility of the definition of 'one China', such as 'One China Divided' released by Wang Daohan, the Chief Representative of mainland's negotiation team.[35] However, in order to weaken any international support for Taiwan independence, China has adopted a hard-line on the issue of one China in international affairs. The Mainland does not hesitate to show it's feeling of 'urgency' to solve the Taiwan problem,[36] and warns Taiwan's against its intention to introduce foreign forces in the unification issue.[37] In response to Taiwan's international propaganda campaigns, Beijing argues that 'there does not exist a country called the Republic of China', and urges Taiwan to 'give up their separatist activities and cooperate with the *Central* government to realize the peaceful reunification of China'.[38]

Mainland China's feeling of 'urgency' on reunification originates from the perception that Taiwan's democratic changes will eventually lead to Taiwan independence. A de facto independent Taiwan may finally result in the separation of the Chinese territory forever. Thus, Beijing's interpretation of Taiwan's quest for autonomy and democracy greatly influences the mainland's policy choices of national unification.

In Taiwan's authoritarian past, charismatic leaders ruled the country under the fantasy that the ROC on Taiwan was still the legal government representing the whole of China. As democratization unfolded, political elites in Taiwan became more pragmatic in dealing with the situation as it is, and began to stress that the 'Republic of China on Taiwan is a sovereign country since 1911' The current territory of ROC, however, is limited to Taiwan. In addition, since Taiwan's democratization is neither a top-down nor a bottom-up revolution, no single force has been able to determine the outcome of democratization, and the result has been cooperation and interaction between the state and society. More recently, it has also been common practice for the ruling KMT to form various alliances with opposition parties, including the pro-independence DPP. Policy outcomes, including the policies toward Mainland China, are always the result of compromise among competing groups. Under the protection of freedom of speech, both integrationist and separatist ideas have support in the Taiwanese society.

Democratic pluralism in Taiwan enhances Mainland China's skepticism about 'indulging Taiwan independence' of Taiwanese leaders.[39] From Mainland China's interpretation, party politics in Taiwan is nothing but the monopoly of power by certain classes. Since the majority of ordinary people are lacking in power and money, they are neither able to reflect their views to the government, nor join the political rules of the game. Hence, Taiwan's drive for 'pragmatic diplomacy' and constitutional reform just reflects the personal wills of individual politicians.[40] Beijing has also launched serious attacks on Taiwan's revision on high-school textbooks that incorporate more materials about Taiwan's historical development. Mainland China argues that the emphasis on the idea 'we are all Taiwanese' implies 'we are not Chinese'. Beijing indicates that the real intention of the textbook revision is to create a young generation, which is anti-Chinese.[41]

In response to Taiwan's initiatives on 'democratic unification', the Mainland argues that the meaning of reunification should be to safeguard the state territorial integrity and sovereignty, not to argue over systems.[42] Differences in social systems should not be the obstacle of reunification. As such it is argued that any political conflict existing between Taiwan and Mainland China are less a result of the differences in political systems, than from the differences on beliefs in terms of separatism and national reunification.[43] In addition to attacking Taiwan's money politics and corruption, Beijing also argues that western or Taiwanese style democracy is not the only form of democracy in the world. Since 1949, the PRC has greatly improved civil rights on political participation through its democratic systems. The Mainland also endeavors to protect human rights, especially to protect Chinese people's 'survival rights' and 'development rights'.[44]

Under the precondition of national integration and the 'one China' principle, the mainland points out that Taiwan's democracy is 'a bridge toward Taiwan independence'.[45] On the other hand, Beijing has also argued that the mainland's 'one country, two systems' formula would allow Taiwan full democratic autonomy and would allow it to maintain the current democratic system of life.

'One country' indicates national integration, and 'two systems' means a high degree (even higher than Hong Kong) of autonomy under the status of a Special Administrative Region. The Mainland proposes that it would not force Taiwan to adopt a socialist system, yet Taiwan continues to put the 'democratic China' as the precondition for reunification. From mainland's perspective then, Taiwan's assertion of 'democratic unification' is 'undemocratic in reality'.[46]

External actor and regional peace

Taiwan's domestic change challenges the compatibility and suitability of Mainland China's one country, two systems formula of integration. The major support behind Taiwan's quest for autonomy and de facto independence is stems from the civil society. This bottom-up pressure is a source of influence on the preferences of the policy choices of Taiwanese decision-makers. Under the consideration of maximizing votes in the elections, Taiwanese politicians have to adapt to grass-root opinions and resist any proposals of political integration that may lead to the demise of the current regimes sovereignty. In other words, Taiwan's domestic changes reinforce the importance of national sovereignty in the process of economic and political integration.

In the international context, Taiwan's domestic changes have come to introduce new factors in the Taipei–Beijing–Washington triangular relationship. Critics argue that Taiwan's democracy and the subsequent quest for autonomy may disturb the current 'status quo' between Taiwan and Mainland China preferred by the United States. For example, former US Deputy Chief of Mission at Beijing Chas Freeman argues that President Lee Teng-hui only came to embrace much of the separatist program of his Taiwanese nationalist opposition during Taiwan's process of democratization. For Freeman, Taiwan's democracy has produced no consensus on what sort of long-term relationship Taiwan should have with the rest of China. Taiwanese public opinion will only permit talks with Beijing about how to preserve and enhance Taiwan's separation from China.[47]

In reality, Taiwan's democracy provides both risks and opportunities for the international society. Since the Nixon administration, the established US policy has been to acknowledge that there is only one China and Taiwan is a part of China. Maintaining the status quo across the Taiwanese Straits matches US national interests. The 'status quo' is interpreted in dynamic terms, adjustable according to different international settings. The ultimate goal of US policy of 'strategic ambiguity' is to maintain flexibility while avoiding direct involvement of cross-Straits conflicts.

It is believed that *de jure* Taiwan independence is against the US principle of maintaining the status quo. The 'strategic ambiguity' in the three communiqués and the Taiwan Relations act is based on the principle that both sides of the Taiwan Straits stick to the 'one China' principle. Any US support for Taiwan, including arms sales, are but an aim to deter mainland China's attempts to destroy the status quo. The 'three noes policy', released during President

Clinton's trip to Beijing in 1988, demonstrates the continuity of US policy of maintaining the status quo. In the three noes policy, President Clinton indicated that the United States (1) does not support two Chinas and one China, one Taiwan; (2) does not support Taiwan independence; (3) does not support Taiwan's participation in international organizations in which statehood is the requirement.[48] In other words, the three noes policy is a declaration that the US support for Taiwan does not equate to US support for Taiwan's independence. From the US perspective, Taiwan's formal announcement of independence may destroy the hard-earned peaceful status quo across the Taiwan Straits. Further evidence of this can be seen in the fact that after the deterioration of the cross-Straits relations after President Lee's 'special state-to-state' talk, the US President reemphasized the three pillars of US policy: one China, cross-Straits dialogue, and peaceful approach.[49]

Hence, Taiwan's democratic pluralism has to be confined within certain international parameters. To a large part, these parameters are being set up by the United States, which is essentially the major protector of Taiwan's security. Nevertheless, Taiwan's democratic changes have made it into an example of political success going beyond that of 'an economic miracle in the third world'. However it is also somewhat problematic, since in the post-cold war world, a democratic Taiwan provides a sharp contrast to its political rival on the other side of Taiwan Straits. Moreover, democracy is a linkage between Taiwan and the 'democratic peace' campaign led by the United States. A 'democratic Taiwan' has continually been emphasized by the US President while in turn reiterating the 'one-China' policy.[50] There is a sense of stability in that the moral power of a democratic Taiwan is an invincible umbrella for Taiwan's security.

However, this doe not imply that moral power will prevail in the U.S.–PRC–ROC triangular relationship. In this unique triangular relationship, democracy plays both a stabilizing and disturbing role. Taiwan's bottom-up democratic changes enhances its moral justice in the western democratic camp, but introduces uncertain factors in the delicate balance of power within this triangular relationship at the same time. This uncertainty originates from the conception (and the misconception) that Taiwan's democracy may lead to Taiwan independence. From the US perspective, the 'dynamic status quo' across the Taiwan Straits must be under firm US control. De Jure Taiwan independence will invite China's military intervention, and thus break up the current status quo. Under this scenario, US decision-makers will meet with the dilemma of needing to choose between continuing a 'comprehensive engagement' policy with an authoritarian regime, or fighting a war for a democracy. From a realist perspective, letting a minor power make decisions for a major power is 'unrealistic' in nature. The reason behind the limitations of Taiwan's democracy and its quest for autonomy is the international reality that power politics is still the dominant force in an interdependent world. From this perspective, external factors play a constraining roles in limiting the efforts of a small power to reshape the regional order and the regional interaction in East Asia.

Conclusion

The preceding analysis illustrates that three major forces determine the scope and direction of informal integration between Taiwan and Mainland China: economic globalization, national sovereignty, and political distrust. Undoubtedly, United States foreign policy has also influenced the interaction between these three factors. The greatest puzzle is that of the widening gap between economic interaction and political differences in the Taiwan-mainland China relationship. Contrary to the 'spillover' argument from low politics to high politics as proposed by the traditional school of 'old regionalism',[51] political conflict remains as the major obstacle against any deepening of economic integration between Taiwan and Mainland China. Asymmetry of power is one, but not the only, factor of the ensuing disintegration in the political sphere. The asymmetry of power between Mexico and United States has not deterred their regional cooperation or the forming of NAFTA. Rather, lack of mutual trust is the major reason behind rising political conflict and the 'reverse spillover effects' into the realm of economic affairs. This mutual-distrust and misunderstanding between Taiwan and Mainland China has also impeded any effort or intention towards institution building and cooperation between the international regimes.

The lack of mutual trust between the two sides of the Taiwan Straits has its historical as well as current origins. From the historical perspective, both Taiwan and Mainland China share the historical heritage of Chinese culture. However, contemporary history of Taiwan signifies the development of cultural pluralism on the island. From 1895 to 1945, under fifty years of Japanese colonial rule, the ensuing political socialization gradually came to shift the political identity toward the 'mother land', and changed the trade pattern with the mainland.[52] Further to this, after 1949, Taiwan and Mainland China belonged to two different camps of ideology in the Cold War era. During this period of time, cross-Straits relations were a zero-sum game. After the collapse of the Berlin Wall and with the end of the Cold War, the large divide between Taiwan's democratic pluralism and the Mainland's nationalist authoritarianism aroused great public distrust toward future unification. Hence, the major source of Taiwan's skepticism toward mainland's 'one country, two systems' formula is the lack of trust toward the communist regime to keep its promises. Cultural as well as historical roots are the determinant factors to achieve any kind of political integration.

In the complex picture of a Taiwan-mainland China sub-regionalism in East Asia, economic globalization weakens the state's role and creates a 'private sphere' of networked firms across the Taiwan Straits. On the other hand, lack of political trust and different interpretation on political integration serves to reinforce the role of the nation state to implement national goals and to protect national interests. To fully understand the dynamism behind regional cooperation and integration, it is necessary to develop a long-term vision on the concepts of cultural and political variables and how they affect competing nation states in the era of 'alliance capitalism'. East Asian regionalism in general and Taiwan-mainland China sub-regionalism in particular must be put in the vertical framework of historical evolution, and in turn under the horizontal framework of economic globalization for analysis.

Another implication of the case of cross-Taiwan Straits relations in East Asian regionalism is that domestic change, especially democratic change, may be a double-edged sword in furthering regional integration initiated by economic relations. For in the case of Taiwan, democratization liberalizes forces within the civil society and leads to the rise of business community in Taiwan. The business community has become a forefront marching into the mainland market regardless of government regulations in Taiwan. To further develop the booming mainland market and reduce political risks, Taiwanese firms internationalize their investment projects and form various commercial alliances with Japanese and American MNCs. International cooperation in economic spheres also leads to de facto integration in Chinese economies. In economic terms, 'civilian governance' is conducive to peace and cooperation across the Taiwan Straits. This civilian momentum has been made possible only after mainland China's opening up to the world and Taiwan's democratization.

However, as a 'democratizing regime', Taiwan is still in the process of searching for new identity and core national interests. Taiwan's efforts of nation building (or rebuilding) emphasize the uniqueness of Taiwan and the importance of national sovereignty. This is a trend opposite to the deepening for regional integration across the Taiwan Straits. In addition, the quest for Taiwan's identity and autonomy is driven by the dynamic civil society that perceives the need to distinguish itself from the authoritarian regime on Mainland China. Mainland China's distrust of Taiwan's recent trend of democratization is based on the perception that Taiwan's democracy will finally lead to an independence movement and subsequently the disintegration of China. The lack of mutual trust is the major reason of rising political conflicts and the 'reverse spillover effects' to the economic affairs. The lack of trust originates from differences in regime types and misperceptions of domestic development on both sides of Taiwan Straits.

The case of Taiwan and Mainland China signifies the importance of improving mutual understanding and perception in shaping regional integration in East Asia. Misperception, regardless of any prior existing common cultural heritage, is a major obstacle towards regional cooperation. Civilian interaction further stimulated by economic globalization and business-networking requires some form of institutionalized channels in order to alleviate hostility in high politics. In conclusion then, among the four levels of analysis–global, regional, national, and individual–individual political elites could play a the greatest role in institution building or even influencing public perception toward regional integration. Regional integration, regional cooperation, and institution building are not natural phenomena. Human efforts, especially elite visions, are the key to the success of cooperation and peace.

Notes

1 Kurt Taylor Gaubatz, 'Democratic States and Commitment in International Relations' in Miles Kahler ed., *Liberalization and Foreign Policy* (New York: Columbia University Press, 1997), pp. 27–67.
2 For an excellent analysis on the relationship between democracy and Taiwan's security, see Vincent Wei-cheng Wang, 'Does Democratization Enhance or Reduce Taiwan's Security? A Democratic-Peace Inquiry', *Asian Affairs: An American Review*, Vol. 23, No. 1 (Spring, 1996), pp. 3–20.
3 *Lienhe Wanbao*, May 27, 1998.
4 For a detailed analysis of this two-track economic interaction, see Tse-Kang Leng, *The Taiwan-China Connection: Democracy and Development Across the Taiwan Straits* (Colorado, Boulder: Westview Press, 1996).
5 *Gongshang Shibao* (April 29, 1998).
6 *Liangan Jingmao Tongxun* (Journal of Cross-Straits Economy), # 49, January 10, 1996 pp. 37–40; *Jingji Ribao*, May 14, 1998.
7 *Jingji Ribao*, March 23, 1998.
8 *Jingji Ribao*, March 3, 1997.
9 Tse-Kang Leng, 1996, p. 114.
10 According to the current Nationality Law in Taiwan, it is legal to have a double nationality.
11 *Zhongguo Shibao*, July 9, 1996.
12 *Zili Zaobao*, May 29, 1996.
13 *Lienhe Bao*, March 31, 1998.
14 For a more detailed discussion of strategic alliance theories, see Paul Vaaler, 'Twilight of the Multinational Firms,' *The Fletcher Forum of World Affairs*, Vol. 22: 1, Winter/Spring, 1998, pp. 117–123; John Dunning, *Alliance Capitalism and Global Business* (New York: Routledge, 1997); Benjamin Gomes-Casseres, *The Alliance Revolution* (Cambridge: Harvard University Press, 1996).
15 For a thorough study on various successful and failed cases on MNCs on mainland China, see *Multinational Companies in China: Winner and Losers* (London: The Economist Intelligence Unit, 1997).
16 Fengshuo Yang, 'Taishang qiye yunyong guoji tselueh lianmeng qianjin dalu zhi fenxi' (An Analysis of Taiwanese Investment to Mainland China by Strategic Alliances), *Jingji qingshi yu pinglun jikan* (Review of Economic Situation), internet edition, November, 1996, pp. 3–5.
17 Jingji Ribao, April 13, 1999.
18 Tse-Kang Leng 'Dynamism of Taiwan-mainland China Economic Relations: The Role of Private Firms', *Asian Survey*, May, 1998, pp. 494–509.
19 Doremus, Keller, Pauly and Reich argue that multinationalization of firms was less market driven than state driven. The global corporation is 'mainly an American myth'. See Paul Doremus, William Keller, Louis Pauly and Simon Reich, *The Myth of the Global Corporation* (Princeton: Princeton University Press, 1998).
20 Bruce Russett, *Grasping the Democratic Peace* (Princeton: Princeton University Press, 1993); Michael Brown, Sean Lynn-Jones, and Steven Miller, eds, *Debating the Democratic Peace* (Cambridge, Mass: MIT Press, 1996); Christopher Layne, 'Kant or Cant: The Myth of Democratic Peace', *International Security*, Vol. 19, No. 2 (Summer 1994), pp. 5–49.
21 For an introductory analysis of empirical data on democratic peace, see Zeev Maoz, 'The Controversy over Democratic Peace', *International security*, Vol. 22, Issue 1 (Summer 1997), pp. 162–199.
22 For a thorough discussion of asymmetric interdependence, see Joseph Nye, *Understanding International Conflicts* (New York: Longman, 1997), Chapter 7;

Joseph Grieco, 'Anarchy and the Limits of Cooperation: A Realist Critique of the Newest Liberal Institutionalism', in David Baldwin ed., *Neorealism and Neoliberalism* (New York: Columbia University Press, 1993), pp. 116–143.

23 Lee Teng-huei, 'Closing Remarks to the Thirteenth Plenary Session of the National Unification Council', July 22, 1998.

24 Ibid.

25 Lee argues that democracy and peace are the pivots of cross-straits interaction. See Lee Teng-hui, 'Closing Remarks to the 14th Plenum of the National Unification Council', April 8, 1999.

26 Lee Teng-hui, 'Remarks on Taiwan Restoration Day', October 24, 1998.

27 Hsin Zaitai, 'On the New Taiwanese', *Zhongyang Rbao* (Central Daily News), December 31, 1998.

28 Lee Teng-hui, 'U.S. Can't Ignore Taiwan', *The Wall Street Journal*, August 3, 1998.

29 'Parity, Peace, and Win–Win' is The Republic of China's Position on the Special State-to-State Relationship', Taipei, Mainland Affairs Council, August 1, 1999.

30 'Mainland Policy of the Republic of China', Mainland Affairs Council, 1998.

31 *Zhongguo Shibao*, April 10, 1999.

32 Jiang Zemin, *Wei Tsujin Zuguo Tonyi Daye De Wancheng Er Jixu Fendou* (Continue to Promote the Reunification of the Motherland), Beijing, Taiwan Affairs Office of the CCP Central Committee, January 30, 1995.

33 *Renmin Ribao* editorials, July 24–27, 1995.

34 Personal attacks on Lee Teng-hui are even harsher than the propaganda campaigns in 1995. For detailed contents of the attacks, please refer to the Renmin Ribao's special section of 'Announcing to Lee Teng-hui and Taiwan Authorities', http://www.peopledaily.com.cn.

35 *Zhongguo Shibao*, April 6, 1999.

36 *Lienhe Zaobao* (Singapore), March 8, 1999.

37 Ibid.

38 Yu Shuning, 'There is only one China', *The Wall Street Journal*, August 13, 1998. Yu is the Press Counselor of The PRC Embassy in Washington D.C.

39 *Renmin Ribao*, June 27, 1995.

40 Mao Zhongwei, 'Lee Denghui yu Taiwan Minyi Qianzai Chongtu Jianxi (An Analysis of the Conflicts Between Lee Teng-hui and Taiwan's Public Opinion)', *Taiwan Yanjiou* (Taiwan Studies) (Beijing), # 1, 1998, pp. 59–61.

41 Peng Xuewei, 'Tai Renshi Taiwan Jiaokeshu Pingxi (An Analysis of Taiwan's New Textbook)', *Taiwan Yanjiou* (Taiwan Studies) (Beijing), No. 4, 1997, pp. 28–33

42 'Qien Qichen Urges Early Cross-Straits Political Talks', Press Release, PRC Embassy in Washington DC, October 18, 1998.

43 Qien Qichen, 'Wei Tueidong Zuguo Heping Tongyi Daye er Nuli Fendou (Struggle for China's Reunification)', *Liangan Guanxi* (Cross-Straits Relations), February, 1999, p. 4.

44 'Yi Jiou Jiou Ba Zhongguo Renquan Shiye De Jinzhan (Progress of China's Human Rights in 1998), PRC State Council, April 13, 1999. Full text cited from *Takungpao*, April 14, 1999.

45 *Renmin Ribao* (overseas edition), December 17, 1998.

46 Ibid.

47 Chas W. Freeman Jr., 'Preventing War in the Taiwan Strait', *Foreign Affairs*, July/August 1998, pp. 9–11.

48 *Washington Post*, June 30, 1998.

49 *New York Times*, July 22, 1999.

50 The White House Office of the Press Secretary, 'Remarks by the President in Foreign Policy Speech', Washington DC, April 7, 1999.

51 Please refer to Dr. Jörn Dosch's chapter in this book for the differences between 'old' and 'new' regionalism.

52 Lin Manhong argues that the Japanese rule in Taiwan not only shifted the trade pattern between Taiwan and mainland China, but also reshaped Taiwan's cultural and political ties with mainland China. See Lin Manhong, 'Jingmao Yu Zhengzhi Wenhua Rentong: Riben Lingtai Qijian Wei Liangan Changcheng Guanxi Suo Touxia De Bianshu (Trade, Politics, and Culture Identity: Impacts of Japanese Colonial Rule on Cross-Straits Relations)', in *Zhongguo Lishi Shang De Fen Yu He Lunwen Ji* (Proceedings of the Conference on Separation and Unification in Chinese History) (Taipei: Linking, 1995, pp. 333–385).

11 Regionalism through interregionalism

East Asia and ASEM

Heiner Hänggi

Introduction

Most comparative analyses of regionalism focus on the internal functioning of particular regions. However, as theorists of regionalism have for long argued, regions are also structured by the way they relate to the outside world. The role of external factors in the development of regional cooperation, such as 'external cogency'[1] or 'external federators',[2] has been widely acknowledged in the traditional literature on regionalism. Accordingly, extra-regional states, great powers in particular, may have a positive or negative impact on the development of intra-regional cooperation. As an illustration, the post-war policy of the United States towards the Western European integration process is generally viewed as an important factor of positive external cogency, whereas the perceived threat posed by the Soviet Union is considered as an element of negative external cogency.[3] Besides external powers, other regions or regional subsystems may also play a role as external factors of regionalism. The impact of regional groupings on the development of regionalism elsewhere has been studied mainly in the context of the phenomenon known as 'extra-regional echoing', which by and large refers to the European prototype of regionalism serving other world regions as a model, either to be imitated or to be avoided. Beyond the 'extra-regional echoing' phenomenon, however, the role of interregional interactions has often been neglected in the literature on regionalism as some authors have noted.[4] Indeed, apart from Kaiser's (1981) study on the interaction of regional subsystems, the relevant literature is conspicuously silent about the impact of interregionalism on regionalism. This may be explained by the systemic bipolarity of the cold-war period which left little room for interregional relations beyond transregional alliances and, therefore, caused little scholarly interest in the subject matter.

In the cold war period, interregional relations were largely confined to the European Community's (EC) so-called group-to-group dialogues with other regional groupings. These dialogue relationships have gradually evolved since the 1970s to cover almost all world regions.[5] The long-standing dialogue partnership between the EC and the Association of Southeast Asian Nations (ASEAN) is considered by some authors as a model of group-to-group interregionalism.[6]

Given the fact that the EC was the most advanced regional organisation and due to the absence of interregional relations among the EC's partner organisations, the interregional network of the cold war period appeared like a 'hub-and-spokes' system[7] gravitating around Brussels. Its dominating position in group-to-group interregionalism made the EC more than just a model which influenced other regions by way of 'extra-regional echoing'. The Community actively used interregional relationships as an instrument for promoting intra-regional cooperation among the dialogue partners.[8]

The impact of external factors – in the form of interregionalism – on regionalism is therefore not an entirely new phenomenon in international relations. But it has come again to the attention of scholars and practitioners alike in recent years against the background of 'new regionalism'[9] and the consequent proliferation of interregional relations beyond the EC's traditional group-to-group approach. Though the EC, now EU, is still the major actor in the expanding network of relations between regional groupings, the number of interregional arrangements without participation of the earlier 'hub' has been increasing. ASEAN has turned out to be a primary mover behind this development.[10] Furthermore, new forms of interregional relations have appeared as a corollary of 'new regionalism'. Membership in such rather heterogeneous arrangements is more diffuse than in traditional group-to-group dialogues; it is not necessarily coinciding with regional groupings and may include member states from more than two regions; therefore, states participate in an individual capacity, although there may be some degree of regional coordination.[11] The Asia Pacific Economic Cooperation (APEC) and Asia-Europe Meeting (ASEM) processes are a good point in case. ASEM in particular illustrates that these new forms of interregionalism, too, may have an impact on the development of regionalism in the areas of their member states.

Against the background of the evolving ASEM process, Camroux and Lechervy have called for the development of a sociology of interregional relations, for, as they argue, 'the composition, structure and behaviour of one region, not only impinges upon, but also serves to structure the evolving nature of other regions'.[12] In other words: under the new systemic conditions, interregional interaction may be an important external factor of regionalism, possibly more so than in the past when this mechanism was confined to the EC's group-to-group dialogue system. In one of the Task Force Reports published by the Council of Asia-Europe Cooperation (CAEC), Maull and Tanaka suggested that the interregional ASEM process could serve as a kind of 'regional integrator' on both sides.[13] Given the much higher level of regional integration in Western Europe as compared to East Asia where regional integration is virtually absent, the impact of Asia-Europe interregionalism on the development of regionalism may be felt much stronger in Asia than in Europe. Indeed, as Maull, Segal and Wanandi have noted, one of the major achievements of ASEM was 'that for the first time the states of Pacific Asia tried to function as a coherent group'.[14] In this context, Jung and Lehmann speak of a regional East Asian rationale for ASEM which 'may result in bring the three Northeast Asian nations in closer dialogue, but more significantly in creating *de facto*, if not *de jure*, the East Asian Economic Caucus (EAEC)'.[15] Already before the launching of the ASEM process, Soesastro and Wanandi had referred to the possibility that, 'a *de-facto*-EAEC is emerging as Asia develops its relations with Europe through the ASEM process'.[16] The EAEC proposal had been put forward by the Malaysian Prime Minister Mahathir as an alternative to APEC but faced strong resistance from the United States and ambivalence of Japan and other East Asian countries.[17]

The fact that Asia-Europe interregionalism has helped East Asian countries to engage in regional cooperation has been noted by East Asian and non-East Asian authors alike.[18] But most of these authors confine themselves to the observation of a possible positive impact of ASEM on East Asian regionalism without further assessing the possible causes and consequences of this 'regionalism-through-interregionalism' phenomenon.[19] Yet, the issue deserves deeper analysis given the fact that the ASEM process has been initiated by East Asian countries for a number of purposes including the facilitation of regionalism in East Asia itself.[20] This is a novelty which goes much beyond the 'extra-regional echoing' mechanism known from the earlier literature on regionalism.

This chapter takes up the 'regional integrator' thesis proposed by Maull and Tanaka[21] and broadens it so as to integrate both aspects, the traditional 'extra-regional echoing' as well as the novel feature mentioned above. It therefore argues that interregionalism may contribute to the development of regionalism in two ways: on the one hand, the dynamics of interregional relations drive regional states to strengthen intra-regional cooperation, in particular so among the members of the regional entity which exhibits a lower degree of cohesiveness; on the other hand, regional states may use interregional relations for their own regionalist objectives, in particular the members of the less cohesive regional entity. In the following, East Asia's interregional interaction with Western Europe in the framework of ASEM is used as a case study to illustrate this double meaning of the 'regional integrator' thesis.

The first part of the chapter introduces the concepts of regionalism and interregionalism in the context of the new Triad comprising North America, Western Europe and East Asia.[22] The second part provides a short overview on the possibilities and constraints of regionalism in East Asia. The third part discusses how ASEM emerged as the main feature of Asia-Europe inter-regionalism and how the participants were chosen. The two following parts explore how an 'Asian' entity emerged in the framework of the ASEM process and how the ASEM process was used to facilitate East Asian regionalism. The chapter concludes that while the Asian members have been driven by the ASEM process to start a mechanism of regional coordination, they have deliberately used ASEM as an instrument of intra-regional cooperation, too – in other words: as a strategy to promote regionalism through interregionalism in a Triadic context. But this strategy will be losing importance as a more genuine East Asian regionalism is developing.

Regionalism and interregionalism in a triadic context

Globalisation and regionalisation are widely seen as the major factors restructuring the post-cold war international system.[23] Ongoing debates notwithstanding, we are witnessing an emerging consensus which views globalisation and regionalisation as by and large complementary processes. This is most evident in the international economic system. The structure of the international economy suggests that globalisation is not really global. On the contrary, the process is characterised by unevenness in terms of geographical scope,[24] which is illustrated by the growing concentration of economic activity in North America, Western Europe and East Asia. The Triad regions account for three-quarters of world trade and provide 90 per cent of global foreign direct investment flows, and their combined share of total world GNP is nearly 85 per cent. Although it may appear contradictory, the process of uneven globalisation is accompanied by a parallel process of uneven regionalisation of economic, political, and societal activities. The end of the cold war helped pave the way for the emergence or resurgence of regional awareness and an increase in intra-regional cooperation on a global scale.[25] Despite its global reach, however, regionalisation just as globalisation is most advanced in the Triad regions and their peripheries. Intra-regional economic transactions have been increasing since the 1960s in all Triad regions, particularly in East Asia. The combined forces of uneven globalisation and uneven regionalisation have resulted in a tripolar configuration, or in a 'Triadisation',[26] of the world economy with three more or less equally powerful regions in terms of accumulated GNP, while the huge 'rest of the world' is left at the margins of the international economy. The Triadisation process may have been slowed down by the East Asian monetary and economic crisis of 1997–98 ('Asian Crisis') because the third and most recent pillar of the world economy has been weakened. But the basic structure of a Triadic world economy remains unchanged.

The processes of globalisation and regionalisation which are largely economic in nature tend to undermine the political control of nation-states and to limit their policy choices. According to Roloff (1998), globalisation and regionalisation can be considered as external challenges which encourage nation-states to engage in enhanced regional cooperation in order to manage jointly the increasingly complex interdependence (liberal-institutionalist explanation) and to balance off regionalist challenges from other world regions (neo-realist explanation).[27] Indeed, since the late 1980s, we have been witnessing an upsurge of regionalism, either through a widening and deepening of existing regional cooperation schemes such as EU, ASEAN, or through new forms of often wider and loser arrangements such as APEC, ASEAN Regional Forum (ARF), ASEAN Free Trade Area (AFTA), and the North American Free Trade Agreement (NAFTA). Against the background of Triadisation, it does not come as a complete surprise that this so-called 'new regionalism' has taken firm roots in the Triad regions and their peripheries:

- Western Europe has seen a deepening as well as a widening of the European Union which has become the major focus of attraction in Europe and is increasingly representing Europe in world affairs, particularly in inter-regional relations.
- North America has seen the United States embracing regionalism in the mid-1980s which finally led to the creation of NAFTA encompassing Canada, Mexico and the USA, and to the project of an even wider Free Trade Area of the Americas (FTAA) encompassing the Western Hemisphere. Unlike the EU, however, NAFTA does not appear as an actor in its own right.
- East Asia has seen the rapid development of *de facto* regionalisation but regionalism did evolve only within subregional (e.g. ASEAN) and transregional schemes (e.g. APEC, ARF) due to considerable constraints on exclusive East Asian regional cooperation such as intra-regional conflicts and dependence on the United States. Contrary to Western Europe, East Asia remains multipolar and still has to develop some sort of 'benign unipolarity' around a 'pluralistic core' (Kupchan 1998). Nevertheless, East Asian countries have albeit hesitantly begun to act as a *de facto* group, particularly so in the interregional ASEM framework and more recently in the regional ASEAN+3 framework.

In retrospect, the rapid economic emergence of East Asia, the launch of the European Single Market programme in 1985 and the Canada-USA Free Trade Agreement in 1988 have been the major causes which triggered off regionalist 'chain reactions' in the sense that an increase in regionalism in one region led to similar reactions in other regions.[28] But these chain reactions did not result in the much feared creation of closed regional blocs. On the contrary, as a consequence of globalisation, 'new regionalism' turned out to be rather open to other regions; hence, the epistemic parlance of 'open regionalism', a concept which has been developed in the context of Asia–Pacific regionalism.[29]

In order to manage and to balance relations among themselves, the Triad regions increasingly began to engage in interregional relations among themselves as well as with other world regions. While interregional relations had been limited to the EU's group-to-group dialogues with other regional organisations in the past, interregionalism in the context of new regionalism took different forms of informal and multi-layered arrangements with a more diffuse membership.[30] Such arrangements first emerged in a Triadic context:

- The APEC forum was created in 1989 in order to manage transpacific economic relations. Though intended by its initiators as a 'mega-regional' endeavour,[31] APEC was widely perceived as an interregional link between North America and East Asia.
- The New Transatlantic Agenda of 1995 and the Transatlantic Economic Partnership of 1998 between the United States and the EU as well as the proposals for creating a Transatlantic Free Trade Area (TAFTA) reflect

the growing interregional network between North America and Western Europe.

- Finally, the ASEM process launched in 1996 was aimed at bridging what was perceived to be the 'missing link' in the Triad, i.e. the relations between Western Europe and East Asia.

Furthermore, Western Europe and East Asia began to establish new interregional links with non-Triadic world regions such as Latin America and Africa. While the formal link between the EU and Mercosur was established as early as 1995, other arrangements such as the Europe-Latin America Summit, the Africa-Europe Summit and the East Asia Latin America Forum (EALAF) are of more recent origin.

These new forms of interregionalism can be explained by two major causes: first, the need to manage the increasingly complex interdependence in a world of Triadic globalisation (liberal-institutionalist explanation), and second, the need to balance regionalism in other regions as well as interregionalism between other regions (neo-realist explanation).[32] Both motivations combined led to a kind of interregionalist chain reactions in the 1990s:

Table 11.1 Membership of East Asian countries in (inter-)regional arrangements

Countries/ 'economies'	ASEAN	ARF	APEC	EAEC*	ASEAN+3	ASEM
PR China		X	X	X	X	X
Japan		X	X	X	X	X
South Korea		X	X	X	X	X
North Korea		X				
Hong Kong			X	(?)		
Taiwan			X	(?)		
Brunei	X	X	X	X	X	X
Indonesia	X	X	X	X	X	X
Malaysia	X	X	X	X	X	X
Philippines	X	X	X	X	X	X
Singapore	X	X	X	X	X	X
Thailand	X	X	X	X	X	X
Vietnam	X	X	X	X	X	X
Cambodia	X	X		X	X	
Laos	X	X		X	X	
Myanmar	X	X		X	X	

* proposed

- The USA saw in APEC a safeguard against the creation of a regional bloc in East Asia whereas East Asians valued APEC as kind of guarantee against possible negative effects of the completion of the European Single Market and the creation of NAFTA.
- The strengthening of the transatlantic relations was partly borne out of the mutual fear of East Asia's economic emergence. Furthermore, the Europeans were much concerned about being left out of APEC.
- The mutual fears of Europeans and East Asians of being left out of APEC and of transatlantic arrangements respectively, led to the creation of ASEM, the third link to complete Triadic relations.

The establishment of interregional links between Triadic and non-Triadic regions had different reasons. Latin America had become attractive for interregional links as a consequence of the US-sponsored FTAA project whereas Africa feared to be marginalized in the context of the emerging interregional network.

To sum up, the 1990s have seen the formation of a Triadic structure of the international system. This has been caused by the joint forces of globalisation and regionalisation which led to a Triadisation of the international economy and triggered off state-led responses to this challenge in the form of regionalism and interregionalism in a Triadic context, with spill-overs to non-Triadic regions. In this perspective, globalisation and regionalisation are seen as causal factors of regionalism and interregionalism. Interregionalism may be understood as a corollary of regionalism in the sense that the more regions become constituting factors of the international system, the more they tend to interact among themselves in order balance and manage relations.

Possibilities and constraints of East Asian regionalism

While NAFTA and the EU make it relatively easy to perceive North America and Western Europe as regions, it is much more difficult in the case of East Asia. Indeed, East Asia is the most heterogeneous and amorphous of the three major world regions, and with considerable constraints on regional cooperation.[33] In terms of security, the East Asian landscape is marked by rival intra-regional powers (China, Japan), by major areas of conflict (Korea, Taiwan, South China Sea), by widespread mutual suspicion among regional states, and by the military presence of the United States as a kind of regional balancer. In terms of politics, governments of the region's states run the gamut from democratic, semi-democratic to authoritarian regimes. In terms of economics, the region comprises of an economic superpower (Japan), four newly industrialised 'Tiger' economies (Hong Kong, South Korea, Singapore, Taiwan), a number of newly industrialising economies as well as developing and even some least developed countries. The disparities within the region could even be further aggravated as a consequence of the Asian Crisis.

Nevertheless, the rapid spread of the Asian Crisis throughout East Asia reflects the high level of economic interdependence which has been achieved in

Table 11.2 Chronology of East Asian regionalism in the ASEAN+3 framework

Date	Event
December 1990	East Asian Economic Grouping (EAEG) proposed by Malaysian Prime Minister
November 1991	East Asian Economic Caucus (EAEC) proposed by Indonesia at ASEAN Economic Ministers' Meeting (AEMM) in Kuala Lumpur
July 1993	ASEAN Foreign Ministers agree that EAEC should be 'a caucus within APEC'
July 1994	First informal ASEAN+3 Foreign Ministers' meeting (ASEAN Foreign Ministers meet with counterparts from China, Japan and South Korea at the ASEAN Post-Ministerial Conferences [PMC] in Bangkok to discuss the EAEC proposal)
October 1994	(East) Asia-Europe summit meeting proposed by Singaporean Prime Minister
March 1995	ASEAN position paper on the proposed Asia-Europe summit meeting suggesting *de facto* the ASEAN+3 format for the Asian side
July 1995	Second informal ASEAN+3 Foreign Ministers' meeting at PMC in Brunei to discuss the Asia-Europe Meeting (ASEM) initiative
November 1995	First informal ASEAN+3 Economic Ministers' meeting (ASEAN Economic Ministers meet with counterparts from China, Japan and South Korea in Osaka to discuss the ASEM initiative)
February 1996	Informal meetings of ASEAN+3 foreign ministers and ASEAN+3 economic ministers in Phuket to prepare ASEM 1
March 1996	ASEM 1 in Bangkok (Asian side represented by ASEAN+3)
November 1997	Asian Monetary Fund (AMF) proposed by Japan at APEC summit meeting
December 1997	First informal ASEAN+3 summit meeting in Kuala Lumpur (in the wake of the Asian Crisis)
April 1998	ASEM 2 in London (Asian side represented by ASEAN+3 minus new ASEAN members [Cambodia and Laos])
December 1998	Second informal ASEAN+3 summit meeting in Hanoi (agreed to make the ASEAN+3 summit meetings an annual event)
November 1999	Third informal and first regular ASEAN+3 summit meeting in Manila (issued a 'Joint Statement on East Asian Cooperation' and agreed to hold an ASEAN+3 Foreign Ministers' Meeting in the margins of the PMC; first trilateral summit talks of China, Japan and South Korea)
May 2000	First ASEAN+3 Economic Ministers' meeting at informal AEMM in Yangon
May 2000	First ASEAN+3 Finance Ministers' meeting in Chiang Mai (discussed AMF proposal and launched the 'Chiang Mai Initiative', i.e. expanded ASEAN Swap Arrangement)
July 2000	First ASEAN+3 Foreign Ministers' meeting at PMC in Bangkok

Date	Event
October 2000	Second ASEAN+3 Economic Ministers' meeting at AEMM in Chiang Mai
October 2000	'Asian Leaders' Meeting' held in Seoul to exchange views prior to ASEM 3
October 2000	ASEM 3 in Seoul (Asian side represented by ASEAN+3 minus new ASEAN members [Cambodia, Laos and Myanmar])
November 2000	Fourth informal and second regular ASEAN+3 summit meeting in Singapore (supporting proposal for an East Asian Study Group on the future of regional integration and an expert group on free trade relations between ASEAN and China; second trilateral summit talks of China, Japan and South Korea)

the region. In the past three decades the so-called 'flying wild geese' pattern of successive industrialisation, led by Japanese multinational corporations, has created a multidimensional network of economic interdependence encompassing Northeast and Southeast Asian countries at different levels of development. The East Asian process of *de facto* economic regionalisation, especially in the fields of trade and direct investment, was essentially driven by the private-sector but supported by a multitude of governmental, semi-governmental and non-governmental actors on various levels. East Asian 'soft regionalism' is not based on an order of harmonised domestic and international law as in Europe but on regimes ruled by similar socio-cultural norms of behaviour and (mainly Overseas Chinese) group networks.[34]

Compared to the other two Triad regions, institutionalisation of regional interstate cooperation has been a rather slow and hesitant process in East Asia, and most regional states prefer 'soft regionalism' which resists exclusive institution-building but features inclusive informal networks instead.[35] The subregional grouping ASEAN which has initiated its own free trade arrangement (AFTA) serves as a nucleus for gradual institutionalisation of economic and security cooperation in the wider region. However, the schemes for economic cooperation (APEC) and security cooperation (ARF) cover a much wider region than East Asia alone and reflect the fact that the conception of East Asia as a region is politically contested, both outside as well as within the region. The only attempt at institutionalising East Asian regionalism has been the proposal of an East Asian Economic Grouping (EAEG), put forward in 1990 by Malaysian Prime Minister Mahathir. It was envisaged as a Japanese-led counterweight to the perceived emergence of trade blocs in Western Europe and North America and as a regionalist alternative to the 'mega-regional' APEC. Due to strong resistance from the non-Asian Pacific rim countries, particularly from the United States, it was revised to a more modest East Asian Economic Caucus (EAEC) version and, although officially supported by ASEAN as a caucus within APEC, it remained a concept far from formal implementation. While the logic of rapid *de facto* economic integration in East Asia appears to increase the long-term prospects of the EAEC concept, the continuing dependence on the US market and on US military power are likely to inhibit the institutionalisation of exclusive East Asian regionalism.[36] Yet, the shared experience that the Asian Crisis has produced amongst regional policy elites, may accelerate the continued development of East Asian regional identity and of more institutionalised regionalism.[37]

Indeed, the Asian Crisis has given an impetus to the nascent East Asian regionalism and, indirectly at least, revitalised the dormant EAEC project.[38] Though ministerial rounds and senior officials meetings between ASEAN member states, China, Japan and South Korea had taken place since 1994 already (mainly in preparation of ASEM),[39] the first ever summit meeting of East Asian heads of state and government took place in December 1997, in the midst of the Asian Crisis. The sensitivity of this approach was reflected by the failure to reach consensus on the ASEAN proposal to hold an annual East Asian summit meeting (Kavi 1998). One year later, in December 1998, a second ASEAN+3 summit meeting was held which resulted in an agreement to make it an annual event to coincide with every formal or informal ASEAN Summit.[40] At their third meeting in November 1999, the East Asian heads of state and government laid the foundations for a soft institutionalisation of the ASEAN+3 process and issued a 'Joint Statement on East Asian Cooperation' in economic, social, political and other fields.[41] This was followed by the initiation of regular meetings of the East Asian foreign, economic and finance ministers. At the fourth ASEAN+3 Summit in November 2000, the 13 leaders commissioned a study on the future shape of East Asian cooperation and discussed the idea of enlarging ASEAN's free trade area AFTA to include all East Asia.[42] Though all these meetings were attended by the supposed member countries of the EAEC except for Taiwan, the participants carefully avoided any reference to the brainchild of Malaysian Prime Minister. But in real terms, the EAEC, albeit under a different heading ('East Asian Cooperation'), is gradually being institutionalised through the ASEAN+3 process, which had first been tested in the framework of the ASEM process.[43]

ASEM as a manifestation of Asia-Europe interregionalism

The ASEM process has been conceptualised by its initiators and proponents in the context of the triangular relationship between North America, Western Europe and East Asia, herein referred to as new Triad.[44] Relations between Western Europe and East Asia were depicted as the 'missing link'[45] and are still perceived to be the 'weak leg' in the new Triad. Compared to transatlantic and transpacific relations, Asia-Europe relations are weak indeed. This is particularly obvious in the case of security relations: While the USA has stationed around 100,000 troops each in Europe and Asia, security links between the two macro-regions are short of non-existent.[46] As for economic relations, while Asia-Europe trade overtook transatlantic trade in the early 1990s, transpacific trade is still much greater. And though the FDI flows to East Asia have clearly increased in the last decade, there is still a disproportionate concentration of capital flows along the transatlantic axis, and even more so since the outbreak of the Asian Crisis. In the field of institutional cooperation, the EU and ASEAN have been involved in a formal group-to-group dialogue since 1978. In the 1990s, the EU has begun to institutionalise bilateral relations with Japan, China and South Korea, too. Asia-Europe relations were put on a broader basis in 1996 when EU and ASEAN member states as well as China, Japan and South Korea launched the interregional ASEM process. In the context of Triadic interaction, it is noteworthy that the creation of ASEM was partly motivated by European concerns of being left out of APEC and Asian concerns of being dominated by the United States in APEC.

The idea of a closer link between 'Asia' and 'Europe' goes back to the early 1990's. The transnational corporate community took the first step in calling attention to the weakness of the Asia-Europe side in the emerging triangle of economic gravity zones. At the first Europe-East Asia Business Summit organised by the World Economic Forum (WEF) in Hong Kong in 1992, it was concluded that a more intensive dialogue between the corporate communities from the two regions was necessary to reduce misunderstandings and to reconcile differences. The idea of an intergovernmental link between the two regions first emerged in November 1993 at a time when US President Bill Clinton succeeded in having the House of Representatives to approve the North American Free Trade Agreement (NAFTA) and in bringing the APEC leaders together for their first informal summit meeting. It was in view of the first APEC summit that French Prime Minister Jacques Chirac proposed regular consultations between the EC and the EAEC countries as representatives of their respective regions.[47] By then, the EAEC had already been re-conceptualised by ASEAN as a caucus within APEC. Consequently, EC-EAEC consultations would have given the Europeans indirect access to APEC since their request for an observer status had been rejected, namely by the United States.

While Chirac's call had no practical impact, Singapore's similar initiative a year later was much more successful. The genesis of the process which was later to be named ASEM took place in August 1994 in Singapore when officials of the Ministry of Foreign Affairs and the Prime Minister's Office were thinking of what kind of project to bring Asia and Europe together could be floated at two major events in October 1994, namely the third WEF Europe-East Asia Business Summit in Singapore, and the visit of Prime Minister Goh Chok Tong to France. The Singaporean officials had 'something like APEC for Europe and East Asia' in mind.[48] From the very beginning, it seemed clear to them that Asia would be represented by the ASEAN countries plus China, Japan and South Korea, at least, and Europe by the member states of the European Union. At the third Europe-East Asia Business Summit in October 1994, Prime Minister Goh publicly proposed that Asia should establish 'Pacific style' ties with Europe in order to bridge the 'missing link' in the global triangle of North America, Western Europe and East Asia. Mr. Goh's proposal was given strong support by the Business Summit, which called for a summit meeting between the political leaders of Europe and East Asia.[49] During his state visit to France later that month, the Singaporean Prime Minister officially proposed the notion of such a meeting to French Prime Minister Edouard Balladur who gave it a warm welcome. Singapore had approached France first because it would hold the EU chair in the first half of 1995. This proved to be the right approach: In late January, the EU General Affairs Council expressed its initial interest in such an Asia-Europe summit meeting, and in June 1995, the European Council under French Presidency in Cannes accepted the principle of such a meeting.[50]

On the Asian side, Singapore's proposal was soon endorsed by the other ASEAN member states. In March 1995, the ASEAN Senior Officials' Meeting adopted a position paper which was transmitted to the EU for comments. The ASEAN position paper said that 'participation would be based on the principle that the EU will select the European participants and that ASEAN will choose the Asian participants and that the two sides would consult each other on that matter.' As to the Asian side, it was said that 'the most important consideration is to include dynamic economies which have contributed to the region's prosperity and growth.'[51] As ASEAN wished to keep the initial meeting small and manageable, it was suggested that the Asian participants would comprise a small group of countries which could eventually be enlarged in subsequent meetings. Though not explicitly mentioned, it was made clear to Brussels that ASEAN wanted to invite China, Japan and South Korea.[52] As to Hong Kong and Taiwan, the ASEAN position paper suggested that their participation could be based on the APEC formula which was in line with the preference of ASEAN for an informal gathering of *economic* leaders.'[53] But China strongly rejected the adoption of the APEC formula and the participation of Taiwan, all the more given the evolving political character of the ASEM initiative.[54]

By July 1995, China, Japan and South Korea had accepted ASEAN's official invitation to join its seven member states in representing 'Asia' at the proposed Asia-Europe meeting. At the annual ASEAN Post-Ministerial Conferences (PMC) in Brunei, the foreign ministers of the seven ASEAN member states and the three Northeast Asian countries met in an EAEC-like format called ASEAN+3 to discuss the ASEM initiative. Concurrently, the first ASEM preparatory meeting was held including the EU Troika and the foreign ministers of ten East Asian countries. At this meeting, the East Asian countries for the first time acted as a regional caucus dealing with another regional grouping. Against the background of the limited number of Asian participants and the high number of European candidates,[55] the EU had little choice but to restrict the European participation to its 15 EU member states.[56] But limitation of the European participants was convenient for the EU, too, as it could rely solely on its existing policy coordination machinery which made the clearing of positions on the European side much easier. In the end, ASEM started at the Bangkok meeting in March 1996 with 'Europe' being represented by the EU and 'Asia' by the *de facto* EAEC. Due to the disagreement among the ASEM participants on whether, when and how enlargement should happen, the same initial EU-EAEC

Table 11.3 Members of the Asia-Europe Meeting (ASEM)

Asian Participants (7+3)	European Participants (15+1)
Brunei (ASEAN)	Austria (EU)
Indonesia (ASEAN)	Belgium (EU)
Malaysia (ASEAN)	Denmark (EU)
Philippines (ASEAN)	Finland (EU)
Singapore (ASEAN)	France (EU)
Thailand (ASEAN)	Germany (EU)
Vietnam (ASEAN)	Greece (EU)
China	Ireland (EU)
Japan	Italy (EU)
South Korea	Luxembourg (EU)
	Netherlands (EU)
	Portugal (EU)
	Sweden (EU)
	Spain (EU)
	United Kingdom (EU)
	European Commission

format was kept at the second meeting in London in April 1998 (ASEM 2) and went unchanged at ASEM 3 in October 2000 in Seoul.[57]

The making of an East Asian regional entity within ASEM

In ASEM, the 'Asian' side represented by ten East Asian countries engages in dialogue and cooperation with the 'European' side represented by the EU member states and the European Commission. This is different from APEC where the East Asian participants do not face a definable (regional) counterpart; and where, therefore, the need of collective regional coordination in preparation for upcoming events does not arise.[58] Indeed, in order to be effective in face of a highly integrated dialogue partner such as the EU, a clearing of positions was needed on the Asian side, thereby necessitating closer intra-regional coopera-tion.[59] The preparations of ASEM already set off a hitherto unknown process of regional coordination in East Asia covering economic, politico-security and socio-cultural issue-areas.[60] Within a couple of months, member states of the proposed EAEC had to meet repeatedly on ministerial and senior officials level in order to co-ordinate their positions.[61] Such coordination has a long tradition among ASEAN countries, of course, but it was a novelty for the three Northeast

Asian countries as well as for ASEAN countries in an East Asian context. For practical reasons, Thailand was asked to co-ordinate the Asian position prior to the Bangkok meeting of which it was the host country. In terms of substance, the Asian participants had to come up with joint positions on a number of contentious issues such as the format of the conference, the topics to be discussed, the principles to be adopted, and the Asian countries to be invited. At the second ASEM preparatory meeting on Senior Officials' level in December 1995 in Madrid, the Asian countries put forward a jointly agreed 'Asian Discussion Paper' which stressed the need to bridge the 'missing link' in the new Triad, and identified priority areas for discussion and cooperation among the ASEM member countries.[62] Though there were conflicts of interest among the East Asian countries, they managed by and large to function as a coherent group in face of the European Union.

What had been developed in an informal and pragmatic manner underwent some sort of 'soft' institutionalisation[63] in the aftermath of the Bangkok meeting during March of 1996. The emerging structure of the ASEM process increased the need for regional coordination on the Asian side. Apart from the meeting of the heads of state and government every two years, the Bangkok Chairman Statement called for meetings of the foreign ministers, the economic ministers, the finance ministers and the senior officials.[64] In preparation of these meetings, East Asian countries had to further engage in regional consultation because the European side would generally come up with a co-ordinated position. Consequently, Asian ASEM participants would hold preparatory meetings, often on an *ad hoc* basis, before the respective ASEM meetings.[65] Furthermore, in order to ensure the continuation of the ASEM process between the ministerial and Senior Officials' meetings, 'Co-ordinators'[66] were selected on both sides.[67] While the EU could rely on a highly institutionalised mechanism for internal coordination and a long tradition of relations with other regional groups, the Asian side had to start from zero. Since it was decided that the second meeting (ASEM 2) would take place in Europe (United Kingdom), the Asian countries had to find some way of co-ordinating their positions other than relying on the host country. This was facilitated by the fact that ASEAN has its own coordination procedures, whereas the three Northeast Asian states were lacking any such experience. Consequently, the Asian ASEM countries decided on joint coordination between one ASEAN and one non-ASEAN, i.e. Northeast Asian state, beginning with Singapore and Japan in March 1996. In July 1997, Singapore passed the torch to Thailand in conformity with ASEAN's internal practice.[68] After ASEM 2 in April 1998, South Korea, the host country of ASEM 3, succeeded to the position of a Northeast Asian co-ordinator; China is expected to be next in line to take over in the aftermath of ASEM 3. Asian Co-ordinators' meetings take place twice to three times a year on senior officials level. In between these meetings, the officials in charge of ASEM affairs in the respective Foreign Ministries contact each other whenever necessary. In practical terms, coordination takes place on a regional as well as on a subregional level. The two co-ordinators would submit their proposals jointly to the other Asian countries but it could also occur that the Southeast Asian co-ordinator informs the ASEAN members while the Northeast Asian co-ordinator informs the other non-ASEAN countries. The results of the coordination process are presented by the two Asian co-ordinators as agreed Asian positions at the ASEM Co-ordinators' group meetings which also include representatives of the EU Presidency and the European Commission as co-ordinators of the European side.

The fact that two countries speak on behalf of the major East Asian countries is certainly a novelty in the region's international relations. But the substance should not be overestimated. First, it seems that not all Asian countries wholeheartedly accept the fact that other countries from their region should represent them in consultations with the European side.[69] Second, coordination on the Asian side is a rather difficult task as the Northeast Asian countries in particular do not always see the necessity to adjust their position to the other East Asian countries. They would rather prefer to partake in the ASEM process based on their own positions. The results of the Asian coordination process therefore do often reflect no more than the lowest common denominator of the ten participating countries.[70] The idea of setting-up a secretariat to improve the coordination of the Asian side has not (yet) been taken up by East Asian policy-makers.[71] Nevertheless, the fact of regional coordination among East Asian states, as modest as it may be, is an achievement in itself taken the legacy of history and the prevailing cleavages of conflict in the region.

Thus, Asia-Europe interregionalism helped to give birth to an informal EAEC-like East Asian regional entity which existed for no other purpose than to take part in ASEM. From a theoretical viewpoint informed by a constructivist approach, the shaping of the Asian grouping within ASEM may be explained by the mere existence of a distinguishable and parallel 'other' (provided by the EU-'Europe') upon which the East Asian participants could create their own regional identity.[72] Europe as represented by the EU had recognised East Asian regionalism by acknowledging that these same states represent 'Asia' in ASEM. As Camroux and Lechervy have argued, 'Eastern Asia – as opposed to an amorphous Asia–Pacific – existed because it was acknowledged to exist by another regional entity, the European Union'.[73] While it has not been feasible so far for East Asian countries and economies to act as a regional group in the framework of APEC,[74] they were even driven to do so in the framework of ASEM. Whereas Europeans encouraged East Asian regionalism through ASEM, Americans tried to undermine it through APEC which was meant to promote Asia–Pacific regionalism at the expense of East Asian regionalism.

East Asian regionalism through Asia-Europe interregionalism

Most observers would stress that the East Asian members of ASEM have been driven to organise themselves on a regional basis by the fact that their counterpart was the most advanced regional grouping in terms of economic and political integration. In face of the well established coordination machinery of the EU, the Asian countries were almost forced to engage in some sort of regional coordination in order to alleviate the sharp asymmetry in internal organisation between the two regions.[75] In other words: 'soft' institutionalisation on the Asian side was necessary in order to match somehow the already existing 'hard' institutionalisation on the European side. This argument suggests that the East Asian countries engaged in intra-regional cooperation in response to external pressure which could be viewed as a blend of positive external cogency and extra-regional echoing emanating from the European side of ASEM.[76]

Apart from such an actor-oriented explanation of the formation of an Asian caucus within ASEM, there is also a system-centred one which reflects a more active East Asian regionalist response to the challenge of Asia-Europe interregionalism in a Triadic context. It suggests that there is what Jung and Lehmann call a 'hidden Asian agenda' of ASEM, i.e. that East Asian countries, Singapore in particular, initiated the interregional dialogue with Europe also for the purpose of enhancing regional cooperation among themselves.[77] If East Asia was to be acknowledged as one of the Triad regions, it needed to reflect a minimum of region-ness.[78] By participating in a region-to-region endeavour such as ASEM, the Asian countries were able to portray themselves as representing the third pole in the North America-Europe-East Asia triangle. For this purpose, the most important consideration was to build the East Asian pole on the 'dynamic economies which have contributed to the region's prosperity and growth',[79] which happened to be the proposed EAEC members.[80]

East Asian countries used ASEM not only for bridging the 'missing link' in the global triangle but also for bridging the 'missing link within East Asia' between the ASEAN and the Northeast Asian countries.[81] While the economies of the two East Asian subregions are already closely linked as a result of *de facto* economic regionalisation,[82] the institutional links are still at an embryonic stage. Consequently, ASEM created an opportunity for major East Asian countries to get together without arousing anxiety in other parts of the world. Furthermore, for the ASEAN countries, ASEM offered an opportunity to increase their collective bargaining power with regard to the EU by including the three Northeast Asian powers into their camp. An East Asian caucus is thought to be a much more powerful voice and potential deterrent in international affairs than ASEAN alone. Indeed, while ASEAN-EU dialogue relations are taking place on the ministerial level only, the inclusion of the three Northeast Asian powers enabled ASEAN to get a heads of state and government meeting with the EU. For the Northeast Asian countries on the other hand, ASEM offered an opportunity to test cooperation among themselves to which they were not used.[83] Thus, ASEM involved the Northeast Asian powers in a process of regional as well as subregional coordination.[84]

Another motivation for the ASEAN countries as well as for Japan and South Korea to partake in ASEM was to engage China, the emerging power in East Asia. It was hoped that, through a multilateral socialisation process such as ASEM, China would be further exposed to the concerns and views of its neighbours and involved in East Asian region-building.[85] This strategy of engaging China in a process of social learning is also applied to other multilateral arrangements such as APEC, ARF, PMC, and most recently, ASEAN+3. The inclusion of China in interregional endeavours such as APEC and ASEM has the advantage of diluting somewhat the overwhelming position which China has in a pure regional (East Asian) context. The need for China as well as Japan to participate in ASEM is not obvious as they have their own bilateral relations with the EU on the highest political level. But by joining their smaller neighbours in ASEM, China and Japan seized an opportunity to portray themselves as benign powers and good neighbours and to alleviate the concerns of the ASEAN countries regarding their long-term ambitions in the region.[86] The other side of this coin is that it offered China and Japan the possibility to influence the future development of Asia-Europe interregionalism and of East Asian regionalism in accordance with their own national interests. China is interested in using ASEM as a device to neutralise American influence, whereas Japan aims at maintaining full transparency of the ASEM process to the USA and other regions (Koshikawa 1996: 3).

Thus, different and partly contradictory objectives motivated China, Japan, South Korea and seven ASEAN countries to use ASEM, *inter alia*, for the purpose of promoting intra-regional cooperation in East Asia. The evolving ASEAN+3 process seems to prove that the interaction of East Asian countries with the EU member states through ASEM has at least facilitated intra-regional cooperation in East Asia. At their third summit meeting in October 2000, ASEM member countries explicitly acknowledged that great progress had been made in East Asian cooperation in the ASEAN+3 framework.[87] In a sense, ASEM served as a training ground for exclusive East Asian regionalism which has taken off in the aftermath of the Asian Crisis of 1997–98.

Conclusion

This chapter started from the proposition that the interregional ASEM process could serve as a 'regional integrator' in East Asia. It argued that, on the one hand, the logic of interregional relations drive regional states participating in such relations to strengthen intra-regional cooperation; on the other hand, it provides regional states with the option of using interregional relations for regionalist objectives. It has been shown that ASEM indeed served as a 'regional integrator' in East Asia in both ways. First, with the EU as the European counterpart, East Asian participants were forced to act as a group which was a novelty to their region. Second, from the very inception of the ASEM initiative, some East Asian governments were determined to promote regional cooperation among their countries by way of ASEM. This indirect approach to (East Asian) regionalism through (Asia-Europe) interregionalism was a consequence of the constraints and deficiencies of regionalism in East Asia, and it seems to have worked to some extent. Indeed, under the umbrella of ASEM, East Asian countries have gradually expanded regional cooperation in a way which was hardly feasible before. Since the inception of ASEM in 1996, when they acted for the first time as a group, East Asian countries have gradually developed their caucus within ASEM and, as a consequence of the Asian Crisis, established their own framework of regional cooperation – the ASEAN+3 process, which could be viewed as a 'soft' institutionalisation of the EAEC proposal under a new name. In a sense, ASEM was used by East Asian governments, making a virtue out of necessity, to pave the way for the regionalist emancipation of East Asia. Yet, the relative success of this approach also shows its limitations: the more East Asian regionalism develops on its own the less ASEM is needed to serve as a facilitator. In conclusion, the promotion of (East Asian) regionalism through (Asia-Europe) interregionalism cannot be considered as a new paradigm but as an original contribution of East Asian policy-makers to the practice of regionalism which may influence policy-makers in other world regions and induce scholars to reconsider the concept of external factors of regionalism.

Notes

1 Joseph Nye, *International Regionalism: Readings* (Boston: Little Brown 1968).
2 Schwarz, Hans-Peter (1971) 'Europa föderieren – aber wie? Eine Methodenkritik der europäischen Integration' ['How to federate Europe? A methodological critique of European Integration'], in Gerhard Lehmbruch, Kurt von Beyme and Iring Fetscher, eds, *Demokratisches System und politische Praxis der Bundesrepublik. Festschrift für Theodor Eschenburg*, München, pp. 377–443.
3 Ruth Zimmerling, *Externe Einflüsse auf die Integration von Staaten [External influences on the integration of states]* (Freiburg and München: Verlag Karl Alber 1991), pp. 139–154.
4 See, for instance, Russett (1967), Cantori and Spiegel (1973) and Kaiser (1981).
5 For an authoritative analysis see Edwards and Regelsberger 1990. An updated version of this volume is under preparation.
6 Andreas Lukas, 'EC-ASEAN in the context of inter-regional cooperation', in Guiseppe Schiavone, ed., *Western Europe and South-East Asia: Co-operation or Competition* (London: Macmillan, 1989), pp. 105–116; Manfred Mols, 'Cooperation with ASEAN: A Success Story', in Geoffrey Edwards and Elfriede Regelsberger, eds, *Europe's Global Links: The European Community and Inter-Regional Cooperation* (London: Pinter Publishers, 1990), pp. 66–83.
7 This term was coined in the context of the United States' bilateral alliance system in the Asia–Pacific region.
8 Nutall, Simon (1990) 'The Commission: protagonists of inter-regional cooperation', in Geoffrey Edwards and Elfriede Regelsberger, eds, *Europe's Global Links: The European Community and Inter-Regional Cooperation*, pp. 143–160.
9 The concept of 'new regionalism' has been introduced by Palmer (1991). For comparisons of 'old regionalism' and 'new regionalism' see the contribution of Jörn Dosch in this volume as well as Yamamoto 1996, pp. 28–30.
10 ASEAN's network of bilateral group-to-group relations now includes linkages with ANCERTA or CER, the Andean Group, ECO, GCC, Mercosur, Rio Group and SAARC, apart from its traditional relationship with the EC/EU.
11 Rüland, Jürgen (1999a) 'The EU as Inter-Regional Actor: The Asia-Europe Meeting (ASEM), Paper Prepared for the International Conference' Asia-Europe on the Eve of the 21st Century, Bangkok, 19–20 August 1999, p. 2.
12 David Camroux, and Christian Lechervy (1996) '"Close Encounter of a Third Kind?" The inaugural Asia-Europe meeting of March 1996', *The Pacific Review*, Vol. 9, No. 3, pp. 450.

13 Hanns W. Maull, and Akihiko Tanaka, 'The Geopolitical Dimension', in *The Rationale and Common Agenda for Asia-Europe Cooperation. CAEC Task Force Reports* (Tokyo/London: Council for Asia-Europe Cooperation, 1997), pp. 34.

14 Hanns Maull, Gerald Segal and Jusuf Wanandi, eds, *Europe and the Asia Pacific* (London and New York: Routledge, 1998), p. xi.

15 Ku-Hyun Jung, and Jean-Pierre Lehmann, 'The Economic and Business Dimension', in *The Rationale and Common Agenda for Asia-Europe Cooperation*. p. 54.

16 Hadi Soesastro, and Jusuf Wanandi, 'Towards an Asia Europe Partnership – A Perspective from Asia, *Indonesian Quarterly*, Vol. 14, No. 1 (First Quarter 1996), p. 50

17 Richard Higgott, and Richard Stubbs, 'Competing conceptions of economic regionalism: APEC versus EAEC in the Asia Pacific', *Review of International Political Economy,* Vol. 2, No. 3 (1995), pp. 516–535.

18 Most of the East Asian authors in question are members of the Council of Asia-Europe Cooperation (CAEC) network which acts as a kind of informal 'track two' of the ASEM process. Among them are Ku-Hyun Jung (Jung and Lehmann 1997, pp. 53–54), Hadi Soesastro (Soesastro and Nutall 1997, pp. 79–80, 82–84; Soesastro and Wanandi 1996, p. 50), Yoshihide Soeya (Soeya and Roper 1997, p. 43), Akihiko Tanaka (Maull and Tanaka 1997, p. 34), and Jusuf Wanandi (Maull, Segal, and Wanandi 1998, p. xi–xii; Soesastro and Wanandi 1996, p. 50).

19 With the partial exception of Soesastro and Nutall (1997) who provide an overview on the coordination mechanisms on the Asian as well as the European side and Gilson (1998) who offers a theoretical explanation of how the EU helped to legitimise the 'Asia' of ASEM.

20 Heiner Hänggi, 'ASEM and the Construction of the new Triad', *Journal of the Asia Pacific Economy,* Vol. 4, No. 1 (1999), pp. 56–80.

21 Maull, and Tanaka, 'The Geopolitical Dimension'.

22 The concept of the Triad has its roots in the trilateral relationship between the USA, the EC/EU and Japan, the three powers of the capitalist world economy during the cold war period. The concept underwent an expansion to embrace the Triad regions (North America, Western Europe and East Asia) as a consequence of several factors such as the end of the cold war, the appearance of 'new regionalism' and the emergence of East Asia as the third centre of the world economy; and it was further strengthened by the establishment of interregional relations among the Triad regions in the 1990s. By the mid-1990s, the new Triad concept had become a major feature in the discourse about the emerging international order in general and about Asia-Europe relations in particular (Hänggi 1999).

23 This section heavily draws on Hänggi/Régnier (2000), pp. 3–6 and Hänggi (1999), pp. 62–69.

24 Hans-Henrik Holm, and Georg Sörensen, eds, *Whose world order? Uneven globalization and the end of the cold war* (Boulder: Westview Press, 1995).

25 Andrew Hurrell, 'Regionalism in theoretical perspective', in Louise Fawcett and Andrew Hurrell, eds, *Regionalism in world politics: regional organization and international order* (Oxford: Oxford University Press, 1995), pp. 37–73.

26 Winfried Ruigrok, and Robert van Tudler, *The Logic of International Restructuring* (London/New York: Routledge, 1995).

27 Ralf Roloff, 'Globalisierung, Regionalisierung und Gleichgewicht' [globalisation, regionalisation and balance of power], in Carl Masala and Ralf Roloff, eds, *Herausforderungen der Realpolitik [challenges of Realpolitik]* (Köln: SYH-Verlag, 1998), pp. 61–94.

28 Yoshinobu Yamamoto, 'Regionalization in Contemporary International Relations', in Van R. Whiting, Jr. (ed.) *Regionalization in the World Economy: NAFTA, the Americas and Asia Pacific* (London and New York: Macmillan, 1996), p. 34.

29 Hadi Soesastro, 'Open Regionalism', in Maull, Segal and Wanandi, eds, *Europe and the Asia Pacific*.

30 Rüland (1999a, pp. 1–2) makes a similar distinction between bilateral interregionalism (group-to-group relations) and transregionalism (dialogue fora which are not
necessarily coinciding with regional organisations).

31 Yamamoto, 'Regionalization in Contemporary International Relations', pp. 29–30.

32 Roloff, Ralf (1998) 'Globalisierung, Regionalisierung und Gleichgewicht' [globalisa-
tion, regionalisation and balance of power], in Carl Masala and Ralf Roloff (eds.)
Herausforderungen der Realpolitik [challenges of Realpolitik], Köln: SYH-Verlag,
pp. 85–94.

33 Rosemary Foot, 'Pacific Asia: The development of regional dialogue', in Fawcett and
Hurrell (eds.) *Regionalism in world politics: regional organization and international
order*, pp. 229–241.

34 Peter J. Katzenstein, and Takashi Shiraishi, eds, *Network Power: Japan and Asia*
(Ithaca and London: Cornell University Press, 1997), pp. 31–41; Richard Higgott, 'De
Facto and De Jure Regionalism: The Double Discourse of Regionalism in the Asia
Pacific', *Global Society*, Vol. 11, No. 2, (1997), pp. 165–183.

35 Peter J. Katzenstein, 'Regionalism in Comparative Perspective', *Cooperation and
Conflict*, Vol. 31, No. 2 (1996), pp. 141, 144.

36 Richard Higgott, and Richard Stubbs, 'Competing conceptions of economic
regionalism: APEC versus EAEC in the Asia Pacific', *Review of International
Political Economy*, Vol. 2, No. 3 (1995), pp. 516–535; Barry Buzan, 'The Asia–
Pacific: what sort of region in what sort of world?', in Anthony McGrew and
Christopher Brook, eds, *Asia–Pacific in the New World Order* (London and New York:
Routledge, 1998)

37 Richard Higgott, 'Shared response to the market shocks?', *The World Today*, January
1998, pp. 4–6.

38 Rüland, Jürgen (1999b) 'APEC, ASEAN and EAEC – A Tale of Two Cultures of
Cooperation', Paper Prepared for the Conference 'The Asia–Pacific Economic
Cooperation (APEC): The First Decade', Freiburg, 21–22 October 1999, p. 13.

39 Since 1994, the Foreign Ministers of ASEAN countries have met regularly at the
annual Post-Ministerial Conferences (PMC) with their counterparts from China,
Japan and South Korea. In November 1995, the ASEAN Economic Minister met for
the first time with their counterparts of the three Northeast Asian countries.

40 'East Asian Leaders hold meetings', http://www.aseansec.org/general/publication/
au199909.htm.

41 *Joint Statement on East Asian Cooperation*, Manila, 28 November 1999.

42 *International Herald Tribune*, 27 November 2000, p. 11.

43 At the time of the third East Asian summit meeting in Manila, South Korean President
Kim Dae Jung was quoted as saying: 'I see a great deal of possibility in this ASEAN-
plus-three group further expanding and further solidifying as a forum for East Asia as
a whole. It will be able to speak for the region *vis-à-vis* the North American Free
Trade Area, Latin America and the European Union, and engage these organizations
in cooperation as well as in competition.' *International Herald Tribune*, 26 November
1999, p. 1.

44 Hänggi, 'ASEM and the Construction of the new Triad', pp. 57–62.

45 At the second ASEM preparatory meeting on senior officials level in December 1995
in Madrid, the East Asian countries came up with a jointly agreed 'Asian Discussion
Paper' which stressed the need to bridge 'the missing link' between Asia and Europe.
It says in its first paragraph: 'When the world is moving towards the 21st century, it is
of great significance that close ties be built up between three centres of economic
growth and power – North America, Europe and Asia. Europe is well linked to North
America through history and rich network of trans-Atlantic institutions. East Asia and
North America are linked by APEC and a growing dense web of Pacific Basin
networks. The missing link is the one between Asia and Europe. The first and
foremost purpose of the Asia-Europe meeting (ASEM) is to bridge this missing link.'

The Asia-Europe Meeting (ASEM): An Asian Discussion Paper (19 December 1995), p. 1 (mimeo).

46 While the EU is a member of the ARF, Japan and South Korea are 'partners of cooperation' of the Organisation for Security and Cooperation in Europe (OSCE). Furthermore, Great Britain is linked to Malaysia, Singapore as well as to Australia and New Zealand in the Five Powers Defence Arrangements (FPDA).

47 *New Straits Times*, 3 November 1993.

48 Ong, Keng Yong 'Why An European-Asian Summit Now? – An Asian Perspective', in B. Singh and N. von Hofmann, eds, *Europe and Southeast Asia: What will be the common future?*, Singapore, p. 4.

49 The final conference document, titled 'A Programme For Action' (Singapore, 14 October 1994), says in its closing paragraph: '... all the existing mechanisms for cooperation between Europe and East Asia ... need to be put in the broader context of a Europe/East Asia summit at the level of heads of government to discuss the issues affecting the relations between the two regions', *ASEAN Economic Bulletin* (March 1995), p. 368.

50 Victor Pou Serradell, 'The Asia-Europe Meeting (ASEM): A Historical Turning Point in Relations Between the Two Regions', *European Foreign Affairs Review*, Vol. 1, No. 2 (1997), pp. 185–210.

51 *Asia-Europe Meeting* (18 March 1995), p. 3 (mimeo).

52 Pou Serradell, 'The Asia-Europe Meeting (ASEM)', p. 191.

53 *Asia-Europe Meeting* (18 March 1995), p. 3 (mimeo). Emphasis added.

54 Following its comprehensive approach, the EU insisted on adding political dialogue to the economic agenda initially envisaged by ASEAN. Pou Serradell 1997, p. 196.

55 Among the European candidates were, apart from the EU member states, Switzerland and Norway as well as a number of Central and Eastern European countries such as Poland, Hungary, the Czech Republic, Romania, and the Ukraine. The interest of Russia and Turkey posed particular problems, as both countries cover European as well as Asian territory.

56 The European format includes in fact the 15 member states of the EU as well as the EU itself, represented by the Presidency (in charge of the Common Foreign and Security Policy) and the Commission (in charge of the Common Commercial Policy).

57 While all ASEAN member states participated in ASEM 1, this was not the case in ASEM 2 and ASEM 3 because ASEAN had twice enlarged its membership in the meantime: Laos and Myanmar joined the Association in 1997, Cambodia followed in 1999.

58 In APEC the members of the regional groupings in North America (NAFTA), Southeast Asia (ASEAN) and Oceania (ANCERTA) act as individual countries only. Soesastro, Hadi, and Simon Nuttall (1997) 'The Institutional Dimension'.

59 Rüland, Jürgen, 'The Future of the ASEM Process: Who, How, Why and What?', in Wim Stokhof and Paul van der Velde, eds, *ASEM. The Asia-Europe Meeting. A Window of Opportunity* (London and New York: Kegan Paul International, 1999) pp. 126–151.

60 The ASEM process covers three broad issue-areas: (1) political dialogue; (2) economic cooperation; and (3) cooperation in other areas (such as culture, education, environment and science). *Chairman's Statement of the Asia-Europe Meeting*, 2 March 1996, Bangkok.

61 The foreign ministers of the Asian participants of ASEM met in July 1995 in Brunei and in February 1996 in Phuket. The 'Asian' Economic Ministers held preliminary discussions on ASEM in November 1995 in Osaka and in February 1996 in Phuket. Asian Senior Officials meetings (SOM) in preparation of ASEM were held in September 1995 in Phuket, in October 1995 in Tokyo and in March 1996 in Bangkok. In November 1995, the Asian Senior Economic Officials met in Jakarta to exchange views on the economic issues to be discussed at ASEM.

62 *The Asia-Europe Meeting (ASEM): An Asian Discussion Paper* (19 December 1995), pp. 1–5 (mimeo).

63 Soesastro, and Nuttall, 'The Institutional Dimension', p. 82.

64 *Chairman's Statement of the Asia-Europe Meeting*, 2 March 1996, Bangkok, para. 19.

65 On the eve of ASEM 3, the heads of state and government of the ten Asian ASEM member countries followed this practice and held an 'Asian Leaders' Meeting' in Seoul to exchange views prior to the official opening of the Summit. See press release under http://www.asem3.org/english/d29.htm.

66 Officials from the Ministries of Foreign Affairs of ASEM member states and the External Relations Directorate of the European Commission.

67 The following section draws from Soesastro and Nutall 1997, and from interviews with Foreign Ministry officials in ASEM member states (between March 1997 and January 1999).

68 For practical reasons, the ASEAN member state in charge of co-ordinating the dialogue partnership relations with the EU is also entrusted with co-ordinating the ASEAN countries in the ASEM framework.

69 Soesastro, and Nuttall, 'The Institutional Dimension', p. 84.

70 Interviews with Foreign Ministry officials, Tokyo (June 1997).

71 This proposal was made by a Chinese scholar at an international conference on ASEM in Seoul in November 1997 (Dai 1997, p. 6). Given the ASEAN+3 format of the evolving East Asian regionalism, it would make sense to set up the proposed Asian ASEM coordination body at the ASEAN Secretariat in Jakarta; such a coordination body could even serve as the nucleus of an eventual future East Asian Cooperation (EAC) secretariat.

72 Julie Gilson, 'Defining Asia through ASEM: The EU Creates a New Partner', Paper Prepared for the Third Pan-European Conference on International Relations, Vienna, 16–19 September 1998, pp. 18–21.

73 Camroux, and Lechervy, '"Close Encounter of a Third Kind?" The inaugural Asia-Europe meeting of March 1996', p. 450.

74 This may change in the future in view of the weakening of APEC in the wake of the Asian Crisis and the evolving East Asian regionalism. It is noteworthy that the East Asian leaders agreed at their third summit meeting in November 1999 'to intensify coordination and cooperation in various international and regional fora such as the UN, WTO, *APEC*, ASEM, and the ARF ...' (emphasis added). *Joint Statement on East Asian Cooperation*, Manila, 28 November 1999, para. 7.

75 The Singaporean officials in charge of drawing up a blueprint for ASEM were aware of this problem: 'So we had to deliberate how this could proceed because all the 10 Asia countries which eventually would participate in this whole initiative, had never heard or dealt with the European Commission as an entity in discussing trade policy. Hence the question of sovereignty on the one hand, the question of socialising with each other on the other.' Ong 1996, p. 5.

76 In her study on external factors of regional integration, Zimmerling (1991, pp. 139–158) identifies three principal mechanisms: (1) negative external cogency, (2) positive external cogency, (3) extra-regional echoing.

77 Jung, and Lehmann, 'The Economic and Business Dimension', p. 53.

78 From a Triadic perspective, five major functions of ASEM can be distinguished (Hänggi 1999, pp. 73–76): (1) to construct an (East) Asian region, (2) to constitute (East) Asia as the third pillar of the new Triad; (3) to promote open regionalism through interregional co-operation: (4) to check and balance US dominance, (5) to avoid coalition-building to the detriment of either of the two regions.

79 *Asia-Europe Meeting* (18 March 1995), p. 3 (mimeo).

80 Hänggi, 'ASEM and the Construction of the new Triad', pp. 73–74.

81 Interview with Foreign Ministry official, Singapore (March 1997).

82 In a speech in Singapore on the eve of the Bangkok Summit, South Korean President Kim Young Sam emphasised the growing cohesion of East Asia following the end of the Cold War. He said that Northeast and Southeast Asia were 'now being unified' into an 'integrated East Asian economic region'. *International Herald Tribune*, 1 March 1996, p. 10.

83 At the margins of the third informal ASEAN+3 Summit in November 1999, the leaders of China, Japan and South Korea held their first trilateral summit talks. *International Herald Tribune*, 29 November 1999, p. 5.

84 Interviews with Foreign Ministry officials, Tokyo (June 1997).

85 Interviews with Foreign Ministry officials in Jakarta, Singapore and Bangkok (February 1997), in Tokyo (June 1997) and in Seoul (July 1998). See also Koshikawa 1996, p. 3; Ong 1996, p. 7.

86 Feng, 'L'ASEM II suscite l'attention mondiale', p. 12.

87 *Chairman's Statement of the Third Asia-Europe Meeting*, Seoul, 20–21 October 2000, para. 5.

12 Conclusion

The renewal of regionalism and an East Asian new order

Fu-Kuo Liu

In this brief concluding chapter, we intend to summarize what we observe to be the most salient features and updated developments of regionalism in East Asia. We began this research by asking whether the arrival of a post-Cold War climate has changed the features of regional cooperation and brought about the need for a new reading of regionalism to the region, and whether there is a change in the nature of regionalism indeed taking shape, and, if so, whether this has resulted in a developing trend of paradigm shifting. Especially since the structural transformation of international relations becomes more salient in the regional setting, there are new factors that are jointly accelerating the regional process. With this new surge of dynamism following the Asian financial crisis, we have found that regionalism in East Asia has not only entered a new era but has now even more dramatically also moved to an era of progressing regional integration.

We are convinced that conventional debate needs to be reviewed and regenerated so as to understand the implications of this new dynamism for East Asian regionalism. The perspective of structural changes to regional cooperation as has been elaborated in this volume has clearly noted that the nature of regionalism is undergoing a transformation, and may need to be spelled out in a few concrete dimensions. Two sets of observations have evolved on structural changes to regionalism. First, the economic structural changes of regional countries in the 1980s have led to the transformation of regionalism, which, in turn, has resulted in the emergence of new regionalism. Second, in the wake of the Asian financial crisis and the epidemic social unrest in the region, the impotency of existing regional mechanisms in coping with this sort of regional challenge has prompted essential structural changes to regional cooperation. Many practical regional initiatives such as the Japanese proposal of the Asian Monetary Funds have been put forward as a result. Now, under the 'ASEAN plus three' process, thirteen heads of states/governments have formed to lead the way in the region, and this could fundamentally change the future course of regionalism in East Asia. Strong involvement among states and the collective intention of searching for a regional identity has accrued profound implications for the process of regional cooperation. Built on the nature of new regionalism, this new dynamism, which incorporates the idea that it is necessary for states to play a greater role in the process, has led to the Second Wave of new Regionalism.

As is apparent in terms of the origins of regional cooperation in East Asia, most of this momentum seems to rest on broader interactions among regional societies such as those initiated through the forms of economic cooperation and networking. In fact, the emergence of the new regionalism as popularized since the 1980s has more to do with overall economic aspiration than with political calculation. This is to suggest that the true features of new regionalism appear to be a spontaneous phenomenon, and are occurring as the region develops further. It is only recently that regional governments have started to take initiatives to push varying regional arrangements. During the 1990s, regional institution buildup in East Asia reached its height with the emergence of ARF, CSCAP, KEDO, ASEM and CAEC on top of the existing PECC, APEC and ASEAN. Among them, ASEAN has initiated regional development proposals and has been at the centre of this wave of new regionalism. From the regionalist perspective of structural strategy, the establishment of APEC and ASEM represents a certain effort to reinforce the internal cohesion of the region by way of developing inter-regionalism.[1] It is true that during the pending global trade negotiation of the Uruguay Round, most East Asian countries became integrated through the APEC process. Relative to other regional blocs, APEC became a single symbolic representative of regional countries in negotiating trade issues. It has also become common practice that leaders of East Asian countries would meet to seek consensus on their policy stand prior to meeting their European counterparts for the ASEM biannual Summit. To a practical extent, inter-regionalism is both a means and an end of strategic arrangements in the region.

In terms of the regionalist process in East Asia, we frequently see that concepts of regional cooperation, regional integration, subregional cooperation and regionalization have been used in varying circumstances. Although they are related to each other and could partly feature some similar developments, they do denote quite different approaches to regionalism. Due to the limited experience of regional cooperation existing in the region, regionalism in East Asia is not characterized by institutional buildup but rather by intensive economic cooperation and regional networking. Strictly speaking, the process of East Asian regionalism cannot be regarded as progressing towards regional integration as yet. Although key regional leaders in the current dynamic of regionalism have advocated strengthening the scope of regional cooperation by pushing through the idea of forming certain effective cooperative mechanisms,[2] it may be highly premature to predict that regionalism in East Asia is about to develop into a European type of regional integration. Mobilized by multiple forces that include economic incentives, political preference and security need, the regionalization process contributes much to enhancing regional coherence in economic and societal fields as well as in the policy arena. There may be some scope for developing an outcome of *de jure* regional arrangements (in political, economic and security forms) and *de facto* regional integration (in economic forms).[3] Since 'regional integration' implies more of a *de jure* regional convergence process with the establishment of regional institutions, we suggest that 'regional cooperation' may be a more relevant term to describe East Asian regionalism, at least for now.

The attempt to define East Asian regionalism has helped to identify the surrounding concepts, which will be critical in conceptualizing a theory-to-be. Reckoning with the main features of regionalism, we have suggested that East Asian regionalism arises out of a unique regional context of great variety and might be depicted as a continuing process undertaken by regional countries to strengthen regional cooperation. Part of our collective effort in this volume has been to stimulate discussion over the implications of present developments in the whole region, and especially to elaborate on the multi-layers of regionalism.

The process of East Asian regionalism

For decades, East Asian regionalism has gradually come to develop its own unique features for pushing ahead regional cooperation. At the core of its developing course there exists more of a loose form of regional cooperation than 'regional integration'. Although it has in general promoted the effect of regional integration along the process of economic development, regionalism in East Asia does not directly reflect a European way of integration. Despite the fact that some analysts have wondered whether a European process of integration might be the optimal goal for Asian regionalism, it is not yet necessary to predict further institutionalized approaches to integration. The question thus remains: In which direction is it heading? Given the great variety of the East Asian community, one would have to be as realistic as possible in reviewing past regional efforts, arguing on basis of the current dynamism or even with regard to foreseeing any further developments. After all, in practice regional identity is far from a full-fledged concept to most East Asian countries. Given this acknowledgement, what kinds of regional cooperation would serve the best interests of East Asian countries? How may regional countries couple their national interests with regional interests? The answers to these pragmatic questions will surely lead to a better understanding of the growing cooperative regional arrangements, and which we imagine are also the basis of the common tendencies of regionalism in the region.

Theoretical arguments on regional integration may provoke challenges in the case of the East Asian region. While it is true to argue that deeper economic interdependence within the region may presumably lead to a natural course of regional integration, the conventional understanding of integration does not anticipate that the will of states may not turn out to be in favour of regional integration. Need we ask why it is that regional integration in East Asia has not reached a threshold over these decades of regional effort, as has been envisaged by many? Clearly, the economic development process, regionalization, and even the globalization process have each enriched the region extensively and have thus enhanced regional coherence. An even more prominent trend is the flourishing development of business networking in the region.[4] Some perceive that the regional developments in East Asia are in place in of any *de facto* regional integration. Others claim that regionalism in East Asia may only be a natural result of economic interdependence and should not be equated with any progress in moving towards an institutionalized regional integration. Besides, there has not yet been a core concept of regional integration able to prevail in the region. The regional institutional building process may have taken place in one particular subregion, but it does not refer to any serious commitment towards a regional process of integration. It seems to be more accurate to comment that states are still far more preoccupied with national interests than with the regional well-being of regional countries. When we consider that many in the region have not thought through the idea of forming a regional union, there seems to be little likelihood of an institutionalized regionalism.

Since the process of regionalism in East Asia has turned out to be more ASEANized and pragmatic oriented (not in the least problem-solving), ASEAN's perspective of regional cooperation and unity will certainly need to be taken into account with regard to the future development of regionalism in East Asia. Based on the 'ASEAN way' or the 'Asia Pacific way' of decision-making to regional cooperation, ASEAN emphasizes that any decision will have to go through consensus, and members will have to abide by three principles of non-interference, mutual respect and responsibility. To many, the ASEAN way has really been devoted to maintaining peace and regional unity for over thirty years.[5] To many others, the slow pace of the ASEAN way may have taken its toll on the efficiency of many related regional mechanisms (e.g. ARF, APEC, ASEM, etc.), especially in times of crisis.

For years, ASEAN has insisted that the nature of regional and transnational cooperation will have to be based on state-to-state interactions rather than 'transnational' types of regional integration. It has also developed various bilateral and multilateral dialogue networks with partners of the region and elsewhere. Regional dialogue forums have been a major focus in its foreign relations. Existing regional mechanisms have been working along the lines of concentrating on exploring opportunity for further economic cooperation and building mutual trust, but not directly on managing regional issues. Despite the fact that the force of economic integration seems to be expanding beyond state boundaries, it is still obvious that ASEAN members would never advocate any cooperation or integration process with a transnational nature, since this would transform the nature of the sovereign state. Nor has any existing effort purposely pointed in that direction so far. The fundamental concept here of regional cooperation (or integration) is still very much trailing the realist view of international politics, which continues to dominate through state-centric theory. It is therefore fair to suggest that due to its particular historical development and with respect to the variety of nations, regionalism in East Asia may be heading for closer regional integration for the sake of common economic interest, but it is certainly not akin to the trend advocated in Europe.

Three general phases of transformation

In the second half of the twentieth century, regionalism in East Asia experienced three general critical periods, which in retrospect may be taken into account as the path of regional development (see Table 12.1 for a detailed comparison of time scale). The process has gradually seen the building of a multi-layered regionalism, within which each layer is seen to complement the others.

First, the 'old regionalism' clearly emerged closely in association with the Cold War spirit. Individual states were limited by the fixed system. There was not much room left for individual countries to act in this context. The main strands of regionalism were actually designated by outside international players (e.g. the United Nations and the United States), rather than activated by regional countries. Throughout East Asia, much of the geographic landscape was overshadowed by the apprehension of the Cold War. In general, regional apprehension about security may well have served as one of the striking impulses for regionalism. On the whole, the development of regionalism was very much initiated, maintained and headed by the superpowers in the hope of collectively defending communist expansionism. It was simply a deliberate effort to promote regionalism without much effective grass-root support around the region. By nature then, regionalism seemed to be given to the region by outsiders. The regional agenda was in accordance with the grand strategy of the superpowers and was undoubtedly meant to serve certain politico-security purposes. At that time both political and military competition were far more significant than economic competition. Since economic interaction among regional countries had not yet been given much credit in bringing about the general regional

Table 12.1 Changing phases of East Asian regionalism

Phases/ timeframes	Representing arrangements	Main features	Paradigms
The old regionalism (1950s to 1970s)	EATO CAFE SEAN (I)	1 Politico-military motivation 2 Superpowers and alliance relationships 3 Motivated by the UN and USA	Cold War paradigm Realist approach
The new regionalism (1980s onwards)	PECC APEC CSCAP ARF ASEM ASEAN(II)	1 Openness 2 Industrial cooperation/division of labour 3 Networking 4 Regional institutions 5 Inter-regionalism/subregionalism	Flying geese model Liberalist approach Market integration Trade competition Corporate integration
The second new regionalism (since 1997)	ASEAN plus three	1 Intra-regional link/inter-regionalism/subregionalism 2 The early stage of regional integration 3 Regional convergence	Security–economic nexus Regional management

interest, the features of regionalism were clearly demonstrated as mission orientated and state centred in tendency.

Second, regionalism prevailed with certain characteristics of open regionalism, which concentrated largely on cooperation through regionalized economic processes. This process of growing economic development in the region against a background of increasing worldwide competition stemming from trade blocs was largely devoted to promoting the dynamism of regionalism in East Asia. The emergence of PBEC, PECC and APEC marked an important era of economic interdependence in the region by which the main features of the 'new regionalism' came to be characterized. Both stimulated by and demanded through the momentum of regional economic development, regionalism gradually came into being. With ever increasing market and industry integration, the impetus for economic development has further involved all countries in a regionalized process in which the groundwork is the basis for the further development of regionalism. Compared to the old regionalism, the new regionalism is characterized mainly by varying economic cooperation formation, both private and official, and, to a lesser extent, by politico-security cooperation.

Since East Asian economies were eager to push ahead in the course of catching up on the developmental ladder, the interactive and transnational cooperation relating to trade, investment and industry became a significant channel of new regionalism. It is understandable that the core idea behind new regionalism should embrace open regionalism and trade liberalization. During the late 1980s, a growing interest in developing regional economic mechanisms was regarded as stimulated by the promising progress of regional integration in the European Community and elsewhere. It also aroused great enthusiasm for discussion on whether East Asia would kick-start the process of regional integration or retain its acquired form of regionalism. The overall picture in East Asia has shown that leaders of regional countries were suspicious of any objective to develop regionalism, even as the new regionalism further evolved and began to overarch matters related to outside the region.[6]

Third, the new dynamism of East Asian regionalism has been nurtured in the post-Cold War and particularly the post-Asian financial crisis settings, especially since the shock wave of Asian financial crisis has to some extent shattered people's anticipation of the existing regionalism. It emerged as an enormous force determinedly pushing through the reformation of national and regional structures. As a result, the focus of regionalism seems to have shifted towards enhancing internal coherence amongst East Asian members, particularly in terms of managing financial systems and procedures.

Due to the fact that the regional environment has generally been shaped by the multiple processes of regionalization and globalization, the pace of economic interaction in the region has also been further accelerated. The desire for security and stability among regional countries is growing in unprecedented terms. In addition, the evolvement of regionalism has also benefited from the development of the regional security cooperative effort, in which the concept of security is broadly defined as 'comprehensive security'. As such, growing regional security concerns and security cooperation have been closely tied with the progress of regional development in various aspects (e.g. economic, environmental, human, social, political, military, etc.). There was even one instance where leaders were tentatively proposing to engage security issues inside the economic-oriented APEC formation. Now, 'ASEAN plus three' leads the way in structuring regional economic and financial cooperation. Analysts have speculated that as long as the process continues to move along, it will soon touch upon not only economic but also security domains.

It is therefore fair to suggest that these developments have enriched the nature of regional cooperation as well as the long-term process of regional integration, since through this there has been a convergence of the regional efforts of economic and security aspects. Although renewing this dynamism has derived from a forceful response to the change in regional circumstances, the present endeavour is taking further steps to push for closer cooperation through inter-regionalism, self-assured regionalism and regional networking, all of which we believe would direct new regional norms and constitute new paradigms to regionalism. Over the past decade, the region has witnessed the flourishing of bilateral and multilateral regional cooperation. With track one and track two establishments playing a substantial role in contributing to general regional coherence and the momentum of regional market integration binding together the region much closer than might have been expected, never before has East Asia been so close to attaining a broad sentiment in regional identity. Apart from the complicated but well-organized business networking, varying regional establishments have also built reticulate networks along with regional governments and organizations, national groups and individuals.

New paradigms of East Asian regionalism to date

What new features of regionalism have been emerging? Differing greatly from previous ideas of regional structures, the present endeavour of the second new wave of regionalism has seen more of a focus on 'intra-regional links', the efforts of which could take East Asia into a new era of regional cooperation. This development has formally structured regionalism in terms of three dimensions: subregionalism, intra-regionalism, and inter-regionalism. This has been a remarkable step, since this current drive is based on regionalism with innovative characteristics, which in general embraces *an East Asia-centred caucus, a process leading to possibly horizontal integration of financial and economic systems* and *convergence of Northeast and Southeast Asian regionalism* through a number of economic complexes. These new features should head the agenda of Asian regionalism and will certainly have profound implications for the future development of regionalism.

An East Asia-centred caucus to lead regional efforts. The long-term effect of the new dynamism may well create a hierarchical complex of regionalism in the region. After almost a decade of advocating East Asian economic caucus by

Malaysian Prime Minister Mahatir Mohamed, the 'ASEAN plus three' process at the Manila Summit of 1999 brought the idea alive. East Asian countries now seem to place much more emphasis on their regional partners than on others. Even more encouraging is the fact that they have started to manage regional cooperation through a multi-layered coalition. At the head of joint decision-making, there is the 'ASEAN plus three' process. Many regional cooperations and issues will be discussed and proposed along ministerial and summit meetings, as have been highlighted during the 'ASEAN plus three' summits. At the lower level, APEC and ARF, with external powers' involvement, will continue to serve as regional-specific functional mechanisms. ASEM will serve as a mechanism outreaching the EU. At the bottom level, varying track 2 arrangements and business networking should continue to pave the way for closer regional cooperation or perhaps even long-term integration.

Horizontal integration of financial and economic systems. In the past, regional efforts embraced trade liberalization, open regionalism and a trust-building process. Under this construct it is envisaged that an individual country may not practise new norms that regional cooperative mechanisms have attempted to set, since the very nature of regionalism should be and has been consultative and cooperative. However, the Asian financial crisis broke through the customary attitude towards regional partnerships. Many regional countries sensed the necessity of enhancing cooperation, and to proposed fixed financial mechanisms in the hope of bringing together all possible resources of the region to combat the future crisis. The 'ASEAN plus three' process has brought about the idea of a regional financial monitoring system in which thirteen countries will try to consolidate their financial operations. Although there has yet to be a clear agenda on integrating financial systems and economic policy, the process of pushing the horizontal integration of financial systems in the region is already underway.

Converging Northeast and Southeast Asian regionalism. One of the salient and important features of regionalism in East Asia to date is the emergence of the natural convergence of Northeast and Southeast Asia, as a result of the emerging new momentum pushing for the making of a more traditional regional community. Regionalism in East Asia used to be quite disparate. The sense of community was limited to such basic structures whereby an individual country may see frequent involvement in others' regional development, for example, Japan in the process of ASEAN economic development. But, at the regional level, Northeast Asia has tended to develop its own economic and security features, in which Southeast Asia found little of a niche to fit itself in and vice versa. The new dynamism, however, has clearly worked to initiate the convergence of two subregions. As such, under the structure of the 'ASEAN plus three' and its vision for the region, abundant capital, high technology and economic development know-how would be brought in from Northeast Asia to help Southeast Asia develop. In return, ASEAN's Northeast Asian partners were able to gain increased access to their markets and natural resources. It is through such steps that the East Asian sentiment of one region is growing much stronger.

Moreover, this new dynamism is also to be found in terms of the security front, since North Korea's latest commitment to the ARF process could prove to be critical to the unity of both subregions. ASEAN has found a role to play in Northeast Asian security matters.

For East Asian countries, building on these multi-layered regional mechanisms could assist their joint efforts towards developing regionalism. Perhaps, by taking on the progressing integration of certain policy initiatives in the region, the new dynamism may even lead to restructuring the ways in which East Asian regionalism is worked through.

Prospective observations

This collective effort has aimed to bring about some practical directions for those seeking to build an understanding of regionalism to date in East Asia. Through this process, we have come to realize that the continuing progress of regionalism will be both advantageous and a determinant of the stability in the region. Although it is clear that over time the development of regionalism in East Asia has further resulted in closer regional interdependence and a growing demand for institutional building of regional mechanisms, it remains, we believe, to be some distance away from fully taking off in the process of regional integration. Despite the fact that regional identity is gradually emerging at an unprecedented pace on both the economic and security fronts, there still has not been the creation of sufficient mutual trust, or at the very least adequate tolerance given among regional countries for the sake of strengthening regional cooperation. In terms of building up regional integration, ASEAN is by far the most advanced regional body in the whole region. It has taken up the endeavour under a widening process, carrying along the image of ten countries in East Asia and in turn working to strengthen the process through a number of integration programmes currently in hand. Over the decades, the regional process has indeed produced a number of promising ambitious regional cooperative plans. Despite the fact that many may have claimed that these were a result of the euphoria of regional integration in the making, there are some obvious outcomes. After all, with ASEAN's presence in the region, there has not been a major regional conflict between states since the termination of the Vietnam War. In any case, the developments we have witnessed in recent times seem to point towards closer regional integration. Nevertheless, others continue to be suspicious of ASEAN's cooperative nature, since one critical aspect of the ASEAN Way has been to deal only with something that will not cause controversy among all members, at the loss of the opportunity to resolve many significant issues. Indeed, beneath the surface of the enthusiastic regional formulae, there remain a score of obstinate disputes and differences among its members. Although praising its contributions to regional peace and cooperation, very few seem to be satisfied with the way it has developed so far. For those leaning towards a more sceptical view there is little scope for optimism about the future of regionalism.

By and large, the further the process progresses, the more we learn that the development of regionalism in East Asia is leading towards something that differs greatly from the *de jure* regional integration in Europe. It may be just and fair to interpret East Asian regionalism as a '*de facto* regional integration' process. In any case, people easily recognize the existing diversity between regional countries, but have not been able to explain why regionalism has appeared to evolve to such an extent nor how future regionalism will develop. Several questions remain: What might be the central thrust, if any, that this East Asian regionalism is lacking? What exactly might be missing in the process now? To be authentic, there has in the past been no commonly shared region-wide plan for regional integration. Although, of late, regional countries have launched this new dynamism of regional cooperation and this new endeavour will surely direct the future, it is clear that the mechanism ('ASEAN plus three') *per se* is mainly designed to counter short-term and future regional economic crises and is still very much a problem-solving orientation. While this new structure may be put forward in a potential effort to take on the harder job of regional cooperation, it does not necessarily lead to an overhaul of the existing understanding of regionalism in East Asia.

Looking ahead, we believe that as the answers to what people in the region really want for regionalism continue to emerge, the steps taken could be decisive. Against the backdrop of the ASEAN way and perhaps that of conventional wisdom,[7] a grand blueprint of regional cooperation or something similar may be called for before any substantial cooperative mechanism can be upgraded. If in the near future there is such an initiative it should prevail, perhaps even quite effortlessly.

Notes

1 This view has been elaborated by Heiner Hänggi in Chapter 11.
2 Through the 'ASEAN plus three' process, President King Dae Jung of South Korea, Premier Zhu Rongji of China and Prime Minister Keizo Obuchi of Japan have on varying occasions advocated the idea of enhancing cooperation in East Asia. The significant statement on 'East Asia cooperation' made in the third 'ASEAN plus three' Informal Summit became a pioneer proposal leading to the 'Chiang Mai Initiative' for 'financial integration'. The 'ASEAN plus three' Informal Summit 'Joint Statement on East Asia Cooperation', Manila, 28 November 1999. http://asean.or.id/summit/inf3rd/js_eac.htm
3 Charles Oman, 'The Policy Challenges of Globalisation and Regionalisation', *Policy Brief*, No. 11 (Paris: OECD, 1996), pp. 6–7.
4 Peter J. Katzenstein, 'Varieties of Asian Regionalisms', in Peter J. Katzenstein, Kozo Kato, Ming Yue, Natasha Hamilton-Hart, *Asian Regionalism* (Ithaca, NY: East Asia Program, Cornell University, 2000).
5 For example, Abdullah Ahmad Badawi, 'Keynote Address', in Stephen Leong, ed., *ASEAN Towards 2020: Strategic Goals and Future Directions* (KL: ISIS Malaysia, 1998), pp. 13–14; Dato' Yusof Hashim, 'ASEAN Cohesion: Issues and Responses', *The Indonesia Quarterly*, Vol. 26 (1998); Hadi Soesastro, 'ASEAN 2030: The Long View', in Simon S.C. Tay, Jesus Estanislao and Hadi Soesastro, eds, *A New ASEAN In A New Millennium* (Jakarta: Centre for Strategic and International Studies, 2000), p. 195.

6 Robert Lawrence, *Regionalism, Multilateralism, and Deeper Integration* (Washington, DC: The Brookings Institution, 1996), p. 83.

7 ASEAN's process is characterized mainly by incrementalism, gradualism and minimalism, which tries to avoid obstacles of 'any sort to costly and grand designs'. Chin Kin Wah, 'ASEAN Institution Building', in Stephen Leong, ed., *ASEAN Towards 2020: Strategic Goals and Future Directions* (KL: ISIS Malaysia, 1998), pp. 13–14.

Bibliography

Sources

ADB. (1997) *Asian Development Outlook 1997 and 1998*. New York: Oxford University Press-Asian Development Bank.
——. (1996) *Asian Development Outlook 1996 and 1997*. New York: Oxford University Press-Asian Development Bank.

APEC. (1994) *Achieving the APEC Vision – Free and Open Trade in the Asia Pacific*. Second Report of the Eminent Persons Group. Singapore: APEC Secretariat.

ASEAN. (2000) 'The Fourth ASEAN Informal Summit'. Singapore. (22–25 November).
——. (2000) 'The Joint Ministerial Statement of the ASEAN + 3 Finance Ministers Meeting (Chiang Mai Initiative)'. Chiang Mai, Thailand. (6 May).
——. (1999) 'Joint Statement on East Asia Cooperation'. Manila. (28 November).
——. (1998) 'Statement on Bold Measures'. 6th ASEAN Summit. Hanoi. (16 December). And 'Hanoi Plan of Action'.
——. (1997) 'Press Statement: The Second ASEAN Informal Meetings of Heads of State/Government of the Member Sates of ASEAN'. Kuala Lumpur. (15 December). And 'ASEAN Vision 2020'.
——. (1996) 'Press Statement: The First Informal ASEAN Heads of Government Meeting'. Jakarta. (30 November).
——. (1984) *A Bibliography*. Singapore: Institute of Southeast Asian Studies.
——. (1978) *10 Years of ASEAN*, Jakarta: ASEAN Secretariat.

ASEAN Secretariat and Philippine Institute for Development Studies. (1992) *ASEAN Economic Cooperation for the 1990s*. A Report Prepared for the ASEAN Standing Committee, Manila, 141 p.

ASEAN Secretariat. (1997a) *ASEAN Economic Co-operation, Transition and Transformation*. Singapore: Institute of Southeast Asian Studies.
——. (1995) *AFTA Reader*. Jakarta. 3 volumes.

ASEAN Standing Committee. (1992) *External Economic Relations, in ASEAN Economic Cooperation for the 1990s: A Report*. Manila: Philippine Institute for Development Studies. pp. 22–30.

IIF. (1999) *Capital Flows to Emerging Market Economies*. Washington, DC: Institute of International Finance. April 24.

JERC. (1966) 'Measures for Trade Expansion of Developing Countries', Japan Economic Research Centre, October, pp. 93–134, Tokyo.

OECD. (1996) *Regionalism and its Place in the Multilateral Trading System*. Paris.

——. (1993) *Regional Integration and Developing Countries.* Paris.

OECD. (1995) *Development Centre, OECD AND ASEAN Economies: The Challenge of Policy Coherence.* Paris.

OECD. (1995) *Foreign Direct Investment, OECD Countries and Dynamic Economies of Asia and Latin America: Regional and Global Gains from Liberalization.* Paris.

UNCTAD. (1997) *Regional Experiences in the Economic Integration Process of Developing Countries.* Geneva: Report by the UNCTAD Secretariat. 25 June.

——. (1995) *Rapidly Emerging Regional Integration Systems: Implications for the Asian Developing Countries and Possible Political Responses.* A Study by Julius C. Parrenas. 15 December.

United Nations. (1974) 'Economic Cooperation among Member Countries of ASEAN', Report of a UN Team. *Journal of Development Planning*, No. 7.

USIP. (1998) *Beyond the Asian Financial Crisis: Challenges and Opportunities for US leadership.* A Special Report of the United States Institute of Peace, Washington, DC: USIP, April.

World Bank. (1998) *East Asia: The Road to Recovery.* Washington, DC: World Bank.

——. (1994) *East Asia's Trade and Investment.* Washington DC.: World Bank

Books and works

Aggarwal, Vinod K. and Charles E. Morrison, eds. (1998) *Institutionalizing the Asia–Pacific: Regime Creation and the Future of APEC.* Houndmills and London: Macmillan.

Akaha, T. ed. (1999) *Politics and Economics in Northeast Asia: Nationalism and Regionalism in Contention.* London: Macmillan.

Akrasanee, Narongchai and David Stifel. (1992) *The Political Economy of the ASEAN Free Trade Area*, in Imada Pearl and Seiji Naya. eds. *AFTA: The way ahead*, Singapore: ISEAS, pp. 27–48.

Alagappa, Muthiah. (1998) 'Asian Practice of Security: Key Features and Explanations', in Muthiah Alagappa, ed. *Asian Security Practice: Material and Ideational Influences.* Stanford: Stanford University Press.

Anand, R.P. and Quisumbing, Purificacion V. eds. (1981) *ASEAN Identity, Development & Culture.* Quezon City: University of the Philippines Press.

Antolik, Michael. (1984) *ASEAN and the Diplomacy of Accommodation.* London: Sharpe, pp. 104–105,

Anwar, Dewi Fortuna. (1995a) *Indonesia in ASEAN: Foreign Policy and Regionalism.* New York/Singapore: St Martin's Press and ISEAS.

——. (1995b) 'Indonesia and ASEAN Extra-Regional Economic Co-operation', in *Indonesia in ASEAN: Foreign Policy and Regionalism.* Singapore: St Martin's Press and ISEAS, pp. 103–107.

Aravena, Francisco Rojas and Paz Buttedahl. eds. (1999) *Open Regionalism: Strengthening the Net – Perspectives from APEC Countries.* Santiago, Chile: FLACSO-Chile.

Ariff, M. (1994) *AFTA: Another Futile Trade Area?* Kuala Lumpur, Syarahan Perdana: University of Malaya.

——. and Loon-Hoe Tan (1988) *ASEAN Trade Policy Options.* Singapore: ISEAS.

Arndt, Heinz W. and Hal Hill, eds. (1999) *Southeast Asia's Economic Crisis: Origins, Lessons, and the Way Forward.* Singapore: ISEAS.

Arthur Andersen Co. (1991) *The Growth Triangle: A Guide to Business*, Singapore.

Ball, Desmond. (2000) *The Council for Security Cooperation in the Asia Pacific: Its Record and Its Prospects.* Canberra Papers on Strategy and Defence No. 139. Canberra: The Australian National University.

Basu Sharma (1985) *Aspects of Industrial Relations in ASEAN*, Singapore. Institute of South East Asian Studies, Occasional Paper, no 78.

Bergsten, Fred. ed. (1997) *Whither APEC? The Progress to Date and Agenda for the Future.* Washington, DC.: Institute for International Economics.

——. (1997) 'Open regionalism'. Working Paper, 97–3. Washington, DC: Institute for International Economics.

Bora, Bijit and Christopher Findlay. eds. (1996) *Regional Integration and the Asia–Pacific.* Melbourne: Oxford University Press.

Boyd, Gavin and Alan Rugman, eds. (1998) *Economic Integration in the Pacific.* Aldershot: Edward Elgar.

Broinowski, Alison, ed. (1982) *Understanding ASEAN.* Hong Kong: Macmillan.

Bull, Hedley. ed. (1975) *Asia and the Western Pacific: Towards A New International Order.* Melbourne: Thomas Nelson.

Bustelo, Pablo. (1998) *The East Asian Financial Crises: An Analytical Survey.* ICEI Working Paper, No. 10/1998, ICEI, Complutense University of Madrid.

Buzan, Barry. (1998) 'The Asia–Pacific: what sort of region in what sort of world?', in Anthony McGrew and Christopher Brook. eds. *Asia–Pacific in the New World Order.* London and New York: Routledge.

Cantori, Louis J. and Steven Spiege. (1973) 'The International Relations of Regions', in R.A. Falk and S.H. Mendlovitz. eds. *Regional Politics and World Order.* San Francisco: W.H. Freeman, pp. 335–353.

Capie, David Paul Evans, and Akiko Fukushima. (1999) *Speaking Asia Pacific Security: A Lexicon of English Terms with Chinese and Japanese Translations and a Note on the Japanese Translation.* Toronto: University of Toronto-York University.

Caporaso, James A. (1998) 'Regional Integration Theory and East Asia', in Kim Chae-Han ed. *Domestic Politics, Trade Negotiations and Regional Integration: the US, Japan and Korea.* Seoul: The Hallym Academy of Sciences, Sowha Publishing Co, pp. 187–212.

Chee, Chang Heng. ed. (1997) *The New Asia–Pacific Order.* Singapore: Institute of Southeast Asian Studies (ISEAS).

Chen, Edward K.Y. & C.H. Kwan. eds. (1997) *Asia's Borderless Economy: the Emergence of Subregional Economic Zones.* St. Leonards, Australia: Allen & Unwin.

Chia Siow Yue and Wendy Dobson. (1997) 'Harnessing Diversity', chapter 11, in same authors eds. *Multinationals and East Asian Integration.* Singapore: ISEAS and International Development Research Centre (Canada), pp. 249–263.

——. Marcello Pacini. eds. (1997) *ASEAN in the New Asia: Issues and Trends.* Singapore: Institute of Southeast Asian Studies.

——. Joseph Tan. eds. (1997) *ASEAN and the EU: Forging New Linkages and Strategic Alliances.* Singapore/Paris: ISEAS and OECD Development Centre.

Chia, Siow Yue. ed. (1994) *APEC Challenges and Opportunities.* Singapore: Institute of Southeast Asian Studies (ISEAS).

Cho, L.J. (1998) *Regional Economic Co-operation and Integration in Northeast Asia for the Twenty-First Century.* paper presented at the Eighth Northeast Asian Economic Forum Conference, 28–30 July 1998, Yonago, Japan.

Choy, Chong Li. (1981) *Open Self-Reliant Regionalism: Power for ASEAN's Development.* Singapore, ISEAS, Occasional Paper No. 65.

Crouch, Harold. ed. (1984) *Domestic Political Structures and Regional Economic Cooperation*. Singapore: ISEAS.

Dai, Bingran. (1997) 'ASEM: Building a Bridge Between Asia and Europe: An Asian Perspective on the Relationship Between APEC and EU', Paper Prepared for the International Conference of EUSA-Korea on 'The Asia Europe Meeting (ASEM): A New Framework for Korea-EU relations in the 21st Century', 14–15 November 1997, Seoul.

De Castro, Renato. (1989) *Decision Making in Regional Organization: The EC and ASEAN Experiences*. Manila: Foreign Service Institute.

De la torre, Augusto and Kelly, Margaret, R. (1992) *Regional Trade Arrangements*. Washington, International Monetary Fund, Occasional Paper 93.

Dent, C.M. (1999) *The European Union and East Asia: An Economic Relationship*. London: Routledge.

Deutsch, Karl. *et. al.* (1957) *Political Community and the North Atlantic Area*. Princeton: Princeton University Press.

Dixon, Chris. (1991) *South East Asia in the World-Economy: A Regional Geography*. London: Cambridge University Press, pp. 2–3.

Djiwandono, J. Soedjati. (1988) 'The Role of ASEAN in the Asia–Pacific Region', in Dalchoong Kim and Noordin Sopiee eds. *Regional Cooperation in the Pacific Era*. Seoul: Institute of East and West Studies,Yonsei University Press, pp. 381–402.

Domenach, Jean-Luc. (1998) *L'Asie en danger.* Paris: Fayard.

Dosch, Jörn. (1998) 'Emerging Multilateralization of Security Cooperation in the Asia–Pacific Region – Following European Experiences and Models or Driven by an Indigenous Approach?' in Joachim Krause and Frank Umbach, eds. *Perspectives of Regional Security Cooperation in Asia–Pacific: Learning from Europe or Developing Indigenous Models?* pp. 143–163. Bonn: Forschungsinstitut der Deutschen Gesellschaft für Auswärtige Politik e. V.

——. (1997) *Die ASEAN. Bilanz eines Erfolges*. Hamburg: Abera.

Dosch, Jörn and Christian Wagner. (1999) *ASEAN and SAARC. Regionale Kooperation in Asien*. Hamburg: Abera.

Dougherty, James E. and Robert L. Pfaltzgraff Jr. (1990) *Contending Theories of International Relations: A Comprehensive Survey*. 3rd edition, New York: Harper Collins.

Drysdale, Peter. (1988) *International Economic Pluralism: Economic Policy in East Asia and the Pacific*. New York: Columbia University Press.

Dutta, M. (1999) *Economic Regionalization in the Asia–Pacific: Challenges to Economic Cooperation*. Cheltenham, UK: Edward Elgar.

Edwards, Geoffrey and Elfriede Regelsberger. eds. (1990) *Europe's Global Links. The European Community and Inter-Regional Cooperation*. London: Pinter Publishers.

Estanislao, Jesus P. (2000) 'ASEAN and APEC: A Post-Crisis Perspective', in *Community Building in Asia Pacific. Dialogue in Okinawa.* edited by Japan Center for International Exchange, pp. 33–38. Tokyo and New York: Japan Center for International Exchange.

Fawcett, Louise and Andrew Hurrell. eds. (1995) *Regionalism in World Politics: Regional Organization and International Order*. Oxford: Oxford University Press.

Fifield Russel H. (1979) *National and Regional Interests in ASEAN: Competition and Cooperation in International Politics*. Singapore, ISEAS, Occasional Paper No. 57.

Frankel, Jeffrey A. ed. (1998) *The Regionalization of the World Economy*. Chicago, Ill.: The University of Chicago Press.

——. and Miles Kahler, eds. (1993) *Regionalism and Rivalry: Japan and the United States in Pacific Asia.* Chicago: the University of Chicago Press.

Fukasaku, Kiichiro. Ed. (1995) *Regional Co-operation and Integration in Asia.* Paris, Organisation for Economic Co-operation and Development (OECD).

Funabashi, Y. (1995) *Asia Pacific Fusion: Japan's Role in APEC.* Washington, DC: Institute for International Economics.

Gamble, Andrew and Anthony Payne. eds. (1996) *Regionalism and World Order.* Basingstoke: Macmillan.

Garnaut, Ross. (1996) *Open Regionalism and Trade Liberalization: An Asia-pacific Contribution to the World Trade System.* Singapore: Institute of Southeast Asian Studies.

Garnaut, Ross and Peter Drysdale. eds. (1994) *Asia–Pacific Regionalism: Readings in International Economic Relations.* Sydney: Harper Educational Publications.

Gerschenkron, A. (1962) *Economic Backwardness in Historical Perspective.* Harvard University Press, Cambridge, MA.

Gilson, Julie. (1998) 'Defining Asia through ASEM: The EU Creates a New Partner', Paper Prepared for the Third Pan-European Conference on International Relations, Vienna, 16–19 September.

Glick, Reuven. (1998) 'Thoughts on the Origins of the Asian Crisis: Impulses and Propagation Mechanisms'. *Pacific Basin Working Paper*, No. 98/07, Federal Reserve Bank of San Francisco, September.

Haas, Michael. (1979) 'Asian intergovernmental organisations and the United Nations', in Berhanykun Andemicael. ed. *Regionalism and the United Nations.* Dobbs Ferry, New York: Oceana Publications, Inc., pp. 400–445.

Halib, Mohammed and Tim Huxley. eds. (1996) *An Introduction to Southeast Asian Studies.* London/Singapore: Tauris Publishers and Institute of Southeast Asian Studies, 254 p.

Hänggi, Heiner. (1991) *ASEAN and the ZOPFAN Concept, Pacific Strategic.* Papers 4. Singapore: ISEAS.

Hänggi, Heiner, and Philippe Régnier (2000) *The Small State and the Triad: the Case of Switzerland's Foreign Policy Towards East Asia.* NFP 42 Synthesis No. 23, Bern: Swiss National Science Foundation.

Hassan, Mohamed Jawhar. ed. (1998) *A Pacific Peace: Issues & Responses.* Kuala Lumpur: ISIS.

Herman, Donald C. and Kenneth B. Pile. eds. (1997) *From APEC to Xanadu: Creating a Viable Community in the Post-Cold War Pacific.* Armonk, NY: M. E. Sharpe.

Hernandez, Carolina G. (1998) 'The Future Role of ASEAN: A View from An ASEAN ISIS Member', in *East Asia at A Crossroads Challenges for ASEAN.* Hanoi: Institute for International Relations.

Hettne, Bjorn. Andras Inotai and Osvaldo Sunkel. eds. (1999) *Globalism and the New Regionalism.* Basingstoke: Macmillan Press Ltd.

Higgott, Richard. (1998) 'The Politics of Economic Crisis in East Asia: Some Longer Term Implications', *CSGR Working Paper*, No. 02/98, University of Warwick, March.

Higgott, Richard and Nicola Phillips. (1999) 'The Limits of Global Liberalisation: Lessons from Asia and Latin America', *CSGR Working Paper*, No. 23/99, University of Warwick, January.

Higgott, Richard and Richard Robison. eds. (1985) *Southeast Asia: Essays in the Political Economy of Structural Change.* London: Routledge and Kegan Paul.

Holm, Hans-Henrik, and Sörensen, Georg, eds. (1995) *Whose World Order? Uneven Globalization and the End of the Cold War.* Boulder: Westview Press.

Hong, Wontck and Lawrence Krause. eds. (1981) *Trade and Growth of the Advanced Developing Countries in the Pacific Basin*, Seoul: Korea Development Institute.

Imada, Pearl and Seiji Naya. eds. (1992) *AFTA: The Way Ahead*. Singapore: Institute of Southeast Asian Studies.

Indorf, Hans H. (1984) *Impediments to Regionalism in Southeast Asia: Bilateral Constraints among ASEAN Member States*. Singapore: Institute of Southeast Asian Studies.

——. (1975) *ASEAN: Problems and Prospects*. Singapore: ISEAS, Occasional Paper No. 38, December.

Ito, Takatoshi and Anne O. Krueger. eds. (1997) *Regionalism versus Multilateral Trade Arrangements*. Chicago, Ill.: The University of Chicago Press.

Jackson, Karl D. ed. (1999) *Asian Contagion: The Causes and Consequences of a Financial Crisis*. Boulder, Colo.: Westview Press.

Jansson, H. (1994) *Transnational Corporations in Southeast Asia, Cambridge*. Cambridge University Press.

Jomo, K.S. ed. (1998) *Tigers in Trouble: Financial Governance, Liberalisation and Crises in East Asia*. London: Zed Books.

Jorgensen-Dahl, Arnfinn. (1982) *Regional Organization and Order in South-East Asia*. London, Macmillan.

Jung, Ku-Hyun and Lehmann, Jean-Pierre. (1997) 'The Economic and Business Dimension', in *The Rationale and Common Agenda for Asia-Europe Cooperation. CAEC Task Force Reports*, Tokyo/London: Council for Asia-Europe Cooperation, pp. 49–73.

Kahler, Miles. (1994) 'Institution-building in the Pacific', in Andrew Mack, Andrew and John Ravenhill eds. *Pacific Cooperation: Building Economic and Security Regimes in the Asia–Pacific Region*. Canberra: Macmillan, pp. 16–39.

Kaiser, Karl. (1981) 'Die Interaktion regionaler Subsysteme' ['The interaction of regional subsystems'], in Günther Doecker and Friedrich Veitl, *Regionalismus und regionale Integration. Zur Theorie der regionalen Integration*, Frankfurt: Peter Lang Verlag, pp. 99–121.

Kamlin, Muhammad. (1991) *The Meaning of Integration in the ASEAN Region*. Bandar Seri Begawan: University Brunei Darissalam, Faculty of Arts and Social Sciences, University Brunei Darussalam, Working Paper No. 8.

Karim, Mohammed Azhari. *et. al.* eds. (1990) *Malaysian Foreign Policy; Issues and Perspectives*. Kuala Lumpur: National Institute of Public Administration.

Kartadjoemena, Hassan S. (1975) *The Politics of External Economic Relations: Indonesia's Options*. Singapore: ISEAS.

Katzenstein, Peter J. *et. al.* (2000) *Asian Regionalism*. Ithaca, New York: East Asian Program, Cornell University.

——. and Takashi Shiraishi. eds. (1997) *Network Power: Japan and Asia*. Ithaca and London: Cornell University Press.

Kawagoe, T. and S. Sekiguchi. eds. (1995) *East Asian Economies: Transformation and Challenges*. Singapore: ISEAS,

Khaw, Guat Hoon. (1977) *An Analysis of China Attitude Towards ASEAN 1967–76*. Singapore: ISEAS, Occasional Paper No. 48, September.

Khoman, Thanat. (1992) 'Conception and Evolution', in Sandhu, K.S. *et. al.* eds. *The ASEAN Reader*. Singapore: Institute of Southeast Asian Studies (ISEAS), pp. xvii–xxii.

Khoo, How San. (1994) 'ASEAN Political and Security Cooperation: Past, Present and Future', Paper presented at the Sixth Southeast Asia Forum on 'One Southeast Asia: Political, Economic and Security Implications', Kuala Lumpur, mimeo.

Kim, Young C. ed. (1995) *The Southeast Asian Economic Miracle.* New Brunswick/ London: Transaction Publishers.

Koh, Tommy. (1998) *The Quest for World Order: Perspectives of a Pragmatic Idealist.* Singapore: Times Academic Press.

Korhonen, Pekka. (1998) *Japan and the Asia Pacific Integration, Pacific Romances 1968–1996.* London: Routledge.

———. (1994) *Japan and the Pacific Free Trade Area.* London: Routledge.

Krause, Joachim and Umbach, Frank. ed. (1998) *Perspectives of Regional Security Cooperation in Asia–Pacific: Learning from Europe or Developing Indigenous Models?* Bonn: Forschungsinstitut der Deutschen Gesellschaft für Auswärtige Politik e. V.

Krauss, Melvyn B. ed. (1974) *The Economics of Integration.* London: Allen and Unwin.

Kreinin, Mordechai. Shigeyuki Abe, and Michael Plummer, 'Regional integration in Asia', in Kohsrow Fatemi. ed. *The New World Order: Internationalism, Regionalism and the Multinational Corporations.* Oxford: Elsevier Science Ltd.

Krishnamra, Nadhavathna. (1997) 'Thailand's Policy towards Cooperation within ASEAN 1967–1979.' Ph.D. dissertation, Geneva: IUHEI, University of Geneva.

Krumar, Sree. (1994) 'Johor-Singapore-Riau Growth Triangle: A Model of Sub-regional Cooperation', in Myo Thant, Min Tang and Hiroshi Kakazu. eds. *Growth Triangles in Asia: A New Approach to Regional Economic Cooperation.* Singapore: Oxford University Press, pp. 175–217.

Kuwahara, Yasuo. (1998) 'Economic development in Asia and its consequences for labour migration'. in OECD Proceedings – *Migration and Regional Economic Integration in Asia.* Paris: OECD.

Kwan, C.H. (1994) *Economic Interdependence in the Asia–Pacific Region.* London: Routledge.

Lake, David A. and Morgan Patrick M. (1997) 'The New Regionalism in Security Affairs', in David A. Lake and Patrick M. Morgan. eds. *Regional Orders: Building Security in a New World.* Pennsylvania: the Pennsylvania State University, pp. 3–19.

Lau, Teik Soon. ed. (1973) *New Directions in the International Relations of Southeast Asia: The Great Powers and Southeast Asia.* Singapore: Singapore University Press.

Lawrence, R. (1996) *Integrating National Economies, Regionalism, Multilateralism and Deeper Integration.* Washington, DC: The Brookings Institution.

———. (1994) *The Global Environment for the East Asian Model.* Cambridge, MA: John F. Kennedy School of Government, Harvard University.

Lee, Chyungly. (1999) 'On Economic Security', in G. Wilson-Roberts. ed. *An Asia–Pacific Security Crisis? New Challenges to Regional Stability.* Wellington, New Zealand: Centre for Strategic Studies,.

Lee, Tsao Yuan. (1991) *Growth Triangle: The Johor-Singapore-Riau Experience.* Singapore: ISEAS and Institute of Policy Studies.

Leifer, Michael. (1996) *The ASEAN Regional Forum.* Adelphi Paper, No. 302. London: IISS.

———. (1983) *Indonesia's Foreign Policy.* London: Routledge.

———. (1972) *Dilemmas of Statehood in Southeast Asia.* Vancouver: University of British Columbia Press.

Lim, Hua Sing. (1994) *Japan's Role in ASEAN: Issues and Prospects.* Singapore: Times Academic Press.

Lindberg, Leon and Scheingold Stuart A. eds. (1971) *Regional Integration: Theory and Research.* Cambridge: Harvard University Press.

Lipsey, Ichard. G. (1971) *The Theory of Customs Unions: A General Equilibrium Analysis.* London: LSE Research Monographs No. 7.

Lucas, Bella R. (1983) *Towards a Methodology for Assessing ASEAN Regionalism: A Study of intra-ASEAN Interactions in 1976–1982.* Quezon City: University of the Philippines Press.

Lukas, Andreas. (1989) 'EC-ASEAN in the context of inter-regional cooperation', in Guiseppe Schiavone. ed. *Western Europe and South-East Asia: Co-operation or Competition.* London: Macmillan, pp. 105–116.

Machetzki, Riger. (1996) 'ASEAN – Politics and Economic Development', in Wolfgang Pape. ed. *Shaping Factors in East Asia by the Year 2000.* Hamburg: Institute of Asian Affairs, pp. 175–207.

Mack, Andrew and John Ravenhill. eds. (1995) *Pacific Cooperation: Building Economic and Security Regimes in the Asia–Pacific Region.* Boulder, Colorado: Westview Press.

Mak, Joon Num. (1998) 'The Asia–Pacific security order', in Anthony McGrew and Christopher Brook. eds. *Asia–Pacific in the New World Order.* London and New York: Routledge, pp. 88–120.

Mansfield, Edward D. and Helen V. Milner. eds. (1997) *The Political Economy of Regionalism.* New York: Columbia University Press

Martin, Linda G. ed. (1987) *The ASEAN Success Story: Social, Economic and Political Dimensions.* Honolulu: East-West Centre, Hawaii University Press.

Masson, Paul. (1998) 'Contagion: Moonsoonal Effects, Spillovers, and Jumps between Multiple Equilibria', *IMF Working Paper*, Vol. 98, No. 142, September.

Matsumoto, S. ed. (1980) *Southeast Asia in a Changing World.* Proceedings and Papers of a Symposium held at the IDE in March 15–17 1978, Tokyo: Institute of Developing Economies.

Maull, Hanns, Gerald Segal and Jusuf Wanandi. eds. (1998) *Europe and the Asia Pacific.* London and New York: Routledge.

Maull, Hanns W., and Akihiko Tanaka. (1997) 'The Geopolitical Dimension', in *The Rationale and Common Agenda for Asia-Europe Cooperation. CAEC Task Force Reports.* Tokyo/London: Council for Asia-Europe Cooperation, pp. 31–40.

Mcleod, Ross H. and Ross Garnaut, eds. (1998) *East Asia in Crisis: From Being a Miracle to Needing One?* London: Routledge.

Menon, Jayant. (1996) *Adjusting towards AFTA: The Dynamics of Trade in ASEAN.* Singapore: Institute of Southeast Asian Studies.

Moellers, Wolfgang and Rohana Mahmood. eds. (1993) *ASEAN Future Economic and Political Cooperation.* Kuala Lumpur: Institute of Strategic and International Studies.

Mols, Manfred. (1996) *Integration und Kooperation in zwei Kontinenten. Das Streben um Einheit in Lateinamerika und in Südostasien.* Stuttgart, Steiner Verlag.

——. (1996) 'Regional Integration and the International System', in Shoji Nishijima and Peter H. Smith, eds, *Cooperation or Rivalry? Regional Integration in the Americas and the Pacific Rim.* Boulder/Colorado: Westview Press. pp. 9–26.

——. (1993) 'The Integration Agenda: A Framework for Comparison' in Peter H. Smith, ed. T*he Challenge of Integration, Europe and the Americas.* New Brunswick: North South Center University of Miami, pp. 51–76.

——. (1990) 'Cooperation with ASEAN: A Success Story', in Geoffrey Edwards and Elfriede Regelsberger. eds. *Europe's Global Links. The European Community and Inter-Regional Cooperation.* London: Pinter Publishers, pp. 66–83.

Mondejar, Reuben. (1988) 'Understanding ASEAN and Other Regional Organizations: An Unfinished Agenda', Conference Paper, September, mimeo.

Moon, C.I. and Rhyu, S.Y. (2000) 'The State, Structural Rigidity, and the End of Asian Capitalism: A Comparative Study of Japan and Korea', in R. Robison, M. Beeson, K. Jayasuriya and H.R. Kim. eds. *Politics and Markets in the Wake of the Asian Crisis.* London: Routledge.

Moon, C.I and Yoo, H. (1997) 'Embedded Mercantilism and Regional Integration in East Asia', paper presented at the 17th World Congress, International Political Science Association.

Nishijima, Shoji and Smith, Peter H. eds. (1996) *Cooperation or Rivalry? Regional Integration in the Americas and the Pacific Rim.* Boulder: Westview Press.

Noordin Sopiee, *et. al.* eds. (1987) *ASEAN at the Crossroads: Obstacles, Options, and Opportunities in Economic Co-operation.* Kuala Lumpur: Institute of Strategic and International Studies.

Nutall, Simon. (1990) 'The Commission: protagonists of inter-regional cooperation', in Geoffrey Edwards and Elfriede Regelsberger. eds. *Europe's Global Links. The European Community and Inter-Regional Cooperation.* London: Pinter Publishers, pp. 143–160.

Nye J.S. (1971) *Peace in Parts: Integration and Conflict in Regional Organization.* Boston: Little Brown and Co.

——. (1968) *International Regionalism: Readings.* Boston: Little Brown and Co.

Ohmae, Kenichi. (1995) *The End of the Nation State: The Rise of Regional Economies.* New York: The Free Press.

Ohno K. and Y. Okamoto (1994) 'Multinational Firms in Market-Led Integration in Asia', in *Regional Integration and Foreign Direct Investment: Implications for Developing Countries.* Tokyo: Institute of Developing Economies.

Olds, Kris. *et. al.* eds. (1999) *Globalisation and the Asia–Pacific.* London and New York: Routledge.

Oman, Charles. (1996) 'The Policy Challenges of Globalisation and Regionalisation', Policy Brief, No. 11. Paris: OECD, 1996, pp. 6–7.

Ong, Keng Yong. (1996) 'Why An European – Asian Summit Now? – An Asian Perspective', in B. Singh and N. von Hofmann. eds. *Europe and Southeast Asia: What will be the common future?* Singapore: ISEAS, pp. 3–9.

Ooi, G.T. (1981) *ASEAN Preferential Trading Arrangements (PTA): An Analysis of Potential Effects on Intra-ASEAN Trade.* Singapore: ISEAS, Research Notes and Discussion Paper No. 26.

Palmer, Norman D. (1991) *The New Regionalism in Asia and the Pacific.* Lexington, MA.: Lexington Books.

Park, Yung-chul. (1996) 'East Asian Liberalization, Bubbles and the Challenges from China'. *Brookings Papers on Economic Activity*, No. 2, pp. 357–371.

Parreñas, Caesar. (1989) *ASEAN im Kräftefeld der Großmächte: Großmachtpolitik und regionale Zusammenarbeit in Südostasien seit 1975.* Frankfurt am Main *et. al.*: Peter Lang.

Paul, Arthur. (1967) 'Regionalism in Asia: A New Thrust for Development', Occasional Paper, No. 1. San Francisco: Asia Foundation.

Phamorabutra, Kriwat. (1997) *Mahathir's Proposal for East Asian Economic Caucus (EAEC).* Tokyo: International University of Japan, MA Thesis.

Radelet, Steven and Jeffrey Sachs. (1998) *The Onset of the Asian Financial Crisis*, Brookings Papers on Economic Activity. No. 1, pp. 1–90.

Rajendran, M. (1986) *ASEAN's Foreign Relations: The Shift to Collective Action.* Kuala Lumpur: Arenabuku.

Regelsberger, Elfriede. (1990) 'The dialogue of the EC/Twelve with other regional groups: a new European identity in the international system?', in Geoffrey Edwards and Elfriede Regelsberger. eds. *Europe's Global Links. The European Community and Inter-Regional Cooperation.* London: Pinter Publishers, pp. 3–26.

Rieger, Hans Christoph. (1991) *ASEAN Economic Co-operation Handbook.* Singapore: Institute of Southeast Asian Studies.

——. (1986) 'The Association of Southeast Asian Nations: Success or Failure in South-South Co-operation?' in *Im Spannungsfeld von Wirtschaft, Technik und Politik.* München: Festschrift für Bruno Fritsch. pp. 79–94.

Roloff, Ralf. (1998) 'Globalisierung, Regionalisierung und Gleichgewicht [globalisation, regionalisation and balance of power], in Carl Masala and Ralf Roloff. eds. *Herausforderungen der Realpolitik* [challenges of Realpolitik, Köln: SYH-Verlag, pp. 61–94.

Ross, Robert S. ed. (1994) *East Asia in Transition: Toward a New Regional Order.* Armonk, NY: M. E. Sharpe.

Ruigrok, Winfried and Robert van Tudler. (1995) *The Logic of International Restructuring.* London/New York: Routledge.

Rüland, Jürgen. (1999a) 'The EU as Inter-Regional Actor: The Asia-Europe Meeting (ASEM)'. Paper Prepared for the International Conference, Asia-Europe on the Eve of the 21st Century, Bangkok, 19–20 August 1999.

——. (1999b) 'APEC, ASEAN and EAEC – A Tale of Two Cultures of Cooperation', Paper Prepared for the Conference on 'The Asia–Pacific Economic Cooperation (APEC): The First Decade', Freiburg, 21–22 October.

——. (1999c) 'The Future of the ASEM Process: Who, How, Why and What?', in Wim Stokhof and Paul van der Velde (eds.), *ASEM. The Asia-Europe Meeting. A Window of Opportunity.* London and New York: Kegan Paul International, pp. 126–151.

Russett, Bruce M. (1967) *International Regions and the International System: A Study in Political Ecology.* Chicago: Rand McNally.

Sandhu, K.S. (1992) 'ASEAN: Achievements and Prospects', Paper presented to the ASEAN Seminar/Roundtable Conference, jointly organized by ASEAN Paris Committee (APC) and Institut Francais des Relations Internationales (IFRI) Paris, 19–20 October.

Sandhu K.S. *et. al.* eds. (1992) *The ASEAN Reader.* Singapore: ISEAS.

Sarasin, Viraphol and Werner Pfennig. eds. (1995) *ASEAN-UN Cooperation in Preventative Diplomacy.* International Studies Centre, Ministry of Foreign Affairs of Thailand.

Saravanamuttu, J. (1985) 'ASEAN Postures and Performances in North-South Negotiations', in Pushpa Thambipillai and J. Saravanamuttu. *ASEAN Negotiations: Two Insights.* Singapore: ISEAS, pp. 29–55.

Satoh, Yukio. (1998) 'Politische Koordination für Sicherheit und Stabilität im asiatisch-pazifischen Raum', in Hanns W. Maull. ed. *Regionalismus in Asien-Pazifik*, Bonn: Forschungsinstitut der Deutschen Gesellschaft für Auswärtige Politik e. V. pp. 59–88.

Schwarz, Hans-Peter. (1971) 'Europa föderieren – aber wie? Eine Methodenkritik der europäischen Integration' ['How to federate Europe? A methodological critique of European Integration'], in Gerhard Lehmbruch, Kurt von Beyme and Iring Fetscher. eds. *Demokratisches System und politische Praxis der Bundesrepublik. Festschrift für Theodor Eschenburg*, München, pp. 377–443.

Shibusawa, Masahide, Z.A. Ahmad and B. Bridges (1992) *Pacific Asia in the 1990s.* London: Routledge (Royal Institute of International Affairs).

Simanjuntak, Djisman S. (1997) 'EU-ASEAN Relationship: Trends and Issues', in Chia Siow Yue and Marcello Pacini. eds. *ASEAN in the New Asia: Issues and Trends.* Singapore: ISEAS, pp. 92–118.

Singh, L.P. (1966) *The Politics of Economic Cooperation in Asia: A Study of Asian International Organizations.* Columbia: Missouri University Press.

Skully, Michael. (1979) *ASEAN Regional Financial Cooperation: Developments in Bankinf and Fianncer.* Singapore: ISEAS, Occasional Paper, No. 56.

Smith, Peter H. ed. (1993) *The Challenge of Integration, Europe and the Americas.* New Brunswick/London: Transaction Publishers.

Soesastro, Hadi. (2000) 'Asia Pacific Trade Arrangements in the New Millennium', in *Community Building in Asia Pacific. Dialogue in Okinawa.* Tokyo: Japan Center for International Exchange. pp. 39–48.

——. (1998) 'Open Regionalism', in Hanns Maull, Gerald Segal and Jusuf Wanandi. eds. *Europe and the Asia Pacific.* London and New York: Routledge, pp. 84–96.

——. (1998) 'Offener Regionalismus im asiatisch-pazifischen Raum', in Hanns W. Maull. ed. *Regionalismus in Asien-Pazifik.* Bonn: Forschungsinstitut der Deutschen Gesellschaft für Auswärtige Politik e. V. pp. 7–58.

——. and Nuttall, S. (1997) 'The Institutional Dimension', in *The Rationale and Common Agenda for Asia-Europe Cooperation. CAEC Task Force Reports.* Tokyo/London: Council for Asia-Europe Cooperation, pp. 75–85.

——. ed. (1995) *ASEAN in a Changed Regional and International Political Economy.* Jakarta: CSIS.

Soeya, Yoshihie and John Roper (1997) *The Political and Economic Security Dimension, in The Rationale and Common Agenda for Asia-Europe Cooperation. CAEC Task Force Reports.* Tokyo/London: Council for Asia-Europe Cooperation, pp. 41–48.

Solidum, Estrella. (1970) *The Nature of Cooperation among ASEAN States as Perceived through Elite Attitudes: A factor of Regionalism.* University of Kentucky, unpublished thesis.

——. (1974) *Towards a Southeast Asian Community.* Quezon City: University of the Philippines Press.

Sopiee, Noordin. (1991) 'ASEAN and Indochina after a Cambodian Settlement', in Dora Alves, ed. *Change, Interdependence and Security in the Pacific Basin*; *The Pacific Symposium.* Washington DC: National Defence University Press. pp. 315–336.

——. Chey Lay See and S.J. Lim. eds. (1987) *ASEAN at the Crossroads: Obstacles, Options and Opportunities in Economic Cooperation.* Kuala Lumpur: Institute of Strategic and International Studies.

Tan, Gerald. (1996) *ASEAN Economic Development and Cooperation.* Singapore: Times Academic Press, pp. 170–196.

Tan, Joseph L.H. (1996) *AFTA in the Changing International Economy.* Singapore: ISEAS, pp. 1–20,

——. ed. (1993) *Regional Economic Integration in the Asia Pacific.* Singapore: ISEAS.

Tang, Min and Myo Thant. (1994) *Growth Triangles: Conceptual Issues and Operational Problems.* Economic Staff Paper, No. 54. Manila: Asian Development Bank.

Tay, Simon S.C. Jesus Estanislo, Hadi Soesastro, eds. (2000) *A New ASEAN in A New Millennium.* Jakarta: Center of Strategic and International Studies.

Thambipillai, Pushpa and J. Saravanamuttu. (1985) *ASEAN Negotiations: Two Insights.* Singapore: Institute of Southeast Asian Studies, p. 55.

——. (1980) *Regional Cooperation and Development: The Case of ASEAN and its External Relations.* Ph.D. Dissertation, Hawaii: University of Hawaii.

Than Mya, *et. al.* eds. (1994) *Growth Triangles in Asia: A New Approach to Regional Economic Cooperation.* Hong Kong: Oxford University Press.

Toh, Mun-Heng and Linda Low. Eds. (1993) *Regional Co-operation and Growth Triangles in ASEAN.* Singapore: Times Academic Press.

Tsao, Yuan. ed. (1991) *Growth Triangle: The Johor-Singapore-Riau Experience.* Singapore: ISEAS and IPS.

Vogel, Ezra and Uchida Ichiro. (1996) *East Asia towards the Year 2000: What the Region should, can and will do.* Kuala Lumpur: ISIS.

Weiss, L. (1998) *The Myth of the Powerless State: Governing the Economy in a Global Era.* London: Polity.

Widyahartono, Bob and Kunio Igusa. eds. (1993) *Indonesian Economy and AFTA: Global Economic Interdependence of ASEAN in the Asia Pacific Era.* Tokyo: Institute of Developing Economies.

Wilcox, Wayne. *et. al.* eds. (1972) *Asia and the International System.* Cambridge: Winthorp Publishers.

Wong, John. (1979) *ASEAN Economies in Perspective.* Hong Kong: MacMillan Press.

Woo-Cumings, M. (1991*) Race to the Swift.* New York: Columbia University Press.

Wurfel, David and Bruce Burton. (1990) *The Political Economy of Foreign Policy in Southeast Asia.* New York: St Martin's Press.

Xuto, Somsakdi. (1982) *In Retrospect; Views and Comments from Selected Writings.* Bangkok.

Yakamoto, Y. and Kikuchi, T. (1998) 'Japan's Approach to APEC and Regime Creation in the Asia–Pacific', in V.K. Aggarwal and C.E. Morrison. eds. *Asia–Pacific Crossroads: Regime Creation and the Future of APEC.* New York: St. Martin's Press.

Yalem, Ronald. (1965) *Regionalism and World Order.* Washington, DC: Public Affairs Press.

Yamakage, S. (1984) 'Japan and ASEAN: are they Really Coming Together?' in W. Pennig and M.B.M. Suh. eds. *Aspects of ASEAN.* Munich: Weltforum Verlag, pp. 293–328.

Yamamoto, Yoshinobu. (1996) 'Regionalization in Contemporary International Relations', in Van R. Whiting, Jr. (ed.) *Regionalization in the World Economy: NAFTA, the Americas and Asia Pacific.* London and New York: Macmillan, pp. 19–42.

Yamaoka, Michio. (1996) *PBEC, PECC and APEC.* Tokyo, Waseda University: Discussion Paper Series, No. 5, March.

Yamazawa, Ippei. (1998) 'Economic integration in the Asia–Pacific region', in Grahame Thompson, ed. *Economic Dynamism in the Asia–Pacific.* London and New York: Routledge, pp. 163–184.

Yuan, Lee Tsao. (1992) *Growth Triangles in ASEAN, Private Investment and Trade Opportunities (PITO).* Economic Brief, No. 10.

Zimmerling, Ruth. (1991) *Externe Einflüsse auf die Integration von Staaten* [External influences on the integration of states]. Freiburg and München: Verlag Karl Alber.

Articles

Abad, Jr., M.C. (1996) 'Re-engineering ASEAN'. *Contemporary Southeast Asia*, Vol. 18, No. 3, pp. 237–253.

Acharya, Amitav. (1998) 'Culture, Security, Multilateralism: the "ASEAN Way" and Regional Order', *Contemporary Security Policy*, Vol. 19, No. 1, pp. 55–84.

——. (1997) 'Ideas, Identity, and Institution-building: from "ASEAN way" to the "Asia–Pacific way"?'. *The Pacific Review,* Vol. 10, No. 1, pp. 319–346.

——. (1991) 'The Association of Southeast Asian Nations: Security Community or "Defence Community"?'. *Pacific Affairs*, Vol. 64, No. 2, pp. 159–177.

Ahn, Chung-Si. (1980) 'Forces of Nationalism and Economics in Asian regional Cooperation', *Asian Pacific Community,* No. 7 (Winter), pp. 106–118.

Alagappa, Muthiah. (1995) 'Regionalism and Conflict Management: A Framework for Analysis'. *Review of International Studies*, No. 21, pp. 359–387.

——. (1991) 'Regional Arrangements and International Security in Southeast Asia: Going Beyond ZOPFAN'. *Contemporary Southeast Asia*, Vol. 12, No. 4, pp. 269–305.

Alburo. Florian A. (1995) 'AFTA in the Light of New Economic Developments'. *Southeast Asian Affairs 1995*, Singapore: ISEAS.

Aldrich, D. (1997) 'If You Build It, They Will Come: A Cautionary Tale About the Tumen River Projects'. *Journal of East Asian Affairs*, Vol. 11, No. 1, pp. 299–326.

Anwar, Dewi Fortuna. (1997) 'ASEAN and Indonesia: Some reflections'. *Asian Journal of Political Science*, Vol. 5, No. 1 (June), pp. 20–34.

Ariff, Mohamed. (1994) 'Open Regionalism a la ASEAN'. *Journal of Asian Economics,* Vol. 5, No. 1, pp. 99–117.

——. and Tan Eu Chye. (1992) 'ASEAN-Pacific Trade Regionalism'. *ASEAN Economic Bulletin*, Vol. 3, No. 8 (March), pp. 258–283.

Arndt, H.W. (1978) 'ASEAN Industrial Projects'. *Asia Pacific Community*, No. 3 (Fall), pp. 118–137.

Arndt, H. W. and Ross Garnaut. (1979) 'ASEAN and the Industrialization of East Asia'. *Journal of Common Market Studies*, Vol. 17, No. 3, pp. 189–211.

Axline, Andrew W. (1977) 'Underdevelopment, dependence and integration: The politics of regionalism in the third world'. *International Organization*, Vol. 31, No. 1, pp. 83–105.

Bandoro, Bantarto. (1998) 'The Implication of Economic Turbulence: ASEAN on the Brink of Depression and Disintegration'. *The Indonesian Quarterly,* Vol. XXVI, No. 4, pp. 298–300.

Barnard, Mitchell and John Ravenhill. (1995) 'Beyond Product Cycles and Flying Geese: Regionalization, Hierarchy and Industrialization in East Asia'. *World Politics*, No. 47, pp. 171–209.

Barnett, Robert. (1980) 'ASEAN's Unguarded Coasts'. *Contemporary Southeast Asia*, Vol. 38, (Spring).

Baughn, C.G. and Yaprak, A. (1996) 'Economic Nationalism: Conceptual and Empirical Development'. *Political Psychology*, Vol. 17, No. 4, pp, 759–778.

Bautista, R.M. (1984) 'Recent Shifts in Industrialisation Strategies and Trade Patterns of ASEAN countries'. *ASEAN Economic Bulletin*, Vol. 1. No. 1, July, pp. 7–25.

Bergsten, C. Fred. (2000) 'East Asian Regionalism: Towards a Tripartite World'. *The Economist* (July 15), pp. 23–26.

Blomqvist, Hans C. (1993) 'ASEAN as a Model to Third World Cooperation?'. *ASEAN Economic Bulletin,* Vol. 9, No. 2.

Bowles, Paul. (2000) 'Regionalism and Development after the Global Financial Crises'. *New Political Economy*, Vol. 5, No. 3 (November), pp. 433–455.

Bustelo, Pablo and Iliana Olivié. (1999) 'Economic Globalisation and Financial Crisis: Some Lessons from East Asia'. *The Indian Journal of Quantitative Economics* (Punjab School of Economics, Amritsar).

Camroux, David and Christian Lechervy. (1996) 'Close Encounter of a Third Kind?: The inaugural Asia-Europe meeting of March 1996'. *The Pacific Review,* Vol. 9, No. 3, pp. 442–453.

Chen, Xiangming. (1995) 'The Evolution of Free Economic Zones and the Recent Development of Cross-National Growth Zones'. *The National Journal of Urban and Regional Research*, No. 19, pp. 593–621.

Chia, Siow Yue. (1998) 'The ASEAN Free Trade Area'. *The Pacific Review*, Vol. 11, No. 2, pp. 213–232.

——. (1996) 'The Deepening and Widening of ASEAN'. *Journal of the Asia Pacific Economy,* Vol. 1, No. 1, pp. 59–78.

——. (1980) 'ASEAN Economic Cooperation: Singapore's Dilemma'. *Contemporary Southeast Asia*, Vol. 2, No. 2 (September), pp. 113–134.

Chin, Kin Wah. (1997) 'ASEAN: The Long Road to One Southeast Asia'. *Asian Journal of Political Science*, Vol. 5, pp. 1–19.

Chirativat, Suthiphand, Pachusanond, Chumporn and Wongboonsin, Patcharawalai. (1999) 'ASEAN Prospects for Regional Integration and the Implications for the ASEAN Legislative and Institutional Framework'. *ASEAN Economic Bulletin*, Vol. 16, No. 1, pp. 28–50.

Chirativat, Suthiphand. (1992) 'ASEAN: Prospects for Growth, Requirements of Structural Adjustment, and Directions for Policy', in *Global Interdependence and Asia–Pacific Cooperation*, Taipei: Chung Hua Institution for Economic Research, pp. 165–202.

Chongkittavorn, Kavi. (1998) 'East Asian Regionalism: So close and yet so far'. *South East Asian Affairs 1998.* Singapore: Institute of Southeast Asian Studies, pp. 45–50.

Chowdury, Abdur R. (1999) 'The Asian Currency Crisis: Origins, Lessons and Future Outlook'. *Research for Action*, No. 47, Helsinki: UNU/WIDER.

Chung, Meng Kang. (1990) 'ASEAN's Institutional Structure and Economic Cooperation'. *ASEAN Economic Bulletin*, Vol. 6, No. 3 (March), pp. 268–282.

Cotton, James. (1999) 'The "Haze" over Southeast Asia: Challenging the ASEAN Mode of Regional Engagement'. *Pacific Affairs*, Vol. 72, No. 3 (Fall), pp. 331–351.

Crane, G.T. (1998) 'Economic Nationalism: Bringing the State Back In' *Millenium*, Vol. 27, No. 1, pp. 55–75.

Crone, Donald. (1983) 'The Management of International Dependence: The Case of ASEAN'. *Contemporary Southeast Asia*, Vol. 5, No. 1 (June), pp. 53–79.

Dent, C.M. (2000) 'What Difference a Crisis? Continuity and Change in South Korea's Foreign Economic Policy'. *Journal of the Asia Pacific Economy*, Vol. 5, No. 3.

——. (1998) 'The ASEM: Managing the New Framework of the EU's Economic Relations with East Asia'. *Pacific Affairs*, Vol. 70, No. 4, pp. 495–516.

De Rosa, D.A. (1993) 'Sources of Comparative Advantage in the International Trade of ASEAN Countries'. *ASEAN Economic Bulletin*, Vol. 10, No. 1, pp. 41–51, July.

Dieter, Heribert. (2000) 'Asia's Monetary Regionalism'. *Far Eastern Economic Review,* July 6.

Dosch, Jörn and Mols, Manfred. (1998) 'Thirty Years of ASEAN: Achievements and Challenges'. *The Pacific Review,* Vol. 11, No. 2, pp. 167–182.

——. (1994) 'Why ASEAN Cooperation Cannot Work as A Model for Regionalism Elsewhere; A Reply'. *ASEAN Economic Bulletin,* Vol. 11, No. 2, pp. 212–222.

Drummond, S. (1982) 'Fifteen Years of ASEAN'. *Journal of Common Market Studies*, Vol. 22, No. 4 (June), pp. 301–321.

Ethier, Wilfred J. (1998) 'The New Regionalism'. *The Economic Journal*, Vol. 108, No. 449 (July), pp. 1149–1161.

Emmerson, Donald K. (1984) '"South East Asia": what's in a name?'. *Journal of South East Asian Studies*, Vol. 15, No. 1, pp. 1–21.

Evans, P. (1997) 'The Eclipse of the State? Reflections on Stateness in an Era of Globalisation'. *World Politics*, Vol. 50 (October), pp. 62–87.

Feng, Zhongpin. (1998) 'L'ASEM II suscite l'attention mondiale' ['ASEM provokes global attention']. *Beijing Information* 20 (11 May), pp. 9–12.

Fujiwara, Ishiro. (1981) 'Japan Southeast Asia Cooperation in the 1980s'. *Asia–Pacific Community* (Summer), No. 13, pp. 1–9.

Funabashi, Yoichi. (1996–97) 'Bridging Asia's Economics-Security Gap'. *Survival*, Vol. 38, No. 4, pp. 101–116.

Funston, John. (1998) 'ASEAN: Out of its Depth?', *Contemporary Southeast Asia*, Vol. 20, No. 1, pp. 22–37.

Glad, James. (1997) 'Regionalism in Southeast Asia. A bridge too far?'. *Southeast Asian Affairs 1997*, Singapore: ISEAS, pp. 3–12.

Haas, E.B. (1977) 'Turbulent Fields in the Theory of Regional Organizations'. *International Organization*, Vol. 31, No. 1, pp. 73–82.

Haas, Michael. (1979) 'The ASEANization of Asian International Relations'. *Asia Pacific Community*, No. 6 (Fall), pp. 72–86.

Haas, Peter. (1992) 'Introduction: Epistemic Communities and International Policy Coordination'. *International Organization*, Vol. 46, No. 1, pp. 1–36.

Habib, Hasnan A. (1995) 'Defining the "Asia Pacific Region"'. *Indonesian Quarterly*, Vol. XXIII, No. 4, pp. 302–312.

Han, Sung-Joo. (1983) 'The Politics of Pacific Cooperation'. *Asian Survey*, Vol. 23, No. 12, pp. 1281–1292.

Hänggi, Heiner. (1999) 'ASEM and the Construction of the new Triad'. *Journal of the Asia Pacific Economy*, Vol. 4, No. 1, pp. 56–80.

Heike, Harald V. (1996) 'Effects of AFTA as a World Market Oriented Regional Integration on Industrial Development of the Participating Countries'. *Indonesian Quarterly*, Vol. XXIV, No. 4, pp. 391–404.

Higgott, Richard. (1998) 'Shared Response to the Market Shocks?'. *The World Today* (January), pp. 4–6.

——. (1997a) 'De Facto and De Jure Regionalism: The Double Discourse of Regionalism in the Asia Pacific'. *Global Society*, Vol. 11, No. 2, pp. 165–183.

——. (1997b) 'Free Trade and Open Regionalism in Asia: *De Facto* or *De Jure* Regionalism?'. *Global Society: Journal of Interdisciplinary International Relations*, Vol. 11, No. 2, pp. 165–183.

Higgott, R. and Stubbs, R. (1995) 'Competing Conceptions of Economic Regionalism: APEC versus EAEC in the Asia Pacific'. *Review of International Political Economy*, Vol. 2, No. 3: pp. 516–535.

Hirono, Ryokichi. (1978–79) 'Towards Increased Intra-ASEAN Economic Cooperation'. *Asia Pacific Community*, No. 3 (Winter), pp. 92–118.

Hughes, C.W. (2000) 'Japanese Policy and the East Asian Currency Crisis: Abject Defeat or Quiet Victory?'. *Review of International Political Economy*, Vol. 7, No. 2, pp. 219–253.

Huxley, Tim. (1996) 'Southeast Asia in the Study of International Relations: the Rise and Decline of a Region'. *The Pacific Review*, Vol. 9, No. 2, pp. 199–228.

Jayasuriya, Kanishka. (1994) 'Singapore: the Politics of Regional Definition'. *The Pacific Review*, Vol. 7, No. 3, pp. 411–420.

Kamiya, Matake. (1996) 'Hopeful Uncertainty: Asia–Pacific Security in Transition'. *Asia–Pacific Review*, Vol. 3, No. 1, pp. 107–130.

Katzenstein, Peter J. (2000) 'Regionalism and Asia'. *New Political Economy,* (November), pp. 353–368.

——. and Takashi Shiraishi. eds. (1997) *Network Power: Japan and Asia.* Ithaca: Cornell University Press.

——. (1996) 'Regionalism in Comparative Perspective'. *Cooperation and Conflict,* Vol. 31, No. 2, pp. 123–159.

Kavi, Chongkittavorn. (1998) 'East Asian Regionalism: So Close and Yet So Far'. *South East Asian Affairs 1998.* Singapore: Institute of Southeast Asian Studies, pp. 45–50.

Kim, Duck Choong. (1992) 'Open Regionalism in the Pacific: A World of Trading Blocs?'. *The American Economic Review,* January, pp. 79–83.

Kim, Y.T. (1999) 'Neoliberalism and the Decline of the Developmental State'. *Journal of Contemporary Asia,* Vol. 29, No. 4, pp. 441–461.

Kojima, K. (1966) 'A Pacific Community and Asian Developing Countries'. *Hitotsubashi Journal of Economics,* Vol. 7, No. 1.

Koshikawa, Kazuhiko. (1996) 'The Asia-Europe Meeting (ASEM) – The First Summit Meeting in Bangkok and Follow-up Activities'. *The Japan Economic Times* (15 November 1996), p. 3.

Krishnamra, Nadhavathna. (1997) 'ASEAN and the New Millenium'. *World Affairs,* Vol. 1. No. 3, pp. 28–36.

Krumar, Sree/Siddique, Sharon. (1994) 'Beyond Economic Reality: New Thoughts on the Growth Triangle'. *Southeast Asian Affairs,* Singapore: ISEAS. pp. 47–56.

Kupchan, Charles A. (1998) 'After Pax Americana. Benign Power, Regional Integration, and the Sources of a Stable Multipolarity'. *Foreign Affairs,* Vol. 23, No. 3 (Fall), pp. 40–79.

Kurus, Bilson. (1995) 'The ASEAN Triad: National Interest, Consensus-Seeking, and Economic Cooperation'. *Contemporary Southeast Asia,* Vol. 16, No. 4, pp. 404–420, March.

Kusumaatmadja, Mochtar. (1990) 'Some Thoughts on ASEAN Security Co-operation: An Indonesian Perspective'. *Contemporary Southeast Asia,* Vol. 12, No. 3, pp. 161–171.

Leifer, Michael. (1973) 'The ASEAN States: No Common Outlook'. *International Affairs,* Vol. 49, No. 3 (October), pp. 600–607.

LeviFaur, D. (1997) 'Economic Nationalism: From Friedrich List to Robert Reich'. *Review of International Studies,* Vol. 23, No. 3, pp. 359–370.

Lin, Chang Li and Ramkishen S. Rajan (1999) 'East Asian Cooperation in Response to the Regional Crisis: A Case of Self-help or No Help?'. Singapore: Institute of Policy Studies (January).

Lubis, Mochtar. (1970) 'A Broad New Conception for Southeast Asia'. *Pacific Community,* Vol. 2, (October), pp. 87–96.

Mahbubani, Kishore. (1997) 'An Asia–Pacific consensus'. *Foreign Affairs,* Vol. 76, No. 5 (Sept/Oct), pp. 149–158.

——. (1995) 'The Pacific Way'. *Foreign Affairs,* Vol. 71, No. 1 (January), pp. 100–110.

Marton, A., McGee, T. and Paterson, D.G. (1995) 'Northeast Asian Economic Cooperation and the Tumen River Area Development Project'. *Pacific Affairs,* Vol. 68, No. 1, pp. 9–33.

Mitchell, Bernard. (1996) 'Regions in the Global Political Economy: Beyond the Local-Global Divide in the Formation of the Eastern Asia Region'. *New Political Economy,* Vol. 1, No. 3, pp. 335–354.

Moon, C.I. (1999) 'Political Economy of East Asian Development and Pacific Economic Co-operation'. *The Pacific Review,* Vol. 12, No. 2, pp. 199–224.

Mutalib, Hussin. (1997) 'At Thirty, ASEAN Looks to Challenges in the New Millennium'. *Contemporary Southeast Asia*, Vol. 19, No. 1, pp. 74–85.

Nakasone, Yasuhiro. (1997) 'The Security Environment of the Asia–Pacific Age'. *Asia–Pacific Review*, Vol. 4, No. 1, pp. 3–16.

Naya, Seiji and Michael Plummer. (1997) 'Economic Co-operation after 30 Years of ASEAN'. *ASEAN Economic Bulletin*, Vol. 14, No. 2, pp. 117–126.

——. (1991) 'ASEAN Economic Cooperation in the New International Economic Order'. *ASEAN Economic Bulletin*, Vol. 7, No. 3 (March), pp. 261–276.

Nor, Aina K. (1995) 'AFTA and Intra-Industry Trade'. *ASEAN Economic Bulletin*, Vol. 12, No. 1 (July), pp. 351–368.

Nye, Joesph S. (1969) 'United States Policy Towards Regional Organization'. *International Organization*, Vol. XXIII, No. 3, pp. 719–740 (Summer).

Ojendal, Joakim. (1997) 'Regionalization in East Asia and the Pacific: An Elusive Process?'. Helsinki: UNU/WIDER *World Development Studies*, No. 11.

Ooi, G.T. (1987) 'Non-Tariff Barriers to Expanding Intra-ASEAN Trade'. *ASEAN Economic Bulletin*, Vol. 3, pp. 97–113.

Pangestu, Mari. (1987) 'The Pattern of Direct Foreign Investment in ASEAN: the USA and Japan'. *ASEAN Economic Bulletin*, Vol. 3, No. 3 (March), pp. 301–328.

Pangestu, Mari. *et. al.* (1992) 'A New Look at Intra-ASEAN Economic Cooperation'. *ASEAN Economic Bulletin*, Vol. 3, No. 8 (March), pp. 333–352.

Paribatra, Sukhumphand. (1994) 'From ASEAN Six to ASEAN Ten: Issues and Prospects'. *Contemporary Southeast Asia*, Vol. 16, No. 3 (December), pp. 243–258,

Pelkmans, J. (1980) 'Economic Theories of Integration Revisited'. *Journal of Common Market Studies*, Vol. 18, pp. 333–354.

Pempel, T.J. (1997) 'Regime Shift: Japanese Politics in a Changing World Economy'. *Journal of Japanese Studies*, Vol. 23(2).

Penaherrera, G. Salgado. (1980) 'Viable Integration and the Economic Cooperation Problems of the Developing World'. *Journal of Common Market Studies*, Vol. 19, No. 1, September, pp. 69–74.

Plummer, Michael G. (1997) 'ASEAN and the Theory of Regional Economic Integration: A Survey'. *ASEAN Economic Bulletin*, Vol. 14, No. 2, pp. 222–214.

Pou Serradell, Victor. (1997) 'The Asia-Europe Meeting (ASEM): A Historical Turning Point in Relations Between the Two Regions'. *European Foreign Affairs Review*, Vol. 1, No. 2, pp. 185–210.

Ramasamy, Bala. (1995) 'Trade Diversion in ASEAN Free Trade Area'. *ASEAN Economic Bulletin*, Vol. 12, No. 1, July, pp. 10–17.

Ravenhill, J. (2000) 'APEC Adrift: Implications for Economic Regionalism in Asia and the Pacific'. *The Pacific Review*, Vol. 13, No. 2, pp. 319–333.

Rieger, Hans Christoph. (1991) 'The Treaty of Rome and its Relevance for ASEAN'. *ASEAN Economic Bulletin*, Vol. 8, No. 2, pp. 160–276.

Risse-Kappen, Thomas. (1996) 'Konfliktprävention durch Theorie?'. *Internationale Politik*, Vol. 51, No. 8, pp. 8–16, August.

Rocamora, Joel. (1994) 'The Philippines and Competing Asian Regionalism'. *Politik. A publication of the Ateneo*, Center for Social Policy and Public Affairs, Vol. 1, No. 1, pp. 33–36.

Rozman, G. (1998a) 'Northeast Asia: Regionalism, a Clash of Civilisations or Strategic Quadrangle?'. *Asia Pacific Review*, Vol. 5, No. 1, pp. 105–126.

——.(1998b) 'Flawed Regionalism: Reconceptualising Northeast Asia in the 1990s'. *The Pacific Review*, Vol. 11, No. 1, pp. 1–27.

——. (1995) 'A Regional Approach to Northeast Asia'. *Orbis*, Vol. 39(1), pp. 65–80.

Salim, Ziad. (1987) 'ASEAN in the United Nations'. *Indonesian Quarterly*, Vol. IX, No. 2, April, pp. 24–38.

Samad, Paridah Abdul/Mokhtar Muhammad. (1995) 'ASEAN's Role and Development as a Security Community'. *Indonesian Quarterly*, Vol. XXIII, No. 1, pp. 67–75.

Saravanamutth, Johan. (1986) 'Imperialism, Dependent Development and ASEAN Regionalism'. Journal of Contemporary Asia, Vol. 16, No. 2, pp. 204–222.

Seki, Hiromoto. (1996) 'APEC: New Paradigm for Asia–Pacific Relations'. *Asia–Pacific Review*, Vol. 3, No. 1, pp. 131–136.

Shee, Poon-Kim. (1977) 'A Decade of ASEAN, 1967–77'. *Asian Survey*, August, Vol. 17, No. 8, pp. 753–770.

——. (1997) 'Singapore and ASEAN: 1967–1997'. *Asian Journal of Political Science*, Vol. 5, No. 1, June, pp. 68–86.

Singh, Ajit. (1997) 'Towards One Southeast Asia'. *ASEAN Economic Bulletin*, Vol. 14, No. 2, Special issue, 126–131.

Singh, Hari. (1997) 'Vietnam and ASEAN. The Politics of Accommodation'. *Australian Journal of International Affairs*, Vol. 51, No. 3, pp. 215–229.

Snitwongse, Kusuma. (1998) 'Thirty Years of ASEAN: Achievements through Political Cooperation'. *The Pacific Review*, Vol. 11, No. 2, pp. 183–194.

Soesastro, Hadi. (1998) 'ASEAN During the Crisis'. *ASEAN Economic Bulletin*, Vol. 15, No. 3, (December), pp. 373–382.

——. (1995) 'ASEAN and APEC: Do Concentric Circles Work?'. *The Pacific Review*, Vol. 8, No. 3, pp. 475–493.

——. (1991) 'Grup Mahathir'. *Tempo*, No. 16, Maret: p. 82.

——. (1983a) 'ASEAN and the Political Economy of Pacific Cooperation'. *Asian Survey*, Vol. 23, No. 12, pp. 1255–1270.

——. (1983b) 'ASEAN and North-South Trade Issues'. *Indonesian Quarterly*, Vol. XI, No. 3 (July).

Soesastro, Hadi and Jusuf Wanandi. (1996) 'Towards an Asia Europe Partnership – A Perspective from Asia'. *Indonesian Quarterly*, Vol. XIV, No. 1 (First Quarter 1996), pp. 38–58.

Sudo, Suedo. (1988) 'The Road to Becoming a Regional Leader: Japanese Attempts in Southeast Asia 1975–1980'. *Pacific Affairs*, Vol. 61, No. 1, Spring, pp. 27–50.

Sumitro, Djojohadkusomo. (1973) 'Foreign Economic Relations-Some Trade Aspects'. *Indonesian Quarterly*, Vol. 1, No. 2 (January), pp. 18–26.

Tan, G. (1982) 'Intra-regional Trade Liberalization: The Case of ASEAN PTA'. *Journal of Common Market Studies*, Vol. 20, No. 4, June, pp. 321–331.

Thambipillai, Pushpa. (1998) 'The ASEAN Growth Areas: Sustaining the Dynamism'. *The Pacific Review*, Vol. 11, No. 2, pp. 249–266.

Thillainathan, R. (1995) 'The ASEAN Financial Sector, A Drag or a Leader?'. *ASEAN Economic Bulletin*, Vol. 12 (July), pp. 1–9.

Toh, Mun-Heng and Linda Low. (1993) 'Is the ASEAN Free Trade Area a Second Best Option?'. *Asian Economic Journal*, Vol. 7, No. 3, pp. 275–298.

Vaitsos, C. (1978) 'Crisis in Regional Economic Cooperation (Integration) Among Developing Countries: A Survey'. *World Development*, Vol. 6, pp. 744–749.

Wade, Robert. (1998) 'The Asian Debt-and-Development Crisis of 1997–? Causes and Consequences'. *World Development*, Vol. 26, No. 8 (August), pp. 1534–1554.

Wanandi, Jusuf. (1995) 'ASEAN's Domestic Political Developments and their Impact on Foreign Policy'. *The Pacific Review*, Vol. 8 No. 3, pp. 440–458.

——. (1995) 'ASEAN'S Informal Networking'. *The Indonesian Quarterly,* Vol. XXIII, No. 1, pp. 56–66.

Wain, Barry. (1998) 'ASEAN is Facing is Keenest Challenges to Date'. *Asian Wall Street Journal Weekly,* 23 February, p. 17.

Weiss, L. (2000) 'Developmental States in Transition: Adapting, Dismantling, Innovating, Not Normalising'. *The Pacific Review,* Vol. 13, No. 1, pp. 21–56.

Wong, John. (1985) 'ASEAN's Experience in Regional Economic Cooperation'. *Asian Development Review,* Vol. 3 No. 1, pp. 78–98.

Index

Date Due

Bock DUE. AUG 1 0 2004		
SEP 0 9 2003		
Bock DUE SEP 0 1 2004		
Bock RET AUG 2 4 '04		
Bock DUE MAY 0 4 2006		
BOOK RET'D JAN 0 9 2006		